Writing Analytically with Readings

SECOND CANADIAN EDITION

David Rosenwasser

Jill Stephen

Doug Babington

NELSON EDUCATION

NELSON EDUCATION

Writing Analytically with Readings, Second Canadian Edition

by David Rosenwasser, Jill Stephen, and Doug Babington

Vice President, Editorial Higher Education:
Anne Williams

Executive Editor:
Laura Macleod

Senior Marketing Manager:
Amanda Henry

Developmental Editor:
Jessica Freedman

Photo Researcher:
Sandra Mark

Permissions Coordinator:
Sandra Mark

Content Production Manager:
Jennifer Hare

Production Service:
Cenveo Publisher Services

Copy Editor:
Jessie Coffey

Proofreader:
Victoria Jones

Indexer:
BIM Indexing & Proofreading Services

Production Coordinator:
Ferial Suleman

Design Director:
Ken Phipps

Managing Designer:
Franca Amore

Interior Design:
Olena Sullivan

Cover Design:
Martyn Schmoll

Cover Image:
ephemera/Getty Images

Compositor:
Cenveo Publisher Services

Printer:
RR Donnelley

Library and Archives Canada Cataloguing in Publication Data

Rosenwasser, David
    Writing analytically with readings/David Rosenwasser, Jill Stephen, Doug Babington. — 2nd Canadian ed.

Includes bibliographical references and index.
ISBN 978-0-17-650446-5

    1. English language—Rhetoric.
2. Academic writing. 3. Critical thinking. I. Stephen, Jill
II Babington, Doug III. Title.

PE1408.R678 2012
808'.042   C2011-907944-5

ISBN-13: 978-0-17-650446-5
ISBN-10: 0-17-650446-X

Contents in Brief

Contents

Part II ❦ Writing the Thesis-Driven Paper 121

Preface

This is not a book that tries to be all things to all teachers and students. Instead, it concentrates on one kind of writing—analysis—which we define as the search for meaningful pattern. This book argues that analysis, rather than dissecting information, fosters an exploratory attitude toward experience. By searching out questions before rushing to answers, analysis aims at a complex understanding of what something means.

Writing Analytically was born of frustration about the gap between, on the one hand, the lively quality of students' thinking in class discussion and informal writing and, on the other hand, the inert, evasive, and simplistic finished products they submitted to us. This book seeks to bridge that gap.

We focus on analysis because it is the skill most often called for in higher education and beyond. Analysis offers alternatives to oversimplified thinking of both the like/dislike, agree/disagree variety and the cut-and-paste compilation of sheer information. Implicit throughout the book is an argument for the value of reflection in an age that seems increasingly unaware of it as an option. Toward this end, *Writing Analytically* teaches students to distinguish between an idea and a mere opinion and to respect the complexity of subjects that have no single right answer. *Writing Analytically* is about how to have and develop ideas in an academic setting.

There are, of course, many causes of mediocre writing, but the primary culprit this book attacks is an overly rigid notion of thesis proffered in many writing textbooks and school settings—that the thesis is an unchanging claim that a paper sets out to prove. In practice, this conception of thesis leads writers to spend most of their time trying to organize superficial ideas rather than testing and evolving them. It leads them to judge prematurely, usually settling for obvious generalizations, rather than use their writing to explore the evidence, finding the questions that intrigue them. And it is at odds with the way that most good writing actually operates. The solution, we believe, is to reorient students from judging to understanding.

How does the book attempt to accomplish these ends? Here is a radically compressed version of the book's project—its essential advice to students.

- Dwell longer than customary on the evidence. Notice more before reducing scope and making the interpretive leap to a thesis.
- Make the thesis evolve in response to evidence. The confrontation with evidence should not only confirm but refine the thesis.
- Converse with sources rather than agreeing/disagreeing or parroting.
- Share your thought process with readers—not just your conclusions but how you arrived at them.

The book does not, by the way, denigrate thesis-driven writing, nor does it slight the importance of producing clear, well-organized finished products. But the book does argue that students should not be pressed to formulate and argue thesis statements without first being taught how to examine evidence in depth, in an open-ended, exploratory way that constant position-taking discourages.

Writing Analytically also acknowledges that various academic disciplines differ in their expectations of student writing. Interspersed throughout the text are boxes labelled "Voices Across the Curriculum." These were written for the book by professors in various disciplines who offer their perspectives on such matters as reasoning back to premises and determining what counts as evidence. In Chapter 10, for example, such "Voices" explain the rationale for disciplinary formats and offer advice on how to use them to arrive at ideas rather than just to arrange the final product.

Finally, the book has more to say about what students shouldn't do than is usually the case in writing texts. While we are sensitive to the dangers of negativism, we have found that students have a hard time developing new skills until they've come to understand what is counterproductive about features of their current practice. We believe in the value of talking overtly with students about where their writing typically goes wrong. So, for example, we discuss at some length the shortcomings of the slot-filler organizational scheme known as five-paragraph form, and we offer a chapter on kinds of weak thesis statements, with explanations of why they are weak and practical advice on how to fix them.

WHAT'S NEW IN THIS EDITION

The Second Canadian Edition of *Writing Analytically* preserves its well-tested strengths—an accessible tone and an emphasis on close reading skills—while introducing several updates and improvements:

- a new sequence of chapters in Part I, in order to place observational skills at the front of the writing process;
- enhanced Canadian content, from a discussion of Alex Colville's art to an academic article on women's prisons by Kelly Hannah-Moffat;
- a streamlined discussion of online research, with improved graphics as well as references to both Google Scholar and the open-access movement;
- the merging of chapters on organization and formatting into a new Chapter 10, which places paragraphing in the foreground; and
- expanded coverage of style and grammar with examples from a nineteenth-century text that illustrates the symbiosis between clear writing and audience.

As in the First Canadian Edition, the readings have been integrated with the content of chapters. That is, the chapters of the book refer—directly and continuously—to the authors' work. Bruce McCall begins with a sentence fragment and Chapter 13 wonders why. Christine Overall argues deductively and Chapter 6 explains how. Furthermore, by introducing new "Voices Across the Curriculum" (those of students as well as professors), this edition underscores the ideal posited by another of its contributing authors, Mark Kingwell: "All claims, if they really are claims, are made on the basis of reason; and a reason is only truly a reason if it can be publicly defended. You may not always actually articulate your justifications to somebody else; but it is essential that you should be *able* to do so, if called upon."

New assignments and "Try This" exercises encourage in-class collaboration and exchange. They also light the students' path through the readings—emphasizing how the principles stressed in *Writing Analytically* are put into practice by both academic and professional writers. In addition, each part of the book—from "Making Meaning" to "The Language of Clarity"—has been updated to reflect current research methodology and composition theory. And, as should go without saying, Canadian content is its own reward: diverse, smart, politically incomparable, able to raze tall idols with a single line.

ABOUT THE AUTHORS

David Rosenwasser and **Jill Stephen** are professors of English at Muhlenberg College in Allentown, Pennsylvania, where they have co-directed a Writing Across the Curriculum (WAC) program since 1987. *Writing Analytically* has grown out of their undergraduate teaching and the seminars on writing and writing instruction that they have offered to faculty at Muhlenberg and at other colleges and universities across the United States.

Doug Babington joined the faculty of Queen's University in 1982, becoming director of the Writing Centre in 1996. In addition to teaching writing courses, he delivers seminars across campus for both undergraduate and graduate students. Doug's work as a teacher and consultant has taken him to a variety of colleges and universities—including the American College of Greece, Trent University, and the University of Mississippi.

ACKNOWLEDGMENTS TO THE SECOND CANADIAN EDITION

Many of my colleagues and students have contributed, knowingly or unknowingly, to the development of this revised edition. In particular, I want to thank Corinne Laverty, head of the Education Library at Queen's University, who wrote and compiled much of the information on finding and citing sources (Chapter 9). Expertise was also provided by Jackie Druery, head of Learning & Research Services at the Joseph S. Stauffer Library.

Several professors and instructors from across Canada offered thorough and insightful reviews of the first Canadian edition:

Lyn Bennett, Dalhousie University

Kit Dobson, Mount Royal University

Aurelea Mahood, Capilano University

Stuart Murray, Ryerson University

Kathleen Shannon, Georgian College

Carmelo Tropiano, Seneca College

Finally, heartfelt thanks—and admiration—go to my colleagues at the Queen's University Writing Centre, without whom I'd know so much less about writing.

Doug Babington

Introduction

This is a book about one type of communication: analytical writing. The definition of that term will grow as the book unfolds, but for now let's say that writing analytically is the process of figuring out what something means. To analyze is to ask how something does what it does—or why it is as it is. Learning to write analytically is primarily a matter of becoming more aware of the act of thinking. Of course, ideas don't just happen—they're made. We have chosen to write about analysis because analysis, more than any other form of thought, is what university and college writing demands. Of all the skills you acquire as a thinker and writer, analysis is likely to have the greatest impact on the way you learn. The more you practise writing analytically, the more actively and patiently you will think.

Analyzing often gets a bad rap. It is sometimes thought of as destructive—breaking things down into their component parts or, to paraphrase William Wordsworth, murdering to dissect. Other detractors attack it as the rarefied province of intellectuals and scholars, beyond the reach of normal people. In fact, we all analyze all of the time, and we do so not simply to break things down but to construct our understandings of the world we inhabit.

If, for example, you find yourself being followed by an Irish wolfhound, your first response—other than breaking into a cold sweat—will be to analyze the situation. What does being followed by this large canine mean for me, here, now? Does it mean the dog is vicious and about to attack? Does it mean the dog is curious and wants to play? Similarly, if you are losing a game of tennis, or if you've just left a job interview, or if you are looking at a painting of a woman with three noses, you will begin to analyze. How can I play differently to increase my chances of winning? Am I likely to get the job, and why (or why not)? Why did the artist give the woman three noses?

If we break things down through analysis, we do so in order to search for meaningful patterns or to uncover what wasn't apparent at first glance—or just to understand more closely how and why the separate parts work as they do. We do this in writing because writing provides a method for expanding our ability to notice things, to have ideas about what we notice, and to arrive ultimately at some plausible interpretation.

In short, writing analytically can make you smarter. It can get you beyond thinking that what things mean is simply a matter of opinion. It can help you understand and synthesize other people's ideas en route to ideas of your own. What's more, analysis is a surprisingly discrete process, one with steps that can be learned and then refined. It consists of a fairly limited set of basic moves. Unfortunately, much of what passes for thinking these days is merely reacting: right/wrong, good/bad, loved it/hated it, couldn't relate to it, boring. Responses like these are habits: reflexes of the mind. And they are surprisingly tough habits to break. See for yourself. Ask someone for a description of a place, a movie, or a new CD, and see what you get. Too often it will be a diatribe. Offer a counterargument and be told, huffily, "I'm entitled to my opinion."

The first step toward writing analytically is to start recognizing and blocking the kinds of mental reflexes that clog perception and substitute prefabricated generic answers for original thoughts.

Why is this so?

We live in a culture of inattention and cliché. It is a culture in which we are perpetually confronted by advertisers' hype (Tim Hortons lures muffin-lovers with a "new Cranberry Orange Explosion"), flip opinions ("Crosby's just a Mama's Boy!"), and easy answers ("A vote for me is a vote for prosperity"). We're awash in what Michael Posner calls "a Disneyfied World" (page 115).

That's one reason for the prominence of the currently popular buzz phrase "thinking outside the box"—which appears to mean getting beyond outworn ways of thinking about things. But more than that, the phrase assumes that most of the time most of us are trapped inside the box—inside a set of prefabricated answers (clichés) and like/dislike responses. This is not a new phenomenon, of course. Two hundred and fifty years ago the philosopher David Hume, writing about perception, asserted that our lives are spent in "dogmatic slumbers," so ensnared in conventional notions of just about everything that we don't really see anything; we just rehearse what we've been told is there.

Growing up, we all become increasingly desensitized to the world around us; we tend to forget the specific things that get us to feel and think in particular ways. Instead we respond to our experience with a limited range of generalizations. And, more often than not, these are shared generalizations—that is, clichés.

The way out of this trap is to adopt an attitude of skepticism, which is the very lifeblood of analysis. Like analysis, skepticism tends to get a bad rap. It is not the enemy of optimism, as people sometimes assume: it's the enemy of blind optimism and of blindness in general. Skeptics believe in asking questions, in not automatically accepting the same old narrow set of answers as accurate and right. A skeptic values doubt because, in the words of one scholar, "everywhere one looks there are those selling their version of the truth as the only version of the truth" (Owens xiii).

Just as analyzing a subject does not mean ripping things apart in a negative way, adopting a skeptical attitude toward life does not mean wallowing in negativity or assuming the futility of everything. The skeptic wants not to deny life but to affirm a version of life that is more accurate—to arrive at a better explanation of what things mean, to locate and solve problems that others don't see. In this sense, skepticism is careful and intelligent optimism.

Perhaps the most infamous skeptic at work today is Julian Assange, the Australian hacker and activist who founded WikiLeaks in 2006. Journalist David Cohen has described WikiLeaks as "a web-based service designed to protect the identity of individuals who want to make sensitive information public." But a service that uses technology to instantaneously disseminate information from anonymous whistleblowers is not necessarily a promoter of careful and intelligent optimism. Indeed, Mr. Assange has stirred up plenty of controversy across the globe. His skeptical attitude towards life has drawn many skeptics.

Writing analytically is one of the most effective ways to articulate the meaning of WikiLeaks—or of any other multifaceted topic. It is a process that requires writers to look attentively at their data, to ask dynamic questions—instead of settling for static answers—and to arrange their words very carefully. This book will help you execute every one of those necessary steps.

PART I

Making Meaning: Essential Skills

CHAPTER

1

Powers of Observation

In the spring of 2011, the Musée des Beaux-Arts in Montréal mounted an exhibit entitled "The Warrior Emperor and China's Terracotta Army." Among the treasures on display—from the Qin Dynasty—was a beautiful bronze swan. An explanatory note complemented the display: "*Like the other life-sized water birds found in what appears to have been a pleasure garden, this bird was based on careful observation of nature.*"

Whoever composed that note was emphasizing a truth that applies as much to modern essay writers as it did to ancient Chinese sculptors: careful observation is the key to communicating clearly.

The meaning of observation, however, is not self-evident. If you got together with five friends and asked them to write down one observation about the room you were all sitting in, it's a sure bet that many of the responses would be generalized judgments—"It's comfortable" or "It's a pigsty." And why? Because the habits of mind that come to most of us most readily and that are further encouraged by our culture tend to shut down the observation stage so that we literally notice and remember less. We go for the quick impression and dismiss the rest.

Of course, we all have methods of observation but most of us are not very aware of these. And so, if we are to become better observers, we need to become more aware of what observation involves. That is the purpose of this introductory chapter, which first explains what gets in the way of observation and then offers several systematic ways of improving your observational skills.

The fundamental principle we want to communicate in this chapter—the key to becoming a better observer and, thus, a better thinker—is that you need to slow down, to stop drawing conclusions before you've spent time openly attending to the data, thereby letting yourself notice more. Better ideas grow out of a richer acquaintance with whatever it is you are looking at. The trick—and it requires both willpower and practice—is to give yourself permission to dwell longer and more closely on the data. A book reviewer once called Margaret Atwood's powers of observation "disconcertingly acute." Better such acute observation, though, than simply rushing to judgment. When we leap prematurely to our perceptions about a thing, we place a filter between ourselves and the "object," shrinking the amount and kinds of information that can get through to our minds and our senses.

Often, it is not just carelessness or a judgmental cast of mind that closes down the information-gathering stage. People sometimes have unreasonable expectations of themselves when it comes to having ideas. They think that they should get to ideas right away, that arriving at a "thesis," some

---

Voices Across the Curriculum

Beginning Early

Like many new faculty members, my approach to writing was best described as long periods of working on everything-else-but, followed by sustained periods of intense writing to meet looming deadlines (the "Procrastination–Binge Model"). The process was usually successful (I finished things on time... just) but never comfortable. It was my experience of writing and seemed to be how many of my colleagues worked—including senior faculty members—so I believed it to be "normal."

It wasn't until my first major book project that I learned about a more balanced, moderate way of writing that is, I discovered, much more sustainable and productive. By beginning early—before feeling "ready"—and working in brief, daily sessions, I was able to complete all that I had to write, edit the contributions of the other authors, and manage the administrative details of the entire project without suffering burnout.

What I found curious was that by organizing my writing sessions into shorter, more frequent periods, other aspects of my work progressed at a similar pace. In effect, they became my "breaks" from writing, and were short, focused, and productive. Not only did my writing benefit: I was less intimidated by all that had to be accomplished, I found it relatively easy to pick up where I had left off, and I had a greater sense of achievement after each session. Now writing is something I look forward to and enjoy.

—Peggy Pritchard, lecturer in microbiology and immunology

---

governing idea about a subject, is a necessary starting point for analysis. We call this kind of idea-first–look-later anxiety the "dogfish problem." In the dogfish problem, a writer trying to start with a thesis before looking more openly at the data is in the same predicament as a scientist being expected to propose a theory about the dogfish after having had only a cursory look at one.

What would a scientist studying a particular species of fish actually do in order to formulate a theory? He or she would start with observation. She'd look at its habitat. She'd watch its habits—how it eats, swims, and reproduces. She'd undoubtedly dissect it. Consider the studies by Jane Goodall and others on apes in the wild. Those scientists spend years observing creatures in their habitats and collecting data before they are ready to start publishing their ideas.

You, on the other hand, don't have years to get your writing done. But you have more time to spend at the data-gathering stage than you are probably accustomed to spending. Slow down; it's worth it. Don't fall victim to the dogfish problem. If you give yourself more time to look at your subject matter and see what you notice, ideas will come.

You will also need to cultivate a more positive attitude toward *not* knowing. Uncertainty—even its more extreme version, confusion—is a productive state of mind, a precondition to allowing yourself to have ideas. For Erna Paris—writing on September 13, 2001—a pressing question helped begin the process of sorting out a terrible confusion (pages 101–103). Rather than court confusion, though, most of us seek the comfort of feeling that we understand. But when people decide too quickly that they understand something, they actually cause themselves to see less. Once they've made a mental note of their general impression and the details that created it, they usually stop looking (and forget the details). A more productive approach is to *deliberately assume that you don't understand*, that you may not yet fully see what is going on in whatever it is you are looking at. By training yourself to be more comfortable with not knowing, you give yourself licence to start working with your material—the data—*before* you try to decide what you think.

In short, the major shift that this chapter asks you to make is to spend more of your time and attention in the observation stage that necessarily precedes the thesis-formulating phase. Train yourself to stay open longer to noticing things in your subject matter. Do this by starting not with "What do I think?" or, worse, with "What do I like/dislike?" but with "What do I notice?"

Here are a few more thoughts about noticing and what gets in its way. Some people, perhaps especially the very young, are good at noticing things. They see things that the rest of us don't see or have ceased to notice. But why is this? Is it just that people become duller as they get older? The poet William Wordsworth, among others, argued that we aren't the victims of declining intelligence but of habit. That is, as we organize our lives so that we can function more efficiently, we condition ourselves to see in more predictable ways and to screen out things that are not immediately relevant to our daily needs.

You can test this theory by considering what you did and did not notice this morning on the way to work or class or wherever you regularly go. Getting where we need to go, following a routine for moving through the day, can be done with minimal engagement of either the brain or the senses. Our minds are often, as we say, "somewhere else." As we walk along, our eyes wander a few feet in front of our shoes or stare blankly in the direction of our destination. Moving along the roadway in cars, we periodically realize that miles have gone by while we were driving on "automatic pilot," attending barely at all to the road or the car or the landscape. Arguably, even when we try to focus on something that we want to consider, the habit of not really attending to things stays with us. We glide over the top. We go for rapidly acquired impressions and then relax our attention.

The deadening effect of habit on seeing and thinking has long been a preoccupation of artists as well as philosophers and psychologists. Some people have even defined the aim of art as "defamiliarization." "The essential purpose of art," writes the novelist David Lodge, "is to overcome the deadening effects of habit by representing familiar things in unfamiliar ways" (53). The man who coined the term "defamiliarization," Victor Shklovsky, wrote, "Habitualization devours works, clothes, furniture, one's wife, and the fear of war…. And art exists that one may recover the sensation of life" (Lodge 53).

In this context we come back around to the perhaps peculiar-sounding suggestion made earlier about not knowing—about accepting uncertainty and even confusion as beneficial states of mind on the way to the discovery of ideas. Curiosity may in fact kill cats, but it has the opposite effect on the human brain.

The problem with convincing ourselves that we have the answers is that we are thus prevented from seeing the questions, which are usually much more interesting than the temporary stopping points we have elected as answers. A strong idea often depends on seeing a question where one seems not to exist or of finding a connection between things that seem not to be connected. In fact, having ideas means allowing yourself to notice things in your subject that you want to better understand rather than glossing over things with a quick and too-easy understanding.

In light of this brief rationale, we now offer two strategies for developing the ability to dwell longer and more insightfully on data, on the stuff of experience, rather than pushing on prematurely to conclusions. The first of these, Notice and Focus, is very basic but nevertheless represents a significant shift for most people. The second procedure, a somewhat more elaborate but still basic set of steps—which we call Five-Step Analysis—is widely applicable to a range of thinking, reading, and writing tasks.

A. NOTICE AND FOCUS (RANKING)

This exercise is governed by a repeated return to the question "What do you notice?" Most people tend to generalize and thus to rapidly move away from whatever it is they are looking at. The question "What do you notice?" redirects attention to the subject matter itself and delays the pressure to come up with answers, with the resultant closing off of the experience.

So the first step is for you to repeatedly answer the question "What do you notice?" Be sure to cite actual details of the thing being observed rather than move to more general observations about it. (Note that this is more difficult than it sounds.) This phase of the exercise should produce an extended, unordered list of details—features of the thing being observed—that call attention to themselves for one reason or another.

The second step is the focusing part in which you *rank* (create an order of importance for) the various features of your subject you have noticed. (Note that sometimes it is useful to start right away with this second step in in-class writing exercises and discussion.) Answer the question "What three details (specific features of the subject matter) are most interesting (or significant or revealing or strange)?" The purpose of relying on "interesting" or one of the other suggested words is that these will help to deactivate the like/dislike switch, which is so much a reflex in all of us, and replace it with a more analytical perspective.

The third step in this process is to say why the three things you selected struck you as the most interesting. We are postponing discussion of this move—the interpretive leap from observation to conclusion—until a later chapter. For now, we ask you only to start looking at things—at everything—using Notice and Focus.

Remember to start by noticing as much as you can about what you are looking at. Dwell on the data. Record what you see. Don't move yet to generalization or, worse, to judgment. What this procedure will begin to demonstrate is how useful description is as a tool for arriving at ideas. Stay at the description stage longer (in that attitude of uncertainty we recommend), and have better ideas. Training yourself to notice is fun. It will improve your memory, your ability to think, and probably also your conversation.

℘*TRY THIS:* This evening, take a careful look at the building you live in— be it a student residence, a house, or an apartment building. List a number of details about it, and then rank the three most important ones. Use in your focusing question any of the four words suggested above: "interesting," "significant," "revealing," or "strange." Bring the results to class and exchange papers with another student. Each of you should then write a one-paragraph response to the other's "Notice and Focus," letting him or her know to what extent the building's image comes through. □

B. FIVE-STEP ANALYSIS

Although in subsequent chapters of this book we offer other procedures for seeing, for dwelling on the data, and for arriving at ideas, Five-Step Analysis underlies them all. Five-Step Analysis, once you've learned how to use it, can become, as it is in our classes, a universal assignment, something you always do with whatever it is you are working on: making sense of something you are reading, contemplating revision of a piece of your own or a friend's writing, or gathering first-hand information on something you plan to write about.

We've been talking about trying to write what you see, starting with details rather than generalizations. It takes most people a while to grasp this idea because they don't readily distinguish between generalizing about a picture, for example, and writing about what is actually in the picture.

We've also tried to suggest that arriving at ideas is not a mystical process— that, in fact, most people already have formulas or mental procedures that they use whenever they're called upon to do analysis. The problem is that people are insufficiently aware of these, so it is difficult to learn to use them more consciously and efficiently.

Finally, we've been saying that people don't spend enough time in the information-gathering stage, nor do they think enough about the discrete activities that information gathering brings into play. That is to say that people need to learn how to notice things. In particular, they need to learn how to go about selecting some things as potentially more important or more interesting than others.

Five-Step Analysis is not about arranging an argument and getting quickly to the bottom line; it's about really looking at things: reducing anxiety by getting rid of the bottom-line mentality and giving yourself something quasi-mechanical to do that will let your mind play freely with the material. Listing is a great form of brainstorming; Five-Step Analysis makes the listing activity more coherent and systematic.

Making Observation Systematic and Habitual

Hold yourself initially to doing the steps one at a time and in order. Start with Step 1 and do it as thoroughly as you can before moving on. As you improve at using Five-Step Analysis, you will be able to record your answers under each of the three steps simultaneously. Use Five-Step Analysis to guide you in circling, underlining, and drawing connecting arrows among things you notice in whatever you are reading or observing. Then make lists following the directions below.

Step 1. Locate exact *repetitions*—identical or nearly identical words or details—and note the number of times each repeats.

> For example, if the word "seems" repeats three times, write "seems × 3." Consider different forms of the same word—"seemed," "seem"—as exact repetitions. Similarly, if you are working with images rather than words, the repeated appearance of high foreheads or of bare midriffs would constitute exact repetitions.

Step 2. Locate repetition of the same kind of detail or word. We call this a *strand*—a grouping of same or similar kind of words or details. (For example, "polite, courteous, mannerly" or "accuse, defence, justice, witness" are strands.)

> Be able to explain the strand's connecting logic: how the words are linked. Some people find it useful to think of strands as clusters or word-detail families that repeat throughout a verbal or visual subject.

Step 3. Locate details or words that form or suggest binary oppositions. We call these *binaries* or *organizing contrasts*. Here are some examples: "open/closed," "naïve/self-conscious," and "grey/brown" (note that the opposition doesn't have to be as stark as "black/white" or "light/dark").

> Start with what's on the page. Gradually move to implied binaries but keep these close to the data. Images of rocks and water, for example, might suggest the implied binary "permanent/ impermanent" or the binary "unchanging/changing."

Step 4. Choose what you take to be the key repetitions, strands, and binaries—which may involve renaming or labelling them—and *rank* them in some order of importance. Notice that deciding which binaries, strands, and repetitions are key is already an interpretive activity.

> At this point in the process (and not before) you can give your-self more space to start making the leap from data to claims (that is, from observations to conclusions). If, for example, you had been analyzing a picture, your leap might answer the question "What does this picture 'say'?" There will always be more than one plausible answer to this question. We say more on this step in Chapter 3, "Interpreting: Asking 'So What?'" For now, you should concentrate on practising the first four steps—the data-gathering phase—and recognize that your choices of what goes with what, what is key, and so forth, already constitute moves toward inter-pretation.

Step 5. Write up the three lists that you have been composing and then write a focused paragraph in which you explain your choice of one repeti-tion or one strand or one binary as especially significant. (We refer to Step 5 as the *Universal Assignment*.)

Looking for Pattern

We have been defining analysis as the search for meaningful pattern, an understanding of parts in relation to each other and to a whole. But how do you know which parts to attend to? What makes some details in the material you are studying more worthy of your attention than others? Here are some principles for selecting significant parts of the whole.

Looking for exact repetition and resemblance, that is, strands (steps 1 and 2)   In virtually all subjects, repetition is a sign of emphasis. In a sym-phony, for example, certain patterns of notes repeat throughout, announcing themselves as major themes. In a legal document, such as a warranty, a reader will quickly become aware of words that are part of a particular idea or pattern of thinking, for instance, disclaimers of accountability.

The repetition may not be exact; in Shakespeare's play *King Lear*, for example, references to "seeing" and "eyes" call attention to themselves through repetition. So a reader of the play would do well to look for various occurrences of words and other details that might be part of this pattern. Let's say you notice that references to seeing and eyes almost always occur with another strand—a pattern of similar kinds of language—having to do with the concept of proof. How might noticing this pattern lead to an idea? You might make a start toward an idea by inferring from the pattern that the play is very concerned with ways of knowing (proving) things with seeing, as opposed to other ways of knowing, such as faith or intuition.

Looking for organizing contrasts (step 3) Sometimes patterns of repetition that you begin to notice in a particular subject matter will be significant because they are part of a contrast—a basic opposition—around which the subject matter is structured. Some examples of organizing contrasts are "nature/civilization," "city/country," "public/private," "organic/inorganic," and "voluntary/involuntary." One advantage of detecting repetition is that it will lead you to discover organizing contrasts, which are central in helping you to locate central issues and concerns in the material you are studying.

Such contrasts, or binaries, are deeply engrained in the ways that we think. Actually, thinking is not possible without them. But discovering binaries is not the end goal.

Why is it useful to find binaries? They are sites of uncertainty, of more than one point of view. As such, they are the breeding ground of ideas. If you can locate and begin to think about—to complicate—the binaries in anything, you will usually be able to detect what is at stake in the subject that you are studying.

Let's think further about what binaries are and what they reveal. When you run into a binary opposition in your own thinking, it is like a fork in the road—a place where two paths going in different directions present themselves and you pause to choose the direction to take. Binaries thus announce a point of tension, a place where something is being opened to decision. When you find a binary opposition in an essay, a film, or a political campaign, you locate the argument—the struggle that the film, essay, or political campaign is having with itself, or the place where something is at issue.

As a general rule, favour live questions, where something remains to be resolved, over inert answers, places where things are already pretty much nailed down and don't leave much space for further thinking. Finding binaries will help you to find the questions around which your subject of study is organized. That's why we call them "organizing contrasts."

⚡*TRY THIS:* Use Five-Step Analysis on the following paragraphs from "Private Investigation and Historical Graduate Studies" by Mary-Kathleen Dunn. Write up the three lists, as well as a focused paragraph in which you explain your choice of one repetition, strand, or binary as most significant. (Note that this is the Universal Assignment as described on page 10). □

Just as the processes of detective work and historical research are similar in structure, so too do the cultures of each profession carry a certain resemblance. Private detectives wear fedoras, smoke stogies and wear loose trenchcoats. They occasionally fortify themselves with Jack Daniels, or some other sort of liquor, either in their local neighbourhood bar or from a flask concealed within their clothing. Similarly, during crunch-time, graduate students in general and history students particularly wear baseball caps (to cover unwashed hair), smoke cigarettes (to promote a nervous buzz) and wear loose, baggy clothing, possibly sweatsuits. They occasionally fortify themselves with pints of beer in their neighbourhood bar—but more often imbibe litres of black coffee to ensure sleeplessness, which they occasionally spike with Jack Daniels, which can be carried concealed in a flask in their clothing. Both private investigators and graduate students experience sleepless nights and observe empty streets drizzled with rain as they try and puzzle out a case or historical problem—while reflecting on past regrets and future possibilities.

As fictional private detective Kinky Friedman once said, "a trail may be old and a trail may be cold, but any trail beats wandering around this Grand Central Station of a world with a busted valise searching for someone who's never there." Ultimately, neither private detectives nor historians can ever know the real truth of a case, if there is indeed such a thing as real truth. Both must start upon an often perilous path, fraught with drudgery and the possibility that one's efforts will be entirely unrewarded. In addition, there is always the possibility that one does not really want to know the so-called truth, as a result of the unsavoury deeds human beings are capable of committing, either in the present or in the past. But for the private detective and the historian, despite all of these dangers and drawbacks, the thrill is truly in the chase.

✦TRY THIS: Do the same assignment as in the "Try this" on page 12, using the following pen and ink drawing.

FIGURE 1.1 *The Dancers,* by Sarah Kersh, pen and ink drawing, 6" × 13.75".

Anomaly

After you have produced your three ranked lists and the paragraph from Five-Step Analysis, you are ready to add an additional step to the process of looking for patterns. Look for anomalies—things that seem unusual or seem not to fit. An anomaly (*a*, meaning "not," and *nom* meaning "name") is literally something that cannot be named—what the dictionary defines as deviation from the normal order. Along with looking for patterns, you should attend to anomalous details—those that seem not to fit the pattern. Anomalies help us to revise our stereotypical assumptions. A recent television commercial, for example, chose to advertise a Major League Baseball team by featuring its star player reading a novel by Dostoyevsky in the dugout during a game. In this case, the anomaly—a baseball player who reads serious literature—is being used to subvert (question, unsettle) the stereotypical assumption that sports and intellectualism don't belong together.

Like searching out binary oppositions, searching out anomalies often takes you to those places in your subject matter where something is going on—where some kind of breaking out of an old pattern or some attempt at "re-seeing" is beginning. Why add anomalies as a separate activity? Anomalies become evident only after you have begun to discern a pattern, so it is best to locate repetitions, strands, and organizing contrasts—things that fit together in some way—before looking for things that seem not to fit. Once you see an anomaly, you will often find that it is part of a strand that you had not detected, a strand that may be the other side of a previously unseen binary. In this respect, looking for anomalies shakes you out of your settled convictions and gets you to consider other possible interpretations.

Just as people tend to leap to evaluative judgments, they also tend to avoid information that challenges (by not conforming to) opinions they already hold. In the desire to make things fit and keep explanations simple, people often screen out anything that would ruffle the pattern they've begun to see. The result is that they ignore the evidence that might lead them to a better theory. (For more on this process of using anomalous evidence to evolve an essay's main idea, see Chapter 6, "The Evolving Thesis.") Anomalies are important because noticing them often leads to new and better ideas. Most advances in scientific thought, for example, have arisen when scientists observed phenomena that do not fit with prevailing theories.

Using Five-Step Analysis: An Example

Examine the following excerpt from a draft of a paper about Ovid's *Metamorphoses*, a collection of short mythological tales dating from ancient Rome. We have included annotations in blue to suggest how the writer's ideas evolve as she looks for patterns (repetition, strands, and binaries) and anomalies, constantly remaining open to reformulation.

The draft actually begins with two loosely connected observations—one, that males dominate females, and another, that many characters in the stories lose the ability to speak and thus become submissive and dominated. In the excerpt, the writer begins to connect these two observations and speculate about what this connection means.

> There are many other examples in Ovid's *Metamorphoses* that show the dominance of man over woman through speech control. In the Daphne and Apollo story, Daphne becomes a tree to escape Apollo, but her ability to speak is destroyed. Likewise, in the Syrinx and Pan story, Syrinx becomes a marsh reed, also a life form that cannot talk, although Pan can make it talk by playing it. *[The writer establishes a pattern of similar detail.]* Pygmalion and Galatea is a story in which the male creates his rendition of the perfect female. The female does not speak once; she is completely silent. Also, Galatea is referred to as "she" and never given a real name. This lack of a name renders her identity more silent. *[Here the writer begins to link the contrasts of speech/silence with the absence/presence of identity.]*
>
> Ocyrhoe is a female character who could tell the future but who was transformed into a mare so that she could not speak. One may explain this transformation by saying it was an attempt by the gods to keep the future

unknown. *[Notice how the writer's thinking expands as she sustains her investigation of the overall pattern of men silencing women: here she tests her theory by adding another variable—prophecy.]* However, there is a male character, Tiresias, who is also a seer of the future and is allowed to speak of his foreknowledge, thereby becoming a famous figure. (Interestingly, Tiresias during his lifetime has experienced being both a male and a female.) *[Notice how the Ocyrhoe example has spawned a contrast based on gender in the Tiresias example. The pairing of the two examples demonstrates that the ability to tell the future is not the sole cause of silencing, because male characters who can do it are not silenced—though the writer pauses to note that Tiresias is not entirely male.]* Finally, in the story of Mercury and Herse, Herse's sister, Aglauros, tries to prevent Mercury from marrying Herse. Mercury turns her into a statue; the male directly silences the female's speech.

The woman silences the man in only two stories studied. *[Here the writer searches out an anomaly—women silencing men—that grows in the rest of the paragraph into an organizing contrast.]* In the first, "The Death of Orpheus," the women make use of "clamorous shouting, Phrygian flutes with curving horns, tambourines, the beating of breasts, and Bacchic howlings" (246) to drown out the male's songs, dominating his speech in terms of volume. In this way, the quality of power within speech is demonstrated: "for the first time, his words had no effect, and he failed to move them [the women] in any way by his voice" (247). Next the women kill him, thereby rendering him silent. However, the male soon regains his temporarily destroyed power of expression: "the lyre uttered a plaintive melody and the lifeless tongue made a piteous murmur" (247). Even after death Orpheus is able to communicate. The women were not able to destroy his power completely, yet they were able to severely reduce his power of speech and expression. *[The writer learns, among other things, that men are harder to silence; Orpheus's lyre continues to sing after his death.]*

The second story in which a woman silences a man is the story of Actaeon, in which the male sees Diana naked, and she transforms him into a stag so that he cannot speak of it: "he tried to say 'Alas!' but no words came" (79). This loss of speech leads to Actaeon's inability to inform his own hunting team of his true identity; his loss of speech leads ultimately to his death. *[This example reinforces the pattern that the writer began to notice in the Orpheus example.]*

In some ways these paragraphs of draft exemplify a writer in the process of discovering a workable idea. They begin with a list of similar examples, briefly noted. As the examples accumulate, the writer begins to make connections and formulate trial explanations. We do not include enough of this draft to get to the tentative thesis the draft is working toward, although that thesis is already beginning to emerge. What we want to emphasize here is the writer's willingness to accumulate data and to locate it in various patterns of similarity and contrast.

C. THINKING RECURSIVELY

Thinking is not simply linear and progressive, from point A to point B to point C, like stops on a train. Careful thinkers are always retracing their steps, questioning their first—and second—impressions, assuming that they've missed something. All good thinking is recursive—that is, it repeatedly goes over the same ground. In a thinking technique called looping, for example, a writer might repeatedly go over the same material but from different starting points, seeing what would happen if he or she reformulates, begins with different details, and moves in a slightly different direction. Imagine writing an autobiographical sketch of your life as a student that begins with getting singled out for winning a spelling bee. Then, imagine beginning instead with getting beaten up on the playground in fourth grade.

For the purposes of using Five-Step Analysis, recursive thinking is essential. You need to view and review the material to find repetition. Working with strands is an inherently recursive activity because you'll tend to first think that one set of words or details fits together as a strand and then you'll find yourself regrouping—reformulating your strands as new patterns begin to strike you. And as you have no doubt already experienced, as you begin to notice repetitions, these tend to suggest strands, and strands tend to beget organizing contrasts.

Nowhere is it more important to reformulate than in working with organizing contrasts. This is because, as you have seen, the habit of mind called binary thinking can retard thought through oversimplification—through a tendency toward rigidly dichotomized (either/or) points of view. But finding binary oppositions as a means of locating what is at issue and then using the binaries to start rather than end your thinking process is not reductive. Notice how in the Ovid example the writer keeps reforming her ways of categorizing her data.

Here are some other examples of what working productively with binaries looks like. Let's consider a brief example in which a writer starts with the binary "Was the pianist Glenn Gould neurotic, or was he a musical genius?" This is a useful, if overstated, starting point for prompting thinking. Going over the same ground, the writer might next decide that the terms "neurosis" and "musical genius" don't accurately name the issue. He or she might decide that artistic genius is often perceived as mental instability by the culture at large and, thus, it's not a viable either/or formulation. This move, by the way, is known as collapsing the binary: coming to see that what had appeared to be an opposition is really two parts of one complex phenomenon. Perhaps the neurosis/musical genius binary would be better reformulated in terms of conventionality/unconventionality—a binary that might lead the writer to start reappraising the ways in which Gould is not as eccentric as he first appeared.

People seem to go through four mental operations when they think recursively with binaries. Here they are with another example.

Step 1. Locate a number of different binaries suggested by your subject.

> Consider, for example, the binaries contained in the following question: Should the Supreme Court of Canada uphold the bylaw in Oakville, Ontario, that bans construction of any commercial signs exceeding 80 square feet in size? The most obvious binary in this question is uphold/deny. But there are also other binaries in the question—judicial/legislative, for example, and corporate welfare/public welfare. These binaries imply further binaries. Insofar as Oakville is one of the country's wealthiest municipalities, the question requires a writer to consider the reality of class distinctions in a democratic society and whether or not rich people are able to control their public spaces in a way that poor people cannot.

Step 2. Analyze and define the opposing terms.

> What, for example, does it mean to ask whether the Supreme Court "upholds" the bylaw in Oakville? Does "uphold" mean refuse to consider amendments to the bylaw? Allow for special appeals? Seek further information from Oakville officials? Too often people start arguing the "either/or" position before they have figured out what the key terms mean.

Step 3. Question the accuracy of the binary.

> Having begun to analyze and define your terms, you would next need to determine how accurately they define the issues raised by your subject. You might consider, for example, to what extent the federal judicial system exercises control over provincial legislation. In the process of trying to determine if there are restrictions on

such control, you could start to locate particular characteristics of our governmental system that might help you to formulate your binary more precisely. Think of the binary as a starting point—a kind of deliberate overgeneralization—that allows you to set up positions that you can then test in order to refine.

Step 4. Substitute "To what extent?" for "either/or."

The best strategy in using binaries productively is usually to locate arguments on both sides of the either/or choice that the binary poses, and then choose a position somewhere in between the two extremes. Once you have arrived at what you consider the most accurate phrasing of the binary, you can rephrase the original either/or question in the more qualified terms that asking "To what extent?" allows. Making this move would not release you from the responsibility of taking a stand and arguing for it. But by analyzing the terms of the binary, you would come to question it and, ultimately, to arrive at a more complex and qualified position to write about.

Admittedly, in reorienting your thinking from the obvious and clear-cut choices that either/or formulations provide to the murkier waters of asking "To what extent?" your decision process will be made more difficult. The gain, however, is that the to-what-extent mind-set, by predisposing you to assess multiple and potentially conflicting points of view, will enable you to address more fairly and accurately the issues raised by your subject.

Applying these steps will usually cause you to do one or more of the following:

a. Discover that you have not adequately named the binary and that another opposition would be more accurate.

b. Weight one side of your binary more heavily than the other, rather than seeing the issue as all or nothing.

c. Discover that the two terms of your binary are not really so separate and opposed after all, but are actually parts of one complex phenomenon or issue (collapsing the binary).

✸*TRY THIS:* Locate some organizing contrasts in a recent news item—something you saw on television or something covered in the newspaper or on the Internet. As we've said, binaries are pervasive in the way we think; therefore, you can expect to find them everywhere. Consider, for example, the binaries suggested by current trends in contemporary music or by the representation of women in birthday cards. Having located the binaries in the news item, pick one and try out the four steps we suggest for working with binaries. Focus especially on Step 4: substituting "To what extent?" for "either/or." In class discussion, share your thoughts on whether or not this final step created a more complex position on the news item. ☐

❧*TRY THIS:* Write a couple of pages in which you work with the binaries suggested by the following familiar expression: "School gets in the way of one's education." Keep the focus on working through the binaries implicit in the quotation. What other terms would you substitute for "school" and "education"? Coming up with a range of synonyms for each term will clarify what is at stake in the binary. Remember to consider the accuracy of the claim. To what extent, and in what ways, is the expression both true and false? ☐

D. THE OBSERVATIONAL BOTTOM LINE

If you persist in working with the observational skills offered in this chapter, you will surprise yourself with all the things you find yourself noticing and with your increasing confidence in your own ability to have ideas. There are, however, certain prerequisites—attitudes and expectations—that you will need to bring to the task of thinking and writing more analytically.

1. Look for questions.

What all of our suggestions have in common is the single requirement that you train yourself to look for questions rather than leaping too quickly to answers. It is this orientation that will move you beyond merely reporting information to thinking with and about it.

The best way to become a better thinker is to actively search out an area of your subject where there are no clear and obvious answers—to look for something that needs explaining rather than to reiterate the obvious.

Although disciplines vary in the kinds of questions they characteristically ask, every discipline is concerned with asking questions, exploring areas of uncertainty, and attempting to solve or at least clarify problems. Rather than leading you to a single or obvious answer, an analytical attitude aims to find a space in which you can have ideas about (explore the questions in) what you've been learning. In short, you are usually better off to begin with something that you don't understand very well and want to understand better. Begin by asking what kinds of questions the material poses.

2. Suspect your first responses.

If you settle for your first response, the result is likely to be superficial, obvious, and overly general. A better strategy is to examine your first response for ways in which it is inaccurate, and then develop the implications of the overstatement (or error) into a new formulation. In many cases, writers go through this process of proposing and rejecting ideas ten times or more before they arrive at an angle or approach that will sustain an essay.

A first response is okay for a start, as long as you don't stop there. For example, many people might agree, at first glance, that no one should be denied health care, that a given film or novel that concludes with a marriage is a happy ending, or that the Canadian government should not pass trade laws that might cause Canadians to lose their jobs. On closer inspection, however, each of these responses begins to reveal its limitations. Given that there is a limited amount of money available, should everyone, regardless of age or physical condition, be accorded every medical treatment that might prolong life? And might not a novel or film that concludes in marriage signal that the society offers too few options or, more cynically, that the author is feeding the audience an implausible fantasy to blanket over problems raised earlier in the work? And couldn't trade laws resulting in short-term loss of jobs ultimately produce more jobs and a healthier economy?

As these examples suggest, first responses—usually pieces of conventional wisdom—can blind you to rival explanations. (See the section entitled "Weak Thesis Type 3: The Thesis Restates Conventional Wisdom" in Chapter 7.)

3. Expect to become interested.

Writing gives you the opportunity to cultivate your curiosity by thinking exploratively. Rather than approaching subjects in a mechanical way or putting off writing to the last possible moment and doing the work grudgingly, try giving yourself and the subject matter the benefit of the doubt. If you can suspend judgment and start writing, you will often find yourself uncovering interests where you had not seen them before. In other words, accept the idea that interest is a product of writing—not a prerequisite.

If you repeatedly reject things because they don't interest you, you will deprive yourself of the opportunity to discover interests. Banish the word "boring," if you can, from your vocabulary for a while. Expect interest to come, and it will. People who are easily bored and not shy about saying so

> ### Voices Across the Curriculum
>
> ### Ode to the All-Nighter
>
> The all-nighter is a mythical beast which prowls through the shadowy halls of the 4:00 a.m. dormitory halls. It is sated by 100-watt light bulbs and powered by cola, juice, water, and loud music in headphones.
>
> The all-nighter is a fickle creature, often providing its victims with a false sense of hope and accomplishment before the adrenaline/caffeine cocktail within them peters out. Lethargy and relief mix in strange manners while the victim valiantly sets out to hand his paper in. But lo, what is that? The all-nighter has nibbled at the coherence of the paper! Oh well... at least it's done.
>
> Evil all-nighter... (grumble, grumble...)
>
> —Jeffrey Osadczuk, second-year political studies major

reveal more about themselves than about the subject matter in which they find no interest. Or as an acerbic colleague of ours marvels, "My students think that when they find Shakespeare boring, they are saying something about Shakespeare."

4. Write all of the time about what you are studying.

Because interest is so often a product and not a prerequisite of writing, it follows that writing informally about what you are studying while you are studying it is probably the single best preparation for developing interesting ideas. By writing spontaneously about what you read, you will accustom yourself to being a less passive consumer of ideas and information, and you will have more ideas and information available to think actively with and about. In any case, you should not wait to start writing until you think you have an idea you can organize a paper around. Instead, use writing to get you to the idea. We say more on this score in the Chapter 3.

ASSIGNMENTS

1. Look at Figure 1.2 carefully, using Notice and Focus in order to rank your three most interesting observations. Remember to "dwell on the data" and record exactly what you see.

   Next, try to determine whether or not your observations are part of any meaningful pattern. In other words, employ Five-Step Analysis to discover a repetition, a strand, or a contrast (that is, a binary).

FIGURE 1.2 *Pierre on the Island of Crete*, 1975 by Doug Babington. Pen and ink drawing.

Finally, compose a focused paragraph in which you explain your choice of one repetition or one strand or one binary as especially significant. This "Universal Assignment"—Step 5 of the Five-Step Analysis—should then be shared with others in your class by reading aloud in groups of three or four. Together, you will appreciate how a nonverbal work of art (nonverbal *except* for its title) can give rise to diverse analyses.

2. Of all rights guaranteed to Canadian citizens, none is more fundamental than the right to free speech. But what binary is suggested by the phrase "free speech"? Is it "enslaved speech," "censored speech," "politically correct speech," "approved speech"? Decide on what *you* consider to be the binary suggested by the phrase "free speech," and then locate arguments on both sides of the either/or choice that the binary poses. Then choose a position somewhere in between the two extremes. In other words, substitute "To what extent?" for "either/or." By collapsing the binary, you should be able to write a few paragraphs that explain how our right to free speech is not only fundamental but also complex. Exchange your paragraphs with a classmate. After reading each other's work, discuss how your "collapsed binaries" converge or diverge.

2

Habitual Thinking

Over sixty years ago, the English writer George Orwell warned against "the invasion of one's mind by ready-made phrases." He realized that even the most observant of people could find their good thinking corrupted by bad usage. Stale phrases anaesthetize the brain, according to Orwell, and—"like cavalry horses answering the bugle call"—they "group themselves automatically into the familiar, dreary pattern."

Our English language may indeed become a foe instead of a friend. Every writer must work hard to avoid an anaesthetized brain, to use words creatively rather than relying on ready-made phrases. To begin that hard work, let's examine six habits of mind that often leave writers open to the sort of invasion described by George Orwell.

A. BANKING

The theorist Paolo Freire is now widely known for his attack on educational practices that he called "banking." In the banking model of education, the student is given information that he or she later gives back in more or less the same form—in other words, there is a deposit, followed by a withdrawal. Like the number-bearing account through which money passes, the learner is a passive conduit taking things in and spitting them back out.

As only one part of the learning process, banking isn't really such a bad habit. We all need information to think with; the worst kind of opinion-mongering is starved of information. Opinion-mongers think what they think because they heard it somewhere, although they often have forgotten where. How can we arrive fairly at ideas and judgments with no information about the world, nothing to go on beyond our own limited experience?

But an education consisting entirely of banking—information in/ information out—does not teach thinking. Being able to recite other people's ideas does not automatically render a person capable of thinking about these ideas or producing them. Of course, repetition, imitation, and memorization can develop our minds and help us retain information, but it is possible to repeat what we don't understand, to merely accept instead of asking questions, and to never learn how to think about all that has been taken in. Passivity is a primary retardant of learning. As we show in a later chapter on reading critically, it is possible to acquire and respect other people's ideas but also to get beyond just cutting and pasting them into mental scrapbooks and just agreeing and disagreeing with them in reflex fashion.

You can try several activities to get beyond banking. One of these is an activity whose usefulness is too often underestimated: paraphrasing. Paraphrasing something is not the same as summarizing it or generalizing about it. Summarizing and generalizing are further removed from the language of the reading than is paraphrasing. A paraphrase takes the language of the reading and restates it in other words.

Why is paraphrasing useful? Why isn't it just a mechanical and labour-intensive form of banking? The answer has to do with words—what they are and what we do with them. When we read, it is easy to skip quickly over the words, assuming we know what they mean. Yet when people start talking about what they mean by particular words—for example, the difference between "assertive" and "aggressive," or the meaning of ordinary words like "polite," "realistic," or "gentlemanly"—they usually find less agreement than they expected. Most words can mean more than one thing and mean different things to different people. Words matter. They are our primary means of negotiating the space between ourselves and others and of figuring out our relation to the world. It pays to take the time to notice words and find ways of thinking more carefully about what they mean. Try, for example, to come up with as many words as you can to name different kinds of anger. What does this reveal?

Because paraphrasing involves more than mechanically reproducing the reading, it is a prime alternative to banking. When you recast a sentence or passage—by finding the best synonyms you can think of for the original language and translating it into an equivalent statement—you are thinking actively about what each word means.

Voices Across the Curriculum

My High-School Writing Career

Early on in my writing career (say, the beginning of high school), I struggled with many an information-banking essay. Back then, the goal was to create a research paper that was a cohesive stew of information. I was to search out the best possible ingredients—the research information itself—and then follow the five-paragraph recipe to arrange those ingredients in a way most pleasing to the teacher's palate. Information banking at its finest: fill the vaults of Sean's bank with as much intellectual capital as possible, and then withdraw it with some semblance of order.

And it went without saying that I, as the cook, should never add my own seasonings to the paper. I even had one history paper where the teacher went as far as to say that any (and every) assertion made in my paper must be cited, because none of what I was saying should be what I myself thought, as I was not the expert here; my sources were. And what's worse, looking back, is that I did well on that paper because I had skill in banking—the order of business for several years.

—Sean Fenlon, first-year software design major

TRY THIS: Select a short paragraph, or even a key sentence, from something you are currently reading. Recast the substantive language in the passage into other words whose meaning is as close to the original as possible. Try not to make the language more general, and don't condense it into a summarizing statement. Then reflect and take some notes on what you notice about the passage that you may not have noticed when you read it the first time. □

The next few chapters offer more tactics for reading actively, but here is another one to start using now. Read with an eye to problems. Virtually all writing can be seen as trying to address some problem or problems. Generally speaking, writers write because they have determined that something needs to be done to correct an idea or situation, whether in their own lives or in the world. You can read more actively by trying to figure out from the use of language in the reading what its author is worried about and what he or she is trying to "fix." Once you figure out what the reading is reacting to, and what it wants to better understand or change, you will have a far clearer understanding of how the reading operates, and why it does what it does. This is true even of textbooks: informational reading still has a point of view. Whenever you can, find the position the reading is trying to resist, revise, or replace.

B. GENERALIZING

When we generalize, we are really saying, "What it all boils down to is…," "What this adds up to is…," or "The gist of her speech was…."

Like banking, generalizing is not always a bad habit. Reducing complex events, theories, books, or speeches to a reasonably accurate summarizing statement requires practice and skill. We generalize from our experience because this is one way of arriving at ideas. The problem with generalizing as a habit of mind is that it removes the mind—usually much too quickly—from the data that produced the generalization in the first place.

People tend to remember their reactions and impressions. The dinner was dull. The house was beautiful. The music was exciting. But they forget the specific, concrete causes of these impressions (if they ever fully noticed them). As a result, people deprive themselves of material to think with—the data that might allow them to reconsider their initial impressions or to share those impressions with others.

One common denominator of an analytical habit of mind is that it pays attention to detail. We analyze because our global responses—to a social problem, for example, or to a film or a speech—are too general to be of much use. To understand a subject, we need to get past our first broad (and usually evaluative) response in order to discover the particulars that best explain the character of the whole.

Consider for a moment what you are actually asking others to do when you offer them a generalization such as "His stories are very depressing." Unless the recipient of this observation asks a question—such as "Why do you think so?"—he or she is being required to take your word for it: the stories are depressing because you say so. What happens instead if you offer a few details to explain what caused you to think as you do? Clearly, you are on riskier ground. Your listener might think that the details you cite are actually not depressing or that this is not the most interesting or useful way to think about the stories. He or she might then offer a different generalization, a different reading of the data, but at least conversation has become possible. There is something available to think with: the actual stuff of experience from which further generalizations can be made.

In a reply to a young writer who had solicited his advice, Ernest Hemingway recommended what he referred to as his "five-finger exercise." The exercise, like playing scales on a piano, is a kind of mental scale playing. In it you train yourself to habitually trace your own responses back to their causes in the concrete stuff of experience. The same five-finger exercise will make you a better reader and learner. Vagueness and generality are major blocks to learning because, as habits of mind, they allow you to dismiss virtually everything you've read and heard except the general idea you've arrived at. Often the generalizations that come to mind are so broad that they tell us nothing. To say, for example, that a poem is about love or death or rebirth, or that the economy of a particular emerging nation is inefficient, accomplishes very little because the generalizations could fit almost any poem or economy. In other words, generalizations are weak ideas, ones that are born prematurely; they always need incubation time in order to gain clarity, precision, and strength.

The simplest antidote to the problem of generalizing is to train yourself to be more self-conscious about where your generalizations come from. In other words, press yourself to trace general impressions back to the particulars that caused them. What three details about a classroom or meeting room (or some public space you regularly spend time in), for example, seem most responsible for the attitude you have toward that place and the way it makes you feel? Why? This tracing of attitudes back to their concrete causes is the most basic—and most necessary—move toward developing an analytical habit of mind. It will help you go through the world in less of a haze. Deciding to be more conscious of our own responses to the world and their causes is also an antidote to the inevitable numbing and desensitizing that take place as habit takes control of our daily lives. Choose to notice more and to keep noticing.

Here's another strategy for bringing your thinking down from high levels of generality. Think of the words you use in terms of an *abstraction ladder*. The more general and vague the word, the higher its position on the abstraction ladder. "Animal," for example, is higher on the abstraction ladder than "mammal," which is higher than "cow." Many years ago, Northrop Frye warned that sitting high on the abstraction ladder meant sitting on "the lowest rung of the literary ladder, on a level with the distributors of gobbledygook, double talk and officialese of all kinds" (106). He defined jargon as "writing in which words do not express meanings, but are thrown in the general direction of their meanings; writing which can always be cut down by two-thirds without loss of whatever sense it has" (106) Furthermore, he came up with a sharp and vivid image for overly abstract language: "verbal cotton wool."

Of course, not *all* jargon is gobbledygook, and not *all* abstract language is verbal cotton wool. As the readings in this book demonstrate, effective writers support their abstract concepts and academic hypotheses with concrete language and clear, detailed examples. We have more to say on this topic in Chapter 11, "The Language of Clarity." You might try applying the tag phrase "level 3 generality" to your first draft generalizations, reminding yourself to steer clear of the higher reaches of abstract generalization—some so high up the ladder from the concrete stuff that produced them that there is barely enough air to sustain the thought. We start with "level 3" instead of "level 2" because there aren't just two categories, abstract and concrete: these categories are the opposite ends of a continuum, a sliding scale. And too often when writers try to concretize their generalizations by just one level, the results are still too general: they change "animal" to "mammal," but they need "cow" or, even better, "Black Angus."

⚡*TRY THIS:* Working with two or three other people, identify all the abstract nouns in the following paragraph—along with any phrases that you think contribute to "verbal cotton wool." Then collaborate to revise the paragraph. Try your best to cut down on verbiage and to replace abstract words with concrete alternatives. At the end of this chapter, you will find the song lyric that provided the source for our paragraph of abstraction. □

> Liberation from the pressures of modern life is sought by many individuals in Canadian society today. Two principal factors contribute to the achievement of a truly personal sense of liberation: on the one hand, the establishment of an environment that allows the individual to perceive the possibility of transcendence or flight; on the other hand, the cultivation of social experiences that accommodate eccentricity and spontaneity while simultaneously establishing a structure of harmony and interdependence.

If you experiment with the abstraction ladder, you will find that it takes some practice to learn to distinguish between abstract words and concrete ones. A concrete word is one that appeals to the senses. Abstract words are not available to our senses of touch, sight, hearing, taste, and smell. "Submarine" is a concrete word. It conjures up a mental image, something we can physically experience. "Peace-keeping force" is an abstract phrase. It conjures up a concept, but in an abstract and general way. We know what people are talking about when they say there is a plan to send submarines to a troubled area. We can't be so sure what is meant when people start talking about a peace-keeping force. Start experimenting to see if you can recognize the rather tricky divide between concrete and abstract words.

⚡*TRY THIS:* Locate a word above (more abstract than) and a word below (more concrete than) each of the following words: "society," "food," "train," "taxes," "school," "government," "cooking oil," "organism," "story," and "magazine." □

C. JUDGING

It would be impossible to overstate the mind-numbing effect that the judgment reflex has on thinking. Why? Consider what we do when we judge something and what we ask others to do when we offer them our judgments: "ugly," "realistic," "pretty," "boring," "wonderful," "unfair," "crazy." Notice that the problem with such words is a version of the problem with all generalizations—lack of information. What have you actually told someone else if you say that X is ugly or boring or realistic?

In its most primitive—most automatic and least thoughtful—form, judging is like an on/off switch. When the switch gets thrown in one direction or the other—good/bad, right/wrong, positive/negative—the resulting judgment predetermines and overdirects any subsequent thinking we might do. Rather than thinking about what X is or how X operates, we lock ourselves prematurely into proving that we were right to think that X should be banned or supported.

The psychologist Carl Rogers has written at length on the problem of the judgment reflex. He claims that our habitual tendency as humans—virtually a programmed response—is to evaluate everything and to do so very quickly. Walking out of a movie, for example, most people will immediately voice their approval or disapproval, usually in either/or terms: I liked it or didn't like it; it was right/wrong, good/bad, interesting/boring. The other people in the conversation will then offer their own evaluations plus their judgments of the others' judgments: "I think that it was a good movie and that you are wrong to think it was bad." And so on.

There are several problems with this kind of reflex move to evaluation. Like the jerk of a knee as a reflex response to the tap from a physician's silver hammer, reflex judgments are made without conscious thought (the source of the pejorative term "knee-jerk thinking"). Reflex judgments close off thinking by categorizing reactions instantly into likes and dislikes. The fact that you liked or didn't like a movie probably says more about you—your tastes, interests, biases, and experiences—than it does about the movie. What makes a movie boring? That it doesn't have enough car chases? That its plot resembles half the plots on cable channels? That the leading man is miscast or the dialogue too long-winded? At the least, in such cases, you should share with readers your criteria for judgment—your reasons and your standards of evaluation. Without such careful explanation, judgments will always appear to be reflex, and others will assume that you are motivated more by your desire to defend your position than by your desire to understand what the film was trying to accomplish.

When people leap to judgment, they usually land in the mental pathways they've grown accustomed to travelling, guided by family or friends or popular opinion. If you can break the evaluation reflex and press yourself to analyze before judging a subject, you will often be surprised at how much your initial responses change. As a general rule, you should seek to understand the subject you are analyzing before moving to a judgment about it. Try to figure out what your subject means before deciding how you feel about it.

This is not to say that all judging should be avoided. Obviously, our thinking on many occasions must be applied to decision making—deciding whether we should or shouldn't vote for a particular candidate, should or shouldn't eat French fries, or should or shouldn't support a ban on cigarette advertising.

A writer needs to take into account how the judgment has been affected by the particular situation (context) and to acknowledge how thinking about these details has led to restricting (qualifying) the range of the judgment: X is sometimes true in these particular circumstances; Z is probably the right thing to do but only when A and B occur. In other words, analytical thinking ultimately does need to arrive at a point of view—which is a form of judgment—but analytical conclusions are usually not phrased in terms of like/dislike or good/bad. They disclose what a person has come to understand about X rather than how he or she imperiously rules on the worth of X.

In some ways, the rest of this book consists of a set of methods for blocking the ever-present judgment reflex in favour of more thoughtful responses. For now, here are two things to try in order to short-circuit the judgment reflex and begin replacing it with a more thoughtful, more patient, and more open-mindedly curious habit of mind. First, try the cure that Carl Rogers recommended to negotiators in industry and government: do not assert an agreement or disagreement with another person's position until you can repeat that position in a way that the other person would accept as fair and accurate. This is surprisingly hard to do because we are usually so busy calling up judgments of our own that we barely hear what the other person is saying.

Second, try eliminating the word "should" from your vocabulary for a while, since judgments so often take the form of recommendations: "We should pass the law" or "We should not consider putting such foolish restrictions into law." By contrast, the analytical habit of mind is characterized by the words "why," "how," and "what." Analysis asks the following: "What is the aim of the new law?" "Why do laws of this sort tend to get passed in some parts of the country rather than in others?" "How does this law compare with its predecessor?"

You might also try eliminating evaluative adjectives—those that offer judgments with no data. "Green" is a descriptive, concrete adjective. It offers something we can experience. "Beautiful" is an evaluative adjective. It offers only judgment.

❧TRY THIS: The dividing line between judgmental and nonjudgmental words is often more difficult to discern in practice than you might assume. Categorize each of the terms in the following list as judgmental or nonjudgmental, and be prepared to explain your reasoning: "monstrous," "delicate," "authoritative," "strong," "muscular," "automatic," "vibrant," "tedious," "pungent," "unrealistic," "flexible," "tart," "pleasing," "clever," "slow." □

❧TRY THIS: One way of keeping tabs on your own habits of mind is to consider the kinds of adjectives and adverbs that you use. Some are neutral in their evaluation, offering information without telling you what to think about it. Others are not neutral; they name evaluative responses, usually offering little or no concrete information. Consider the following sentence: "The politician grinned at the camera, running his fingers through his hair like some vain, silly starlet." The words in this sentence do each of the four different things that can happen when we describe: they offer details, make comparisons, name, and overtly judge. Locate an example of each of these four different descriptive activities in the sentence. Then, write a paragraph of description—on anything that comes to mind—without using any evaluative adjectives or adverbs. Alternatively, analyze and categorize the word choice in a piece of your own recent writing. □

D. DEBATE-STYLE ARGUMENT

People are customarily introduced to writing arguments through the debate model. They are taught to argue pro or con on a given position or issue, with the aim of defeating an imagined opponent and convincing an audience of the rightness of one side of the argument. To its credit, the debate model teaches writers to consider more than a single viewpoint: their opponent's as well as their own. But unfortunately it can also train them, even if inadvertently, to see the other side only as the opposition and to concentrate their energy only on winning the day. The problem with this approach is that it overemphasizes the bottom line—aggressively advancing a claim for or against some view—without first engaging in the exploratory interpretation of evidence that is so necessary to arriving at thoughtful arguments.

Thus, debate-style argument produces a frame of mind in which defending a position matters more than taking the necessary time to develop ideas worth defending. And, very possibly, it nourishes the mudslinging and opinionated mind-set of "attack first" that proliferates in editorials and television talk shows, not to mention the conversations you overhear in going about your life. We are not saying that people should forget about making value and policy decisions and avoid the task of persuading others. We are saying that too many of the arguments we all read, hear, and participate in every day are based on insufficient analysis.

In sum, adhering to the more restrictive, debate-style definition of argument can create a number of problems for careful analytical writers:

1. By requiring writers to be oppositional, the debate model inclines them to discount or dismiss problems with the position they have chosen; they cling to the same static position rather than testing it as a way of allowing it to evolve.
2. The debate model leads writers toward either/or thinking rather than encouraging them to formulate more qualified positions (carefully limited, acknowledging exceptions, and so forth) that integrate apparently opposing viewpoints.
3. The debate model overvalues convincing someone else at the expense of developing understanding.

The remedy, we suggest, is the temporary suspension of the pro/con, debate-style habit of mind. Argument and analysis are profoundly connected, but their stances toward subject matter and audience differ so much that most people need to learn them separately before being able to put them back together. And because the argumentative habit of mind is so aggressively visible in our culture, most people never get around to experimenting with the more reflective and less combative approach that analysis embraces. Thus, this book asks you to turn off the argument switch—not forever, but for as long as it takes for you to cultivate other habits of mind that argument might otherwise overshadow.

Although analysis and argument proceed in essentially the same way, they differ in the kinds of questions they try to answer. Argument, at its most dispassionate, asks, "What can be said with truth about X or Y?" In common practice, though, the kinds of questions that argument more often answers are more committed, directive, and "should"-centred, such as "Which is better, X or Y?" "How can we best achieve X or Y?" "Why should we stop doing X or Y?"

Analysis, by contrast, asks, "What does X or Y mean?" In analysis the evidence (your data) is something you wish to understand, and the claims are assertions about what that evidence means. The claim that an argument makes—for example, readers should or shouldn't vote for bans on smoking in public buildings, or they should or shouldn't believe that gays can function effectively in the military—is often an answer to a "should" question. The writer of an analysis is more concerned with discovering how each of these complex subjects might be defined and explained than with convincing readers to approve or disapprove of them.

The factor that most clearly separates argument and analysis is the closer association of argument with the desire to persuade. A writer concerned with persuading others may feel the need to go into the writing process with considerable certainty about the position he or she advocates. The writer of an analysis, on the other hand, usually begins and remains for an extended period in a position of uncertainty. Analysis is thus more exploratory, more tentative, and more dispassionate than argument (especially debate-style argument).

Analytical writers are frequently more concerned with persuading *themselves*, with discovering what they believe about a subject, than they are with persuading others. The writer of an analysis is thus more likely to begin with the details of a subject he or she wishes to better understand than with a position he or she wishes to defend. Analysis, in sum, is concerned with having clearer ideas about how things operate rather than with whether or not we should approve or disapprove of them.

It's important to remember that, in practice, analysis and argument are inevitably linked. Even the most tentative and cautiously evolving analysis shares with argument the aim of having readers accept a particular interpretation of a set of data. Similarly, even the most passionately committed argument engages in analysis, arranging details into patterns and explaining what they mean. But as should now be clear, the aims of analysis and argument can sometimes be in conflict.

E. EITHER/OR THINKING (BINARIES)

Analytical thought is unthinkable without categories. Categorical thinking is an unavoidable and distinctive feature of how all human beings make sense of the world: in order to generalize from particular experiences, we try to put those experiences into meaningful categories. When we contract an illness, for example, doctors diagnose it by type. When we study personality theory, different behaviours are grouped by personality type. Subject areas in school are categorized into divisions: the natural sciences, the social sciences, and the humanities.

But categorical thinking can also be dangerous. It can lead us into oversimplification. This is especially the case with one of the most common forms of categorical thinking: the use of binaries.

In human thinking, as in a computer, a binary is a pair of elements, usually in opposition to each other, such as off/on, yes/no, right/wrong, agree/disagree, approve/disapprove, real/unreal, accurate/inaccurate, believable/unbelievable, and so on. As the philosopher Herbert Marcuse says, "We understand that which is in terms of that which is not": light is that which is not dark; masculine is that which is not feminine; and civilized is that which is not primitive. We can't help but think in binary terms—creating opposing categories is fundamental to defining things.

Binaries become a problem when they are used uncritically, leading to what is called reductive thinking. Reductive thinking oversimplifies a subject, eliminating alternatives between two extremes—for example, that women are either virgins or whores, or that teachers either instill a love of learning in students or alienate them from their feelings.

Because binaries are part of how humans think, we can't avoid the problem of reductive thinking by just avoiding binaries altogether. In fact, noticing and naming binaries is an excellent way to improve your reading skills and to generate ideas. The issue is how to make productive rather than reductive use of binaries. You can start by keeping the following two points in mind:

1. Most subjects cannot be adequately considered in terms of only two options—either this or that, with nothing in between.
2. The arrangement of two terms into opposing categories usually implies a value hierarchy even when the valuing of one side of the binary over the other is not intended. The binaries black/white or primitive/civilized may in the writer's mind be value neutral, but the fact that the terms appear in opposed pairs suggests that one side is right, the other wrong, one side is desirable, the other less so.

In sum, it is useful and necessary to construct binaries, but it is dangerous to ignore the grey areas in between and the value judgments that binaries tend to conceal.

Often the trouble starts with the ways that binaries are phrased. Two of the most common and potentially counterproductive ways of phrasing binaries are either/or and agree/disagree. In most cases, there are more than two alternatives, but the either/or or agree/disagree phrasing prevents you from looking for them. And it does not acknowledge that both alternatives may have some truth to them. A new environmental policy may be both visionary and blind, or some combination of the two. And there may be more accurate categories than visionary and blind for considering the merits and demerits of the policy.

Framing an issue in either/or terms can be useful for stimulating a chain of thought, but it is usually not a good way to end one. Consider the following either/or binary: "Was Quebec separatism fuelled by political concerns or linguistic concerns?" You could begin this way, but if you're not careful—not conscious of the all-or-nothing force of binary formulations—you could easily get trapped in an overly dichotomized position; in this case, that political concerns caused separatism and that linguistic concerns have nothing to do with it, or vice versa.

You can't analyze without binaries, but you need to be wary of putting everything into large, undifferentiated categories, labelled all black or all white, with nothing in between.

⚡TRY THIS: In his essay "The Scavenger of Highway #3" (which follows Chapter 4), Bruce McCall describes how we Canadians used to regard our neighbours to the south: "The Americans talked too much, mainly about themselves. Their torrid love affair with their own history and legend exceeded—painfully—the quasi-British Canadian idea of modesty and self-restraint. They were jammed permanently in extroverted high gear, confident to the brink of, if not over the edge of, arrogance; strident, take-charge, can-do—fatiguing … They were forever busting their buttons in spasms of insufferable yahoo pride or all too publicly agonizing over their crises." Should McCall be faulted here for generalizing, for judging, and for ignoring grey areas that binaries tend to conceal? Formulate your answer by talking with another person in your class and by paying close attention to McCall's choice of words. □

F. OPINIONS (VERSUS IDEAS)

Perhaps no single word causes more problems between students and teachers, and among people in general, than the word "opinion." As the saying goes, most everyone feels "entitled" to have one. But are there limits to that entitlement? Do opinions stand up to comparison with, say, ideas—or beliefs—or great notions?

Many of the opinions people fight about are actually clichés—pieces of much-repeated conventional wisdom; for example, "People are entitled to say what they want. That's just my opinion." But, of course, this assertion isn't a private, personal revelation. It is an exaggerated and oversimplified version of the right to freedom of expression in the Canadian Charter of Rights and Freedoms. Much public thinking has gone on about this essential democratic right, and it has thus been carefully qualified. A person can't, for example, say publicly whatever he or she pleases about other people if what he or she says is false and damages the reputation of another person.

Our opinions are learned. They are products of our culture and our upbringing—not personal possessions. It is okay to have opinions. Everyone does. It is not okay, however, to give too many of our views and opinions protected-species status by walling them off into a reserve, not to be touched by reasoning or evidence.

Some things, of course, we do have to take on faith. Religious convictions, for example, are more than opinions, though they operate in a similar way: we believe where we can't always prove. But even our most sacred convictions are not really harmed by thinking. The world's religions are constantly engaged in interpreting and reinterpreting what religious texts mean, what various traditional practices mean, and how they may or may not be adapted to the attitudes and practices of the world as it is today.

For purposes of writing analytically, you need to think about the difference between an idea and an opinion. The discovery and careful wording of ideas is one of the primary aims of analysis. To arrive at ideas, we have to learn to see the questions that are suggested by whatever it is we are studying. Opinions, particularly for people who have a lot of them, get in the way of having ideas because opinions are so often habitual responses—mental reflexes.

G. IDEAS ACROSS THE CURRICULUM

This is a book about how to have ideas. It's one thing to acquire knowledge, but you also need to learn how to produce knowledge, to think for yourself. The problem is that people get daunted when asked to arrive at ideas. They dream up ingenious ways to avoid the task. Or they get paralyzed with anxiety.

What is an idea? Must an idea be something that is entirely "original"? Must it revamp the way you understand yourself or your stance toward the world?

Such expectations are unreasonably grand. Clearly, a writer in the early stages of learning about a subject can't be expected to arrive at an idea so original that, like one in a Ph.D. thesis, it revises complex concepts in a discipline. Nor should you count as ideas only those that lead to some kind of life-altering discovery.

What, then, does it mean to have an idea? We can probably best understand what ideas are by considering what ideas do and where they can be found. Here is a partial list:

- An idea may be the discovery of a question where there seemed not to be one.
- An idea usually starts with an observation that is puzzling, with something that you want to figure out rather than with something that you think you already understand.
- An idea may make explicit and explore the meaning of something implicit—an unstated assumption upon which an argument rests or a logical consequence of a given position.
- An idea may connect elements of a subject and explain the significance of that connection.
- An idea often accounts for some *dissonance*—that is, something that seems not to fit together.
- An idea provides the answer to a good question; it explains something that needs to be explained.

Most strong analytical ideas launch you in a process of resolving problems and bringing competing positions into some kind of alignment. They locate you where there is something to negotiate, where you are required not just to list answers but also to ask questions, make choices, and engage in reasoning about the significance of your evidence.

When we wrote this book, our aim was to serve the needs of writers not just in English courses but across the curriculum and beyond school altogether. Some would argue that ideas are in fact discipline-specific, which is to say that what counts as an idea in psychology is quite different from what counts as an idea in history or philosophy or business. And surely the context does affect the way that ideas are shaped and expressed. As you go through your education, you will find it interesting to think about how different disciplines seem to define what an idea is, what it does, and how you recognize one.

This book operates on the premise, however, that ideas across the curriculum share common elements. All of the items in the list above, for example, seem to us to be common to ideas and to idea making in virtually any context. As you read the book, we hope that you will try to add to our list—to develop your own sense of what it means to have an idea.

H. CREATIVE ANALYSIS

We conclude this chapter on habits of mind with our short answer to a long-standing vicious dichotomy—that between creativity and analysis. This version of the head/heart false dichotomy, which has been making trouble since before the Enlightenment (circa 1750), is absolutely disabling to people on both sides of the supposed analytical/creative divide.

It has been one project of this chapter to show that analysis and creativity go hand-in-hand. A person who possesses an analytical cast of mind aims to notice more; is more inclined to see the questions rather than to settle for clichéd answers or to leave his or her own assumptions unacknowledged; is suspicious of rigid dichotomies (heart/head, creative/analytical, feeling/thinking); is slow to leap to generalizations and judgments, instead choosing to dwell longer with detail in an open, exploratory way; knows that formulating an idea—searching out what something means—is creative; recognizes that creative writing isn't just about feelings but is also a way of thinking about feelings. In future chapters we explore—and we hope, explode—the myths that artificially separate analytical from creative writing. All good writing, we believe, is both.

ASSIGNMENTS

1. Among the habits of mind that this chapter recommends, one of the most useful (and satisfying) is to trace impressions, reactions, sudden thoughts, moods, and so forth back to their probable causes. Practise this skill for a week by recording entries in a journal. Amy Addison explains the process in her article "Pre-writing: Keeping a Journal" (written for the University of Richmond's Writer's Web): "This journal may be as formal or informal as you wish; it is for you and should be written as if you are addressing yourself or a very close friend. The idea is to get things down on paper as you think of them. When making an entry, write from beginning to end before rereading." Record at least one impression or reaction each day, along

with three specific things that caused it. Try to focus on concrete, sensory details. In class, share your journal entries with a few other students—in peer groups of four or five—and compare the range of details covered by the group.

2. Visit a professor on campus and interview him or her about what constitutes an idea in that discipline. Ask for one or two single-sentence statements of ideas that the professor may have seen lately in a journal—or in his or her current research. You might also ask the professor to share some ideas generated by students. Write a brief account of the interview, including examples of what the professor considered to be sound ideas and why.

❧*TRY THIS:* Solution, page 28

The song lyric that provided the source for the paragraph of abstraction is:

"Like a bird on the wire,

Like a drunk in a midnight choir,

I have tried in my way to be free."

—Leonard Cohen, "Bird on the Wire"* □

3

Interpreting Your Data

Let's assume that you have begun to practise the skills laid out in the book so far. You've begun to catch yourself when leaping to judgments, using level 3 generalities and clichés, and adopting rigidly dichotomized points of view. You've been trying to avoid words like "should" and "shouldn't" that prompt a move to judgment rather than to analysis and interpretation. You've been practising dwelling on the data using various tools: Notice and Focus, Five-Step Analysis (repetitions, strands, and binaries), looking for anomalies, and reformulating binaries. Inevitably, these observational strategies will have led you to begin experimenting with ways of generating ideas. In this chapter, we want to get more specific about this phase of the thinking process—the phase in which you make an interpretive leap from your data to ideas and, ultimately, to theories about the meaning of your data.

An interpretation is a theory, a hypothetical explanation (which means it is still open to question and to testing) of what something means. An interpretation offers a reading of what is at stake, or what is driving or motivating the character of something that you have been observing. Since interpretations are always shaped by context, it is difficult to generalize about the interpretive process. But we can start by saying simply that interpretation is what happens when you make certain kinds of moves with your data. Later on in this chapter—in a section called "The Making of Meaning"—we'll tackle interpretation anew in more complexity. But for now, let's talk about why certain moves are useful in getting to interpretation.

A. PROMPTS: "INTERESTING" AND "STRANGE"

Consider, for example, the verbal prompts that we proposed in Chapter 1: "interesting," "strange," "revealing," and "significant." What do these do? First of all, they offer alternatives to the judgment reflex (like/dislike, right/ wrong, and should/shouldn't). The prompts shift attention from pro/con argument to thinking aimed at understanding, at theorizing about the nature of things. The same words also press you to notice and to stay more aware of the connections between your responses (moods, attitudes, beginnings of ideas) and the particulars that gave rise to them.

What does it mean to find something "interesting"? Often we are interested by things that have captured our attention without our clearly knowing why. Interest and curiosity are near cousins. Interest is also related to confidence. When you can allow yourself to feel that you don't have to have all the answers immediately, you can trust yourself to dwell on questions, a primary characteristic of good thinking.

The word "strange" is a useful prompt because it gives us permission to notice oddities, the things we called anomalies in the preceding chapter. "Strange" invites us to defamiliarize, rather than to normalize, things within our range of notice. "Strange," in this context, is not a judgmental term but one denoting features of a subject or situation that aren't readily explainable. Where you locate something strange, you will have something to interpret—to figure out what makes it strange and why.

Along similar lines, the words "revealing" and "significant" work by requiring you to make choices that can lead to interpretive leaps. If something strikes you as revealing, even if you're not yet sure why, you will eventually have to produce some theories on what it reveals. If something strikes you as significant, you will motivate yourself to come up with some things that it might signify or "say." Words matter: your choice of some words as verbal starting points can direct you onto more productive pathways.

❦*TRY THIS:* Choose one of Canada's prominent cities and write one or two paragraphs on what makes it "interesting," "strange," "revealing," or "significant." This is a freewriting exercise; in other words, there's no need to edit for correct grammar and spelling. Share your work, by reading aloud, with three or four other students. In follow-up discussion, try to identify any interpretative leaps that were made by any of the freewriters concerning the nature of Canadian urban life. □

B. PUSHING OBSERVATIONS TO CONCLUSIONS: ASKING "SO WHAT?"

A prompt we now want to add to your repertoire is what we call the "So what?" question. Asking "So what?" forces the issue, so to speak. It presses you to make some kind of claim about something you've noticed in your data.

Asking "So what?" is a *calling to account*, which is why, in conversation, its force is potentially rude. That is, the question intervenes rather peremptorily with a "Why does this matter?" It is thus a challenge to make meaning through a creative leap—to move beyond the patterns and emphases you've been observing in the data to what tentative conclusions these observations suggest. Michael Posner challenges himself, in "Image World," to understand *why* the crowd at the Air Canada Centre is glued to the in-house screen instead of the ice rink (page 113). He writes in a "So what?" frame of mind.

Asking yourself "So what?" is a central way to spur yourself to leap, to hazard an interpretation. It can and should be posed all of the time as you think and write, not just at the end of your thinking process. At the very least, consider asking and answering "So what?" at the ends of paragraphs. And then, if you ask "So what?" again of the first answer you've offered, you'll often tell yourself where your thinking needs to go next.

For example, let's say you make a number of observations about the nature of email communication—it's cheap, informal, often grammatically incorrect, full of abbreviations ("IMHO"), and ephemeral (impermanent). You rank these and decide that its ephemerality is most interesting. So what? Well, that's why so many people use it, you speculate, because it doesn't last. So what that its popularity follows from its ephemerality? Well, apparently we like being released from the hard-and-fast rules of formal communication; email frees us. So what? Well,...

The pushiness of the "So what?" question can, we think, be liberating. Okay, take the plunge, it says. Start laying out possible interpretations. And, when you are tempted to stop thinking too soon, asking "So what?" will press you onward. In Part II, "Writing the Thesis-Driven Paper," we have more to say about what to do when your answer to "So what?" calls to mind conflicting data or an opposing idea, and thus interferes with the forward flow of your thinking. For now, start experimenting with asking, "So what?"

Voices Across the Curriculum

Gathering Material

The planning stage is the most time-consuming part of the writing process; it involves a great deal of reading, scribbling, mulling, and back-tracking. And then more scribbling. And more mulling. However, this stage is crucial to creating a successful paper. Time spent considering your own ideas, exploring new approaches, following hunches, and comparing observations will lead to a more thoughtful, substantial (and, thus, persuasive) piece of writing.

Begin by gathering your own thoughts. There are any number of ways to do this, depending on your own learning style. Some people scribble notes on paper. Others draw. Still others pace the room, thinking out loud. The most important thing is to find a method that works for you. Here are some suggestions:

- Keep a notebook (separate from your class notes) as a running log-book for all your ideas.
- Record your ideas on cue cards, using a separate card for each point. The cards will give you room to jot down thoughts about each point, while still keeping your ideas separate from one another. They also give you something physical to work with as you start grouping ideas and organizing the flow of your paper.
- Map out your thoughts on large sheets of paper using pictures, arrows, lists of words, different coloured pens or markers, etc. As you work, stick the pages up on the wall so that you can see everything you're thinking at once. (You may want to check with your house-mates before overtaking the living room.)
- Keep verbal notes on a tape recorder. Think out loud. Later, play the tape back and take written notes of your ideas.

Once you've taken time to brainstorm your initial ideas, arm yourself with the necessary pens, cards, or crayons and reread your primary materials with an eye to the essay topic. As you read, ask yourself questions: *what* is being said here? *how* do these ideas fit together? If a passage leaps out at you, mark it so that you can go back and examine it more closely. Ask yourself *why* a passage or point seems significant. *Keep asking why* until you come up with a satisfactory response; press your analysis. The more you can articulate for yourself why something matters, the more you will be able to explain your thoughts in the essay.

When it comes to gathering ideas, there are no right or wrong methods. The only rule is to do it. You must keep track of your thoughts. By not keeping a record, you may forget ideas, misplace quotations, or lose track of insights or creative touches that could become central points later on. Furthermore, maintaining a tangible record of your thoughts may help you get some sleep—when it's time for a break, it is much easier to set aside notebooks and cue cards than it is to shut off an overworked brain scrambling to keep track of details.

—Leslie Casson, writing instructor

Moving from Description to Interpretation: An Example

Where does interpretation begin? When does analysis become interpretation? What we have suggested thus far is that the processes of noticing and of recording selected details and patterns of detail are already the beginning of interpretation. Analysis and interpretation are, by and large, inseparable. Analysis implies a *search for meaning*.

Let's work through a more extended example, using as our subject matter a painting by Maritime artist Alex Colville: *Family and Rainstorm*, shown in Figure 3.1. We chose a painting for our example because it is a relatively compact subject, one that can fit on a single page (like Figure 1.2). The ways of thinking about the painting are, we believe, applicable to most kinds of subject matter. First, spend some time at the observation phase.

❦ ***TRY THIS:*** Apply Five-Step Analysis to the painting. What details repeat in the picture? What patterns of similar detail (strands) can you find? What details and patterns of detail seem to fall into organizing contrasts? Compile your three lists in writing; then rank the top three in each category and write a paragraph on why you would choose one of these as most important. ☐

A primary aim of the observation practice we call Five-Step Analysis, as you will recall, is to shift your attention from premature generalizing about a subject—in this case the painting—to recording detail that actually

FIGURE 3.1 Alex Colville *Family and Rainstorm*, 1955. Glazed tempera on Masonite, 57.1 x 74.9 cm. National Gallery of Canada, Ottawa Photo © NGC Copyright A.C.Fine Art Inc.

appears in it. Description is the best antidote to what we call in Chapter 1 the "dogfish problem"—trying to start with an idea about your subject without first really looking at it. What do you notice about the picture? Not what do you *think*, but what do you notice?

Using Five-Step Analysis will produce a description of the painting. We offer our own description in Figure 3.2, but we urge you to do yours first. That way you will more easily discover a cardinal rule of interpretation: there is always a range of plausible interpretations, depending, in part, on the differing descriptions that underlie them.

Once you have finished your description, you will see that the observations in the "interpretive leaps" column in Figure 3.2 go beyond describing what the painting contains, moving on to ideas about what its details imply, what the painting invites us to make of it and by what means. Notice how intertwined the descriptive analysis is with the interpretations. Laying out the data is key to any kind of analysis not simply because it keeps the analysis accurate but also because, crucially, it is *in the act of carefully describing a subject that analytical writers often have their best ideas.*

Here is a sample interpretive analysis of the painting, based on the details we chose to emphasize and the leaps we initially made in response to the "So what?" prompt:

Descriptive Analysis	**Prompt**	**Interpretive Leaps**
Most significant detail: Subjects viewed from behind, not looking at us	→ So what? (speculate about what the detail might suggest)	→ Figures strike us as distant and inscrutable
Repetitions: two torrential downpours, two white dresses, two black swimsuits (?)	→ So what?	→ Nature's force is extreme; darkness is connected to water
Most significant strand: departure: the open car door, stepping into the car, the approaching (?) storm	→ So what?	→ The family members are calm and methodical when confronted by the storm—emotionless?
Most significant (and related) organizing contrasts: white garments versus black garments; mother's left arm versus mother's right arm	→ So what?	→ Contrasting colours emphasize gender difference; the mother appears to simultaneously guide and conceal
Most significant anomalies: the car door, which opens one space while closing off another	→ So what?	→ The mother appears to be shutting the door on our view of the seascape

FIGURE 3.2 Summary and Analysis of *Family and Rainstorm*

The painter's decision to portray his subjects from behind contributes to our sense of their distance from us and their inscrutability. We look at them, but they do not look back at us. The stark contrast between black and white clothing suggests differences—or similarities—among the three visible members of this family (Colville's title assures us that they are indeed members of the same family). What is the attraction of this painting (this being one of the questions that an analysis might ask)? What might draw a viewer to the sight of two children and a woman, lined up to enter the front door of an automobile? Perhaps it is the very starkness of the painting, as well as the ominous storm clouds in the distance, that attracts us.

You may not agree with this reading of the painting, neither the details we have emphasized nor the conclusions ("their inscrutability") we have drawn about them. Nor is it necessary that you agree, because there is no single right answer to what the painting means. The absence of a single right answer does not, however, mean that "anything goes," or that any reading is as good as any other. Some readings *are* better—better evidenced, better reasoned—than others.

A reader's willingness to accept an analytical conclusion is powerfully connected to his or her ability to see its *plausibility*—that is, how it follows from both the supporting details that the writer has selected and the language used in characterizing those details. The writer who can offer a plausible description of a subject's key features is likely to arrive at conclusions about possible meanings that others would share. This is often the best you can hope for: not that others will say, "Yes, that is obviously right," but rather, "Yes, I can see where it might be possible and reasonable to think as you do."

❧*TRY THIS:* Return to your own lists of key details, and write the interpretive leaps that they might plausibly prompt. Then, generate in a paragraph or two your own interpretation of *Family and Rainstorm*. □

C. THE MAKING OF MEANING

Our last example, the interpretation of the painting *Family and Rainstorm*, raises some theoretical questions about interpretation; that is, about where meanings come from. The discussion may also have raised in you some of the reservations that the interpretive process tends to evoke. We will now pause to consider a few issues about the making of meaning.

Although analysis is an activity we call on constantly in our everyday lives, many people are deeply suspicious of it. "Why can't you just enjoy the movie rather than picking it apart?" they'll say. Or, "Oh, you're just making that up!" You may even be accused of being an unfeeling person if you adopt an analytical stance, because it is typical of the anti-intellectual position to insist that feeling and thinking are separate and essentially incompatible activities.

Though he was among the most astutely analytical of thinkers, the nineteenth-century English romantic poet William Wordsworth wrote the famous line that we mention in the Introduction, "we murder to dissect," giving voice to the still-common anxiety that analysis takes the life out of things. This anxiety—so common in romanticism as to be virtually a defining characteristic of that intellectual and artistic movement—arose in reaction against an equally extreme position from the eighteenth century (the so-called Age of Reason or Enlightenment), known for its indictment of emotion as the enemy of rationality. In response to the eighteenth century's elevation of reason over all other human faculties, the nineteenth century sought to correct the imbalance by elevating the faculties of feeling and imagination. Few thinkers of either century really adhered to these positions in such extreme forms, but suffice it to say that analysts of human beings seem always to have been perplexed about how our various capacities fit together into a functional whole. One aim of this book is to demonstrate that taking refuge in either side of the opposition between thinking and feeling is not only counterproductive but also unnecessary.

The Limits on Interpretation

The first thing to understand about meanings is that they are made. They are not preexistent in the subject matter. That is to say, they are the product of a transaction between a mind and the world, between a reader and a text or texts. The making of meaning is a process to which the observer and the thing observed both contribute. It is not a product of either alone.

If meanings aren't ready-made, there to be found in the subject matter, what's to prevent people from making things mean whatever they want them to—say, for example, that *Family and Rainstorm* is a painting about parental abuse, with the sadistic mother locking her kids in a steamy car rather than letting them frolic on the expansive beach? There are, in fact, limits on the meaning-making process.

- Meanings must be reasoned from sufficient evidence if they are to be judged plausible. Meanings can always be refuted by people who find fault with your reasoning or who can cite conflicting evidence. In the case of the parental–abuse theory, for example, no account is taken of the intense rainstorm on the horizon.

- Meanings, to have value outside one's own private realm of experience, have to make sense to other people. Asserting that the little girl in the painting is about to do a somersault is unlikely to be deemed acceptable by enough people to give it currency. In every instance, the relative value of interpretive meanings is socially (culturally) determined. Although people are free to say that things mean whatever they want them to mean, simply saying it doesn't make it a reasonable explanation.

Multiple Meanings and Interpretive Contexts

In the last section, we demonstrated that there are certain limits on interpretation, chiefly that interpretation has to follow the rules of evidence. It is useful and reassuring to know that a person can't just make up meanings and say they are true simply because he or she says so. As you've already seen, however, meanings are multiple. Evidence usually will support more than one plausible interpretation.

Consider, for example, a reading of *Family and Rainstorm* that a person might produce if he or she began by noticing the date of composition: 1955. From this starting point, a person might focus on the cultural context of North American life following World War II. The "baby boom" of that era, combined with economic growth, led to an emphasis on family values and material well-being. From this perspective, a viewer of Colville's painting might assume that Dad is already behind the wheel, ready to treat his young family to a delicious seafood lunch. Perhaps Mom and the kids are grinning ear-to-ear (only the boy's face is at all visible, after all). While plausible, this idea for an interpretation would require consideration of conflicting evidence—as is the case with all viable ideas.

To generalize: two equally plausible interpretations can be made of the same thing. It is not the case that our first reading (focusing on the three figures being viewed from behind and suggesting distance and inscrutability) is right, while the historical view (building from the date of composition) is wrong. They operate within different contexts. As these examples illustrate, very often the starting point for an interpretation (the viewing angle, the date of composition) in effect determines its context. However the context is arrived at, an important part of getting an interpretation accepted as plausible is to argue for the appropriateness of the interpretive *context* you use, not just the interpretation to which it takes you.

What About the Writer's Intentions?

Let's turn now to an interpretive context that frequently creates problems: authorial intention. People relying on authorial intention as their interpretive context typically assert that the author—not the work itself—is the ultimate and correct source of interpretations. The work means what its author says it means, and even without his or her explicit interpretation, we are expected to guess at it.

Let's say that an enterprising person had recently been reading about Alex Colville's "magic realism" and about the importance that the artist placed on "what happens to us every day in our immediate familial and physical surroundings." That person might reasonably conclude that *Family and Rainstorm* was intended by Colville to celebrate the magical significance of family vacations along the coast of the Atlantic. Whether or not that was actually the artist's intention, it is not more correct than, say, the "inscrutability" reading. Whatever an author thinks he or she is doing is often a significant part of the meaning of what he or she creates, but it does not outrank or exclude other interpretations. Authorial intention is simply another context for understanding.

Why is this so? In our earlier discussion of personalizing, we suggested that people are not entirely free agents, immune to the effects of the culture they inhabit. It follows that when people produce things, they are inevitably affected by that culture in ways of which they both are and are not aware. The culture, in other words, speaks through them. In the early 1960s, for example, a popular American sitcom entitled *Leave It to Beaver* portrayed the mother, June Cleaver, usually impeccably dressed in heels, dress, and pearls, doing little other than dusting the mantelpiece and making tuna fish sandwiches for her sons. Is the show then intentionally oppressing June by implying that the proper role for women is that of domestic helper? Well, that meaning is in the show, if we choose to view it in this gendered context. But to conclude that *Leave it to Beaver* promoted a particular stereotype about women does not mean that the writers got together every week and asked, "How should we oppress June this week?" It is cultural norms asserting themselves here, not authorial intent.

It is interesting and useful to try to determine from something you are analyzing what its makers might have intended. But, by and large, you are best to concentrate on what the thing itself communicates as opposed to what someone might have wanted it to communicate. As a rule, intention does not finally control the implications that an event, a text, or anything else possesses.

Look at the drawing entitled *The Dancers* in Chapter 1 (Figure 1.1). What follows is the artist's statement about how the drawing came about and what it came to mean to her.

> This piece was created completely unintentionally. I poured some ink onto paper and blew on it through a straw. The ink took the form of what looked like little people in movement. I recopied the figures I liked, touched up the rough edges, and ended with this gathering of fairy-like creatures. I love how in art something abstract can so suddenly become recognizable.

In this case, interestingly, the author initially had no intentions beyond experimenting with materials. As the work evolved, she began to arrive at her own interpretation of what the drawing might suggest. Most viewers would probably find the artist's interpretation plausible, but this is not to say that the artist must have the last word and that it is somehow an infraction for others to produce alternative interpretations. Suppose the artist had stopped with her first two sentences. Even this explicit statement of the artist's lack of intention would not prohibit people from interpreting the drawing in some of the ways that the artist later goes on to suggest. The artist's initial absence of a plan doesn't require viewers to interpret *The Dancers* as only ink on paper.

Where, then, do meanings reside? In the maker? In the thing itself? While the maker's personal intentions don't control meaning, it is interesting and useful to infer from the material itself what a creator might have been trying to accomplish.

What about analyzing things that were not intended to mean anything, like entertainment films and everyday things like blue jeans and shopping malls? Writers sometimes resist analysis on the grounds that some things were not intended to have meaning outside of a limited context, such as entertainment, and so should not be analyzed from any other point of view. Barbie dolls are toys intended for young girls. Should the fact that the makers of Barbie intended to make money by entertaining children rather than trying to create a cultural artifact rule out analysis of Barbie's characteristics (built-in earrings and high-heeled feet), marketing, and appeal as cultural phenomena?

What the makers of a particular product or idea intend is only a part of what that product or idea communicates. The urge to cordon off certain subjects from analysis on the grounds that they weren't meant to be analyzed unnecessarily excludes a wealth of information—and meaning—from your range of vision. It is right to be careful about the interpretive contexts we bring to our experience. It is less right—less useful—to confine our choice of context in a too-literal-minded way to a single category. To some people, hockey is only a game, and clothing is only there to protect us from the elements.

Notice how in the following analysis the student writer's interpretation relies on his choice of a particular interpretive context, post–World War II Japan. Had he selected another context, he might have arrived at some different conclusions about the same details. Notice also how the writer perceives a pattern in the details and queries his own observations (asking "So what?") to arrive at an interpretation.

The series entitled *Kamaitachi* is a journal of [Japanese photographer Eikoh] Hosoe's desolate childhood and wartime evacuation in the Tokyo countryside. He returns years later to the areas where he grew up, a stranger to his native land, perhaps likening himself to the legendary Kamaitachi, an invisible sickle-toothed weasel, intertwined with the soil and its unrealized fertility. *Kamaitachi #8* (1956), a platinum palladium print, stands alone to best capture Hosoe's alienation from and troubled expectation of the future of Japan. *[Here the writer chooses a biographical approach as his interpretive context.]*

The image is that of a tall fence of stark horizontal and vertical rough wood lashed together, looming above the barren rice fields. Straddling the fence, half-crouched and half-clinging, is a solitary male figure, gazing in profile to the horizon. Oblivious to the sky above of dark and churning thunderclouds, the figure instead focuses his attentions and concentrations elsewhere. *[The writer selects and describes significant detail.]*

It is exactly this elsewhere that makes the image successful, for in studying the man we are to turn our attention toward him and away from the print. He hangs curiously between heaven and earth, suspended on a makeshift man-made structure, in a purgatorial limbo awaiting the future. He waits with anticipation—perhaps dread?—for a time that has not yet come; he is directed away from the present, and it is this sensitivity to time which sets this print apart from the others in the series. One could argue that in effect this man, clothed in common garb, has become Japan itself, indicative of the post-war uncertainty of a country once dominant and now destroyed. What will the future (dark storm clouds) hold for this newly humbled nation? *[Here the writer notices a pattern of "in-between-ness" and locates it in a historical context in order to make his interpretive leap.]*

Remember that regardless of the subject you select for your analysis, you should directly address not just "What does this say?" but also, as this writer has done, "What are we invited to make of it, and in what context?"

"Hidden" Meanings: What "Reading Between the Lines" Really Means

"You're reading between the lines" is a claim we've all heard. Depending on the context, it can be an accusation or a compliment, though it's usually the former. When it's uttered as an accusation, it implies that the accused is not actually reading the words on the page but the white space between the sentences. So, presumably, the charge means that the person producing the analysis is basing it on nothing—on white space. In other words, it's all in his or her imagination, not really "there."

Indeed, all of our interpretations of *Family and Rainstorm* could be attacked as "reading between the lines": pulled out of thin air, imposed upon the painting. The attacker would maintain that the painting is only what the title declares, a portrait of family members trying to stay dry, and that any further interpretation is "reading into" the painting things that are not there. But what does "not there" really signify? It signifies that the *meanings are not overt, not tangible, not extractable and ready-made (like fortune-cookie fortunes) from the thing being analyzed.* As we've seen, this is a worthwhile approach to analysis: creative interpretation is always the product of a leap.

The naïveté of people who make the reading-between-the-lines attack lies in their unstated assumption that all communication is or *should* be a matter of direct statement. In effect, they are committing themselves to the position that everything in life means what it says and says what it means— that meanings are always obvious and understood the same by everyone and thus don't require interpretation.

This view—that all communication is a matter of direct statement—is easily open to question. You need think only of what people's body positions "say" in addition to (sometimes in opposition to) the words they speak in order to see the error in assuming that all things can be communicated directly.

It is in fact an inherent property of language, linguists tell us, that it always means more than, and thus other than, it says. How often have you heard a person respond to a challenging personal question with "I don't know," when what he or she really means is "I don't want to talk about it"? And doesn't the "How you doin'?" that we toss at others as we pass them in the hallway really mean "I acknowledge that you and I are acquaintances"—because in most cases we have neither the time nor the inclination to find out how they are really doing? If you don't believe this, the next time someone asks you how you're doing, give him or her a line of Ernest Hemingway's—"Sometimes I see me dead in the rain"—and see what kind of response you get.

As these examples demonstrate, people are remarkably adept at sending and receiving complex and subtle—that is, indirect—signals. Though we may not pause to take notice, we are continually processing the information around us for the indirect or suggested meanings it contains. If you observe yourself for a day, you'll find yourself interpreting even the most direct-seeming statements. There's an old cartoon about the anxiety bred by the continual demands of interpretation: a person who says, "Good morning," causes the one addressed to respond, "What did she mean by that?"

The truth to which this cartoon points is that a statement can have various meanings, depending on various circumstances and how it is said. *The relationship between words and meaning is always complex.* Marshall McLuhan, one of the fathers of modern communication theory, noted that communication always involves determining not just what is being said, but also "what kind of message a message is." Depending on tone and context, "Good morning" can mean a number of things.

Why does so much communication take place indirectly? When we want to understand a complex subject like love or death, we sometimes need to arrive at that understanding indirectly—by comparison with more tangible and accessible subjects like the weather, the seasons, hockey, or chess. This is because sometimes it is possible to communicate complex ideas or feelings or situations only through comparison with something that is more immediate and more concrete. It is also the case that human beings seem inclined to think by *association* and by *analogy* (likeness). A compelling example is Roger Martin's editorial essay, "The Wrong Incentive" (pages 420–423). At the root of indirect communication lies *metaphor*—a mode of expression in which one thing stands for (represents) something else that remains unnamed.

Metaphor is not confined to the arts; it is a pervasive feature of communication. Many linguists argue that all language is metaphor; that is, that we are always talking about things in terms of other things. This is the case not only when we say, "My love is like a red, red rose," but also when we say, "That movie was a piece of trash" or "I could kill you for that." The leap to language is itself metaphorical: the word spelled *c-a-t* is not the same thing as the four-legged feline that purrs.

You can easily test some of these assertions yourself as you go through an ordinary day. What, for example, does your choice of wearing a baseball cap to a staff meeting or a class—rather than no hat or a straw hat or a beret—"say"? Note, by the way, that a communicative gesture such as the wearing of a cap need not be premeditated and entirely conscious in order to communicate something to those who see it. The cap is still "there" and available to be "read" by others as a sign of certain attitudes and a culturally defined sense of identity, with or without your intention. Things communicate meaning to others whether we wish them to or not, which is to say that the meanings of most things are always to some extent socially rather than privately and individually determined.

As we have repeatedly argued, it helps to remember that *interpretive leaps*—conclusions arrived at through analysis about what some gesture or word choice or clothing combination or scene in a film means—follow certain established rules of evidence. One such rule is that the conclusions of a good analysis do not rest on details taken out of context; you should instead test and support claims about the details' significance by locating them in a pattern of similar detail (see "Five-Step Analysis" in Chapter 1). In other words, analytical thinkers are not really free to say whatever they think, as those who are made uneasy by analysis sometimes fear.

We should acknowledge, with respect to the reading-between-the-lines charge, that analysis sometimes does draw out the implications of things that are not there because they have been deliberately omitted. Usually we recognize such omissions because we have been led to expect something that we are not given, making its absence conspicuous. An analysis of the Nancy Drew mysteries, for example, might attach significance to the absence of a mother in the books, particularly in light of the fact that biological mothers, as opposed to wicked stepmothers, are pretty rare in many kinds of stories involving female protagonists, such as fairy tales ("Hansel and Gretel," "Cinderella," and "Snow White"). Taking note of mothers as a potentially significant omission could lead to a series of analytical questions, such as the following: How might this common denominator of certain kinds of children's stories be explained? What features of the stories' social, psychological, historical, economic, and other possible contexts might offer an explanation? As this example suggests, things are often left out for a reason, and a good analysis should therefore be alert to potentially meaningful omissions.

But what about meanings that are neither intentionally omitted nor directly and overtly present, such as the baseball cap worn backward—are they hidden or not?

The Fortune-Cookie School of Interpretation versus The Anything-Goes School

The Fortune-Cookie School of Interpretation believes that things have a single, hidden, "right" meaning, and if a person can only "crack" the thing, it will yield an extractable and self-contained "message." There are several problems with this conception of meaning. First of all, the assumption that things have single hidden meanings interferes with open-minded and dispassionate observation. The thinker looks solely for clues pointing to the hidden message and, having found these clues, discards the rest. But worse, the fortune-cookie approach forecloses on the possibility of multiple plausible meanings, each within its own context. When you assume that there is only one right answer, you are also assuming that there is only one proper context for understanding and, by extension, that anybody who happens to select a different starting point or context and who thus arrives at a different answer is necessarily wrong.

Most of the time, practitioners of the fortune-cookie approach aren't even aware that they are assuming the correctness of a single context because they don't realize a fundamental truth: interpretations are always limited by contexts. In other words, we are suggesting that claims to universal truths are always problematic, if not downright dubious. Things don't just mean in some simple and clear way for all people in all situations; they always mean within a network of beliefs, from a particular point of view. The person who claims to have access to some universal truth, beyond context and point of view, is either naïve (unaware) or, worse, a bully—insisting that his or her view of the world is obviously correct and must be accepted by everyone.

At the opposite extreme from the single-right-answer-obsessed Fortune-Cookie School lies the completely relativistic Anything-Goes School. The problem with the anything-goes approach is that it tends to assume that all interpretations are equally viable—that meanings are simply a matter of individual choice, irrespective of evidence or plausibility. Put another way, it overextends the creative aspect of interpretation to absurdity, arriving at the position that you can see in a subject whatever you want to see.

As we suggest throughout this book, it is simply not the case that meaning is up to the individual. Some readings are clearly better than others: the "inscrutability" reading of *Family and Rainstorm* is better than the "parental-abuse" reading. Better interpretations have more evidence and rational explanation of how the evidence means what they claim—qualities that make these meanings more public and negotiable because they are more plausible. Plausible interpretations are multiple but not infinite: anything *doesn't* go.

It is probably worth noting here that in the field of logic there is a principle known as *parsimony*, which holds that "no more forces or causes should be assumed than are necessary to account for the facts" (*Oxford English Dictionary*). In other words, the explanation that both explains the largest amount of evidence (accounts for facts) and is the simplest (no more than necessary) is the best. There are limits to this rule as well: sometimes focusing on what appears to be an insignificant detail as a starting point can provide a revelatory perspective on a subject. But, as rules go, parsimony is a useful one to keep in mind as you start sifting through your various interpretive leaps about a subject.

Implication and Inference: Hidden or Not?

Sometimes, as earlier noted, the ability to read between the lines is commended as a talent. In this context, the assumption is not that the reader is inventing meanings that are not there but rather that he or she is *making explicit* (overtly stated) *what is implicit* (suggested but not overtly stated). This is a definition of analytical writing to which this book will return repeatedly. The process of converting suggestions into direct statements is essential to analysis. It's one of the activities that makes analysis valuable.

Let's look at a hypothetical example of this process of drawing out implications, but pause first to offer a couple of definitions. The process of drawing out implications is also known as *making inferences*. "Inference" and "implication" are related but not synonymous terms, and the difference is a useful one to know. The term "implication" is used to describe something suggested by the material itself. The term "inference" is used to describe your thinking process. In short, *you infer what the subject implies*.

Now, let's move on to the example, which will suggest not only how the process of "making the implicit explicit" works but also how often we do it in our everyday lives. Imagine that you are driving down the highway and find yourself analyzing a billboard advertisement for a brand of beer. Such an analysis might begin with your noticing what the billboard photo contains; that is, its various "parts"—six young, athletic, and scantily clad men and women drinking beer while pushing kayaks into a fast-running river. At this point, you have produced not an analysis but a summary—a description of what the photo contains. If, however, you go on to consider what the particulars of the photo imply, your summary would become analytical.

You might infer, for example, that the photo implies that beer is the beverage of fashionable, healthy, active people, not just of older men with large stomachs dozing in armchairs in front of the television. Thus, the advertisement's meaning goes beyond its explicit contents; your analysis would lead you to *convert to direct statement those meanings that are suggested but not overtly stated*, such as the advertisement's goal of attacking a common, negative stereotype about its product (that only lazy, overweight men drink beer). The naming and renaming of parts that you undertake when analyzing should carry you from the actual details to the meanings they imply. By making the implicit explicit (inferring what the ad implies), you can better understand the nature of your subject.

ᕯTRY THIS: Locate any magazine ad that you find interesting. Ask yourself, *"What are we invited to make of this and by what means?"* Use our hypothetical beer ad as a model for making the implicit explicit. Don't settle for just one or even three answers. *Keep answering the question in different ways*, letting your answers grow in length as they identify and begin to interpret the significance of telling details. Attend to your choice of language, because your word choice as you summarize details will begin to suggest to you the ad's range of implication. Remember to *write about what you see*, the details of the ad, rather than generalizing too soon about it. □

Seems to Be About X but...

This chapter, along with Chapter 1, has focused your attention on three prerequisites to becoming a more perceptive analytical thinker:

1. Training yourself to observe more fully and more systematically— dwelling longer on the data before leaping to generalizations, using Notice and Focus (ranking) and Five-Step Analysis, looking for anomalies, and reformulating binaries.
2. Pushing yourself to make interpretive leaps by describing carefully and then querying your own observations by repeatedly asking "So what?"
3. Getting beyond common misconceptions about where meanings come from: that meanings are hidden, that they are "read into" something but are really "not there" (reading between the lines), that there are single right answers or that anything goes, that meanings are determined by a writer's intentions, that some things should not be analyzed because they weren't meant to be, and so forth.

A useful verbal prompt founded on these prerequisites is "seems to be about X but is really (or could also be) about Y."

This formula can open up your thinking about all manner of thinking and writing situations: analysis of reading, problems, complex situations, behaviour, art, popular culture, current events, and so forth. Here's why the formula works. Frequently, the nominal (in name only) subject matter— what a book or speech or X appears to be about, or what it says it is about—is not what the book or speech or X is most interested in. The nominal subject, in other words, is a means to some other end; it creates an opportunity for some less overtly designated matter to be put forward. This is so, regardless of intention. Consider the following example.

A recent highly successful television ad campaign for Nike Freestyle shoes contains sixty seconds showing famous basketball players dribbling and passing and otherwise handling the ball in dextrous ways to the accompaniment of court noises and hip-hop music. The ad seems to be about X (basketball or shoes) but is *really* (or could also be) about Y. Either a rapid-fire list might follow or a filling in of the blanks (for Y) might prompt a more sustained exploration of a single point.

Here is one version of a rapid-fire list, any item of which might be expanded.

Seems to be about basketball but is really about dance

Seems to be about selling shoes but is really about artistry

Seems to be about basketball but is really about race

Seems to be about basketball but is really about the greater acceptance of racial minorities in North American media

Seems to be about the greater acceptance of racial minorities in North American media but is really about targeting black basketball players as performing seals or freaks

Here is one version of a more sustained exploration of a single seems-to-be-about-X statement.

The Nike Freestyle commercial seems to be about basketball but is really about the greater acceptance of racial minorities in North American media. Of course it is a shoe commercial and so aims to sell a product, but the same could be said about any commercial. What makes the Nike commercial distinctive is its loving embrace of black culture. The hip-hop soundtrack, for example, which coincides with the rhythmic dribbling of the basketball, places music and sport on a par, and the dexterity with which the players (actual NBA stars) move with the ball—moonwalking; doing 360s on it; balancing it on their fingers, heads, and backs—is nothing short of dance. The intrinsic cool of the commercial suggests that Nike is targeting an audience of basketball lovers, not just blacks. If I am right, then it is selling blackness to white as well as to black audiences. Of course, the idea that blacks are cooler than whites goes back at least as far as the early days of jazz and might be seen as its own strange form of prejudice.... In that case, maybe there is something a little disturbing in the commercial, in the way that it relegates the athletes to the status of trained seals. I'll have to think more about this.

Note: Don't be misled by our use of "really" in the prompt into thinking that there should be some single hidden right answer. Rather, "really" aims to prompt you to think recursively, to come up with a range of less obvious landing sites for your interpretive leap. The word "really" is in the prompt in order to get you past a recitation of the obvious—for example, that the ad appears to be about basketball but is really about selling shoes. Both basketball and shoe sales are the ad's nominal subjects, what it is overtly about. But as we demonstrate, nominal subjects allow for the expression of other less immediately obvious ideas and attitudes. To look for these ideas and attitudes is not to condition yourself to see sinister and manipulative plots everywhere. It is instead to recognize that communication is not simple but, rather, that most things we want to understand are complexly embedded in particular cultural contexts. It is this embedding and the complexity of the verbal and visual gestures permeating our world that analysis equips us to better understand and enjoy.

As we say in our discussion of where meanings come from, meanings are not simply "there" to be found, ready-made and directly stated in what you are studying. They are the product of a transaction between a mind and materials. "Seems to be about X…" can give you practice at making the implicit explicit and at accepting the existence of more than one plausible meaning for the same thing, depending on interpretive context or starting point. "Seems to be about X…" gives you licence to try on all kinds of interpretive possibilities, but the one you pick will most likely not say that the ad appears to be about basketball but is really about aliens in professional sport today.

TRY THIS: "Seems to be about X…" can be applied to one of the most common reading experiences in everyday life: the newspaper. Choose a front-page story from the past week—in either a local or national newspaper—and, after reading it carefully, make a rapid-fire list (as we did for the Nike Freestyle shoes campaign). Then move on to a more sustained exploration of one of your seems-to-be-about-X statements by writing a paragraph that elaborates on the idea. □

ASSIGNMENT

Write a brief essay, approximately 500 words, in which you make observations about the ROOTS chain of clothing stores. If you're familiar with ROOTS, think about its products, image, market, advertising, and logo. If you're not familiar, spend some time searching for such details. Push your observations to tentative conclusions by repeatedly asking "So what?" Be sure to query your initial answers to the "So what?" question with further "So what?" questions, trying to push further into your own thinking and into the meaning of ROOTS.

4

Readers' Writing

A. HOW TO READ: WORDS MATTER

In a sense, the world is a text. As any child psychology textbook will tell you, as we acquire language, we acquire knowledge of the world. We can ask for things, or say what's on our mind. But it's language, arguably, that fills our minds and gives us something to say in the first place. A well-known twentieth-century philosopher, Ludwig Wittgenstein, noted that we cannot make a proposition about the world; we can only make a proposition about another proposition about the world. Think about that remark for a minute. Try paraphrasing it.

The statement implies that we live in a world of language. This is not to say that everything is words, that words are the only reality. But to an enormous extent, we understand the world and our relation to it by working through language, "reading." Words matter: they are how we process the world.

As you have probably noticed, this book has been using the word "reading" to mean "interpreting." This usage hearkens back to the idea of the world as a text. The idea wasn't new with Wittgenstein, by the way. Several North American religious communities—from the French Calvinists to the Puritans—also envisioned the world as a text in which God read their lives, and so, predictably, they started reading their lives too: reflecting on events that befell them and querying whether events happening in their lives were signs of salvation or damnation. (The stakes for being a good reader couldn't have been higher!) In short, reading for them meant gathering evidence and analyzing it to arrive at ideas or conclusions.

That more generalized notion of reading remains with us today. In interpreting the world, we are reading it as a text that is largely made knowable to us through words. And, obviously, for most of us a significant amount of that interpretation actually consists of the more literal act of reading—that is, moving our eyes along a line of printed words and processing what the words signify ("reading comprehension," as the standardized tests call it). And so reading suggests two related activities: (1) reading in the literal sense of tackling words on the page, and (2) reading in the metaphorical sense of gathering data that can be analyzed as primary evidence to produce ideas.

Considering how central both kinds of reading are in our lives, it's amazing how little we think about words themselves. We use words all the time, but often unthinkingly. We don't plan out our sentences before we utter them, for example, and the same goes for most of the ones that we write. In the last chapter, we put forth the notion that things often have multiple meanings. So do words; check any dictionary, and you will find more than one definition for virtually every word.

Most of us live, however, as if there were a consensus about what words mean. More often than you would suspect, there isn't a consensus. We tend to assume that things have simple or single meanings. Don't believe it. Words are promiscuous; they won't stay put, won't stick to a single meaning. This is often a source of amusement. On Internet comedy sites and in books on humour in the English language, headlines such as the following illustrate how double meanings can produce comical results: "Teacher Strikes Idle Kids," "Panda Mating Fails: Veterinarian Takes Over," "New Vaccines May Contain Rabies," "Local High School Dropouts Cut in Half," and "Include Your Children When Baking Cookies" (or, if you prefer, "Kids Make Nutritious Snacks"). Other lists include sentences such as "The bandage was wound around the wound" and "After a number of injections my jaw got number." It's often a nutty language, and we need to remember this fact whenever we start getting too complacent about the meanings of words being singular and obvious.

If you want to better understand something that you're reading—or revising in your own writing—ask yourself what certain key words mean, even if you think you know what they mean. As was mentioned in our discussion of banking in Chapter 2, paraphrasing—the act of recasting words—is one of the best ways to make the move to analysis. Whether you are in a school setting or not, paraphrasing is a great way to figure out how to respond to questions. Consider, for example, the question "Is feminism good for Judaism?" You would first want to figure out what "good" means and in what interpretive context. (For another example, look back at the treatment of the word "uphold" in the section called "Thinking Recursively" in Chapter 1.) So, if you want to read more effectively, then two guidelines are (1) to expect complexity and (2) to ask yourself what the words mean and paraphrase them (which will reveal the complexity you may not have noticed initially).

Becoming Conversant Versus Reading for the Gist

Many readers operate under the dubious impression that they are to "read for the gist"—for the main point that is to be gleaned through speed-reading. Quite simply, you cannot expect to demonstrate your control of the information without getting closer to it than generalizations allow. One of the most crippling and frustrating things for many students is to expect that, if they read through something once and then look away, they should be able either to accurately and productively restate it or to have an idea about it. The vast majority of writing tasks that you will encounter require as a prerequisite your *conversancy* with material that you have read, not inert generalizations about it.

It is a reasonable expectation both in academic courses and in the workplace that you should become *conversant* with the material. To become conversant means that

1. after a significant amount of work with the material, you should be able to talk about it conversationally with other people and answer questions about it without having to look everything up; and
2. you should be able to converse with the material—to be in some kind of dialogue with it, to see the questions the material asks, and to pose your own questions about it.

Few people are able to really understand things they read or see without making the language of that material in some way their own. We can learn, in other words, only by finding ways to actively engage material rather than to move passively through it. This is why skills such as note taking, paraphrasing, and outlining—all forms of summary—are not just empty mechanical tasks. They are the mind's ways of acquiring material, both the ideas and the language, which make it possible to work with these ideas. Let's pause to examine a few of these key tools; if you want to improve your reading, they will be useful.

Paraphrase × 3

The exercise we call *Paraphrase × 3* offers the quickest means of seeing how writing a little about what you're reading can lead to having ideas about it. (Paraphrasing is an activity we introduce in our discussion of banking in Chapter 2.) Paraphrase is commonly misunderstood as summary—a way of shrinking an idea you've read about—or perhaps as simply a way to avoid plagiarism by "putting it in your own words." Rather, *the goal of paraphrase* is to open up the possible meanings of the words; it's a mode of inquiry.

If you force yourself to paraphrase a key passage from a reading three times, you will discover that it gets you actually working with the language. But you have to work slavishly at it. Don't go for the gist; aim to replace all of the key words. The new words you will be forced to come up with represent first stabs at interpretation, at having (small) ideas about what you are reading by unearthing a range of possible meanings embedded in the

---

Voices Across the Curriculum

When Reading Becomes a Chore

I used to do a lot of writing when I was younger, as well as a lot of reading. By about age 12, my collection of R.L. Stine books had grown out of control, and whenever I had a free minute, I would bury my face between the pages. It was all this reading that inspired my writing—I had produced page after page of morbid events and mysterious circumstances—but I eventually ran out of time for both.

Now, almost ten years later, I've begun to wonder what happened to that child who used to worry her family with all of her gory stories. I never pick up a pen to just write anymore, or even a book to curl up with and read. Life has become too busy. I read now only when assigned to, and I write only when a paper is due. School leaves little time for leisure, but even when I *do* have a free minute, the last thing I want to do is continue reading or writing. The activities I used to love now have an overpowering association with the activities I've grown to hate. Sadly, both of them have become chores and after being bombarded with pages I *have to read*, I've decided that I would much rather go out and play.

—Daina Astwood-George, second-year French studies major

---

passage. Then, you will have *something to do* with your writing about the reading beyond simply recording it or agreeing/disagreeing with it.

❧ *TRY THIS:* Do Paraphrase × 3 with the following sentence: "Clarity, as a norm for speech and writing, presents a paradox: although the burden of achieving it falls on the speaker, the achievement itself apparently falls to the hearer." Resist the temptation to talk about the words on the page. Instead, use synonyms to make the words speak. Next, write a paragraph about what you've discovered through your paraphrases. □

Summary

Summary is the standard way that reading—not just facts and figures but also other people's theories and observations—enters your writing. The aim of summary is to recount (in effect, to reproduce) someone else's ideas, to achieve sufficient understanding of them to productively converse with what you have been reading.

Summary and analysis go hand in hand. Neither aims to approve or disapprove of its subject; the goal for both is to understand rather than evaluate. Summary is a necessary early step in analysis because it provides *perspective* on the subject as a whole by explaining the meaning and function of each of that subject's parts. Within larger analyses—papers or reports—summary performs the essential function of contextualizing your subject accurately. It creates a fair picture of what's there. If you don't take the time to get your whole subject in perspective, you will be more prone to misrepresenting it in your analysis.

But summarizing isn't simply the unanalytical reporting of information; it's more than just shrinking someone else's words. To write an accurate summary, you have to ask analytical questions, such as

- Which of the ideas in the reading are most significant? Why?
- How do these ideas fit together?
- What do the key passages in the reading mean?

Summarizing is, like paraphrasing, a tool of understanding and not just a mechanical task. But summary stops short of in-depth analysis because summary typically makes much smaller interpretive leaps. A summary of a picture, for example, would tell readers what the picture includes, which details are the most prominent, and even what its overall effect seems to be. A summary of the painting *Family and Rainstorm* (discussed in Chapter 3) might say that it possesses a certain austerity, that it is somewhat subdued. This kind of language still falls into the category of *focused description*, which is what a summary is.

Strategies for Making Summaries More Analytical

What information should be included and what excluded? That's the perennial question that summarizing raises. When summaries go wrong, they are just lists. A list is a simple "this and then this and then this" sequence. Sometimes lists are random, as in a shopping list compiled from the first thing you thought of to the last. Sometimes they are organized: fruit and vegetables here, dried goods there. At best, they do very little logical connecting among the parts beyond "next."

Summaries that are just lists tend to dollop the information monotonously. They omit the thinking that the piece is doing—the ways it is connecting the information, the contexts it establishes, and the implicit slant or point of view. Be aware that the thinking the piece is doing is not necessarily the same as the ideas it may contain. Two articles on European attitudes toward Canada–U.S. relations, for example, may contain essentially the same information but vary widely in how they assemble it, how they connect the dots. Writing analytical summaries can teach you how to read for the connections, the lines that connect the dots. And when you're operating at that level, you are much more likely to have ideas about what you are summarizing.

Here are five strategies for seeing and connecting the dots in what you are reading and, by extension, for deciding what to include and exclude in your summaries.

1. Look for the underlying structure.

Use Five-Step Analysis. Even if you just apply Five-Step Analysis (see Chapter 1) to a few selected paragraphs, it will provide you with the terms that get repeated, and these will almost always suggest strands, which in turn make up the organizing contrasts. Five-Step Analysis, in other words, works to categorize and then further organize information and, in so doing, to bring out the underlying structure of the reading that you are summarizing.

2. Select the information that you wish to discuss on some principle other than general coverage (usually "and-then" lists) of the material.

Use Notice and Focus to rank these items in some order of importance (see Chapter 1). Let's say that you are writing a paper on proposed changes to health care legislation or on recent developments in European economic policy. Rather than simply collecting the information, try to arrange it into hierarchies. What are the least or most significant changes or developments, and why? Which are most overlooked or most overrated or most controversial or most practical, and why? All of these terms—"significant," "overlooked," and so forth—have the effect of *focusing* the summary. In other words, they will guide your decisions about what to include and exclude. As you rank, however, it is important to distinguish between the rankings that are implicit within the piece (for a strict summary) and your own rankings of the material (for beginning to use the summary in a context of your own).

3. Reduce the scope of what you choose to summarize, and say more about less.

Both Five-Step Analysis and Notice and Focus inevitably involve some loss of breadth; you won't be able to cover everything. But this is usually a trade-off worth making. Your ability to rank parts of your subject or choose a particularly revealing feature or pattern to focus on will give you surer control of the material than if you just reproduced what was in the text. You can still begin with a brief survey of major points to provide context, before narrowing the focus.

Reducing scope is an especially efficient and productive strategy when you are trying to understand a reading you find difficult or perplexing. It will move you beyond just banking and toward having ideas about the reading. If, for example, you are reading Chaucer's *The Canterbury Tales* and start cataloguing what makes it funny, you are likely to end up with an unanalyzed plot summary—a list that arranges its elements in no particular order. But narrowing the question to "How does Chaucer's use of religious commentary contribute to the humour of 'The Wife of Bath's Tale'?" reduces the scope to a single tale and the humour to a single aspect of humour. Describe those as accurately as you can, and you will begin to notice things.

4. Get some detachment: shift your focus from *what* to *how* and *why*.

Most readers tend to get too single-minded about absorbing the information. That is, they attend only to the *what*: what the reading is saying or what it is about. They take it all in passively. But through an act of will, as a tool in your repertoire, you can deliberately shift your focus to *how* it says what it says, and *why*. If, for example, you were asked to discuss the major discoveries that Darwin made on the *Beagle*, you could avoid simply listing his conclusions by redirecting your attention to how he proceeds. You could choose to focus, for example, on Darwin's use of the scientific method, examining how he builds and, in some cases, discards hypotheses.

Or you might select several passages that illustrate how Darwin proceeded from evidence to conclusion, and then rank them in order of importance to the overall theory. Notice that in shifting the emphasis to Darwin's thinking—the *how* and *why*—you would not be excluding the *what* (the information component) from your discussion.

Let's take one more example. If you were studying the influence of the Group of Seven on Canadian art and culture, such a broad subject would tend to produce passive summary—a list of standard generalizations about nature and landscape painting. But what if you narrowed the focus to their stylistic innovations and considered *how* their use of colour and shape helped redefine our national identity? Note that this question would still enable you to address, though in much more focused form, the broader question of why the Group of Seven has had such an enduring influence.

5. Attend to the pitch, the complaint, and the moment.

Consider that whatever you are reading—and this is even true in such apparently neutral material as textbooks—is at least three things other than just an assemblage of information.

A reading is an argument, a presentation of information that makes a case of some sort, even if the argument is not explicitly stated. When you write a summary, look for language that reveals the position or positions the piece seems interested in having you adopt. As we say in Chapter 1, it is not only debate-style argument that makes a case for things. Analysis, for example, argues for understanding a subject in a particular way. In her critique of the global economy, for example, Linda McQuaig in her article "A Matter of Will" repeatedly cues her reader concerning what she "would argue" (pages 108–112).

A reading is a reaction to some situation, some set of circumstances, that the piece has set out to address. An indispensable means of understanding and summarizing someone else's writing is to figure out what seems to have caused the person to write the piece in the first place. Writers write, presumably, because they think something needs to be addressed. What? Take a close look at the introduction to Robert Fulford's "My Life as a High School Dropout" (pages 98–100). Look for language in the piece that reveals the writer's starting point. If you can find the position or situation he is trying to correct, you will find it much easier to locate the argument—the position the piece asks you to accept.

A reading is a response to the world conditioned by the writer's particular moment in time. In your attempt to figure out not only what a piece says but where it is coming from (the causes of its having been written in the first place and the positions it works to establish), history is significant. When was the piece written? Where? What else was going on at the time that might have shaped the writer's ideas and attitudes? You don't necessarily have to run to a history book for every summary you write, but neither do you want to ignore the extent to which writers are conditioned by their times.

Passage-Based Focused Freewriting

Passage-based focused freewriting is one of the best analytical exercises you can do in order to get ideas about what you are reading. It works on the assumption that you'll be ready to have a smarter appreciation of how the whole works when you've seen how a piece works.

In general, freewriting is a method of arriving at ideas by writing continuously about a subject for a specified period of time (usually ten to twenty minutes) without pausing to edit or correct or bite your pen or stare into space. The rationale behind this activity can be understood through a well-known remark by the novelist E.M. Forster (in regard to the "tyranny" of prearranging everything): "How do I know what I think until I see what I say?" Freewriting gives you the chance to see what you'll say.

In passage-based focused freewriting, you narrow the scope to a single passage, a brief piece of the reading (at least a sentence, at most a paragraph), to anchor your analysis. You might choose the passage in answer to the question, "What is the one passage in the reading that needs to be discussed, that poses a question or a problem, or that seems (in some way that is perhaps difficult to pin down) anomalous or even just unclear?" You can vary this question by selecting the passage that you find most puzzling, most important, most dissonant, or whatever.

One advantage of focused freewriting is that it forces you to articulate what you notice as you notice it, not delaying—or, as is more common, simply avoiding—thinking in a persistent and relatively disciplined way about what you are reading. There is no set procedure for such writing, but it usually involves the following:

- It selects out key phrases or terms in the passage and paraphrases them, trying to tease out the possible meanings of these words.
- It relentlessly asks "So what?" about the details: "so what" that the passage uses this language, moves in this way, arrives at these points? and so forth.

- It addresses how the passage is representative of broader issues in the reading; perhaps it will refer to another similar passage.
- It attends briefly to the context surrounding the passage, summarizing the larger section of which the passage is a part.

As you can see, passage-based focused freewriting thus makes use of the other skills that we have been discussing in this chapter as well: paraphrasing, summarizing, and narrowing the focus. It is an effective way of preparing for class discussion and of testing possible target areas of concentration for a paper.

❧*TRY THIS:* Select a passage from any of the materials that you are reading and copy it at the top of the page. Then do a twenty-minute focused freewrite on it, using the bulleted items on page 69–70 as guidelines. Strive by the end of the time allotted to make some kind of interpretive leap, some consolidation of what you have learned about the reading by doing the exercise. □

Voices Across the Curriculum

Finding Your Subject and Your Voice

Nothing to say. No ideas. Blank. Blocked. Deadline looms; you're thinking as hard as you can, but nothing comes to mind. In fact, the more you try to concentrate, the more anxious you feel. Have you been there? If so, you know that sometimes the more analytical you work to be, the less analytical you become. Paradoxically, the way out of this mess can be temporarily to give up being analytical, to stop worrying about every word and phrase, to stop looking over your own shoulder at every thought—to get all the critics crowding your brain to give you a break and take some time off. And allow your ideas to surface from the underside of your mind.

How to do that? Try *freewriting*, putting your pen to paper or your hands to the keyboard and writing or typing for ten minutes without stopping. Freewriting involves what Peter Elbow calls "first-order thinking," thinking that's "intuitive and creative, that doesn't strive for conscious direction and control." It's the opposite of "second-order thinking," which is also known as critical thinking. Critical thinking is what teachers often expect in analytical essays, so how can first-order thinking help produce it? Well, first-order thinking helps us lock up our editors, helps us separate the two essential, but contradictory, dimensions of effective writing: creativity and critical thinking. In using it, we often surface deeper, stronger, more authentic and—consequently—more persuasive arguments. It helps us get past our counter-productive fears of looking foolish and making mistakes.

—Mark Weisberg, professor of law

B. WHAT TO DO WITH THE READING: AVOIDING THE MATCHING EXERCISE

What does it mean "to do something with the reading"? Well, obviously, you can paraphrase, summarize, or do a focused freewrite with it, but these exercises aim primarily to establish an accurate understanding of what the reading is doing and saying. This is why they are included under the heading "How to Read: Words Matter." When, by contrast, you *do* something with the reading, you use it for purposes that are different from the aims of the reading itself. This distinction holds for all kinds of reading, not just the academic or literary varieties. In reading a guide to bike repair, you might paraphrase the directions for replacing the brakes to make sure your understanding of this complex procedure is sufficiently clear. But if you use the knowledge you gained to fix the brakes on some other machine, adapting what you learned, you'd be doing something with the reading.

Since analysis relies so heavily on reading, we address in much of the rest of this book, either directly or implicitly, ways of negotiating what you read. In a later chapter, for example, we concentrate on how to use secondary research. For now, we will discuss three basic approaches to doing things with the reading:

- Applying a reading as a lens for examining something else
- Comparing one reading with another
- Uncovering the assumptions in a reading—where the piece is "coming from"

We'll introduce and do basic troubleshooting on the first two approaches, foregrounding the major problems and how to solve them. But we'll concentrate on the third, with which you are probably least familiar.

Applying a Reading as a Lens

We apply what we read about all the time. It's a standard academic assignment. You read an article on gender and blue jeans and then connect its ideas to something else—how, for example, magazine ads represent jeans-wearing with respect to gender. Or you study Freud's *The Interpretation of Dreams* and then analyze a dream of your own or a friend's as you project what Freud would have done. Or you apply his theory of repression to the behaviour of a character in a novel or to some newfound realization about your mother's occasional bouts of frenzied housecleaning or your father's zealous weeding when he's upset. Freud thus becomes a lens for seeing the subject.

But what about taking an article on liberation theology as practised by certain Catholic priests in Latin America and applying it to the rise of Islamic fundamentalism in the Middle East? Or for that matter, what about applying the directions for fixing the brakes on a bicycle to the analogous task on a car? Obviously, the original texts may be somewhat useful, but there are also significant differences between the two religious movements and between the two kinds of brakes.

So what should you do? When using a reading as a lens to see better what is going on in something you are studying, assume that the match between the lens and your subject will never be exact. It is often in the area where things don't match up exactly that you will find your best opportunity for having ideas. Here are two guidelines for applying lens A to some subject matter B.

1. Think about how lens A both fits *and* does not fit subject B: avoid the matching-exercise mentality.

The big problem with the way most people apply a reading is that they do so too indiscriminately, too generally. They essentially construct a matching exercise in which each of a set of ideas drawn from text A is made to equate with a corresponding element (an idea or a fact) from subject B, often in virtual list-like fashion. Matching exercises are more useful in some contexts than in others (great for fixing your bike's brakes, less so for analyzing your parents). At their worst, matching exercises are static, mindlessly mechanical, and, worst of all, inaccurate. This is because they concentrate on similarities and forget the rest. As a result, the lens screens out what it cannot bring into focus, and the writer applying it distorts what he or she sees. Like an optometrist figuring out the new prescription for your glasses, you need to constantly adjust the lens whenever you bring it to new material. Don't just apply A as a blanket: really think about how A both fits *and* doesn't fit B.

Remember that whenever you apply lens A to a new subject B, you are taking A from its original context and using its ideas in at least somewhat different circumstances for at least somewhat different purposes. Don't just nod to the shift in context; really think about how this shift changes things and, thus, how it may require you to refocus the lens. Freud's theory of repression wasn't actually talking about your father, after all. And there are probably other explanations for his weeding frenzies to be explored. Again, the goal is not to dismiss Freud but to adjust his thinking to the particular case. You don't want to use the reading that you are applying as a club to bludgeon your subject into submission.

2. Actively seek out the differences between lens A and subject B; use these differences to probe both A and B ("Yes, but...").

If you undertake applications assuming that A does not fit B completely and accurately, then you are bound to find areas of mismatch—ideas in the reading that don't apply and information and ideas in your subject that don't fit. This is not a problem. It's an opportunity, giving you something to do with the reading. On the basis of the differences you detect, you can probe both A and B.

Say, for example, you are applying an article on the racist implications of the recent vogue for black/white buddy films to a film you've seen recently that was not discussed in the article. "Yes, but...," you find yourself responding: there are places where the film does appear to fit within the pattern that the article claims, but there are also exceptions to the pattern. What do you do? What not to do is either choose a different film that "fits better" or decide that the article is wrong-headed.

Instead, start with the "yes"; talk about how the film accords with the general pattern. Then, focus on the "but"; talk about the claims in the reading (the lens) that seem not to fit, or material in your subject not adequately accounted for by the lens. Although you're not out to attack the reading you have been applying, neither should you believe that applying a reading as a lens is a process of merely nodding repeatedly about how neatly everything fits. In fact, a careful application of a reading will usually lead you to refine one or more of its ideas (to adjust the lens) and bring you to new, small additions to or changes in the thinking offered by the reading. We have more to say about this subject—the reciprocal relationship between claims and evidence—in later chapters.

❦*TRY THIS:* Using the two guidelines described above, apply the following observation by Jeffrey Simpson ("lens A") to your own university ("subject B"): "Too many undergraduate students are taught by teaching assistants or find themselves in cavernous lecture halls with hundreds of fellow students or watching classes on closed-circuit television." Strive to produce several paragraphs in which you avoid the matching exercise and instead probe both lens A and subject B. □

Comparing and Contrasting One Reading with Another

Comparing and contrasting is another traditional assignment done with readings that falls flat when it turns into a mechanical matching exercise. Comparing readings resembles applying a reading as a lens. These activities are not intended as ends in themselves; they almost always contribute to some larger process of understanding.

The rationale for working comparatively is that you can usually discover ideas about a reading much more easily when you are not viewing it in isolation. You can observe it from a different perspective: in relation to something else. When used in this way, the comparison is usually not a 50–50 split; you've moved to a comparison of A with B because you want to better understand A.

In short, a *good comparison* should open up a reading, not close it down. It does more than demonstrate that you've "done the reading." We're all completely familiar with the formulaic conclusions to the comparisons produced by the matching-exercise mentality: "Thus, we see there are many similarities and differences between A and B." Perfunctory, pointless, and inert lists: that's what you get if you stop the process of comparing and contrasting too soon, before you've focused and explored something interesting that you notice.

How do you avoid the ubiquitous matching-exercise habit? Here are three guidelines for productively comparing A with B:

1. Focus the comparison to give it a point.

A comparison won't have a point inherently—you need to consciously give it one. It's often useful to assume that what you have originally taken for a point has not yet gone far enough, is still too close to summary. Rather than sticking with a range of broad comparisons, try to focus on a key comparison, one that you find interesting or revealing. (Five-Step Analysis, Notice and Focus, and other tools can help you here to select your focus.) Although narrowing the focus in this way might seem to eliminate other important areas of consideration, in fact it usually allows you to incorporate at least some of these other areas in a more tightly connected, less list-like fashion.

If, to return to an earlier example about the Group of Seven, you were to compare the artistic styles of Tom Thomson and Arthur Lismer, you would begin but not stop with identifying similarities and differences. The goal of your analysis would be to focus on some particular matches that seem especially revealing—for example, that the two artists shared subject matter but grew to approach it in different ways. Then, in response to the "So what?" question, you could attempt to develop some explanation of what these differences reveal and why they are significant. You might, for example, decide that Lismer's use of twisted shapes reveals an ominous facet of the Canadian experience, while Thomson's rich colours evoke the pastoral quality of our bountiful landscape.

2. Look for significant differences between A and B, given their similarity.

One of the best ways to arrive at a meaningful and interesting focus is to follow a principle that we call looking for difference within similarity. The procedure is simple but virtually guaranteed to produce a focused idea.

   a. First, deal with the similarity. Identify what the essential similarity is and then ask and answer, "So what?" Why is this similarity significant?

   b. Then, in this context, identify the differences that you notice.

   c. Choose one difference you find particularly revealing or interesting, and again ask, "So what?" What is the significance of this difference?

You can repeat this procedure with a range of key similarities and differences. If you do so, look for ways that the various differences are connected.

The phrase "difference within similarity" is to remind you that once you have started your thinking by locating apparent similarities, you can usually refine that thinking by pursuing significant, though often less obvious, distinctions among the similar things. In Irish studies, for example, scholars characteristically acknowledge the extent to which contemporary Irish culture is the product of colonization. To this extent, Irish culture shares certain traits with other former colonies in Africa, Asia, Latin America, and elsewhere. But instead of simply demonstrating how Irish culture fits the general pattern of colonialism, these scholars also isolate the ways that Ireland *does not fit the model.* They focus, for example, on how its close geographical proximity and racial similarity to England, its colonizer, have distinguished the kinds of problems it encounters today from those characteristic of the more generalized model of colonialism. In effect, looking for difference within similarity has led them to locate and analyze the anomalies.

3. Look for unexpected similarity between A and B, given their difference.

A corollary of the preceding principle is that you should focus on *unexpected similarity rather than obvious difference.* The fact that, in 2003, Jean Chrétien's Liberals differed from Stephen Harper's Canadian Alliance on tax policy is probably a less promising focal point than their surprising agreement on a new health accord with the provinces. Most readers would expect the political parties to differ on taxes, and a comparison of their positions would likely involve mostly summarizing. But a surprising similarity, like an unexpected difference, necessarily raises questions for you to pursue: do the parties' shared positions on health policy, for example, stem from the same motives?

❦*TRY THIS:* Choose any item from the list below, and practise reading comparatively. After you've done the research necessary to locate material to read and analyze, list as many similarities and differences as you can: go for coverage. Then, review your list, and select the two or three most revealing similarities and the two or three most revealing differences. At this point, you are ready to write a few paragraphs in which you argue for the significance of a key difference or similarity. In so doing, you may find it interesting to focus on an unexpected similarity or difference—one that others might not initially notice. (We recommend trying the "unexpected" gambit.) □

1. Accounts of the same event from two different newspapers or magazines or textbooks
2. Two CDs (or even songs) by the same artist or group
3. Two ads for the same kind of product
4. Graffiti in men's bathrooms versus graffiti in women's bathrooms
5. The political campaigns of two opponents running for the same or similar office

Uncovering the Assumptions in a Reading

Everything you read has basic assumptions that underlie it. What are "assumptions" in this context? They are the basic starting points for beliefs from which a position springs, its "givens" or basic operating premises. The *Oxford English Dictionary* defines a "premise"—from a Latin word meaning "to put before"—as "a previous statement or proposition from which another statement is inferred or follows as a conclusion." All arguments or articulations of point of view have premises—that is, they are based in a given set of assumptions, which are built upon to arrive at conclusions. A clearly stated premise—or assumption—in Leslie Millin's "Idols of the Tribe" is that "Virtually all new technologies have unintended consequences" (pages 277–284). Millin works from this premise in order to build his multifaceted analysis of communications technology.

Much of the time, though, the assumptions are not visible; they're implicit (which is why they need to be inferred). They're usually not actively concealed—writers hiding from readers the subterranean bases of their outlooks—which might be considered unethical. Rather, many writers (especially inexperienced ones) remain unaware of the premises that underlie their points of view—probably because they were never taught to be aware of them. Similarly, most readers don't know that they should search out the starting points of what they read and so, of course, they also don't know how.

Especially if it's in a book, most readers tend to credit what they read as true, or at least relatively neutral. In other words, most people aren't aware that everything they read (and write) comes from given sets of assumptions. It follows that the ability to uncover assumptions is a powerful analytical procedure to learn—it gives you insight into the roots, the basic givens that a piece of writing (or a speaker) has assumed are true. When you locate assumptions in a text, you understand the text better—where it's coming from, what else it believes that is more fundamental than what it is overtly declaring. You also find things to write about; uncovering assumptions offers one of the best ways of developing and revising your own work. Uncovering assumptions can help you to understand why you believe X, or it may reveal to you that two of your givens are in conflict with each other.

To uncover assumptions, you need to read "backward"—to ask what a reading must also already believe, given that it believes what it overtly claims. In other words, you need to imagine or reinvent the process of thinking by which a writer has arrived at a position. You can do this by employing some of the skills already discussed in this chapter; in particular, identifying the underlying structure of a reading, asking what particular words mean, and shifting your focus from *what* to *how* and *why*.

Say you read a piece that praises a television show for being realistic but faults it for setting a bad example to the kids who watch it. What assumptions might we infer from such a piece? Here are some:

- Television should attempt to depict life accurately (realistically).
- Television should produce shows that set good examples.
- Kids imitate, or at least have their attitudes shaped by, what they watch on television.
- Good and bad examples are clear and easily recognizable by everyone.

Note that none of these assumptions is self-evidently true—each would need to be argued for. And some of the assumptions conflict with others—for example, that shows should be both morally uplifting and realistic, given that in "real life" those who do wrong often go unpunished. These are subjects an analytical response to the piece (or a revision of it) could bring out.

Procedure for Uncovering Assumptions

How do you actually go about uncovering assumptions? Here's a fairly flexible procedure, which we will apply step-by-step to the claim "Tax laws benefit the wealthy."

1. Paraphrase the explicit claim.

This activity will get you started interpreting the claim, and it may begin to suggest the claim's underlying assumptions. We might paraphrase the claim as "The rules for paying income tax give rich people monetary advantages" or "The rules for paying income tax help the rich get richer."

2. List the implicit ideas that the claim seems to assume to be true.

Here are two: "Tax laws shouldn't benefit anybody" and "Tax laws should benefit those who need the benefit, those with the least money."

3. Determine the various ways that the key terms of the claim might be defined, as well as how the writer of the claim has defined them.

This process of definition will help you to see the key concepts upon which the claim depends. How does the writer intend "benefit"? And does he or she mean that tax laws benefit only the wealthy and presumably harm those who are not wealthy? And where does the line between wealthy and not wealthy get drawn?

4. Try on an oppositional stance to the claim to see if this unearths more underlying assumptions.

Regardless of your view on the subject, suppose for the sake of argument that the writer is wrong. This step allows you to think comparatively, helping you to see the claim more clearly, to see what it apparently *excludes* from its fundamental beliefs. Knowing what the underlying assumption leaves out helps us to see the narrowness upon which the claim may rest; we understand better its limits. Two positions that the claim appears to exclude are "Tax laws benefit the poor" and "Tax laws do not benefit the wealthy."

Whether you encounter a claim such as "Tax laws benefit the wealthy" in your reading or start writing a paper from that position, you will get into trouble as you develop your claim (move it forward) if you don't move backward as well, for the claim conceals a set of more fundamental assumptions about the purpose of tax laws. To find these assumptions, you need to query the claim before going on to make some kind of argument about it. Is the purpose of tax laws to redress economic inequities, as the claim seems to imply? Is the purpose of tax laws to spur the economy by rewarding those who generate capital, in which case tax laws don't benefit only the wealthy? You might go to the Canadian Constitution Acts and/ or to legal precedents to resolve such questions, but our point here is that regardless of the position your paper adopts—attacking tax laws, defending them, showing how they actually benefit everyone, or whatever—you risk proceeding blindly if you have failed to question the purpose of tax laws in the first place.

❧*TRY THIS:* Apply the four-step procedure for uncovering assumptions to the following brief excerpt from a student paper: paraphrase, list implicit assumptions, define key terms, and try on an oppositional stance. The result of this process should be a list of the premises upon which the writer's argument operates and which the paragraph has not made sufficiently clear. At this point, if you wish, you might write a page about the paragraph, providing the results of your analytical reading. ☐

> In all levels of trade, including individual, local, domestic, and international, both buyers and sellers are essentially concerned with their own welfare. This self-interest, however, actually contributes to the health and growth of the economy as a whole. Each country benefits by exporting those goods in which it has an advantage and importing goods in which it does not. Importing and exporting allow countries to focus on producing those goods that they can generate most efficiently. As a result of specializing in certain products and then trading them, self-interest leads to efficient trade, which leads to consumer satisfaction.

❧*TRY THIS:* Here's another statement for uncovering assumptions. In the reference application sent to professors for students who are seeking to enter a student-teaching program, the professor is asked to rank the student from one to four (unacceptable to acceptable) on the following criterion: "The student uses his/her sense of humour appropriately." Use the procedure for uncovering assumptions to compile a list of the assumptions embedded in the quotation. ☐

A Sample Essay: Having Ideas by Uncovering Assumptions

As an analytical activity, uncovering assumptions is not limited to reading. Like other tools we discuss, it can also lead you to have ideas and formulate a point of view about the reading—in effect, to become a writer. We'll now examine a newspaper editorial (from Montreal's *The Gazette*) that demonstrates this process. The editorial illustrates how a writer reasons forward to his own conclusions by reasoning backward to the premises assumed in the positions of others. As you will see, the piece also shows how the strategy of refocusing binaries (discussed in Chapter 2) operates in tandem with uncovering assumptions.

As you read this editorial on the 1995 Quebec referendum, try to focus not only on the content of the argument but also on its form—that is, how the writer moves from one phase of his thinking to the next. Toward this end, we have added our own summaries of what each paragraph of the editorial accomplishes. At the end of the editorial we sum up the writer's primary developmental strategies as guidelines that you can apply to your own reading and writing.

"Why Blame Ethnics for Referendum Loss, and Not Women?"

by Joseph Heath

Why blame just ethnic voters for the failure of the 1995 referendum? Why not blame women as well? The fact that Jacques Parizeau recently repeated his famous line about "the ethnic vote" being responsible for the failure of the 1995 Quebec referendum suggests that he still doesn't see what's wrong with these comments. *[The writer names the issue: responsibility for the defeat of the Separatist position in the 1995 Quebec referendum.]*

On this point, I have some sympathy for the man. After all, in the midst of the anger and denunciation, people tend to lose sight of the fact that what he's saying is true: if all non-francophone voters had mysteriously disappeared on the day of the referendum, the Yes side would have won. Among francophone voters, 61 percent supported the Yes side. In this sense, "the ethnic vote" is responsible for the failure of the sovereignist project. So what could be wrong with pointing that out? *[The writer concedes that, despite his announced disagreement with Parizeau, the two of them share some surprising common ground.]*

Yet Parizeau's comments never seem to go over very well. To help him see the problem, I would like to draw a little analogy. While it's true that a majority of francophones voted for the Yes side and a majority of non-francophones voted No, it is also the case that a majority of men voted Yes, while a majority of women voted No. In other words, if all of the women in Quebec had mysteriously disappeared on the eve of the referendum, then the Yes side would have won. In fact, if only just francophone women had supported the Yes side as strongly as francophone men did, the Yes side would have won with a 55 percent majority. So obviously it is not just "money and the ethnic vote" that's responsible for the failure of the referendum; it's women as well. *[The writer uses analogy to question the assumption that a single bloc of voters can be held responsible for the referendum's outcome.]*

Now imagine that after the results of the referendum had been announced, Premier Jacques Parizeau had got up before the assembled crowd and said: "My friends, once again our dreams have been frustrated. And we all know who is responsible; let us not mince words. By Jove, it's the women who are to blame. Like Delilah, they have shorn us of our locks. If it weren't for them, our dream of an independent Quebec would be at hand." And imagine that, later in the evening, Finance Minister Bernard Landry was overheard berating a female clerk at a hotel, saying "I hope you women are happy. Is this why we let you out of the kitchen?" *[The writer dramatizes, playfully, cultural assumptions concerning gender relations and roles.]*

If either of them had done such a thing, people would have immediately concluded that they were misogynists. Why? Because a majority of the population of Quebec voted for the No side. To single out one group that voted strongly against and to hold it responsible is arbitrary and unreasonable. *[The writer states his thesis by rejecting the premise that the collective action of any subgroup can be held responsible for a larger group's action.]*

Anyone who singles out women and blames them for the defeat obviously has an axe to grind with women. Yet the decision to blame ethnic voters, rather than female voters, is just as unreasonable. Thus anyone who goes around blaming ethnic voters for the loss must have an axe to grind with ethnics. *[The writer returns to his analogy in order to expose Parizeau's assumption concerning ethnic voters in Quebec.]*

Of course, I'm sure it never crossed Parizeau's mind to blame women for the defeat in 1995. Part of the reason is undoubtedly that he is not a misogynist. But the other reason is that blaming women would be outrageously divisive and hurtful. He would be able to see this quite easily because it's easy for him to imagine himself in a woman's shoes, and to see how such an accusation would be perceived. Yet blaming the ethnic vote is just as hurtful and divisive as blaming women. *[The writer reiterates his own assumption that, in order to ensure fair analysis, each subgroup must be viewed similarly.]*

What are we to conclude from this? It suggests that Parizeau, and his many supporters in the Parti Québécois, have difficulty putting themselves in the shoes of non-francophones and seeing how their actions look from the perspective of their fellow citizens. If they could, they would think twice about engaging in such hurtful and divisive political rhetoric. *[The writer develops the implication of assuming that one subgroup bears responsibility: political divisiveness.]*

Of course, some might argue that singling out ethnic groups, rather than women, is justified, because in the former case, it is precisely their allegiance to the group that motivated them to vote No. In other words, allophones voted No because they were allophones, whereas women did not vote No because they were women. *[The writer tries on an oppositional stance in order to unearth an underlying premise of his own position: that members' allegiance to their subgroup is a constant across subgroups.]*

This conclusion would be overly hasty. Perhaps there is a reason "men are from Quebec, women are from Canada." Women tend to have fairly consistent political preferences: as a group they are less right-wing than men, less confrontational, less territorial, less punitive and less intolerant. They are also less nationalistic. Is that pure coincidence? *[The writer concludes by defending the underlying premise; he does so by invoking assumptions about gender differences.]*[*]

The strategies that direct the thinking in this editorial offer a model for reading to uncover assumptions in the service of arriving at ideas. If you examine what the writer has done—not just what he has said—you might arrive at the following primary moves, which can be phrased as general guidelines for reading analytically:

1. Paraphrase the explicit claims; search out the meanings of key terms.

The writer devotes the first half of his editorial to recasting Parizeau's famous statement. He slows down the forward momentum toward judgment by conceding that the votes of non-francophones carried indisputably significant weight. His analogy between native language and gender illustrates vividly just how complicated the meaning of "responsibility" is when it comes to analyzing the referendum results.

2. Uncover assumptions to decide what is really at issue.

By imagining verbal attacks on women by Parizeau and Landry (paragraph 4), the writer dramatizes not only cultural assumptions about gender roles but also the central "given" of the Separatist government's thinking: that the collective action of any subgroup can be held responsible for a larger group's action. Beneath the attack on ethnic voters, therefore, lies an unreasonable premise concerning political responsibility. It's one thing to appear racist or sexist in the aftermath of a referendum; it's still another to

---

[*]Joseph Heath, MONTREAL GAZETTE on Monday, April 7, 2003. Reprinted with permission from the author.

assume that ethnic voters—or female voters—may bear sole responsibility for the referendum's outcome.

3. Attend to organizing contrasts; but be alert to the possibility that they may be false dichotomies, and reformulate them as necessary.

A false dichotomy (sometimes called a false binary) inaccurately divides possible views on a subject into two opposing camps, forcing a choice between black and white when some shade of grey might be fairer and more accurate. As we discuss under the section "Either/Or Thinking (Binaries)" in Chapter 2, it is always a good strategy to question any either/or dichotomy. Consider whether its opposing terms define the issue fairly and accurately before accepting an argument in favour of one side or the other.

Consider, too, how you might reject both choices offered by an either/ or opposition in order to construct an alternative approach that is truer to the issues at hand. (See the section "Thinking Recursively" in Chapter 1.) This is what the author of the editorial does. He outlines and then rejects as a false dichotomy the assumption held by the Separatist leadership—that the 1995 referendum can be viewed as a division between francophones and allophones.

It is here, evidently, that reasoning back to premises and reformulating binaries has led the writer to his primary idea. He argues, by analogy, that responsibility for the outcome of the referendum rests no more with allophones ("ethnics") than it does with women. The only binary that holds fast is the one between the Yes side and the No side; in other words, voters express a choice, and that choice is the one indisputable dichotomy. Notice, though, that in his final paragraph the writer makes a case for a distinction between women ("less right-wing") and men. He reformulates this dichotomy (a politically incorrect one in modern society) and leaves his reader with a question: "Is that pure coincidence?" He may not have all the answers, but he encourages his reader to consider the shades of grey that come with every "black and white" binary.

4. When you write your analysis of the reading, rehearse for your readers the thinking process by which you have uncovered the assumptions—not just the conclusions to which the process has led you.

Notice that virtually the entire editorial has consisted of uncovering assumptions as a way of arriving at new ways of thinking. This matter of sharing your thinking with readers as you develop and fine-tune your ideas is the primary subject of Part II of this book.

C. PERSONALIZING (LOCATING THE "I")

Before getting to Part II, though, let's think about the personal relationship that every writer inevitably builds with his or her audience. No matter how formal your voice, no matter how objective your analysis, the fact remains that a connection between people is at the heart of every essay. As the title of this chapter suggests, the most successful writers keep their audiences clearly in view; in the end, it's the readers who take possession of your writing.

So what about using the first-person "I"? In his editorial for *The Gazette*, Joseph Heath does so repeatedly. He's an editorialist, after all. He can get away with it. For academic essay-writers, however, the matter always seems to be a bit more complicated.

In one sense all writing is personal: you are the one putting words on the page, and inevitably you see things from your point of view. Even if you were to summarize what someone else had written, aiming for maximum impersonality, you would be making the decisions about what to include and exclude. Most effective analytical prose has a strong personal element—the writer's stake in the subject matter. As readers, we want the sense that a writer is engaged with the material, cares about what he or she says about it, and is sharing what he or she finds interesting about it.

But, in another sense, no writing is strictly personal. As contemporary cultural theorists are fond of pointing out, the "I" is not a wholly autonomous free agent who writes from a unique point of view. Rather, the "I" is always affected by forces outside the self—social, cultural, educational, historical, and so forth—that shape the self. The extreme version of this position allots little space for what we like to think of as individuality: the self is a site through which dominant cultural ways of understanding the world (ideologies) circulate. That's a pretty disarming notion, but one worth pondering. From this perspective, we are like actors who don't know that we're actors, reciting various cultural scripts that we don't realize are scripts.

This is, of course, an extreme position. A person who believes that "civil rights for all" is an essential human right is not necessarily a victim of cultural brainwashing. The grounds of his or her belief, shaped by participation in a larger community of belief (ethnic, religious, family tradition, and so forth), are, however, not merely personal.

What every academic writer must keep in mind, though, is that overpersonalizing substitutes merely reacting for thinking. Rather than open-mindedly exploring what a subject might mean, the overpersonalizing writer tends to use a limited range of culturally conditioned likes and dislikes to close the subject down. Is a person who dislikes a character in a novel or television show—Madame Bovary or Jerry Seinfeld—doing any useful analytical thinking? If Jerry reminds her of her own self-centred brother and so she dislikes him, who cares? If a viewer hates a film because the film's star divorced his wife and left his children as did her own father, is that reasonable? These are responses that, however valid in themselves, are merely personal.

Along similar lines, it's a mistake for a person to assume that because he or she experiences X, everyone else does too. It is surprisingly difficult to break the habit of treating our points of view as self-evidently true—not for just us but for everyone. What seems to be common sense for one person and not even in need of explanation can be quite uncommon and not so obviously sensible to someone else. More often than not, "common sense" really means "what seems obvious to me and therefore should be obvious to you."

❦TRY THIS: Paraphrase the phrase "common sense." Your aim is to extend our discussion of what people are doing when they fall back on the idea of common sense. You also may wish to think of recent situations in which someone you know has appealed to common sense or remarked on its absence from a discussion. ☐

One telltale sign of an overpersonalizing writer is his or her tendency to let personal narratives substitute for careful consideration of a subject. When you substitute personal narrative for analysis, your own experiences and prejudices tend to become an unquestioned standard of value. Your own disastrous experience during an ice storm may predispose you to ridicule the provincial government's handling of power plants, but your writing needs to examine in detail the administrative problems—not simply evoke the six hours you spent shivering in your apartment. Paying too much attention to how a subject makes you feel or how it fits your previous experience can seduce you away from paying attention to how the subject itself operates.

This is not to say that there is no learning or thinking value in telling our experiences. Storytelling has the virtue of offering concrete experience rather than just the conclusions the experience led to. Personal narratives can take us back to the source of our convictions. The problem comes when "relating" to someone's story becomes a habitual substitute for thinking through the ideas and attitudes that the story suggests. What do people mean when they say, "I can relate to that"? By and large, "relating" to someone else's experience is an overly generalized response, one in which you do not stop to isolate either the precise grounds of the emotional identification or the various assumptions that the story rests on but does not make overt.

If our experience is not necessarily applicable to others and if our feelings about X are not self-evident truths about it, what then is the role of "the personal" in thinking and writing analytically? The problem with the personal has to do with how that term is commonly (mis)understood. It is usually located as one-half of a particularly vicious binary that might be shown thus:

subjective		objective
personal expression	*versus*	impersonal analysis
passionately engaged		detached, impassively neutral
genuinely felt		heartless

Like most vicious binaries, this one overstates the case and obscures the considerable overlap between the two sides. Analysis is not separate from feeling and engagement; these are attitudes necessary to energize it. Analysis is always personal but not overly personal; it is somewhat detached but not cold and heartless.

The antidote to the overpersonalizing habit of mind is, as with most habits you want to break, to become more self-conscious about it. If you keep in mind that the "I" you tend to lead with is not simply a free agent but also a product of cultural influences, you will be more likely to notice your first responses and become curious about them. Is this what you really believe? Asking that question is a healthy habit to cultivate and one that can often help you see the logic of other possible responses to the position you've initially taken. And, of course, some intuitive responses provide valuable beginnings for constructive thinking; so get in the habit of tracing your own responses back to their causes. If you find an aspect of your subject irritating or funny or disappointing, locate the exact details that evoked your emotional response, and begin to analyze those details.

ASSIGNMENTS

1. After reading and rereading Robert Fulford's "My Life as a High School Dropout" (pages 98–100) narrow your scope to his final paragraph and do fifteen minutes of focused freewriting. Try paraphrasing

---

Voices Across the Curriculum

Using the First-Person "I" in Academic Writing

In high school, many students seem to have been told never to use "I." They acquire the impression that there is something wrong with giving their own opinions. If they do find themselves having to advance their own point of view, they engage in linguistic contortions in order to disguise it, using such convoluted expressions as "it might be thought that..." or "one might then conclude that...."

Instead, it is much clearer, simpler, and more honest to say "I believe..." or "I will argue..." or some variant, such as "My thesis is...." As a scholar, I use "I" when it is both relevant and necessary in my own published work, and I see no reason that students should not also use "I" when relevant and necessary in their papers. However, using the first-person singular pronoun need not and should not mean that your paper is only "subjective" or that it is "nothing more than opinion." What you must do, as an academic writer, is to develop and then communicate the evidence and the reasons that led to your point of view. You present the evidence and the reasons in the form of arguments. Therefore, when you write "I believe..." you are not simply stating an unjustified opinion; you are introducing what should be a carefully developed argument.

—Christine Overall, professor of philosophy, Queen's University

---

key phrases or terms. Or ask yourself "So what?" In other words, aim to know what you think by seeing what you have to say. And remember: freewriting is continuous writing—there's no need to pause over spelling, usage, or proper grammar. Afterward, share your freewriting in a small-group exchange (four to five students).

2. Use Michael Posner's "Image World" (pages 113–120) as a lens for examining a particular film, television show, or musical group. Keep in mind that applying a reading as a lens involves more than doing a matching exercise. The objective should be to write two paragraphs that test Posner's claims by applying them to evidence you've selected.

3. Keeping in mind the editorial on the 1995 referendum (pages 80–82), write an essay (750 words) in which you develop a position by uncovering the assumptions in Linda McQuaig's "A Matter of Will" (pages 108–112). As she builds her argument concerning Canada's role in the global economy, what premises does McQuaig rely upon? Are they stated explicitly? Are they convincing? Team up with someone else in your class in order to elicit peer response: after reading each other's essay, write one or two paragraphs of response,

letting your partner know how convincing you find his or her reading of McQuaig.

4. Write a personal essay that develops a thesis by reasoning back to premises. Use as an example (but not as a model) Bruce McCall's "The Scavenger of Highway #3" (pages 91–97). In other words, see if you can detect any concealed assumptions that come into view as McCall writes about his own childhood. Your own essay need not be a childhood reflection, but you should try to examine some idea or attitude of your own, preferably one that has undergone some kind of change in recent years (for example, your attitude toward the world of work, toward marriage, toward family life, toward community, toward religion, and so forth).

D. THE ULTIMATE *TRY THIS*

Each of the three parts of *Writing Analytically* includes "The Ultimate *Try This*"—which brings together a few of the key concepts discussed in the preceding chapters. For Part I (Making Meaning: Essential Skills), those concepts are *observation* and *use of the first-person*:

What follows is the Introduction to an article by Betty Bednarski entitled "Sameness and 'difference' in *Les Belles-soeurs*: A Canadian spectator's reflections on two Polish productions of Michel Tremblay's play." Published in an academic journal, Professor Bednarski's analysis is written from the perspective of "I" and is developed on the basis of her own observations or, as the title states, her "spectator's reflections."

Locate each usage of "I" in Bednarski's Introduction and notice the action (the verb) connected to each one. Do those actions combine to clearly present the main point of the article? Does the first person contribute positively to your sense of the article's intentions? Why or why not?

In her third paragraph, Bednarski uses, repeatedly, another term to describe her reflections, namely, impressions. Do you think that the word "impressions" differs in any significant way from the word "reflections"? How effectively does the Introduction to this article present the writer's powers of observation?

Introduction

As a teacher of literature and a literary translator, I am interested in how works "travel", where and why they travel, and what happens to them along the way—how, in the course of their reception by other cultures, they can be "changed". When it comes to theatrical works, that reception will involve not only translation into another language, but also the potentially "othering" physical manifestations of performance and staging. In the context of a recent Canadian Studies conference session, where discussion centred on issues of cultural diversity *within* particular works, I chose to consider some of the ways in which a work of Québécois theatre could, so to speak, itself be "diversified", once it was taken *outside* of Quebec.†

There is probably no Québécois playwright whose work has travelled more than Michel Tremblay's. In the recent film *Entre les mains de Michel Tremblay* (Wills 2007), we are told that his plays have been translated into 31 languages and staged all over the world (no figures are given, but the number of foreign productions must be very high). I shall reflect here on my own experience as a Canadian spectator of two Polish productions of Tremblay's *Les Belles-soeur*—a national television production from 1993 and a live stage production from 2000–2001, which was a musical adaptation of the play—two very different productions, occurring seven years apart, at two very different moments in the post-Communist era, as change was sweeping through Polish society and the gap between Polish and North American cultures was narrowing.

What I have to offer are above all impressions. Impressions that go back a long way—sixteen years and eight years respectively—*remembered* impressions, then, that have taken on some of the inevitable vagueness of memory, but also some of the perspective of retrospect. They are the impressions of a Canadian with a keen interest in literary translation, who was, in 1993 and 2001, already very familiar with the original French version of Tremblay's play, a Canadian familiar with Poland and its culture, and who could claim to have a reasonable working knowledge of the Polish language.

I shall make some reference to the language of the Polish translation, particularly at the beginning. But my reflections are, first and foremost, those of a theatre-goer and spectator, based on my viewing of the two productions rather than on a reading of the Polish text (or texts). Both productions, as it happens, took as their starting point the same translation by University of Warsaw professor Józef Kwaterko (Kwaterko 1990), even though they were given different titles and were, as I have indicated, quite unlike each other in a number of striking ways.

Finally, as notions of historical timing will be central to the tentative conclusions I draw and to the arguments I make, I shall attach considerable importance to *dates*—among others, the date of the translation itself, and those two production dates.

---

†Bednarski, Betty. "'Sameness' and 'difference' in Les Belles-soeurs: A Canadian spectator's Reflections on two Polish productions of Michel Tremblay's play." *International Journal of Francophone Studies* 13 (2): 515–25.

READINGS FOR PART I

Making Meaning: Essential Skills

As we stress in Chapter 4, most effective analytical prose has a strong personal element. The first two readings for Part I are fine examples of this fact. **Bruce McCall** uses his boyhood experiences to illuminate the difference between Canadian and American outlooks on life. "The Scavenger of Highway #3" is a personal essay whose playful tone of voice and vivid metaphors are complemented by the rigorous thinking of a writer who constantly asks, "So what?" In "My Life as a High School Dropout," **Robert Fulford** recalls his academic struggles as a young man. Conveying concrete details to his reader, Fulford brings fresh insight to the puzzle of attention deficit disorder.

Some experiences can be simultaneously personal and communal, such as the extraordinary morning of September 11, 2001. Just two days after the devastation in New York City, Pennsylvania, and Washington, **Erna Paris** published "What Sort of People Did This?"—asking a question that haunted countless North Americans. Her answers are interpretive leaps that strive to place 9/11 in the contexts of twentieth-century warfare and international politics.

While interviewers always rely upon interpersonal exchange, **David Cohen** moves beyond the questions posed to Julian Assange in order to probe the very nature of WikiLeaks. Like all analytical writers, he interrogates not only his subject but also himself. Another persistent analyst is **Linda McQuaig**. In "A Matter of Will," she develops ideas to account for some dissonance—that is, something that seems not to fit together (as we explain in Chapter 1). The global economy is threatening Canada's autonomy, according to McQuaig, and she is determined to not only examine the dilemma but also propose necessary action.

The readings for Part I conclude with "Image World" by **Michael Posner**. Like the other contributing essayists, he is not an academic by trade. Nevertheless, Posner shares with each of them an analytical habit of mind that searches out the implications of what he calls "the mesmerizing power of the visual."

The Scavenger of Highway #3‡
Bruce McCall

Another spacious summer afternoon in 1946 in Simcoe, Ontario, pop. 6,000. Most local youngsters not off at camp, lolling on the nearby Lake Erie beaches, or picking strawberries in the surrounding farm fields are gallivanting at the municipal swimming pool. Half a mile north, as cars hurtle by, inches away, a lone eleven-year-old boy slowly patrols the shoulder of the two-lane highway that cuts through town. He looks only down. He sporadically scoops this or that small object from the gravel and dirt of the shoulder and inspects it. Most he casts aside after a cursory look, but a few go into a pocket of his short pants, which he then fondly pats each time, as if it were money in there, or jewels.

Provincial Highway #3 is a heavily traveled shortcut between the American Midwest and the northeastern states in these pre-interstate days; and the boy—me—is pocketing a connoisseur's selection of matchbooks, Camel packs, Schlitz bottle tops, and Baby Ruth wrappers flung from passing cars bound from Detroit to Buffalo and vice versa.

To me, they are no mere roadside detritus. They are to be fondled, savored, prized. They are rare and priceless artifacts delivered fresh from a higher civilization. They are American.

Meanwhile, a carton of freshly printed books has arrived at the Eva Brook Donly Museum on Norfolk Street near the center of town: the first copies of *The Genealogy and History of the Norfolk McCall Family and Associate Descendants, 1796–1946,* by Delbert T. McCall, a distant relation.

The dedicatory poem on the first page sets the tone:

Dear were the homes where they were born
    Where slept their honored dead;
And rich and wide, on every side,
    Their fruitful acres spread;
But dearer to their faithful hearts
    Than home, and gold, and lands,
Were Britain's laws, and Britain's crown,
    And grip of British hands.

Delbert's genealogy is mainly a proud and detailed recapitulation of 150 unbroken years' worth of fealty to God and the Crown—not always necessarily in that order—by the generations of Norfolk County McCalls that are his subject matter.

The patriarch was Donald McCall—"Old Donald," "Noble Donald," "Noble Old Donald," as his hagiographer variously exults—late of what is now Basking Ridge in Somerset County, New Jersey; before that, of His Majesty King George III's army; before that, of the Isle of Mull in Scotland. On a July day in 1796 Donald stepped ashore from the boat that had brought him and his family to Lake Erie and a clearing on its northern shore, on the final stage of their long voyage from temporary refuge in Nova Scotia.

Regional history would classify Old Donald as something more than a patriot and a pioneer. He was a prototypical United Empire Loyalist—a kind of inverted but non-gender-specific member of the Canadian version of the Daughters of the American Revolution—and as such a super-patriot and founding Canadian. His was the classic U.E.L. story. He had sailed to America from Scotland in 1756 as an enlistee in the Forty-second Highlanders. He fought the Indians, he fought the French, he fought with General Wolfe at Quebec in the successful battle to raise the Union Jack over Canada and forever lower the Fleur-de-Lis. His enlistment period finally over, Donald—then in barracks at Philadelphia—did as many other such British Army veterans did upon discharge: Eschewing a return to the old world, he settled in the Colonies to farm and to raise a family.

But not for long. Staunch British loyalties were rapidly becoming more than a social handicap in places like Basking Ridge. They were halfway to treason. Donald took the hint. "The abuse and persecution these old stalwarts were subjected to," fumes Delbert, "was more than they could endure and they finally yielded to the fates, sacrificed their humble and happy homes to share the lot of numerous refugees in the far-away northland, where British laws and assurances restored them to that peace of mind so relished by honorable people."

Donald's reward for his loyalty to the Crown was twofold: a six-hundred-acre land grant in the Long Point Settlement in what is now Norfolk County, Ontario, and immortality—among those who value such things—as a United Empire Loyalist.

Old Donald would be gathered to his ancestors in 1818. His immediate and later descendants largely chose to stay close to the original homestead and spread their roots not wide but deep. Delbert's history records McCalls, generation after generation, clustering there in Norfolk County—farmers working the fertile land, lumbermen, millwrights, storekeepers, innkeepers. Fellow Scots by the hundreds had migrated there in Donald's wake to spread across southwestern Ontario like marmalade; McCalls married almost exclusively within the local Scots immigrant colony and spawned large families. By the mid-nineteenth century, barely fifty years after Donald's advent, the Norfolk McCall family tree was already an impenetrable thicket.

A drunk, profligate, slow-witted, or deviant McCall never appears in Delbert's circumspect family chronicle. They are an unfailingly pious, sober, civic-minded line, these Duncans and Jameses and Daniels and their Phoebes and Charitys and Jemimas. And patriotic. They had but to hear the word *war,* or even *rebellion,* or only *raid,* before the clang of McCalls dropping their adzes and scythes and saws to pick up their muskets reverberated across the country. Delbert proudly recounts in his chronicle the rallying to arms of seven successive McCall generations, beginning eons ago with Noble Old Donald's father at the Battle of Culloden and up to my own father's R.C.A.F. service in World War Two. Donald's sons, chips off the old soldier, made almost an avocation of Yankee-potting in the early 1800s, in the course of defending local settlements from marauding intruders in the skirmishing that preceded the all-out Canadian–American War of 1812–14. A McCall was there—indeed often more than one, and one often in charge—at every call to arms through the nineteenth century. One was a captain in the Home Guard during the Fenian Raid; another was a boatman on Kitchener's Sudan expedition of 1883. My own Grandfather Walt sailed off with the Canadian Army contingent to the Boer War in 1899, to be captured—shades of young Winston Churchill—then to escape. The first Norfolk County soldier to be killed in World War One, a few days after reaching the front in September 1915, was a McCall.

As Delbert's genealogical reconstruction makes vivid, the McCalls of Norfolk County embraced the British review of events on the North American continent from the Revolutionary War onward: The American colonists were seen as an ingrate rabble so infected with their zeal for independence that they itched to drive the British not only out of their own colonies but off the map of North America, annexing Canada at the first opportunity as part of the process. The greedy Yanks had been plotting to do just that until 1812, when, as every Canadian schoolchild learned in history class, it came to a head in all-out war. Canada, valiant David against the American Goliath, thereupon (with, er, a little help from the British) trounced the bastards, and for good measure torched the White House.

Fears of a Yankee takeover subsided somewhat in the aftermath, but the suspicion that they might try it again sometime lingered with surprising persistence for much of the rest of the nineteenth century, especially in places like Norfolk County, within easy raiding distance; and the residue of that suspicion fueled the faint hostility, the sense of having to always be on guard, that colored Canadian attitudes—certainly McCall attitudes— toward the U.S.A. well into the twentieth. By my father's generation that impulse had metamorphosed into a hot but largely dormant little glob of bile lodged somewhere in the Canadian craw.

I grew up in a world where the average Canadian would rather be trampled by the R.C.M.P. Musical Ride than be found publicly admitting anything American to be superior, or even much good. Nobody, not even the most rabidly anti-American Canadian nationalist, could or would deny the economic and cultural facts of life that all but swamped our nation in Americana. But that didn't mean Canadians had to like it. That would mean accepting and even liking Americans, and wait just a minute, eh? If the general attitude of Canadians toward their mighty neighbor to the south could be distilled into a single phrase, that phrase would probably be "Oh, shut up." The Americans talked too much, mainly about themselves. Their torrid love affair with their own history and legend exceeded—painfully—the quasi-British Canadian idea of modesty and self-restraint. They were jammed permanently in extroverted high gear, confident to the brink of, if not over the edge of, arrogance; strident, take-charge, can-do—fatiguing. There was about the American style something, indeed plenty, that jarred the Canadian love of calm. Americans spent far too much of their vaunted energy out at the extremes of feeling. They were forever busting their buttons in spasms of insufferable yahoo pride or all too publicly agonizing over their crises.

The patriotic Canadian should keep his distance, then. Snuggle in the warmth and safety of the British institutions and customs and attitudes that have always underpinned Canadian life, lending it dignity and order, helping shield it from the obnoxious blowhards forever yelping and banging and partying next door, way past bedtime.

This was the view of the Americans I had breathed as part of the very air of Simcoe and Canada since infancy. Evidence that ours was a superior civilization was obvious, at least to us: We had the Imperial gallon, two-dollar bills, Mounties, the more scenic part of Niagara Falls, grade thirteen in high school, a governor-general, Eskimos, three downs in football, the Toronto Maple Leafs and the Montreal Canadiens, our Deanna Durbin in Hollywood and our Max Aitken, Lord Beaverbrook, in London, and a permanent private pipeline to Buckingham Palace.

And yet, even by age eleven I was beginning to secretly backslide. I had begun to find myself privately questioning my faith and putting it to the test. I was beginning to wonder if, despite all the evidence, Canada really was so inherently superior and the way of the U.S.A. really was so inherently intolerable. I was feeling the first pangs of envy arising from a strong and growing suspicion that not all that far away over the border, the average eleven-year-old American kid was having lots more fun. From all appearances, indeed, being first in fun was part of the American boy's birthright.

Reminders were as plentiful as the comparisons that inevitably followed. American kids got whistles, rings, glittering prizes in their cereal boxes; all we got was cereal. They could goggle at page after page of color comics—"Prince Valiant," "The Katzenjammer Kids," "Smokey Stover"— in their Sunday papers; we didn't even have Sunday papers. The comic book, that archetypal American expressive form—splashy, loud, rowdy, and manic, boiling with superheroes and supervillains, a TNT charge to the boyish imagination—had only a pallid, pathetic Canadian counterpart. The few Canadian comic books were black-and-white, vapid, and hopelessly wholesome. American kids, as I vicariously feasted along with them via the comic-book ads, guzzled Royal Crown Cola, rode balloon-tired Schwinn bikes with sirens and headlights or deluxe coaster wagons or futuristic scooters. They shot pearl-handled cap guns drawn from tooled-leather holsters or Daisy air rifles, wore aviator goggles, flew gasoline-powered model airplanes. American kids even had their own exclusive boys' mail-order department store in the form of the Johnson & Smith catalog. Rushed to your front door C.O.D. from Racine, Wisconsin—ventriloquism kits, genuine onyx signet rings, whoopee cushions, treasure Made in the U.S.A.

But not for me; not for Canadians. In the fine-print legalese, in the radio announcer's dream-smashing disclaimer, four words would serve to keep every son of the Maple Leaf empty-handed and brokenhearted, with his nose pressed enviously to the glass that separated him from the delirious ongoing American carnival of plenty and fun: "Not Available in Canada."

I was beginning to discern that this bounty showered down upon American boyhood was a mere by-product of a system so inconceivably rich and generous that it was almost carelessly throwing off wealth in every direction, nonstop.

The American cars swishing through the north of town weren't the dusty old Fords and Chevrolets Simconians drove. They were big Buicks and Packards and Chryslers and Oldsmobiles with whitewall tires and metallic paint jobs, the brightest colors ever seen in Norfolk County. They drove fast—naturally, as brother Mike explained; everybody knew the Americans had better gasoline. The Bakelite model of the Empire State Building on the desk of Dr. Sihler, the family dentist, had transfixed me from about age five; I now realized why. Canada had no Empire State Building, no Hoover Dam, no Golden Gate Bridge; Canada declined to soar in any way.

The Americans had Franklin Delano Roosevelt at the helm. We had a dyspeptic-looking old bachelor, Mackenzie King. Canada lacked the energy to make it through a week without closing down on Wednesday afternoons and all day Sunday to rest. The U.S.A. was open twenty-four hours a day, seven days a week, and even that was barely time enough for them to cram in all the things they were up to. The more I pondered it, the more true it seemed to be: Everything exciting, bold, glamorous in life could be traced back to America. To New York, Hollywood, Detroit, and Washington, D.C.

It was probably foreordained, such a view, when the picture of America was obtained exclusively through the peephole of mass media by an eleven-year-old kid whose familiarity with Canada was limited to his small home-town. The duel for affection between America and Canada was rigged from the outset. Canada, its thin population strung out across four thousand miles, one in ten Francophone and thus out of the action, could never generate the cultural combustion that made a country buzz. Canada couldn't afford a domestic movie industry, or even a commercial radio network, and its few national magazines couldn't compete economically or editorially with their giant American counterparts.

It was superficial, but my handful of empirical evidence was all I needed to decide that whatever their failings in the dour Canadian view, the Yanks seemed to be doing things bigger, bolder, better, and reaping the rewards by way of a richer and more exciting life than anybody north of the 49th Parallel could ever hope to live.

And in fairness, something about my growing disenchantment was real: the growing discrepancy between Simcoe's and Canada's metabolism and mine. Being a true son of the strong, north, brave, and free required a calmer, steadier, more controlled temperament than the one beginning to jell within me. Canadianism seemed to require, beneath everything, contentment with the world as it was. Not so—emphatically not so—down south amid those amber waves of grain. In fact, you could take almost any random Canadian trait, invert or reverse it, and—presto!—you had an American trait. And U.E.L. ancestors, generations of proudly anti-American McCalls, "O Canada," and all the sturdy virtues it celebrated notwithstanding, in the American style I was coming to recognize the greater part of myself.

So let them gibe and rant and call me a turncoat. Give me the shoulder of Highway #3 any day.

My Life as a High School Dropout§
Robert Fulford

No book on sex is complete without an account of those who don't get any, and no discussion of formal education should omit the many citizens who mostly lack it, such as me. The other day, while testifying as an expert witness in a copyright case, I was asked about my education. "Completed Grade 11 in high school," I replied. The lawyer cross-examining me raised his eyebrows and, just to be sure, asked whether I had any further education. No, I said. As he moved on to his next question, my mind floated back to 1950, when I was 18 years old and concluding my career as the most dismal academic failure I had ever met.

If this delicate subject comes up, kind friends treat my high-school life as mildly comic, a cute eccentricity. I don't discourage that interpretation, but nor do I agree with it. It was, in fact, horrible. One history teacher called me the best student he had ever taught but in the same breath made it clear he didn't expect me to go anywhere, educationally speaking. How right he was. When finally I made my escape, I had some of the worst marks in Malvern Collegiate, which may have been the least-demanding high school in Toronto.

Failed Grade 10, repeated it, then passed Grade 11 (in only one year!), then failed again in Grade 12. But I wrote the Grade 13 provincial exams in history and English without taking the courses, and passed them. It has since occurred to me that if only there had been a school that taught nothing but history and English, I might be a high-school graduate today.

None of this should be considered a complaint; things didn't work out badly. But it appears now that I was living with a condition whose name was then unknown, attention deficit disorder. Since the mid-1990s ADD has become a suspiciously fashionable diagnosis. Any idea that so quickly invades our collective consciousness, accompanied by convenient drug therapy, should be scrutinized with care. Even so, ADD demands to be taken seriously, and there is no question I displayed, floridly, a crucial tell-tale sign.

Aside from a tendency to be easily distracted, my most obvious ADD characteristic was an acute version of something that remains merely chronic in most adolescents: I didn't feel like paying attention to what I didn't feel

---

§Robert Fulford. *National Post,* 18 April 2001. Material reprinted with the express permission of National Post Inc.

like paying attention to. It was considered laziness at the time, and part of me still thinks of it that way, but its extreme form falls within the ADD spectrum.

Experts in ADD try to state it gently. Dr. Sam Goldstein, a University of Utah child psychologist, says that people with ADD "do not respond well to repetitive, effortful, uninteresting activities that others choose for them." Dr. Gabor Maté of Vancouver, in his engrossing book, *Scattered Minds: A New Look at the Origins and Healing of Attention Deficit Disorder*, says that among people with ADD, "Active attention, the mind fully engaged and the brain performing work, is mustered only in special circumstances of high motivation." Dr. Maté's discovery that he himself suffers from ADD, even though he made his way through medical school, makes his book especially persuasive.

The ADD mind can't arouse itself when it should be attending to a subject it finds uninteresting. In those circumstances it is (Dr. Maté says) "immobilizingly difficult" to marshal the brain's motivational apparatus. Immobilized: That was me when confronted by chemistry, irregular French verbs, geometry and many other mandatory subjects. Anyone could see they weren't that hard and had to be conquered, but I couldn't manage.

Still, I was a long-time heavy reader, and my reading was slowly growing serious. I could write a little, and I could type like the wind. Though poorly coordinated, I performed better in typing than in any other subject. A student of ADD could easily explain. I wanted passionately to be a newspaperman and had seen newspapermen typing fast, so I simply bulled my way through, emotionally motivated.

I had been working part-time in the sports department of *The Globe and Mail* during summers and weekends, and the sports editor agreed to take me on, at 18, as the lowliest sports writer. My older colleagues, some stern and some friendly, generously assumed the responsibility of making me reliable enough to remain employed, screaming when necessary. Thirty months later, the paper shifted me to the news pages, at my request, and my education grew more interesting. Whatever law I learned, for instance, was acquired sitting as a reporter in courtrooms. Jury trials were best, because you could hear the same legal principles explained three times, by judge, Crown attorney and defence lawyer. Covering City Hall was even more rewarding. Many aldermen had little idea of what was going on, so the city solicitor had to explain to them the subtleties of "enabling legislation" and "legal non-conforming use" and many other concepts. A man of infinite patience, he did this so slowly even I caught on.

Meanwhile, I was pursuing private studies elsewhere. My art education was obtained in galleries and the studios of artists, my literary education in books, magazines and ferocious arguments. Later I became a reviewer of books and read somewhere that literary critics are people who conduct their education in public. In my own case, this was true in a more than usually literal sense.

Once or twice I've been asked whether I missed much by failing to go to university. The answer is yes and no. I missed all those subjects a university teaches best: classics, ancient history, the sciences, philosophy. But on the other hand, I wouldn't have studied any of them. I would have picked modern literature, modern history, political science, maybe even journalism—all, in my opinion, subjects you study best at your own pace, according to your own inclination and more or less on your own. At 18, I wasn't nearly smart enough to choose the really useful subjects. That's one of the flaws I long ago noticed in the education system: All the truly vital decisions are made by people too young to know exactly what they're doing. Maybe I should be grateful to ADD for saving me from folly.

What Sort of People Did This?[1]
Erna Paris

In a culture that ignores the past, Tuesday's devastating attacks on the military and financial nerve centers of Western power are portrayed as having emerged out of a void. Today, the finger seems to point to Saddam Hussein, or to someone called Osama bin Laden. Saddam is familiar, but who is Osama bin Laden? In photos, he is rather handsome. We are told that he is a fanatic and that he is protected by another group of fanatics called the Taliban who live in Afghanistan and wear turbans.

But there is a thread that connects us to Mr. bin Laden and to other haters of the West. Here are two strands.

Picture the world in 1955, a decade after the end of the Second World War and the Holocaust (the attempted genocide that will, as the years pass, increasingly color Western perceptions of the 20th century). The ancient territories of the Middle East have recently undergone a fatal change: The State of Israel is just seven years old, but its arrival has effectively displaced most of the Arabs who had lived for centuries on that tiny sliver of land. The Palestinian refugee camps are already in place. And they are breeding a generation of angry children nourished on stories of family loss and exile.

In Europe and North America, the postwar West is ascendant. The special relationship between Israel and the United States is already firm, largely because the former is perceived by the latter as a geographical and ideological bulwark in the emerging Cold War struggle. In Western Europe, especially Germany, what matters are the pleasures of a booming economy.

Then in April, 1955, a key event occurs: A conference whose echo will be heard across many decades is held in Bandung, Indonesia. Delegates from 29 African and Asian countries (representing half the world's population) come to discuss racism, nationalism, and the struggle against colonialism. Britain has been separating from its colonies relatively peacefully, but France's eight-year war to hold onto Indochina (Vietnam) has just ended. Its war to maintain control over Algeria is still ahead.

The meeting concludes with a statement about economic and cultural cooperation, human rights, and anti-imperialist self-determination, but

---

[1] Erna Paris. *The Globe and Mail*, September 13, 2001. Reprinted with permission from the author.

the single common theme among the Arab delegations is hatred of Israel. The Iraqi representative calls Zionism "one of the blackest, most somber chapters in human history." An Arab-sponsored resolution against Israel is one of the few that everyone can agree on. Israel, the conference concludes, is a base for imperialism and a threat to world peace.

Bandung gave birth to the idea of the Third World and concentrated efforts to achieve stability that continue to this day (they were visible in the buildup to the recent Durban conference). At the same time, Bandung was the first comprehensive, international opposition to Israel, Zionism, and eventually the entire West—an ideology that would soon mobilize elements of the radical right as well as the Marxist left in terrorist movements that paralyzed parts of Western Europe in the 1970s and 1980s.

Otto Ernst Remer, an ex-Nazi who lived in Cairo after the war, clearly expressed the developing anti-Zionist/anti-Western thinking in an 1980s interview: "There is a problem concerning who holds the real power in the United States," he said. "Without a doubt, the Zionists control Wall Street, and as a result, the Middle East foments war."

Since he voiced these words, the equation has been repeated: Zionism + Wall Street + U.S. military power = the enemy. Though we don't yet have all the evidence that this is what drove Tuesday's suicidal attackers to murder thousands of innocent people, the likelihood is high.

In a global world united by instant technologies—a world that ought to be increasingly rational—how is it that a culture of terror and martyrdom continues into the 21st century?

The easy response is to dismiss those who choose to die as fanatics. But a deeper answer may emerge from the unfinished business first articulated at Bandung. North Americans tend to think little about colonialism, but its aftermath has not yet been resolved.

Another answer is despair. In 1987, I traveled to the West Bank to research my book (*The Garden and the Gun*) about the shifting ideologies of Israel. In the dusty Balata refugee camp, I encountered young Palestinians who were enraged or numbed by the thwarted circumstances of their lives. I remember their rousing, well-rehearsed chorus of "Death to Israel." And I shall never forget the boy of 18 who said, "Our daily life is what you see here. We have no hope.... Maybe death is that way out." Nor shall I forget the soft-spoken professor at An Najah University near Nablus who said, "I believe that if the Palestinians continue to live as deprived as they are now, the younger, more radical generation will initiate a new round of terrible violence."

A few months after I left Israel, the first *intifada* began. Now that violence has evolved into suicide bombings—martyrdom in the war against the hated West. Such martyrs struck again this week.

Who is Osama bin Laden—this man who can (we presume) command young people to die for his cause? And when the West retaliates against him or against others, will anything really change? If we paid more attention to the currents of the past that shape the present, would we have been less surprised than Tuesday revealed us to be?

Julian Assange: The End of Secrets?**

Lifting the lid on the whistle-blowing website WikiLeaks and its enigmatic hacker-turned-activist founder

David Cohen

"**Q**UICK, you've got to come now or you'll miss him," says the press officer. I'm being ushered down a corridor in the back of the Randolph hotel, Oxford, UK, to meet Julian Assange, an Australian hacker and the founder of the whistle-blower's website WikiLeaks.

I find Assange sitting on a red leather armchair surrounded by journalists and holding a makeshift press conference. He looks wary, like a man on the run, and speaks in a hushed, deep tone—his voice barely audible above the general hubbub—carefully choosing every word. He seems ill at ease, and I can't work out whether he dislikes the press attention, is genuinely scared for his life, or is just a bit socially awkward.

Assange was thrust into the limelight in April after WikiLeaks posted a video of U.S. forces killing civilians in Iraq in 2007. For three years the news agency Reuters had tried, fruitlessly, to get hold of the classified official documents and video describing these events using the U.S. Freedom of Information Act. WikiLeaks—a tiny ad hoc organization headed by Assange and run by an undisclosed number of volunteers—scored a coup, striking a goal for citizen journalism and invoking the U.S. government's ire in the process.

"Is there a threat to your security coming from the United States?" one journalist asks.

"There have been unreasonable statements made in private by certain officials in the U.S. administration," Assange replies.

"How would you define 'unreasonable'?"

"Statements which suggest that they may not follow the rule of law."

Assange says he hasn't any direct physical threats, but adds that he cancelled a recent trip to the U.S. on the advice of an investigative journalist. It is classic cloak-and-dagger stuff, and it gets more so by the day.

**Cohen, David. "Julian Assange: The end of secrets?" *New Scientist* 16 August 2010.
(c) New Scientist

Ten days after I met Assange at the press conference in July, his fame mushroomed overnight with the publication of the Afghan War Diary. This collection of over 91,000 documents chronicled virtually every battle and skirmish in the war in Afghanistan. Around 75,000 of them were releases on WikiLeaks (the remainder were withheld for security reasons), with simultaneous coverage in *The Guardian*, *Der Speigel* and *The New York Times*. Assange agreed to give all three newspapers access to the documents six weeks in advance of publication on his website, a new tactic for the previously little-known organization. This advance access has proved to be a shrewd move, bringing Assange and WikiLeaks fame on an international scale. Then came the backlash, with several front-page stories in other newspapers echoing U.S. government criticism that leaks potentially endanger the lives of Afghans working with NATO forces.

Though the War Diary held crucial details about the war in Afghanistan, it didn't alter our understanding of it. The real story revolved around the way the material had been leaked. Something fundamental about how information reaches the public arena has changed. "WikiLeaks underlines to government that simply stamping something secret isn't a solution, because it will come out," says Ross Anderson, a computer security researcher at the University of Cambridge.

What, exactly, has changed? Whistle-blowers may always have chosen what to leak, but the big difference here is that WikiLeaks is able to publish and promote this information to a global audience on a system that makes correction, or post hoc removal, virtually impossible. How did such a system come about?

Assange founded WikiLeaks in 2006. It offers a way for whistle-blowers to anonymously reveal sensitive material to the public. "WikiLeaks is a combined technical, legal and political tool," he says. Since its inception it has published several high-profile leaks, including revelations of corruption in the Kenyan government, the membership list of the British National Party, and the operating procedures manual for Guantanamo Bay prison. But the leaks this year have truly marked its coming of age.

Assange was born in Australia 39 years ago, in Townsville, Queensland. He reportedly moved 37 times by the age of 14, and his schooling was largely done at home. In his teens he developed an interest in computers and became a keen hacker, breaking into several government and corporate servers. Australian police eventually caught up with him, and in his early

20s he stood trial for hacking. Around that time his marriage fell apart, and after a lengthy custody case over his son was concluded he made a trip through Vietnam. When he returned to Australia he wound up studying physics at the University of Melbourne. There his nascent interest in activism developed and the seeds for WikiLeaks were sown.

The site is hosted by Swedish Internet provider PRQ. Sweden was seen as the ideal jurisdiction for WikiLeaks because of the country's stringent laws protecting whistle-blowers. The content is mirrored on several other web servers around the globe, and on peer-to-peer networks where content is virtually impossible to censor. To protect the identity of its sources, it uses a computer network based on a system called Tor. Tor is a successor to Onion Routing, developed by U.S. naval intelligence as a way for its field operatives to communicate anonymously over the internet. All messages in the network are encrypted, so covert communications cannot be distinguished from ordinary messages. "It's a delicious irony that a system first developed by the U.S. government has now come back to haunt them," says Anderson.

Once WikiLeaks receives a submission, Assange says there is a rigorous process to check that the information is genuine. This can involve contacting the subject of the leak, and—as in the case of the Iraq video footage—sending people to verify details on the ground. "As far as we know, we've never released false information," he says.

What is less clear is who decides what information is released and when. In fact, Assange has refused to answer any questions about how his organization works (it is yet another irony that the mission of such a secretive organization is to enforce openness on others). However, someone I contacted via the WikiLeaks webserver, who claimed to be a WikiLeaks volunteer, told me that a core of five staff coordinate the analysis of the content on the site, and that "to an extent" Assange has editorial veto over what gets published.

As *New Scientist* went to press, another twist emerged. A 1.4-gigabyte encrypted file labelled "insurance" appeared on WikiLeaks, prompting speculation that it contained the full, unedited War Diary, and that the pass code to access the files would be released if any action were taken against the site by U.S. authorities. If true, Assange has dramatically upped the ante. Whether this helps in his mission to make the world a more transparent place remains to be seen.

Background

WikiLeaks, founded in 2006 by Australian hacker and activist Julian Assange, is a web-based service designed to protect the identity of individuals who want to make sensitive information public. Its mission is to promote transparency in government and reduce corruption and promote democracy.

A Matter of Will††

Linda McQuaig

It is fair to say that, in general, we are not becoming a society focused on the public good. Instead, I would argue, we are increasingly organizing our society around the principles of the marketplace, giving precedence to the rights of investors and private interests. More and more, we are adopting the attitude that everyone should fend for herself or himself, adopting Margaret Thatcher's vision of society as simply a collection of individuals and their families. In this view, society is nothing but a collection of private interests.

But I would also argue that most Canadians do not like the direction we are headed in, and have only reluctantly accepted it because they have come to believe there is no alternative. For years, this lack of alternative has been blamed on the government deficit. Yet now, with the deficit gone, it still appears that there is no alternative. We are still told that we cannot have the social programs we want and that governments can do very little to fight high unemployment. We are told that we—and the governments we elect—are pretty powerless in the global economy.

I argue that this is wrong, that this is really nothing more than what I like to call a "cult of impotence," which amounts to a celebration of the weakening of democracy, the transfer of power from popularly elected governments to powerful private interests. Basically, there are two parts to my argument.

First, governments have considerably more manoeuvring room in the global economy than is commonly believed. The popular belief is that Canada must do what international investors want, or they will withdraw their capital, leaving us in difficult circumstances. Yet the truth is that even in this world of full capital mobility, Ottawa has more options in its choice of policies than this version of events suggests.

One piece of evidence to illustrate this point invokes a 1994 report on Ottawa's finances by Goldman Sachs, one of the most prestigious firms on Wall Street. The report, which was not distributed outside government and financial circles, contradicted much of the cant emanating from the Canadian

---

††Linda McQuaig. *Queen's Quarterly*, 106/1 (Spring 1999): 9-15. Reprinted with permission from the author.

business community about the severity of Canada's deficit problems. It seemed to provide evidence that the international investment community was not particularly alarmed by Canada's finances and was not about to withdraw capital from Canada. All this suggested that the policy constraints on Ottawa were therefore not as severe as was widely believed. One might have expected that Ottawa would have been delighted by this favourable assessment of its fiscal situation and would have been keen to publicize it.

But, as it turned out, Ottawa had little interest in publicizing the report. That would have opened up a genuine debate within Canada about the possibilities and alternatives, and risked weakening public willingness to go along with government spending cuts. As Ottawa plowed ahead with its plans for deep cuts in its next budget, the concern inside the finance department was over how to prevent the Goldman Sachs report from getting out to the public.

The point is that the constraints on the Canadian government in the global economy are often exaggerated. And this exaggeration has acted to convince Canadians that they have fewer options than they really do.

The second part of my argument is that, to the extent that there are constraints on governments in today's global economy, it is largely because governments have chosen to cede power to the financial markets. But this power could be reclaimed. In the last several decades governments, in Canada and elsewhere, have surrendered a significant amount of power to private financial capital through domestic deregulation and also through international arrangements and trade deals that enhance the rights of investors at the expense of governments. This transfer of power from democratically elected governments to the private sector has taken place in response to enormous pressure from that same private sector.

This transfer of control could not have occurred without public acquiescence. But while the Canadian public has tacitly gone along with this change, I would argue that this is not because Canadians want to see themselves or their governments stripped of power, but because they have come to believe—falsely—that nothing else is possible in the global economy, that globalization has changed things in some fundamental way that eliminates the democratic options that once existed.

Perhaps this sounds like I am skirting dangerously close to ignoring the hard reality of globalization. Few arguments seem to be able to shut down political debate faster these days than the accusation that one is not facing up to the reality that we are living in a global economy. When accused of this, it is hard not to feel like a buffoon, like someone who's advocating a return to feudalism or some pre-industrial society.

But I believe that this sort of accusation misses the mark. Of course we are living in a global economy! We have been living in one for more than a hundred years. Ever since the laying of the transatlantic cable in the late 1860s, the world has been a highly interconnected place, in terms of trade and capital flows. The real issue is not whether we live in a global economy; the issue is *what kind of global economy will we have?*

In the last fifty years alone, we have seen two very different global economies, which have produced significantly different results. There is a strong tendency these days to forget about the global economy that existed in the first three decades following the Second World War, roughly from the mid-1940s to the mid-1970s. It was more regulated, and the power of markets was more restricted. The rights of capital and investors in general were given less precedence than today, and were often made to take a back seat to the rights of the broader public. At the very least, it can be said that there was a greater balance between the rights of private interests and those of the public at large—a balance that is missing today.

This greater focus on the public interest was the deliberate intent of the key architects of the early postwar system—John Maynard Keynes of Britain and Harry Dexter White of the U.S. and, to a lesser but notable extent, Louis Rasminsky of Canada—who were determined to avoid a return to the Depression, with its devastatingly high unemployment and serious lack of social supports. Keynes and White therefore constructed a system—known as the Bretton Woods Accords—that, among other things, gave governments a key role in managing their own economies, including the power to control the flow of financial capital across their borders. The financial elite was fiercely opposed to these capital controls, but Keynes and White argued that without such restraints this financial elite would constantly be using the threat of capital withdrawal to intimidate governments into doing what it wanted.

Capital controls made a significant difference. Insulating governments from the threat of capital withdrawal enabled them to be far more responsive to demands from the electorate—demands that usually involved policies aimed at achieving full employment and developing strong social programs. The result was the attainment of an unprecedented level of equality amongst citizens in most Western nations, including Canada. There was also widespread prosperity, partly because capital controls created stable currency values which helped promote world trade. While a number of huge problems remained largely unaddressed in this early postwar period—the environment, Third World poverty, the position of women, and militarism, to name a few—the overall progress in the direction of equality, democratic empowerment, and prosperity was significant. With some reservations, this could be termed "good globalization."

What has replaced it, I would argue, is what loosely could be termed "bad globalization"—a global economy in which the rights of capital holders are increasingly given precedence over the rights of the broader public. In this new form of globalization, the international marketplace is still regulated by international treaties and agreements, but it is regulated now more in the interests of capital than in the public interest. And the result has been growing inequality. So the key question is: why was the "good globalization" possible in the early postwar period, but apparently is no longer possible today?

The conventional answer is that technology has changed everything. The computer now makes it possible to move money around the world so quickly that no governments could possibly control capital movements today.

But this only tells part of the story. The computer also gives us enormous power to trace the movement of money, and therefore to monitor it and even to control it. In other words, governments could still today impose controls on the movement of capital *if they wanted to*—or rather, if we demanded that they do so. There is no reason we could not have a form of "good globalization" today if, as citizens, we insisted on it. The obstacles in our way are not technological—as is often asserted—but merely political. The real obstacle is the fierce opposition of the financial elite.

But while the power of this elite is real, it is not insurmountable—as the architects of the early postwar system discovered in their showdown with the financial elite of their day. Indeed, this is clearly the perfect moment for Canada, along with other nations, to be pushing for fundamental reforms to the global economy. "Bad globalization" is in crisis. It has been revealed not only to cause greater inequality, but also to create enormous instability—as we have seen during the world financial crisis over the past year.

Indeed, this crisis is integrally linked to the free movement of capital, which causes the kind of boom-and-bust scenario that unfolded in Asia. As financial markets have become increasingly focused on moving around huge pools of speculative capital, rather than on making serious long-term investments, the international financial system has become more volatile and unstable. Asia and Russia are now bearing the devastating consequences of that instability; even Canada felt the ripple effects as our dollar plummeted in the summer of 1998. Perhaps the damage will be contained this time. But today's global financial system, with its free-flowing capital, is clearly less stable than the one that prevailed in the postwar period. Unfortunately, most reforms proposed so far, including those advanced by our own finance minister, Paul Martin, do little to address the fundamental problem of free-flowing capital.

But recognition of the serious flaws in the current global economy could be the beginning of real change. It is also crucial that the public come to believe, once again, that goals like full employment and properly funded social programs are attainable. Indeed, the obstacles that prevent us from attaining them now are not, as is often suggested, forces beyond our control—things like technological change or globalization. Rather, the major obstacle in our path is the same obstacle we have always faced—the enormous power of the financial elite, its determination to block change that would favour the interests of the broader public.

The important thing to remember is that we have overcome that obstacle before—in the early postwar period. And in doing so, we became a more egalitarian society. We can overcome that obstacle again today—if we want.

Image World‡‡
Michael Posner

Not long ago, a friend invited me to accompany him to a Toronto Maple Leafs hockey game at the Air Canada Centre. We had front-row seats behind the goalie, the best in the house. Yet, perversely, I found myself repeatedly glancing up at the vast in-house screen positioned over centre ice. Somehow, the big pixel board seemed to frame the action on the ice in a more optically manageable way. And I wasn't alone; all around me, I noticed, other eyes were doing the same. The gritty, hard-contact reality was right before us, yet we were essentially watching the game on television, exactly as we've been conditioned to do.

Hockey—indeed almost any professional sport today—may be taken as an example of what the late French philosopher Guy Debord called the "triumph of visual spectacle": reality constantly filtered through the distorting prism of contrived images. And it's a pernicious development. It warps our core sensibility, making us confuse the image with the real thing. It forces us to encounter and comprehend our environment indirectly. And—most significantly, perhaps even ominously—it makes all of us easy prey to manipulation—to what Debord termed "hypnotic behaviour."

Consider, for a moment, pornography. Last year, in the U.S. alone, there were more than 700 million rentals of porn videos, roughly two million a day. That figure, incidentally, does not include Web-based porn sites (the biggest, most profitable business on the Internet) or pay-per-view movies. At a conservatively estimated $10 billion a year and growing, the American porn industry is now a more lucrative enterprise than professional football, basketball, and baseball—combined. For millions of people, what passes for sexual gratification can only be achieved through the act of watching paid performers do it for them.

"The world of media fantasies is more real than everyday life," writes French philosopher Jean Baudrillard.

Video or computer games are more compelling than school or work. Porno videos or web sites simulate sex in abstraction from the problems of real relations with others, while simulated environments

---

‡‡Michael Posner. *Queen's Quarterly,* 110/2 (Summer 2003): 229–41. Reprinted with permission from the author.

like Las Vegas, Disney World or shopping malls are cleaner and prettier than the actual world.

According to Baudrillard, "This is the artificial universe of the hyper-real and the hyper-real is thus the death of the real."

It is no exercise in profundity to say that we now live in what Canadian uber-designer Bruce Mau has termed a "global image economy," a world dominated by the mesmerizing power of the visual. Its principal product and expression, of course, is film—diced, spliced and rendered in myriad forms: television, movies, video, photography. But Mau's phrase also embraces the iconic phenomenon of branding—goods and services that we instantly identify by virtue of logos, typefaces, and graphic design. Think of Nike's "swoosh," a trademark so universally recognizable that the company's ads no longer need even to use the word "Nike." Think of McDonald's golden arches, or Starbuck's mermaid, or Coca-Cola's flowing red and white script.

Logos, billboards, banks of televisions, video monitors, camcorders, games downloadable to cell phones—one might be forgiven for thinking that the modern world has become afflicted by the tyranny of the visual. The importance of this hegemony ought not to be underestimated, or explained away as simply the dominant modality of Western popular culture. Indeed, it *is* the dominant modality of Western popular culture, but its implications transcend the purely cultural.

To keep us interested, and hypnotically responsive, the ante of visual culture is always being raised. Everything, it seems, has been turned into a pageant, a distended, mind-numbing, synthetic, high-octane visual glorification. On Broadway, in London's West End, and in other major urban centres the nightly curtains rise on the theatre of spectacle—enduring megamusicals such as *The Lion King, Mamma Mia!, Aida.* In Cannes, the annual orgiastic prayer rituals in worship of the Armani-suited gods of cinema have recently concluded—although somewhere on the planet, at any given moment, another film festival is opening, closing, or being announced. On any given weekend, before television audiences in the many millions, the sweat-soaked deities of hockey and baseball, tennis and golf, perform. This is what professional sport has become—spectacle. In Paris and Milan, New York and London, the paparazzi assemble, jostling to capture stick-thin women draped in the latest absurdities of fashion designers, while their previous creations are being advertised by celebrities at some gala television awards show, an almost weekly spectacle of self-congratulation.

Even for ordinary Joes and Janes, the modern world more and more resembles a movie set. We take our children to theme parks, a fraudulent, antiseptic universe of enforced gaiety. The highest rated show on TSN is professional wrestling—a two-hour extravaganza of garish costume, dry ice, pounding heavy metal, soap opera, and bad grammar (the scripts right out of some low-budget B-movie)... and, of course, twelve minutes of fake fighting. Our political campaigns and conventions, once occasions for legitimate policy debate, have been utterly transformed and devalued, now resembling a cacophonous swirl of balloons, placards, marching bands and stump speeches, every candidate's appearance carefully programmed for sound bytes and the six o'clock news.

More examples? Rock concerts (another venue where more people watch the screen facsimile than the real performer)—elaborate sound and light shows that have less to do with music (ear-shattering regardless) than with the Event. The Olympics, now staggered so that every two years we have a winter or summer fever of nationalism that grips athletes and global television audiences: stirring anthems, flag-raising ceremonies, torch-lit parades. Video games, now a bigger business than the movies, and tutoring an entire generation in the dubious principles of virtual reality. Buses turned mobile billboards. The Rainforest Café and comparably themed restaurants. The sham universe of shopping malls. It's a Disneyfied World, indeed—one marathon photo opportunity.

In the Nevada desert, an entire city, Las Vegas, has been turned into spectacle, a neon-lit 24-hour wonderland of ersatz experience, complete with fake Eiffel Tower, fake Venetian canals. Annual tourist traffic: roughly 35 million. One of its best draws is a made-in-Canada tenant—Cirque du Soleil, the circus rendered as sumptuous visual feast.

But Las Vegas' virtual city is simply the logical extension of New York City's Times Square, Miami's South Beach, Paris' Champs Elysées, Tokyo's Roppongi, Berlin's Kurfuerstendamm, and the dazzling streetscapes of Hong Kong. According to Princeton professor M. Christine Boyer,

> ... these carefully manipulated visual and social environments make the real city and its chaos, class distinctions... disappear from view. Our optic nerves blinded by glitter, we fail to see highways in disrepair, charred and abandoned tenements, the scourge of drugs, the wandering homeless, subway breakdowns and deteriorating buses.

Even those who rail against this trend are increasingly ensnared by it: as writer Naomi Klein has observed, the now routine brick-throwing demonstrations against the evils of free trade and corporate branding (Seattle, Quebec City, Genoa) have made social protest itself a commodified spectacle. To get attention, demonstrators must invoke theatre: not long ago, some 7,500 women in London walked 26 miles stripped to their ornament-decorated bras to raise funds for breast cancer. The power of theatre: it's a safe bet they raised more money half-naked than they would have fully clothed. More recently, the entire world became spectators to the first war in history to be fought—live—in our living rooms: the American-led attack on Saddam Hussein's Iraq, a genuine reality show about survival.

In the modern conditions of production, said Guy Debord presciently, all of life announces itself as an immense accumulation of spectacles. Or as Seth Feldman of York University puts it: "Every day is Halloween."

It wasn't that long ago that literature—novels, poetry, essays, drama—stood at the very acme of artistic expression. It wasn't that long ago that literary critic F.R. Leavis called the notion of filming D.H. Lawrence's *Women in Love* "an obscene undertaking," as if the simple act of transforming a classic novel into mere celluloid was by definition a desecration. Today, Leavis' sentiment seems almost laughably out-dated. Today, as social critic Camille Paglia has put it, "… the rhythms of our thinking in the pop culture world, the domination by image, the whole way the images are put together… are way beyond the novel at this point."

In a recent book, *Lifestyle*, Bruce Mau argues that film (and its progeny) now colonize all social space, a process he calls "cinematic migration." By this he means that in order to be understood, or even recognized, artists from diverse disciplines feel compelled to express themselves through the language of film. Certainly, over the past several decades, its influence has seeped ever more steadily into other genres. The impact that film language and technique have had on literary novelists is probably deserving of a PhD thesis, but there is no doubt that more commercial writers increasingly write—and publishers increasingly publish—with a view to the sale of film rights. So much of commercial fiction reads like movies rendered into prose that half the fun of reading a book is mentally casting the film.

Older literary modes, richer in memory, psychology, and interior monologue, are now deemed too slow and complicated for film. In a preface to a recent anthology of fifteen short stories, editors Matt Thorne and Nicholas Blincoe argue that the problem with contemporary literature is that it isn't more like the movies. "Today," they maintain, "fiction should be focusing on visual culture, and attempting to prove itself the equal to these mediums." It's a jejune viewpoint, obviously, but arresting in its brazen dismissal of textual narrative.

But it's not only writers who find themselves drawn into the cinematic force field. The same holds true in the visual arts. Postmodern painters like Julian Schnabel (*Before Night Falls, Basquiat*), Matthew Barney (the Cremaster series), David Salle (*Search and Destroy*), Robert Longo (*Johnny Mnemonic*) and Cindy Sherman (*Office Killer*) increasingly use film and video to express their ideas. Sherman's photographic oeuvre is virtually inseparable from film: it's her essential vocabulary. Her most famous collection, *Untitled Film Stills*, consists of small black-and-white photographs of Sherman impersonating various female character types from old B-movies.

A few years ago, in a catalogue essay for a retrospective of Robert Longo's work, Los Angeles curator Howard Fox cited the artist's fascination with fascism. "Fascism isn't just dictatorial regimes," Fox wrote. "It's a way of thinking. And it doesn't just come in on leather jackets and motorcycles; it comes in on bumper stickers and television. Fascism is our visual culture."

Everyone from sculptors to advertising designers is struggling to find cinematic correlatives for their work. "What links film to contemporary visual art practice… is its twin ability to reach large audiences and to evoke that ephemeral quality I call glamour," says Mark Betz, professor of film and media studies at the University of Alberta. As Betz notes, the art world has experimented with film before. Avant-garde painters such as Fernand Léger, Salvador Dali, Hans Richter and Marcel Duchamp did it in 1920s Europe. Four decades later, the Situationists and Lettrists in France and Pop movements in Britain and the U.S. did it again. "Andy Warhol is the key figure here," Betz contends, "as he was able to address both the mechanically reproducible features of film… and the glamour of film that visual artists were clamouring for." Today's cutting edge artists, he argues, "recognize that Warhol was right: [visual] art now is, simply put, popular culture." Not surprisingly, the visual imperative is particularly pronounced in youth culture—in the silos of pop music and video games. Few songs today become major hits without a simultaneous big-budget video release—in effect, a three-minute movie, however nonsensical its content. The emphasis on visuals means that the manufactured stars, more and more, must resemble Britney Spears or Ricky Martin, musical Barbies and Kens, air-brushed, acne-free and dripping sexuality.

Ugliness is allowed—even mandated—in rap or heavy metal music; it's the tattoo of admission. But, even here, the performers are usually draped with chorus lines of under-attired women. In all of this, the actual music becomes secondary. Does anyone really know what such performers as Janet Jackson or Madonna sound like? The truth is that how well pop stars sing is almost irrelevant—the music is largely massaged in the engineering studio. What counts is visual: cleavage, buns, smiles, how well they move. Unable to separate the sound from its glossy video wrapping, the younger generation is losing the ability to appreciate the art of listening to music.

But even more serious musical exponents have been affected by film's gravitational pull. Not long ago, electric guitarists Tom Verlaine (founder of the now-defunct rock band Television) and Jimmy Ripp improvised soundtracks to several films screened live in a Boston auditorium. Minimalist composer Philip Glass has done the same with written scores, playing live to screenings of films like Cocteau's *La Belle et la Bête*, and writing scores for old silent films like *Dracula*. "This has really become the main thing that I do," Glass said in an interview, "combining images and music." And the work of other composers—such as soundscape artist Brian Eno, godspeed you black emperor, and Glenn Branca—play like soundtracks for non-existent films.

And then there are the vast, omnipresent, Cyclopian eyes: television and the Internet. According to A.C. Neilsen, the average American spends almost four hours a day (more than 52 days a year) watching TV. It is our chief source of news, information and, especially, what passes for entertainment. By age 65, most of us have spent nearly nine years thus passively engaged, roughly 15 percent of our life. Internet use is climbing steadily. As of last March, almost 50 percent of the English-speaking world had Internet access, and in Canada 64 percent of adults aged 19–54 surf the Web at least an hour a day.

Thus, like Prairie Wheeler, a character in Thomas Pynchon's *Vineland*, most of us now reside in a world mediated by layer upon layer of film and television. We don't confront reality so much as we encounter it through screens, large and small. "Film rolls up the mat of the world," observes media critic Nelson Thall. "You reel up the real world and reconfigure it for presentation. TV is a new meme for reality." Thall quotes Marshall McLuhan: "… the new media are not ways of relating us to the old real world; they are the real world and they reshape what remains of the old world at will."

A picture, according to the old cliché, is worth a thousand words. That's because the message it communicates is unmistakable and instantaneous. We relate to images in more direct ways than we do to words. Text requires another level of mediation, a mental or intellectual filter of some kind that distances us from what we are reading. Images are immediate. They require less judgment, less interpretation. They appeal not to our reason but to our intuition, not to thought but to feeling. Inevitably, therefore, the ascendancy of the image economy, and the concomitant decline of print culture, means that ever larger percentages of the population are being conditioned to respond emotionally and viscerally to the daily blizzard of images that bombard them. Both literally and figuratively, these images are carefully manipulated to achieve desired effects—whether it's a tearful, sympathetic reaction to a *cinéma vérité* film about child prostitution or the illusion of freedom that the average television commercial for cars tries to create; the exhilaration of the open road or the promise of easy sex embedded in so many contemporary rock and rap music videos.

This trend, long underway but gathering momentum, is weighted with serious social and indeed political implications. That it marches hand-in-hand with two other worrisome developments—the relentless dumbing down of the population through the deliberate erosion of standards in learning and culture and, under the pretext of greater security, the increasing subjection of people to video surveillance in public spaces—constitutes additional grounds for concern.

These, it need hardly be said, are the formative, incipient grammars of fascism. A liberal or neo-fascism, to be sure, where the expected smorgasbord of consumer choice—in politics, automobiles, or what to watch on television—remains more or less intact. But fascism nonetheless, in its essential anti-humanistic form, where society is increasingly susceptible to top-down governance, often in the seemingly innocuous name of public safety or health, or in whatever name the moment requires. The concern, baldly stated, is that we are moving at pace toward a much higher degree of social control and engineering, responsive to omnipresent, officially mandated iconography and to which, more and more, we will lack the wherewithal, the intellectual capital, needed to resist. Witness the 150,000 video cameras that monitor the world of central London, keeping watchful eyes over the citizenry, and with negligible protest.

Media gurus Arthur and Marilouise Kroker have called this the post-alphabetic reality. Mere writing can't keep up to the speed of electronic society, they have said. The result is the end of the Gutenberg Galaxy and the beginning of the Image Millennium.

Images moving at the speed of light. Images moving faster than the time it takes to record their passing. Iconic images. Special-effect images. Images of life past, present and future as culture is fast-forwarded into the electronic nervous system. Images that circulate so quickly and shine with such intensity that they begin to alter the ratio of the human sensorium.

Visual culture, Bruce Mau maintains, is more primitive, more tribal, than its print-based antecedent, in that it works directly on the ancient nervous system. In other words, it is pre-rational, harkening back to an epoch in which meaning was communicated by pictographic symbols. "Unless we recognize the techniques being used to manipulate us," Mau warns, "we are doomed to a life of decorating and redecorating."

Debord went further. He rightly considered the spectacle of a tool of pacification and depoliticization—a permanent opium war designed to stupefy and distract us. Even now, long after his death, in an age of mindless interactivity, we remain consumers, increasingly disconnected from reality and our own lives—and mesmerized by images.

PART II

Writing the Thesis-Driven Paper

CHAPTER 5
Linking Evidence and Claims: 1 on 10 Versus 10 on 1

CHAPTER 6
The Evolving Thesis

CHAPTER 7
Recognizing and Fixing Weak Thesis Statements

CHAPTER 8
Writing the Researched Paper

CHAPTER 9
Finding and Citing Sources

CHAPTER

5

Linking Evidence and Claims:
1 on 10 Versus 10 on 1

Thus far, we have been concerned with developing the primary skills and habits of mind that go into thinking and writing analytically. Now, in Part II of this book, we turn to ways of using those skills to write a thesis-driven paper.

Perhaps no aspect of writing causes more problems and attracts more unsound advice than the question of how to construct an effective thesis. In Part I we deliberately skirt this subject for a good reason: a primary problem in thesis construction is that people think about it too early in the analytical process, leaping to a thesis too soon. And so we haven't even used the word "thesis," instead opting for a synonym, "claim."

By way of definition, a *claim* is an assertion that you make about your evidence—an idea that you believe the evidence supports. The primary claim in a paper is the *thesis*. In analytical writing, the thesis is a theory that explains what some feature or features of a subject mean. The subject itself, the pool of primary material (data) being analyzed, is known as *evidence*.

Of course, we have, using different terms, been talking about approaches to evidence and thesis all along. The chapter on observation (Chapter 1), for instance, is about ways of looking at evidence; the chapter on interpretation (Chapter 3) is about making claims; and the chapter on reading (Chapter 4) is vitally concerned with the connection between evidence and claims. *If we were to summarize the whole point of the book so far, it would be that you should avoid settling for premature leaps to generalities and then looking at evidence only to find things that fit the claim.* Instead, the approach we suggest is to look at evidence more openly. When you find yourself arriving at generalizations, don't stop with these. Go back to the details, look for patterns, find the organizing contrasts, and come up with a range of synonyms to describe what is there. These tactics will give rise to better ideas.

At some point, however, you are going to need to move from exploratory evidence-gathering and preliminary interpretation to producing a more finished paper, one with a thesis and an introduction, a conclusion, and an orderly review of your evidence. This is not to say that Five-Step Analysis, Notice and Focus, and asking "So what?" won't get you to a paper—they will, if you will stick with them.

But when the time comes to compose a formal paper with a thesis, it is very common for writers who have been thinking well while doing these preliminary activities to abandon both the thinking they have been doing and the skills that have produced it. Faced with the challenge of constructing a *thesis*, they panic and revert to old habits: "Now I better have my one idea and be able to prove to everybody that I'm right." So, out goes careful attention to detail. Out goes any evidence that doesn't fit. Instead of analysis, they substitute the kind of paper we call a *demonstration*.

Demonstrations are the result of two primary mistaken assumptions about what an analytical paper is, one having to do with thesis, the other with evidence.

- The misconception about a thesis is that a thesis should be static and unchanging.
- The misconception about evidence is that the sole function of evidence is to corroborate (confirm) the thesis—in other words, that evidence is limited to "the stuff that proves I'm right."

If these are misconceptions, then what are the better, more accurate understandings to acquire about the thesis and the use of evidence? Here's the short answer, after which we take up these matters in more detail:

- A strong thesis evolves: it changes as a paper progresses. The changes in the thesis are galvanized by its repeated encounters with evidence. A strong thesis is not static.
- Evidence has a second function beyond corroborating claims: to test and develop and evolve the thesis, making the thesis more precise. Evidence is not to be treated as static, as just a means of confirming and reasserting unchanging ideas.

Now let's slow down and explore these two misconceptions, starting with what's wrong with the idea of a static thesis.

A. DEVELOPING A THESIS IS MORE THAN REPEATING AN IDEA ("1 ON 10")

Perhaps the most common misunderstanding about the thesis is that it must appear throughout the paper in essentially the same form. In fact, this absence of change is the primary trait of a weak thesis. Like an *inert* (unreactive) material, a weak thesis neither affects nor is affected by the evidence that surrounds it.

A paper produced by repeating a single idea generally follows the form we call 1 on 10: the writer makes a single and usually very general claim ("History repeats itself," "Exercise is good for you," and so forth) and then proceeds to affix it to ten examples (see Figure 5.1). The problem with 1 on 10 is that it tries to cover too much ground and often ends by noticing little more than some general similarity that might be the starting point but should not be the final outcome of a paper. The number ten, we should add, is arbitrarily chosen. You could cite four, five, or seven examples. Whatever the number, the evidence would remain insufficiently analyzed, the thesis would remain inert, and the paper would amount to little more than a list if all you did was reassert the same idea about each example. By contrast, in nearly all good writing the thesis evolves by *gaining in complexity* and, thus, in accuracy as the paper progresses.

Even in cases where, for disciplinary reasons, the thesis itself cannot change, there is still movement between the beginning of the paper and the end. In the report format of the natural and social sciences, for example, the hypothesis as initially worded must be either confirmed or denied, but it still undergoes much conceptual development. Rather than *simply* being confirmed or rejected, its adequacy is considered from various angles; and

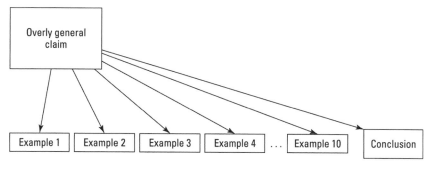

FIGURE 5.1 Doing 1 on 10. The horizontal pattern of 1 on 10 (in which "10" stands arbitrarily for any number of examples) repeatedly makes the same point about every example and in the conclusion. Its analysis of evidence is superficial.

alternatives, along with alternative methodologies for testing the original hypothesis again, are often proposed. (We discuss later, in a section of Chapter 6 entitled "Locating the Evolving Thesis in the Final Draft," the differences and especially the similarities in the ways various disciplines locate and use thesis statements.)

Weak thesis statements (poorly formulated and inadequately developed) are most easily detected not only by their repetitiveness but also by their predictability. The writer says the same thing again and again, drawing the same overgeneralized conclusion from each piece of evidence ("And so, once again we see that…"). A thesis that functions as an inert formula closes down a writer's thinking rather than guiding and stimulating it.

Inert thesis statements are, at least in part, products of a writer's adhering to an overly rigid and mechanical organizational scheme. Such schemes have the advantage of guaranteeing order, which they achieve by arranging everything under some single unifying point. Any data that do not conform, however, remain unnoticed or are studiously ignored. Thus, a thesis such as "Government welfare programs stifle initiative" will exclude welfare success stories, and a thesis such as "Marlowe's *Doctor Faustus* is a play about greed" will screen out the main character's moments of generosity.

Where do writers get the idea in the first place that a thesis should be static? In most cases they learned it early in their writing careers as part of a stubbornly inflexible organizational scheme known as five-paragraph form.

What's Wrong with Five-Paragraph Form?

Perhaps the best introduction to what's wrong with five-paragraph form can be found in Greek mythology. On his way to Athens, the hero Theseus encounters a particularly surly host, Procrustes, who offers wayfarers a bed for the night but with a catch. If they do not fit his bed exactly, he either stretches them or lops off their extremities until they do. This story has given us the word "procrustean," which the dictionary defines as "tending to produce conformity by violent or arbitrary means."

Five-paragraph form is a procrustean formula that most students learn in high school. While it has the advantage of providing a mechanical format that will give virtually any subject the appearance of order, it usually lops off a writer's ideas before they have the chance to form, or stretches a single idea to the breaking point. In other words, this simplistic scheme blocks writers' abilities to think deeply or logically, restricting rather than encouraging the development of complex ideas.

A complex idea is one that has many sides. To treat such ideas intelligently, writers need a form that will not require them to cut off all of those sides except the one that most easily fits the bed. Most of you will find the basic five-paragraph form (also known as the hamburger model) familiar:

1. An introduction—the top bun—that announces the writer's main idea, about which he or she will make three points.
2. Three paragraphs—the meat patties—each on one of the three points.
3. A conclusion—the bottom bun—beginning "Thus, we see" or "In conclusion" that essentially repeats the introduction.

Here is an example in outline form:

Introduction: The food in the school cafeteria is bad. It lacks variety, it's unhealthy, and it is always overcooked. In this essay I will discuss these three characteristics.

Paragraph 2: The first reason cafeteria food is bad is that there is no variety. (Plus one or two examples—no salad bar, mostly fried food, and so forth)

Paragraph 3: Another reason cafeteria food is bad is that it is not healthy. (Plus a few reasons—high cholesterol, too many hot dogs, too much sugar, and so forth)

Paragraph 4: In addition, the food is always overcooked. (Plus some examples—the vegetables are mushy, the "mystery" meat is tough to recognize, and so forth)

Conclusion: Thus, we see... (Plus a restatement of the introductory paragraph)

Most high school students write dozens of themes using this basic formula. They are taught to use five-paragraph form because it seems to provide the greatest good—a certain minimal clarity—for the greatest number of students. But the form does not promote logically tight and intellectually aggressive writing. It is a meat grinder that can turn any content into sausage. The two major problems it typically creates are easy to see.

1. The introduction reduces the remainder of the essay to *redundancy*. The first paragraph tells readers, in an overly general and list-like way, what they're going to hear; the succeeding three paragraphs tell the readers the same thing again in more detail and carry the overly general main idea along inertly; and the conclusion repeats what the readers have just been told (twice). The first cause of all this redundancy lies with the thesis. As in the example above, the thesis (cafeteria food is bad) is too broad—an unqualified and obvious generalization—and substitutes a simple list of predictable points for a complex statement of idea.

2. The form arbitrarily divides content: why are there three points (or examples or reasons) instead of five or one? A quick look at the three categories in our example reveals how arbitrarily the form has divided the subject. Isn't overcooked food unhealthy? Isn't a lack of variety also conceivably unhealthy? The format invites writers to list rather than analyze, to plug supporting examples into categories without examining the examples or how they are related. Five-paragraph form, as is evident in our sample's transitions ("first," "another reason," and "in addition"), counts things off but doesn't make logical connections. At its worst, the form prompts the writer to simply append evidence to generalizations without saying anything about it.

The subject, on the other hand, is not as unpromising as the format makes it appear. It could easily be redirected along a more productive pathway. (If the food is bad, what are the underlying causes of the problem? Are students getting what they ask for? Is the problem one of cost? Is the faculty cafeteria better? Why or why not?)

Now, let's look briefly at the introductory paragraph from a student's essay on a more academic subject. Here we can see a remarkable feature of five-paragraph form—its capacity to produce the same kind of say-nothing prose on almost any subject.

> Throughout the film *The Tempest*, a version of Shakespeare's play *The Tempest*, there were a total of seven characters. These characters were Calibano, Alonso, Antonio, Aretha, Freddy, the doctor, and Dolores. Each character in the film represented a person in Shakespeare's play, but there were four people who were greatly similar to those in Shakespeare, and who played a role in symbolizing aspects of forgiveness, love, and power.

The final sentence of the paragraph reveals the writer's addiction to five-paragraph form. It signals that the writer will proceed in a purely mechanical and superficial way, producing a paragraph on forgiveness, a paragraph on love, a paragraph on power, and a conclusion stating again that the film's characters resemble Shakespeare's in these three aspects. The writer is so busy *demonstrating* that the characters are concerned with forgiveness, love, and power that she misses the opportunity to analyze the significance of her own observations. Instead, readers are drawn wearily to a conclusion; they get no place except back where they began. Further, the demonstration mode prevents her from analyzing connections among the categories. The writer might consider, for example, how the play and the film differ in resolving the conflict between power and forgiveness (focusing on difference within similarity) and to what extent the film and the play agree about which is the most important of the three aspects (focusing on similarity despite difference).

These more analytical approaches lie concealed in the writer's introduction, but they never get discovered because the five-paragraph form militates against sustained analytical thinking. Its division of the subject into parts, which is only one part of analysis, has become an end unto itself. The procrustean formula insists upon a tripartite list in which each of the three parts is separate, equal, and, above all, *inert*.

Here are two *quick checks* for whether a paper of yours has closed down your thinking through a scheme such as five-paragraph form:

1. *Look at the paragraph openings.* If these read like a list, each beginning with an additive transition like "another" followed by a more or less exact repetition of your central point ("Another example is…" or "Yet another example is…"), you should suspect that you are not adequately developing your ideas.

2. *Compare the wording in the last statement of the paper's thesis (in the conclusion) with the first statement of it in the introduction.* If the wording at these two locations is virtually the same, you will know that your thesis has not responded adequately to your evidence.

An Alternative to Five-Paragraph Form: The All-Purpose Organizational Scheme

Five-paragraph form sacrifices thinking for organization—a losing bargain—but organization does matter. The various analytical techniques and prompts that we offer in its place, from "interesting" and "strange" to looking for difference within similarity, will encourage thinking, but how do you go about organizing that thinking? We address many aspects of organization in Part III of the book, "Organization and Style"; but for now, let's leap ahead to a template that you can adapt to many kinds of analytical writing. It is constructed upon several premises that we have already mentioned in Part I:

• An analytical writer approaches evidence to refine and sharpen his or her thesis, not just to support it.
• A productive thesis changes (evolves) as it encounters evidence.
• The paper itself should re-enact in more polished form for the reader the chains of thought that led the writer to his or her conclusions (the editorial, "Why Blame Ethnics for Referendum Loss, and Not Women?" on page 80 in Chapter 4 being a case in point).

Some of the steps below will become clearer by the end of the chapter, and there will be further discussion of organization in succeeding chapters. In any case, here is the template:

1. Write an introduction.

Begin analytical papers by defining some issue, question, problem, or phenomenon that the paper will address. An introduction is not a conclusion. It lays out something you have noticed that you think needs to be better understood. Use the introduction to get your readers to see why they should be more curious about the thing you have noticed. Aim for half a page.

2. State a working thesis.

Early in the paper, often at the end of the first paragraph or the beginning of the second (depending on the conventions of the discipline you are writing in), make a tentative claim about whatever it is you have laid out as being in need of exploration. The initial version of your thesis, known as *the working thesis*, should offer a tentative explanation, answer, or solution that the body of your paper will go on to apply and develop (clarify, extend, substantiate, qualify, and so on).

3. Begin querying your thesis.

Start developing your working thesis and other opening observations with the question "So what?" This question is shorthand for questions like "What does this observation mean?" and "Where does this thesis get me in my attempts to explain my subject?"

4. Muster supporting evidence for your working thesis.

Test its adequacy by seeing how much of the available evidence it can honestly account for. That is, try to prove that your thesis is correct, but also expect to come across evidence that does not fit your initial formulation of the thesis.

5. Seek complicating evidence.

Find evidence that does not readily support your thesis. Then explore—and explain—how and why it doesn't fit.

6. Reformulate your thesis.

Use the complicating evidence to produce new wording in your working thesis (additions, qualification, and so forth). This is how a thesis evolves: by assimilating obstacles and refining terms.

7. Repeat steps 3 to 6.

Query, support, complicate, and reformulate your thesis until you are satisfied with its accuracy.

8. State a conclusion.

Reflect on and reformulate your paper's opening position in light of the thinking that your analysis of evidence has caused you to do. Culminate rather than merely restate your paper's main idea in the concluding paragraph. Do this by getting your conclusion to again answer the question "So what?" In the conclusion, this question is shorthand for "Where does it get us to view the subject in this way?" or "What are the possible implications or consequences of the position the paper has arrived at?" Usually the reformulated (evolved) thesis comes near the beginning of the concluding paragraph. The remainder of the paragraph gradually moves the reader out of your piece, preferably feeling good about what you have accomplished for him or her.

As should be apparent, following the template will require you to shift your approach not only to a thesis (abandoning the notion of a fixed and static one) but also to evidence. Let's turn now to consider more carefully the nature and function of evidence.

B. LINKING EVIDENCE AND CLAIMS

Evidence matters because it always involves authority: the power of evidence is, well, *evident* in the laboratory, the courtroom, the classroom, and just about everywhere else. Your high school grades are evidence, and they may have worked for or against you. If they worked against you—if you believe yourself smarter than the numbers indicate—then you probably offered alternative evidence, such as extracurricular achievements, when you applied to university. As this example illustrates, there are many kinds of evidence; and whether or not something qualifies as acceptable evidence, as well as what it may show or prove, is often debatable.

The types and amounts of evidence necessary for persuading readers and building authority also vary from one discipline to another, as does the manner in which the evidence is presented. While some disciplines—the natural sciences, for example—will require you to present your evidence first and then interpret it, others (the humanities and some social sciences) will expect you to interpret your evidence as it is presented. But in all disciplines—and virtually any writing situation—it is important to support claims with evidence, to make your evidence lead to claims, and especially

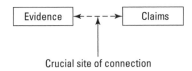

FIGURE 5.2 Linking Evidence and Claims

to be explicit about *how you've arrived at the connection between your evidence and your claims* (see Figure 5.2).

The first step in learning to explain the connection between your evidence and your claims is to remember that *evidence rarely, if ever, can be left to speak for itself.* When you leave evidence to speak for itself, you are assuming that it can be interpreted in only one way and that others will necessarily think as you do.

Writers who think that evidence speaks for itself generally do very little with it. Sometimes they will present it without making any overt claims, stating, for example, "There was no alcohol at the party," and expecting the reader to understand this statement as a sign of approval or disapproval. Alternatively, they may simply place the evidence next to a claim. Such writers will say, for example, "The party was terrible: there was no alcohol," or "The party was great: there was no alcohol." Merely juxtaposing the evidence to the claim (just putting them next to each other) leaves out the *thinking* that connects them and thereby implies that the logic of the connection is obvious. But even for readers prone to agree with you, just pointing to the evidence, assuming it will speak for itself, is not enough.

Of course, before you can attend to the relationship between evidence and claims, you first have to make sure to include both of them. The two most fundamental problems that writers must surmount, then, are unsubstantiated claims and pointless evidence. Let's pause to take a look at how to remedy these problems.

Unsubstantiated Claims

Problem: Making claims that lack supporting evidence.
Solution: Learning to recognize and support unsubstantiated assertions.

Unsubstantiated claims occur when you concentrate only on conclusions, omitting the evidence that led to them. At the opposite extreme, pointless evidence results when you offer a mass of detail attached to an overly general claim. To solve both of these problems, remember two rules. Whenever you make a claim, make sure that you (1) offer your readers the evidence that led you to it and (2) explain how the evidence led you to that conclusion. The word "unsubstantiated" means "without substance." An unsubstantiated claim is not necessarily false; it just offers none of the concrete "stuff" upon which the claim is based. When you make an unsubstantiated claim, you assume that readers will believe you just because you say this or that.

Perhaps more important, unsubstantiated claims deprive you of details. Without details, you're left with nothing concrete to think about. If you lack some actual "stuff" to analyze, you can easily get stuck in a set of abstractions, which tend to overstate your position, inhibit your thinking, and leave your readers wondering exactly what you mean. The further away your language gets from the concrete, from references to physical detail—things that you can see, hear, count, taste, smell, and touch—the more abstract it becomes. An aircraft carrier anchored outside a foreign harbour is concrete; the phrase "intervening in the name of democracy" is abstract.

You can see the problem of unsubstantiated assertions not only in papers but also in everyday conversation. It occurs when people get in the habit of leaping to conclusions—forming impressions so quickly and automatically that they have difficulty even recalling what it was that triggered a particular response. Ask such people why they thought a party

---

Voices Across the Curriculum

Earning Your Conclusions

Typically, when we write analytically, we write for others. What would induce them to read what we've written, grab their attention, make them keep reading? Detail, for one. Too often, feeling inadequate, fearing being mistaken, we hide behind labels, abstract phrases, and technical jargon, refuse to be present in what we write, and—consequently—nothing distinguishes our essay from any other.

Better to step forward, risk being there, making ourselves and our thinking visible. Details do that. As poet, novelist, and writing teacher Natalie Goldberg reminds us: *"Be specific. Not car, but Cadillac. Not bird, but wren. Not a codependent, neurotic man, but Harry, who runs to open the refrigerator for his wife, thinking she wants an apple, when she is headed for the gas stove to light her cigarette. Be careful of those pop-psychology labels. Get below the label and be specific to the person (or to the experience)"* (3).

Details persuade; rather than tell, they show. They make our subsequent abstractions and conclusions count.

—Mark Weisberg, professor of law

was boring or a new acquaintance pretentious, and they will rephrase the generalization rather than offer the evidence that led to it: the party was boring because nobody did anything; the person is pretentious because he puts on airs.

Rephrasing your generalizations rather than offering evidence tends to starve your thinking; it also has the effect of shutting out readers. If, for example, you defend your judgment that a person is pretentious by saying that he puts on airs, you have ruled on the matter and dismissed it. (You have also committed a logical flaw known as a *circular argument*, because "pretentious" and "putting on airs" mean virtually the same thing and using one in support of the other is arguing in a circle.) If, by contrast, you include the *grounds* upon which your judgment is based—the fact that he uses big words or that he always wears a bow tie—you have given readers a glimpse of your criteria. Readers are far more likely to accept your views if you give them the chance to think *with* you about the evidence. The alternative—offering groundless assertions—is to expect them to take your word for it.

There is, of course, an element of risk in providing the details that have informed your judgment. You leave yourself open to attack if, for example, your readers wear bow ties or speak in polysyllables. But this is an essential risk to take, for, otherwise, you leave your readers wondering why you think as you do or, worse, unlikely to credit your point of view. Moreover, in laying out your evidence, you will be more likely to anticipate your readers' possible disagreements. This will make you more inclined to think openly and carefully about your judgments.

In order to check your drafts for unsubstantiated assertions, you first have to know how to recognize them. One of the most fundamental skills for a writer to possess is the ability to *distinguish* evidence from claims. It is sometimes difficult to separate facts from judgments, data from interpretations of the data. Writers who aren't practised in this skill can believe that they are offering evidence when they are really offering only unsubstantiated claims. In your own reading and writing, pause once in a while to label the sentences of a paragraph as either evidence (E) or claims (C). What happens if we try to categorize the sentences of the following paragraph in this way?

> The NHL Players Association is ruining professional hockey in North America. Although players claim that they are underpaid, they are really just being greedy. Seventeen years ago, they delayed the start of the season for fifteen weeks, because the commissioner refused to buckle to their demands. Hockey is a sport, not a business, and it is a sad fact that it is being threatened by selfish athletes.

The first and last sentences of the paragraph are claims. They draw conclusions about as yet unstated evidence that the writer will need to provide. The middle two sentences are harder to classify. If particular players have stated publicly that they are underpaid, the existence of the players' statements is a fact. But the writer moves from evidence to claims when he suggests that the players are motivated by greed. As it stands, the assertion is an unsubstantiated claim. Unless the writer proceeds to ground it in evidence—relevant facts—it amounts to little more than name-calling. Similarly, it is a fact that the 1994–95 season was delayed for fifteen weeks, but the assertion that "the commissioner refused to buckle" is another unsubstantiated claim. The writer needs to offer evidence in support of this claim, along with his reasons for believing that the evidence means what he says it does.

Without evidence and the reasoning you've done about it, your writing asks readers to accept your opinions as though they were facts. The central claim of the hockey paragraph—that greedy players are ruining the sport—is an example of an opinion treated as though it were factual information. While many readers might be inclined to accept some version of the claim as true, they should not be asked to accept the writer's opinion as a self-evident truth.

The word "evident" comes from a Latin verb meaning "to see." To say that the truth of a statement is "self-evident" means that it does not need proving because its truth should be plainly seen by all. The problem is that very few ideas—no matter how much you may believe in them—readily attest to their own truth. And precisely because what people have taken to be common knowledge ("Women can't do math," for example, or "Men don't talk about their feelings") so often turns out to be wrong, you should take care to avoid unsubstantiated claims.

You need to be stingy, therefore, about treating your claims and evidence as factual. The more concrete information you gather, the less likely you will be to accept your opinions, partial information, or misinformation as fact. The writer of the hockey paragraph, for example, offers as fact that the players claim they are underpaid. If he were to search harder, however, he would find that his statement of the players' claim is not entirely accurate. The players have not unanimously claimed that they are underpaid; they have acknowledged that the problem has to do with poorer "small-market" teams competing against richer "large-market" teams. This more complicated version of the facts might at first be discouraging to the writer, since it reveals his original thesis ("greed") to be oversimplified. But then, as we have been saying, the function of evidence is not just to corroborate your claims; it should also help you to *test* and *refine* your ideas and to *define* your key terms more precisely.

TRY THIS: Take an excerpt from your own writing, at least two paragraphs in length—perhaps from a paper you have already written or a draft you are working on—and label each sentence as either evidence (E) or claim (C). For sentences that appear to offer both, determine which parts of the sentence are evidence and which are claim, and then decide which one, E or C, predominates. What is the ratio of evidence to claim, especially in particularly effective or particularly weak paragraphs? ☐

Pointless Evidence

Problem: Presenting a mass of evidence without explaining how it relates to the claims.

Solution: Making details speak; explaining how evidence confirms and qualifies the claim.

Your thinking emerges in the way that you follow through on the implications of the evidence you have selected. You need to interpret it for your readers. It is not enough to insert evidence after your claim, expecting readers to draw the same conclusion about its meaning that you have. You cannot assume that the facts can speak for themselves. You have to make the details speak, conveying to your readers why the details mean what you claim they mean.

The following paragraph illustrates what happens when a writer leaves the evidence to speak for itself:

The use of computers is ruining the concentration powers of most Canadian teenagers today. For example, one of the most popular games, *Diablo II*, throws a confusing array of visual signals in front of the player's eyes. Also of concern is the fact that many young people admit to having no appetite for reading books. It takes a great deal of focus and determination to wade through a 350-page novel. In addition to not appreciating the insights of our many fine novelists, such as Margaret Atwood and Hugh MacLennan, teenagers seem oblivious to the physical effects of spending countless hours glued to a screen, seated on a chair. Studies suggest that office workers who spend all day at their desks and at their keyboards suffer not only muscle problems but also psychological ones in the long term. Without the ability to concentrate on something other than the kaleidoscope of colours, images, and noise that emanates from high-tech games and other computerized diversions, an entire generation will face years of recuperation, once those teenagers become adults who must work to support a family and to earn a decent living.

Unlike the paragraph on greedy athletes, which was virtually all claims, this one offers a loose parade of evidence that is both preceded and followed by a redundant claim about teenagers and their dwindling powers of concentration. In essence, this paragraph is built like a miniature five-paragraph hamburger. The three meat patties of evidence—*Diablo II*, Canadian literature, and office-worker ailments—are sandwiched between twin buns of interpretation.

Unfortunately, the formula works no better at the paragraph level than it does at the essay level. Lining up evidence in a series of three (or four, or five) will be unconvincing if that evidence is left to speak for itself. If readers are to accept the writer's implicit claim—that teenagers are both inattentive and sedentary—he will have to show *how* and *why* the evidence supports that conclusion. The rule that applies here is that *evidence can almost always be interpreted in more than one way.*

You might, for instance, formulate at least three conclusions from the evidence offered in this hamburger paragraph. You might decide that the writer believes teenagers spend office workers' hours at their computers— or that lack of exercise takes away one's ability to concentrate. Quite possibly, you might disagree with his claim and conclude that video games have positive effects on those who enjoy them; *Diablo II* could be read as a stimulant to the imagination. Since the connection between claim and evidence is not clearly stated, readers are left to fend for themselves.

How can you ensure that your readers will at least understand your interpretation of the data? Begin by constantly reminding yourself that the thought connections that have occurred to you will not automatically occur to others. This doesn't mean that you should assume your readers are stupid, but you shouldn't expect them to read your mind and to do for themselves the thinking that you should be doing for them.

You can make the details speak if you take the time to stop and look at them, asking questions about what they imply. The two steps to follow are (1) to say explicitly what you take the details to mean and (2) to state exactly how the evidence supports or qualifies your claims.

The writer of the hamburger paragraph leaves his claim and virtually all of his reasoning about the evidence implicit. What, for example, is the connection between teenagers who don't like to read and teenagers who like to play computer games? Are they one and the same? Does the writer presume that the two activities are mutually exclusive? Due to its overly loose construction, the paragraph generates more questions than it answers.

There is a final lesson to glean from this example. Notice that when you focus on tightening the links between evidence and claim, the result is almost always a "smaller" claim than the one you set out to prove. This is what evidence characteristically does to a claim; it shrinks and restricts its scope. This process, also known as *qualifying a claim*, is the means by which a thesis evolves.

Sometimes it is hard to give up on the large, general assertions that were your first response to your subject. But your sacrifices are exchanged for greater accuracy and validity. The sweeping claims you lose ("an entire generation will face years of recuperation") give way to less resounding but also more informed, more incisive, and less judgmental ideas.

C. ANALYZING EVIDENCE IN DEPTH: "10 ON 1"

How do you move from making details speak and explaining how evidence confirms and qualifies the claim to actually composing a paper? One way is through the practice we call *10 on 1*: a focused analysis of a representative example (see Figure 5.3). Doing 10 on 1 is the opposite of doing 1 on 10—the phrase we introduced at the beginning of this chapter to describe the static demonstration paper that repeats the same point as its "answer" for ten similar examples or issues.

Phrased as a general rule, 10 on 1 holds that it is better to make ten observations or points about a single representative issue or example than to make the same basic point about ten related issues or examples (as in 1 on 10). The number "10," let us hasten to add, is arbitrarily chosen. You could make four or five or seven observations and points.

We bring together in 10 on 1 the various skills that the book has been discussing thus far. It offers an efficient and productive way to look at evidence, to formulate claims about it, and, ultimately, to organize your analysis into a paper. We get to the organizational element shortly; for now the important idea we intend 10 on 1 to communicate is that you should draw out as much meaning as possible from your best examples. Doing 10 on 1 depends, in other words, upon narrowing your focus and then analyzing in depth.

Once most writers decide that all the evidence points to the same conclusion, they tend to stop really looking at the evidence. If you were to use all of your examples to repeatedly corroborate the same point, the repetition would deter you from exploring the evidence in more depth. Writing would then become not a matter of finding things out or developing an idea but simply of dropping each example into place next to an unchanging conclusion. Here is a brief example: say that you were writing an essay on the symbolism of monsters in Japanese popular cinema. You locate a number of examples that all point to the same conclusion: since World War II, monster movies have expressed Japan's ongoing anxiety over the atomic and hydrogen bombs. Rather than catalogue all of the instances of Godzilla's trampling on cities, you would do better to scrutinize the most revealing instance and then locate it in a pattern of other like instances. By drawing out its implications, you would more likely discover the questions and understand the cultural issues that surround the symbolism of monsters, or that exist in any subject.

❦*TRY THIS:* In March of 2011, Oxford University researcher Peter Wynn Kirby composed an article about Japanese B-movies entitled "Japan's Long Nuclear Disaster Film." His writing was inspired by the earthquakes and tsunami that had recently devastated that island nation. Read the article carefully (it appears on pages 262–264) and assess for yourself how well Kirby analyzes

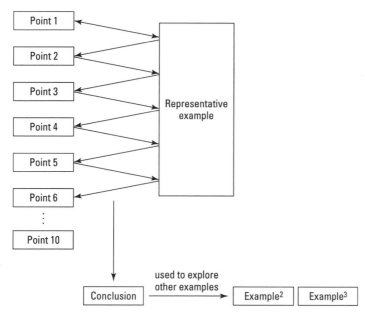

FIGURE 5.3 Doing 10 on 1. The pattern of 10 on 1 (in which "10" stands arbitrarily for any number of points) successively develops a series of points about a single representative example. Its analysis of evidence is in-depth.

his evidence. The following questions will aid in your assessment, which you can then compare with those of your classmates: □

- Does the analysis focus on a representative example of Japanese B-movies?
- If so, does the writer conduct a version of "10 on 1"?
- Which historical and cultural issues (if any) inform Kirby's analysis?
- Does the article succeed in presenting an evolving thesis?

In sum, you can use 10 on 1 to accomplish various ends: (1) to locate the range of possible meanings your evidence suggests; (2) to make you less inclined to cling to your first claim inflexibly, thereby opening the way for you to discover a way of representing more fully the complexity of your subject; and (3) to slow down the rush to generalization and thus help to ensure that when you arrive at a working thesis, it will be more specific and better able to account for your evidence.

But what exactly are the "1" and the "10," and how do you go about finding them? The "1" is a representative example of what you have narrowed your focus to. How do you select the "1"? One of the best ways is to use Five-Step Analysis to identify a strand or pattern and then to choose the example of it you find most interesting, strange, revealing, and so forth. Here, in effect, you do 1 on 10 as a preliminary step—locating ten examples that share a trait—and then focus on one of these for in-depth analysis. Proceeding in this way would guarantee that your example was representative. It is essential that your example be representative because in doing 10 on 1 you will take one part of the whole, put it under a microscope, and then generalize about the whole on the basis of your analysis. In the preceding section we used the hockey example in this way, doing 10 on 1 with the student's paragraph as a way of anchoring our generalizations about giving evidence a point. We address the issue of representativeness in more detail shortly.

As for the "10," they are comprised of both observations and interpretive leaps that you make about the "1," both what you notice about the evidence and what you make of what you notice. To get the "10"—to analyze in depth—use the various tools, prompts, and procedures that have been introduced in this book thus far:

- Look at the example and ask yourself what you notice.
- Use Five-Step Analysis to identify patterns of repetition and contrast.
- Locate anomalies and query them.
- Locate, name, and reformulate binaries.

- Try saying that something "seems to be about X but is *also* about Y."
- Employ Paraphrase × 3 on key sentences or phrases if your evidence has a verbal component.
- Actively seek to uncover the assumptions in your example.
- As you try on different interpretations, repeatedly ask, "So what?" to develop the implications of your thinking.
- As a major claim begins to emerge (and it will), seek out conflicting evidence to enable you to qualify the claim still further.

Pan, Track, and Zoom: The Film Analogy

To understand how 10 on 1 can generate the form of a paper, let's turn to an analogy. The language of filmmaking offers a useful way for under-standing the different ways that a writer can focus evidence. The writer, like the director of a film, controls the focus through different kinds of shots.

The pan—The camera pivots around a stable axis, giving the viewer the big picture. Using a pan, we see everything from a distance. Pans provide a context, some larger pattern, the "forest" within which the writer can also examine particular "trees." Pans establish the repre-sentativeness of the example the writer later examines in more detail, showing that it is not an isolated instance.

The track—The camera no longer stays in one place but follows some sequence of action. For example, whereas a pan might survey a room full of guests at a cocktail party, a track would pick up a particular guest and follow along as she walks across the room, picks up a photograph, pro-ceeds through the door, and throws the photo in a trash can. Analogously, a writer tracks by moving in on selected pieces of the larger picture and following them in order to make telling connections among them.

The zoom—The camera moves in even closer on a selected piece of the scene, allowing us to notice more of its details. For example, a zoom might focus in on the woman's hand as she crumples the photograph she's about to throw away or on her face as she slams the lid on the trash can. A writer zooms by giving us more detail on a particular part of his or her evidence and by making the details say more. The zoom is the shot that enables you to do 10 on 1.

In a short paper (three to five pages), you might devote as much as ninety percent of your writing to illustrating what one example (the "1"—your zoom) reveals about the larger subject. Even in a paper that uses several examples, however, as much as fifty percent might still be devoted to analysis of and generalization from a single case. The remaining portion of the paper would *make connections with other examples, testing and applying the ideas you arrived at from your single case.* In-depth analysis of your best example thus creates a centre from which you can move in two directions: (1) toward generalizations about the larger subject and (2) toward other examples, using your primary example as a tool of exploration.

Faced, for example, with writing a paper about the role the Reform Party played in the creation of the Canadian Alliance, an inexperienced writer might offer a broad survey with a few paragraphs on Preston Manning, a few paragraphs on various grassroots initiatives, and a few paragraphs on economic rivalries between Ontario and Alberta. You could cover the same body of information in far more depth, however, by focusing almost entirely on the Canadian Alliance Leadership Election of 2000 as a representative instance. Your analysis of this leadership battle would necessarily include discussion of Manning's role and the economic interests of Western Canada, but it would do so within a tightly focused framework. Your assumption would be that if readers can see the collision of interests that led to the ascendance of the Canadian Alliance, they will obtain a deeper understanding of the Reform Party than a survey could provide.

This same model, applicable across a wide variety of writing situations, can be reduced to a series of steps:

1. Find (using Five-Step Analysis) a revealing pattern or tendency in your evidence.
2. Select a representative example.
3. Provide in-depth analysis (doing 10 on 1) of your example.
4. Test your results in similar cases.

An analysis of the representation of females on television, for example, would fare better if you focused on one show—say, *Nikita*—narrowed the focus to teenage girls, and tested your results against other shows with teenage girl characters, such as *Glee, Gossip Girl,* and *The Secret Circle.* Similarly, a study of the national debt might focus on Social Insurance, analyzing it in order to arrive at generalizations to be tested and refined in the context of, say, health care or military spending. A close look at virtually anything will reveal its complexity, and you can bring that complex understanding to other examples for further testing and refining.

It is, of course, important to let your readers know that you are using the one primary example in this generalizable way. Note how the writer of the following discussion of the people's revolt in China in 1989 sets up his analysis. He first explains how his chosen example—a single photograph (shown in Figure 5.4) from the media coverage of the event—illuminates his larger subject. The image is of a Chinese man in a white shirt who temporarily halted a line of tanks on their way to quell a demonstration in Tiananmen Square in Beijing.

The tank image provided a miniature, simplified version of a larger, more complex revolution. The conflict between man and tank embodied the same tension found in the conflict between student demonstrators and the People's Army. The man in the white shirt, like the students, displayed courage, defiance, and rebellious individuality in the face of power. Initially, the peaceful revolution succeeded: the state allowed the students to protest; likewise, the tank spared the man's life. Empowered, the students' demands for democracy grew louder. Likewise, the man boldly jumped onto the tank and addressed the soldiers. The state's formerly unshakable dominance appeared weak next to the strength of the individual. However, the state asserted its power: the People's Army marched into the square, and the tanks roared past the man into Beijing.

The image appeals to American ideology. The man in the white shirt personifies the strength of the American individual. His rugged courage draws on contemporary heroes such as Rambo. His defiant gestures resemble the

FIGURE 5.4 Tiananmen Square, Beijing, 1989

demonstrations of Martin Luther King Jr. and his followers. American history predisposes citizens to identify strongly with the Chinese demonstrators: Americans have rebelled against the establishment, they have fought for freedom and democracy, and they have defended the rights of the individual. For example, the *New York Times* reported that President George Bush watched the tank incident on television and said, "I'm convinced that the forces of democracy are going to overcome these unfortunate events in Tiananmen Square." Bush represents the popular American perspective of the Chinese rebellion: support for the student demonstrators.

This analysis is a striking example of doing 10 on 1. In the first paragraph, the writer constructs a detailed analogy between the particular image and the larger subject of which it was a part. The analogy allows the writer not just to describe but also to interpret the event. In the second paragraph, he develops his focus on the image as an image, a photographic representation tailor-made to appeal to American viewing audiences. Rather than generalizing about why Americans might find the image appealing, he establishes a number of explicit connections (does 10 on 1) between the details of the image and typical American heroes. By drawing out the implications of particular details, he manages to say more about the significance of the American response to the demonstrations in China than a broader survey of those events would have allowed.

The rule of thumb here is to say more about less, rather than less about more, to allow a carefully analyzed part of your subject to provide perspective on the whole.

Demonstrating the Representativeness of Your Example

Problem: Generalizing on the basis of too little and unrepresentative evidence.

Solution: Surveying the available evidence and arguing overtly for the representativeness of the examples on which you focus.

One significant advantage of concentrating on your single best example is its economy: you can cut quickly to the heart of a subject. But with this advantage comes a danger: that the example you select will not in fact be representative. Thus, it's not enough just to select an example you think is representative. You also need to overtly demonstrate its representativeness. In other words, you must *show that your example is part of a larger pattern of similar evidence and not just an isolated instance.*

In terms of logic, the problem of generalizing from too little and unrepresentative evidence is known as an *unwarranted inductive leap*. That is, the writer leaps from one or two instances to a broad claim about an entire class or category. For example, just because you see an economics professor and a biology professor wear corduroy jackets, you should not leap to the conclusion that all professors wear corduroy jackets.

The surest way you can guard against the problem of unwarranted inductive leaps is by reviewing the range of possible examples to make certain that the ones you choose to focus on are representative. If you were writing about faith as it is portrayed in the book of Exodus, for example, you might suggest the general trend by briefly panning across instances in which the Israelites have difficulty believing in an unseen God. Then you could concentrate (zoom in) on the best example.

Not all illogical leaps are easy to spot. Here is a brief example from a writer who makes an unwarranted inductive leap.

> Some people feel that rock music videos are purely sexist propaganda and that they stereotype women as sex objects. I feel this is a generalization and far from the truth. Many types of videos exist, a lot of which show no women in them at all. Others do contain women and could be considered sexist only if you choose to look at them from that point of view.

The writer of this paragraph next offers three examples in support of her generalization that rock videos do not stereotype women as sex objects. One video consists entirely of concert footage. In another, the lead singer hugs and kisses his mother. The third shows a female passenger in a Jaguar trying to get the attention of the male singer, who is driving—a scenario that leads the writer to assert, "If anyone is being presented as the sex object, it is he."

Clearly, this writer is trying to correct the overgeneralization that all rock videos are sexist in their depiction of women, but her argument falls prey to the same kind of overgeneralization. Her *sample is too small*. Three examples of videos that do not depict women as sex objects constitute too small a sample to dismiss the charge of sexism. Also, her *sample is too selective*. It does not confront examples that would challenge her point of view, examples that an opponent might use to prove that videos do stereotype women as sex objects. In other words, she avoids the difficult evidence, deliberately picking videos that may well be exceptions to the rule and then arguing that they are the rule.

Most of the time, unwarranted leaps result from making too large a claim and avoiding examples that might contradict it. As a rule, you should *deliberately seek out the single piece of evidence that might most effectively oppose your point of view and address it.* Doing so will prompt you to test the representativeness of your evidence and, in many cases, to qualify the claims you have made for it. The writer of the rock video example, for instance, can argue on the basis of three videos for a *more limited* version of her claim—that the representation of men and their relationship to women in rock videos is more varied and complex than the charge of sexism has allowed. In sum, if you select more complicated examples or actively search out complication in evidence that at first seems simple and obvious, then you will be less likely to use unrepresentative examples to arrive at a claim that does not respond to the full range of relevant evidence.

❧*TRY THIS:* Study the photograph in Figure 5.5 and do 10 on 1. The key to doing 10 on 1 successfully is to slow down the rush to conclusions so that you can allow yourself to notice more about the evidence and make the details speak. The more observations you assemble about your data *before* settling on your main idea, the better that idea is likely to be. Remember that you should be striving to say more about less rather than less about more. A skilled photographer such as Henri Cartier-Bresson presents a lot of detail in a relatively small space. Try to notice and focus on as much of that detail as possible. □

FIGURE 5.5 *London, 1938*

10 on 1 and Disciplinary Conventions

In some cases, the conventions of a discipline would appear to discourage doing 10 on 1. The social sciences in particular tend to require a larger set of analogous examples to prove a hypothesis (tentative claim). Especially in certain kinds of research, the focus of inquiry rests on discerning broad statistical trends over a wide range of evidence. The inexperienced writer is likely to obey this disciplinary convention by providing a list of unanalyzed examples. But some trends deserve more attention than others, and some statistics similarly merit more interpretation than others. The best writers learn to choose examples carefully—each one for a reason—and to concentrate on developing the most revealing ones in depth; the interpretive and statistical models for analyzing evidence are not necessarily opposed to one another.

For instance, proving that tax laws are prejudiced in particularly subtle ways against unmarried people might require a number of analogous cases along with a statistical summary of the evidence. But even with a subject such as this, you could still concentrate on some examples more than others. Rather than moving through each example as a separate case, you could use your analyses of these primary examples as *lenses* for investigating other evidence.

A Template for Using 10 on 1

Here is a variant on the template offered earlier as an alternative to five-paragraph form. It is adapted for use with 10 on 1. Think of it not as a rigid outline but as a way of moving from one phase of your paper to the next.

1. In your introduction, start by noting (panning on) an interesting pattern or tendency you have found in your evidence. Explain what attracted you to it—why you find it potentially significant and worth looking at. This paragraph would end with a tentative theory (working thesis) about what this pattern or tendency might reveal or accomplish.

2. Zoom in on your representative example, some smaller part of the larger pattern. Argue for the example's representativeness and usefulness in coming to a better understanding of your subject.

3. Do 10 on 1—analyze your representative example—sharing with your readers your observations (what you notice) and your tentative conclusions (answers to the "So what?" question).

4. In a short paper, you might at this point move to your conclusion, with its qualified, refined (evolved) version of your thesis and brief commentary on what you've accomplished—that is, the ways in which your analysis has illuminated the larger subject.

5. In a longer paper, you would move from your initial zoom to another zoom on a similar case, to see the extent to which the thesis you evolved with your representative example is in need of further adjusting to better reflect the nature of your subject as a whole. This last move is the primary topic of our next chapter.

ASSIGNMENT

The technique we call 10 on 1 is the primary thinking strategy we offer in this chapter. Write a paper in which you do 10 on 1 with the following paragraph by Margaret Wente. Brainstorm your "1" on the page, making observations and tracking your own responses as a reader. Is Wente's writing deliberately provocative and "impolite"? If so, "So what?" Draw out as much meaning as possible from this example. Aim for depth and detail.

> It's ironic that not so long ago, female students were objecting that the university administration had no business being sex police. My girlfriends would have been insulted by the notion that they couldn't make such decisions for themselves. And they were well aware of the special power they possessed. Campus harassment codes have mostly put an end to the days of lecherous professors. But they also perpetuate the myth that sexual advances all go one way. Anyone with any experience of campus life knows otherwise, and any charismatic professor can tell you how often it's his students who do the chasing. Although it's impolite to say so, erotic bonds have sprung up between teachers and pupils since Socrates started giving philosophy lessons in the agora. And they aren't always a bad thing.*

---

*Margaret Wente, *The Globe and Mail*, Feb. 24, 2004, p. A19. Reprinted with permission from The Globe and Mail.

CHAPTER

6

The Evolving Thesis

You now know what a thesis is—a claim about the meaning of some feature or features of your subject—but what does a thesis *do*? What is its function?

A thesis focuses inquiry, providing a principle of selection that makes some evidence more relevant than other evidence. It also works to guide development of your ideas, leading you to greater precision and accuracy about what things mean. The static thesis, as we demonstrate in the previous chapter, provides organization but sacrifices thinking. By contrast, the evolving thesis both prompts and organizes your thinking.

The first step in composing a productive working thesis is to recognize that one will not appear to you, ready-made, in the material you are analyzing. In other words, a restatement of some idea that is already clearly stated in your subject is not itself a thesis (though summarizing analytically may help you to find a thesis). The process of finding a thesis—an idea about the facts and ideas in your subject—begins only when you start to ask questions about the material, deliberately looking for places where there is something to be curious about—something, in short, that seems to you to require analysis.

The second step in composing a productive working thesis is to recognize that a working thesis will only be relatively adequate. It won't explain all of the relevant evidence equally well. More often than not, when inexperienced writers face a situation in which evidence seems to be unclear or contradictory, they tend to make one of two unproductive moves: they either ignore the conflicting evidence, or they abandon the problem altogether and look for something more clear-cut to write about.

In fact, you should *expect* to find evidence that will complicate your thesis. *Complicating evidence is something for which your thesis does not account.* When you don't seek to complicate—to find exceptions to and questions about—your claims, you inevitably oversimplify. As we note in Chapter 3, meanings are multiple, which is to say that most things—even the simplest everyday objects and gestures—mean different things at the same time, depending on context.

If you are doing 10 on 1 and using Five-Step Analysis (see Chapters 5 and 1, respectively) in a genuinely exploratory fashion, rest assured that you will find things for which your thesis does not account. Often these emerge when you look for what we have called difference within similarity. The examples in the strands you detect won't be *exactly* alike, and the very act of deciding that your "1" is a representative case will have made you aware of subtle differences among the examples from which you have chosen the typical one. So, too, the organizing contrasts you find will point to conflicts, to issues that are at stake within your subject. These are all sources of complication. Alternatively, the complicating evidence may at first have seemed not to fit within the scope of your thesis, or it may actually lie outside your scope—in either case, it is evidence that will help you to specify more accurately the limits of your thesis.

Faced with evidence that complicates your thesis, the one thing *not* to do is run away. The "problem" you have discovered offers a chance to modify your thesis rather than abandon it. *The complications you encounter are an opportunity to make your thesis evolve.* Formulating a claim, seeking out conflicting evidence, and then using these conflicts to revise the claim are primary movements of mind in analytical writing. The savvy writer will take advantage of opportunities to make complications overt in order to make his or her claim respond more fully to the evidence. This is precisely what Christine Overall does in "Karla Homolka Has a Right to Study at Queen's" (pages 265–267). By engaging the complications, Overall strengthens her evolving thesis.

A. RE-CREATING THE CHAIN OF THOUGHT

Let's begin with an example of how to make a thesis evolve. Say that you're looking for a trend (strand) in contemporary films you've seen and, as a working thesis, you claim that "women are more sensitive than men." If you were to seek out data that would complicate this overstated claim, you would soon encounter evidence that would press you to make some distinctions that the initial formulation of this claim leaves obscure. You would need, for example, to clarify what you mean by "sensitive" and how you were assessing its presence and absence.

Evidence might also lead you to consider whether men, although not demonstrative about certain kinds of tender feelings, nonetheless show them in ways different from the ways women do. And surely you would want to think about how the films represent women's sensitivity. Are women punished for it in the plots? Are they rewarded with being liked (approved of) by the films, even if this trait does cause them problems?

Such considerations as these would require significant reformulation of the working thesis. By the end of the paper, the claim that "women are more sensitive than men" should have evolved into a more carefully defined and qualified statement that reflects the thinking you have done in your analysis of evidence. This, by and large, is what good concluding paragraphs do; they reflect back on and reformulate your paper's initial position in light of the thinking you have done about it (see Figure 6.1).

But, you might ask, isn't this reformulating of the thesis something a writer does before he or she writes the essay? Certainly some of it is accomplished in your prewriting—the exploratory drafting and note taking you do before you begin to compose the first draft of the essay. But your finished paper will necessarily be more than a list of conclusions. To an extent, all good writing re-creates the chains of thought that lead writers to their conclusions. Your revision process will have weeded out various false starts and dead ends that you may have wandered into on the way to your finished ideas, but the main routes of your movement from a tentative idea to a refined and substantiated theory should remain visible for readers to follow. (See the section "Locating the Evolving Thesis in the Final Draft" later in this chapter for a more extensive discussion of how much thesis evolution to include in your final draft.)

❧TRY THIS: Using as a model of inquiry the treatment of the example thesis "Women are more sensitive than men," seek out complications in one of the overstated claims in the following list. These complications might include conflicting evidence (which you should specify) and questions about the meaning or appropriateness of key terms (again, which you should exemplify). Illustrate a few of these complications, and then reformulate the claim in language that is more carefully qualified and accurate.

Welfare encourages recipients not to work.

Religious people are more moral than those who are not religious.

FIGURE 6.1 The Evolving Thesis. A strong thesis evolves as it confronts and assimilates evidence; the evolved thesis may expand or restrict the original claim. The process may need to be repeated a number of times.

School gets in the way of education.

Herbal remedies are better than pharmaceutical ones.

The book is always better than the film. □

The Reciprocal Relationship Between Thesis and Evidence: The Thesis as a Camera Lens

What we have said so far about the thesis does not mean that all repetition is bad or that a writer's concluding paragraph should have no reference to the way the paper began. One function of the thesis is to provide the connective tissue, so to speak, that holds together a paper's three main parts—its beginning, middle, and end. Periodic reminders of your paper's thesis, its unifying idea, are essential for keeping both you and your readers on track.

But, as we also argue, developing an idea requires more than repetition. It is in light of this fact that the analogy of a thesis to connective tissue proves inadequate. A better way of envisioning how a thesis operates is to think of it as a camera lens. This analogy more accurately describes the relationship between the thesis and the subject it seeks to explain: while the lens affects how we see the subject (what evidence we select and what questions we ask about that evidence), the subject we are looking at also affects how we adjust the lens.

Here is the principle that the camera-lens analogy allows us to see: the relationship between thesis and subject is *reciprocal* (see Figure 6.2). In good analytical writing, especially in the early, investigatory stages of writing and thinking, *not only does the thesis direct the writer's way of looking at evidence, but the analysis of evidence should also direct and redirect (bring about revision of) the thesis.* Even in a final draft, writers are usually fine-tuning their governing idea in response to their analysis of evidence.

The enemy of good analytical writing is the fuzzy lens—an imprecisely worded thesis statement. Very broad thesis statements, those that are made up of imprecise (fuzzy) terms, make bad camera lenses. They blur everything together and muddy important distinctions. If your lens is

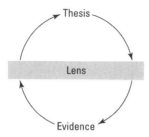

FIGURE 6.2 The Reciprocal Relationship Between Thesis and Evidence. Like a lens, the thesis affects the way a writer sees evidence. Evidence should also require the writer to readjust the lens.

insufficiently sharp, you are not likely to see much in your evidence. If you say, for example, that the economic situation today is bad, you will at least have some sense of direction, but the imprecise terms "bad" and "economic situation" don't provide you with a focus clear enough to distinguish significant detail in your evidence. Without significant detail to analyze, you can't develop your thesis, either by showing readers what the thesis is good for (what it allows us to understand and explain) or by clarifying its terms.

A writer's thesis is usually fuzzier in a paper's opening than it is in the conclusion. As we argue in our critique of five-paragraph form, a paper ending with a claim worded almost exactly as it is in the beginning has not made its thesis adequately responsive to evidence. The body of the paper should not only substantiate the thesis by demonstrating its value in selecting and explaining evidence, but also bring the opening version of the thesis into better focus.

Moving Through a Series of Complications

This section of the chapter presents an extended example that illustrates how the initial formulation of a thesis might evolve—through a series of complications—over the course of a draft.

The procedure for evolving a thesis can be described in the following steps:

1. Formulate an idea about your subject.

This *working thesis* should be some claim about the meaning of your evidence that is good enough to get you started.

2. See how far you can make this thesis go in accounting for evidence.

Use the thesis to explain as much of your evidence as it reasonably can. Try it on. This initial application of thesis to evidence will already begin the process of pressing you to develop your thesis—to ponder the accuracy of key terms, and so forth.

3. Locate evidence that is not adequately accounted for by the thesis.

You will need to look actively for such evidence because the initial version of the thesis will incline you to see only what fits and not to notice the evidence that doesn't fit.

4. Ask "So what?" about the apparent mismatch between the thesis and selected evidence.

Explain how and why some pieces of evidence do not fit the thesis.

5. Reshape your claim to accommodate the evidence that hasn't fit.

This will mean rethinking (and rewording) your thesis to resolve or explain apparent contradictions or the way your thesis first led you to see the evidence. Perhaps you will discover that what seemed to be contradictory in the evidence actually isn't. If the contradiction cannot be resolved, it will put pressure on you to evolve your claim.

6. Repeat steps 2, 3, 4, and 5 several times.

Repeat these steps until you are satisfied that the thesis statement accounts for your evidence as fully and accurately as possible. This is to say that the procedure for making a thesis evolve is *recursive*: it requires you to go over the same ground repeatedly, formulating successive versions of the thesis that are increasingly accurate in wording and idea.

As an overarching guideline, acknowledge the questions that each new formulation of the thesis prompts you to ask. Keep asking "So what?" relentlessly of each new formulation. Remember that the thesis develops through successive complications. Allowing your thesis to run up against potentially conflicting evidence ("But what about this?") enables you to build upon your initial idea, extending the range of evidence it can accurately account for by clarifying and qualifying its key terms.

Let's consider the stages you might go through within a more finished draft to evolve a thesis about a film (see Figure 6.3). In *Educating Rita*, a working-class English hairdresser (Rita) wants to change her life by taking courses from a professor (Frank) at the local university, even though this move threatens her relationship with her husband (Denny), who burns her books and puts pressure on her to quit school and get pregnant. Frank, she discovers, has his own problems: he's a divorced alcoholic who is bored with his life, bored with his privileged and complacent students, and bent on self-destruction. The film follows the growth of Frank and Rita's friendship and the changes it brings about in their lives. By the end of the film, each has left a limiting way of life behind and has set off in a seemingly more promising direction. She leaves her constricting marriage, passes her university examinations with honours, and begins to view her life in terms of choices; he stops drinking and sets off, determined but sad, to make a new start as a teacher in Australia.

Formulate an idea about your subject (step 1)

Working thesis: *Educating Rita* celebrates the liberating potential of education.

The film's relatively happy ending and the presence of the word "educating" in the film's title make this thesis a reasonable opening claim.

See how far you can make this thesis go in accounting for evidence (step 2)

The working thesis seems compatible, for example, with Rita's achievement of greater self-awareness and independence. You would go on to locate more data like this that would support the idea that education is potentially liberating. She becomes more articulate, thereby freeing herself from otherwise disabling situations. She starts to think about other kinds of work she might do, rather than assuming that she must continue in the one job she has always done. She travels, first elsewhere in England and then to the Continent. So, the thesis checks out as viable: there is enough of a match with evidence to make it worth pursuing.

Locate evidence that is not adequately accounted for by the thesis and ask "So what?" about the apparent mismatch between the thesis and selected evidence (steps 3 and 4)

Other evidence troubles the adequacy of the working thesis, however: Rita's education causes her to become alienated from her husband, her parents, and her social class; at the end of the film she is alone and unsure about her direction in life. In Frank's case, the thesis runs into even more problems. His boredom, drinking, and alienation seem to have been caused, at least in part, by his education rather than by his lack of it. He sees his book-lined study as a prison. Moreover, his profound knowledge of literature has not helped him to control his life: he comes to class drunk, fails to notice or care that his girlfriend is having an affair with one of his colleagues, and asks his classes whether it is worth gaining all of literature if it means losing one's soul.

Reshape your claim to accommodate the evidence that hasn't fit (step 5)

Question: What are you to do? You cannot convincingly argue that the film celebrates the liberating potential of education, since that thesis ignores such a significant amount of the evidence. Nor can you "switch sides" and argue that the film attacks education as life-denying and disabling, because this thesis is also only partially true.

What not to do. Faced with evidence that complicates your thesis, you should not assume that it is worthless and that you need to start over from scratch. View the "problem" you have discovered as an opportunity to modify your thesis rather than abandon it. After all, the thesis still fits a lot of significant evidence. Rita is arguably better off at the end of the film than at the beginning: we are not left to believe that she should have remained resistant to education, like her husband Denny, whose world doesn't extend much beyond the corner pub.

What to do. Make apparent complications—the film's seemingly contradictory attitudes about education—explicit, and then modify the wording of your thesis in a way that might resolve or explain these contradictions. You might, for example, be able to resolve an apparent contradiction between your initial thesis (the film celebrates the liberating potential of education) and the evidence by proposing that there is more than one version of education depicted in the film. You would, in short, start qualifying and clarifying the meaning of key terms in your thesis.

In this case, you could divide education as represented by the film into two kinds, enabling and stultifying. The next step in the development of your thesis would be to elaborate on how the film seeks to distinguish true and enabling forms of education from false and debilitating ones (as represented by the self-satisfied and status-conscious behaviour of the supposedly educated people at Frank's university).

Revised thesis: *Educating Rita* celebrates the liberating potential of enabling—in contrast to stultifying—education.

Repeat steps 2, 3, 4, and 5 (step 6)

Having refined your thesis in this way, you would then repeat the step of seeing what the new wording allows you to account for in your evidence. The revised thesis might, for example, explain Frank's problems as being less a product of his education than of the cynical and pretentious versions of education that surround him in his university life. You could posit further that Frank, with Rita as inspiration, rediscovers at least some of his idealism about education.

What about Frank's emigration to Australia? If we can take Australia to stand for a newer world, one where education would be less likely to become the stale and exclusive property of a self-satisfied elite, then the refined version of the thesis would seem to be working well. In fact, given the possible thematic connection between Rita's working-class identity and Australia (associated, as a former frontier and English penal colony, with lower-class vitality as opposed to the complacency bred of class privilege), the thesis about the film's celebration of the contrast between enabling and stultifying forms of education could be sharpened further. You might propose, for example, that the film presents institutional education as desperately in need of frequent doses of "real life" (as represented by Rita and Australia)—infusions of working-class pragmatism, energy, and optimism—if it is to remain healthy and open, as opposed to becoming the oppressive property of a privileged social class. This is to say that the film arguably exploits stereotypical assumptions about social class.

> Revised thesis: *Educating Rita* celebrates the liberating potential of enabling education, defined as that which remains open to healthy doses of working-class, real-world infusions.

Similarly, you can make your supporting ideas (those on which your thesis depends) more accurate and less susceptible to oversimplification, by seeking evidence that might challenge their key terms. *Sharpening the language of your supporting assertions will help you develop your thesis.*

Consider, for example, the wording of the supporting idea that *Educating Rita* has a happy ending. Some qualification of this idea through consideration of possibly conflicting evidence could produce an adjustment in the first part of the working thesis, that the film celebrates education and presents it as liberating. At the end of the film, Frank and Rita walk off in opposite directions down long, empty airport corridors. Though promising to remain friends, the two do not become a couple. This closing emphasis on Frank's and Rita's alienation from their respective cultures, and the film's apparent insistence on the necessity of each going on alone, significantly qualifies the happiness of the "happy ending."

Once you have complicated your interpretation of the ending, you will again need to modify your thesis in accord with your new observations. Does the film simply celebrate education if it also presents it as being, to some degree, incompatible with conventional forms of happiness? By emphasizing the necessity of having Frank and Rita each go on alone, the film may be suggesting that in order to be truly liberating, education—as opposed to its less honest and more comfortable substitutes—inevitably produces and even requires a certain amount of loneliness and alienation. Review the successive revisions of the thesis in Figure 6.3.

❧*TRY THIS:*   Go home, settle into a comfortable chair (with good lighting), and read Kelly Hannah-Moffat's "Gendering Risk at What Cost: Negotiations of Gender and Risk in Canadian Women's Prisons" (pages 285–291). As you read, pick out sentences that demonstrate the evolution of her thesis. Keep in

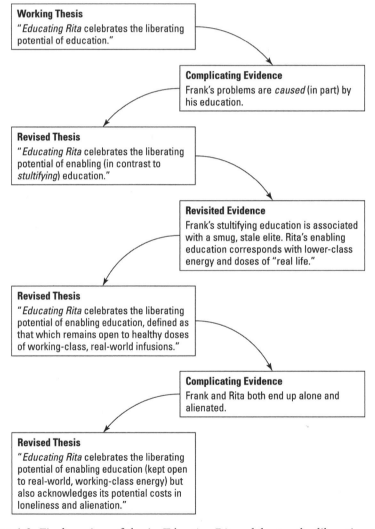

FIGURE 6.3 Final version of thesis: *Educating Rita* celebrates the liberating potential of enabling education (kept open to real-world, working-class energy) but also acknowledges its potential costs in loneliness and alienation.

mind that we have defined *thesis* as "a claim about the meaning of some feature or features of [her] subject" (page 149). Look especially for moments where the writer re-works her thesis in order to account for complicating evidence. Also notice to what degree the language of Moffat's title reappears in her paragraphs: does the title simply announce the subject of the article or does it also indicate the writer's evolving thesis? ☐

Whether or not there's a comfortable chair at home, make sure that you put aside time to read slowly and attentively. The article was written for an academic journal, after all; most of us are not part of Moffat's intended audience. Nevertheless, the article is accessible to any serious reader. Through the upcoming chapters of this book, we will return to its analytical content repeatedly.

B. LOCATING THE EVOLVING THESIS IN THE FINAL DRAFT

An evolving thesis not only stimulates analytical thinking but provides a form. Having achieved a final version of a thesis, such as the one above, *what next?* How and where do you locate the fully evolved thesis in the final draft? Why, for example, wouldn't a writer just offer this last statement of the thesis in his or her first paragraph and then prove it?

One answer to this last question has to do with the reader. The position articulated in the fully evolved thesis is in most cases too complex and too dependent on the various considerations that preceded it to be stated intelligibly and concisely in the introduction. By the time you get to drafting the final, or close-to-final, version of the essay, you will be writing with a reasonably secure sense of how you will conclude, but even then it is not always possible or desirable to try to encapsulate in a paper's first couple of sentences what it will actually take the whole paper to explain.

Another answer has to do with the writer: writing is a matter not just of communicating with and persuading readers but of communicating with and persuading yourself. The evolution of a thesis involves the discovery of new ways of thinking brought about by successive confrontations with evidence. *The history of your various changes in thinking is what the evolving thesis records (and, in some cases, it's the essay itself).*

A full answer to the questions of where to locate the fully evolved thesis in a final draft and how much of its evolution to include involves two separate but related issues: (1) the location of the thesis statement in relation to the conventional shapes of argument—induction and deduction—and

(2) the customary location of the thesis according to the protocols (ways of proceeding) of different disciplines.

The Evolving Thesis and Common Thought Patterns: Deduction and Induction

The standard definition of "deduction" is "a process based on inference from accepted principles" or "the process of drawing a conclusion from something known or assumed." A deductive argument draws out the implications—infers the consequences—of a position you already agree to. As a thought process, deduction reasons from the general to the particular.

For example, a deductive paper might state in its first paragraph that attitudes toward and rules governing sexuality in a given culture can be seen, at least in part, to have economic causes. The paper might then apply this principle, already assumed to be true, to the codes governing sexual behaviour in several cultures or to several kinds of sexual behaviour in a single culture. The writer's aim would be to use the general principle as a means of explaining selected features of particular cases. (She or he would, it should be added, thereby articulate what is implicit in the general principle as well.)

A deductive paper will thus state at or near its beginning the general principle governing its examination of evidence. For example, Mark Kingwell establishes—at the outset of "The Mirror Stage: Infinite Reflections on the Public Good"—the deductive path of his writing: "Before we can say what *the* public good is, or even whether there is one, we have to ask what *a* public good might be" (page 268). *It is important to note that the general principle stated at the beginning of the paper and the idea stated as the paper's conclusion are usually not the same.* Rather, the conclusion presents the idea that the writer has arrived at through the application of the principle.

An inductively organized paper typically begins not with a principle already assumed to be true but with particular data for which it seeks to generate some explanatory principle. While deduction moves by applying a generalization to particular cases in point, induction moves from the observation of individual cases to the formation of a general principle.

Ideally, the principle arrived at through inductive reasoning is not deemed a workable theory until the writer has examined all possible instances (every left-handed person, for example, if he or she wishes to theorize that left-handed people are better at spatial thinking than right-handers). But since this comprehensiveness is usually impossible, the thesis of an inductive paper (the principle or theory arrived at through the examination of particulars) is generally deemed acceptable if a writer can demonstrate that the theory is based on a reasonably sized sampling of representative instances. This matter of a writer's establishing the representativeness of his or her examples is taken up in detail in the previous chapter. For present purposes, suffice it to say that a child who arrives at the thesis that all orange food tastes bad on the basis of squash and carrots has not based that theory on an adequate sampling of available evidence.

Keep in mind, though, that an analytical essay's "thought process" is never one hundred percent deductive or inductive. As noted in Chapter 2 of this book, such binaries can become straitjackets if taken to an extreme: "Most subjects cannot be adequately considered in terms of only two options—either this or that, with nothing in between" (page 34). So don't become a binary reader or, for that matter, a binary writer; instead, work on developing your awareness of how these two patterns of reasoning interweave and overlap.

We argue in this chapter that a thesis—the governing idea of an analysis—evolves through successive confrontations with evidence. *This evolution occurs whether the paper is primarily deductive or inductive.* Because the full version of the thesis statement doesn't emerge until the end in our procedure "Moving Through a Series of Complications," it might appear that the six steps will work only if you are thinking inductively. But in fact, as the *Educating Rita* example illustrates, in most cases induction and deduction operate in tandem.

It's true that in some disciplines (philosophy, for example), something close to an entirely deductive pattern of argument prevails. But writers using this thought pattern still, for the most part, repeatedly rearticulate and develop their deductive claims through a series of smaller, essentially inductive moves. In other words, the examination of particular cases that constitute a writer's evidence will be both deductive and inductive—clearly reflective of the general principle but also leading to new formulations that will in various ways modify the general principle.

✶TRY THIS: Study a group of like things inductively. You might, for example, use greeting cards aimed at women versus greeting cards aimed at men, a group of poems by one author, or ads for one kind of product (jeans) or aimed at one target group (teenage girls). Make use of Five-Step Analysis to compile and organize a set of significant details about the data and then leap to a general claim about the group that you think is interesting and accurate. This generalization is your inductive principle. Then use the principle to examine deductively more data of the same kind. That is, you will be using your claim

not only to explain the pool of data but also to explore and evolve the claim more fully. □

The Evolving Thesis as Hypothesis and Conclusion in the Natural and Social Sciences

It is important to note that the way a thesis functions in a paper—whether it must be stated in full at the outset, for example, and what happens to it between the beginning of the paper and the end—is not the same for all disciplines. Disciplinary differences appear greatest as you move back and forth between courses in the humanities and courses in the natural and certain of the social sciences.

Not only do patterns of induction and deduction vary across academic disciplines, but so too does the terminology describing these patterns. The natural and social sciences typically use a pair of terms, *hypothesis* and *conclusion*, for the single term *thesis*. Because writing in the sciences is patterned according to the scientific method, writers in disciplines such as biology and psychology must report how the original thesis (hypothesis) was tested against empirical evidence and then conclude on this basis whether or not the hypothesis was confirmed.

The gap between this way of thinking about the thesis and the concept of an evolving thesis is not as large as it may seem. In fact, one of this chapter's main points—if not *the* main point—is that something must happen to the thesis between the introduction and the conclusion so that the conclusion does more than just reassert what has already been asserted in the beginning. To put this concept in the language of the sciences, the paper's hypothesis needs to be carefully tested against evidence, the results of which allow the writer to draw conclusions about the hypothesis's validity. So, in the sciences, while the hypothesis itself does not change, the testing of it and subsequent interpretation of those results produces commentary on and, often, qualifications of the paper's central claim.

So, in the natural and social sciences, successive reformulations of the thesis are less likely to be recorded and may not even be expressly articulated. But, as in all disciplines, the primary analytical activity in the sciences is to repeatedly reconsider the assumptions upon which a conclusion is based.

The Evolving Thesis and Introductory and Concluding Paragraphs

If you are not using the hypothesis/conclusion format, your final drafts could often begin by predicting the evolution of their theses. Thus, the

---

Voices Across the Curriculum

The Hypothesis in the Sciences

It should go without saying that if the empirical evidence doesn't confirm your hypothesis, you rethink your hypothesis, but it's a complex issue. Researchers whose hypotheses are not confirmed in fact often question their method ("if I had more subjects," or "a better manipulation of the experimental group," or "a better test of intelligence," etc.) as much as their hypothesis. And that's often legitimate. Part of the challenge of psychological research is its reliance on a long array of assumptions. Failure to confirm a hypothesis could mean a problem in any of that long array of assumptions. So failure to confirm your hypothesis is often difficult to interpret.

—Alan Tjeltveit, professor of psychology

The thesis in Experimental Psychology papers is the statement of the hypothesis. It is always carefully and explicitly stated in the last few sentences of the introduction. The hypothesis is usually a deductive statement such as: if color does influence mood, then an ambiguous picture printed on different colors of paper should be interpreted differently, depending on the color of the paper. Specifically, based on the results of Jones (1997), the pink paper should cause participants to perceive the picture as a more calm and restful image, and the green paper should cause the picture to be interpreted as a more anxious image.

—Laura Snodgrass, professor of psychology

The thesis is usually presented in the abstract and then again at the end of the introduction. Probably the most frequent writing error is not providing a thesis at all. Sometimes this is because the student doesn't have a thesis; other times it is because the student wants to maintain a sense of mystery about the paper, as if driving toward a dramatic conclusion. This actually makes it harder to read. The best papers are clear and up-front about what their point is, then use evidence and argument to support and evaluate the thesis. I encourage students to have a sentence immediately following their discussion of the background on the subject that can be as explicit as: "In this paper I will argue that while research on toxic effects of methyl bromide provides troubling evidence for severe physiological effects, conclusive proof of a significant environmental hazard is lacking at this time."

I try to avoid the use of the term "hypothesis." I think it gives the false sense that scientists always start with an idea about how something works. Frequently, that is not the case. Some of the best science has actually come from observation. Darwin's work on finches is a classic example. His ideas about adaptation probably derived from the observation.

—Bruce Wightman, professor of biology

(continued)

> Economists do make pretense to follow scientific methodology. Thus we are careful not to mix hypothesis and conclusion. I think it's important to distinguish between what is conjectured, the working hypothesis, and what ultimately emerges as a result of an examination of the evidence. Conclusions come only after some test has been passed.
>
> —James Marshall, professor of economics

Educating Rita paper might open by using a version of the seems-to-be-about-X gambit, claiming that *at first glance* the film seems to celebrate the liberating potential of education. You could then lay out the evidence for this view and proceed to complicate it in the ways we've discussed.

What typically happens is that you lead (usually at the end of the first paragraph or at the beginning of the second) with the best version of your thesis that you can come up with that will be understandable to your readers without a lengthy preamble. If you find yourself writing a page-long introductory paragraph to get to your initial statement of thesis, try settling for a simpler articulation of your central idea in its first appearance. As you move through the paper, substantiate, elaborate on, test, and qualify your paper's opening gambit.

The most important thing to do in the introductory paragraph of an analytical paper is to lay out a *genuine issue*, which is to say, something that seems to be *at stake* in whatever it is you are studying. Preferably, you should select a complex issue—one not easily resolved, seeming to have some truth on both sides—and not an overly general one. Otherwise you run the risk of writing a paper that proves the obvious or that radically oversimplifies.

Set up this issue as quickly and concretely as you can, avoiding generic (fits anything) comments, throat clearing, and review-style evaluations. As a general rule, you should assume that readers of your essay will need to know on page 1—preferably by the end of your first paragraph—what your paper is attempting to resolve or negotiate.

The first paragraph does not need to—and usually can't—offer your conclusion; it will take the body of your paper to accomplish that. It should, however, provide a quick look at particular details that set up the issue. Use these details to generate a *theory*, a *working hypothesis*, about whatever it is you think is at stake in the material. The rest of the paper will test and develop this theory.

Your concluding paragraph will offer the more carefully qualified and evolved version of your thesis that the body of your paper has allowed you to arrive at. Rather than just summarizing and restating what you said in your introduction, the concluding paragraph should leave readers with what you take to be your single best insight, and it should put what you have had to say into some kind of *perspective*. Peter Wynn Kirby accomplishes these objectives in "Japan's Long Nuclear Disaster Film" (pages 262–264): in a concise concluding paragraph, he presents his seminal insight and connects it to the need for action. See Chapter 10 for a more extended discussion of introductions and conclusions.

Voices Across the Curriculum

Recognizing Your Thesis

A thesis statement can be thought of in a number of ways: an opinion that needs backing up; a conclusion of an argument that the essay will make; what you have learned through your thinking/research; the answer to a question; what you are trying to persuade the reader to accept. Regardless of how you think of it, however, remember that a thesis statement names the point/purpose/goal of the essay.

Think of yourself as a judge in a courtroom; like a judge, you examine and weigh the opposing and often conflicting arguments (research) and develop your own perspective. In essence, your thesis is the judgment that you make after hearing and considering all of the evidence. In the essay itself, you then explain what evidence you examined, how you interpreted it, and why your interpretation—and your judgment/conclusion—is reasonable.

To develop a thesis statement, start with the topic—look at it, think about it, use the nature of the discipline to get at the main issue(s) surrounding it. Then, examine the assignment instructions. Ask yourself, *What is the point that I am trying to make in this essay? What am I trying to "prove"? What's my purpose for writing?* Specifically...

- Develop a "research question" (something that you want to know about the topic)
- Conduct your research (gather the relevant information)
- Answer the question *(Aha! Now I understand! This is the answer!)*
- Complete the following statement of purpose in a single phrase: PURPOSE: to show that...

This completed statement of purpose will be (more or less) your thesis statement. Your task in the essay then becomes to demonstrate to your reader that this statement is reasonable and that he or she should believe you or, at least, understand why you have come to think that this is so.

—Paul Gamache, writing instructor

C. PUTTING IT ALL TOGETHER

Let's look at one more example, this time using it to bring together all of the strategies that we have suggested so far for writing an analytical paper. The example is a student writer's exploratory draft on a painting called *Las Meninas* (Spanish for "the ladies-in-waiting") by the seventeenth-century painter Diego Velázquez. We have, by the way, selected a paper on a painting because all of the student's data (the painting) is on one page where you can keep referring back to it, trying to share in the writer's thought process. In a similar fashion, all of the visual data was on one page for the Notice and Focus assignment in Chapter 1 on the drawing "Pierre on the Island of Crete, 1975."

Look at the painting (Figure 6.4), and then read the student's draft. As you read, you will notice that much of the essay is still unfocused, relying

Figure 6.4 *Las Meninas* by Diego Velázquez, 1656, approximately 10'5" × 9', Museo del Prado, Madrid

upon a list-like description, but as we note in our chapter on interpretation (Chapter 3), careful description is a necessary stage in moving toward interpretations of evidence, especially in an exploratory draft where the writer is not yet committed to any single position. Notice how the writer's word choice in her descriptions prompts various kinds of interpretive leaps. We have added in blue our observations about how the writer is proceeding.

Velázquez's Intentions in *Las Meninas*

[1] Velázquez has been noted as being one of the best Spanish artists of all time. It seems that as Velázquez got older, his paintings became better. Towards the end of his life, he painted his masterpiece, *Las Meninas*. Out of all of his works, *Las Meninas* is the only known self-portrait of Velázquez. There is much to be said about *Las Meninas*. The painting is very complex, but some of the intentions that Velázquez had in painting *Las Meninas* are very clear. *[The writer opens with background information and a broad working thesis (underlined).]*

[2] First, we must look at the painting as a whole. The question which must be answered is, who is in the painting? The people are all members of the Royal Court of the Spanish monarch, Philip IV. In the centre is the daughter of the king who would eventually become Empress of Spain. Around her are her *meninas* or ladies-in-waiting. These *meninas* are all daughters of influential men. To the right of the *meninas* are dwarfs who are servants, and the family dog who looks fierce but is easily tamed by the foot of the little dwarf. The more unique people in the painting are Velázquez himself who stands to the left in front of a large canvas, the king and queen whose faces are captured in the obscure mirror, the man in the doorway, and the nun and man behind the *meninas*. To analyze this painting further, the relationship between characters must be understood. *[The writer describes the evidence and arrives at an operating assumption—focusing on the relationship between characters.]*

[3] Where is this scene occurring? Well, most likely it is in the palace. But, why is there no visible furniture? Is it because Velázquez didn't want the viewers to become distracted from his true intentions? I believe it is to show that this is not just a painting of an actual event. This is an event out of his imagination. *[The writer begins pushing observations to tentative conclusions by asking "So what?"]*

[4] Now, let us become better acquainted with the characters. The child in the centre is the most visible. All the light is shining on her. Maybe

Velázquez is suggesting that she is the next light for Spain and that even God has approved her by shining all the available light on her. Back in those days there was a belief in the divine right of kings, so this just might be what Velázquez is saying. *[The writer starts ranking evidence for importance and continues to ask "So what?"; she arrives at a possible interpretation of the painter's intention.]*

[5] The next people of interest are the ones behind the *meninas*. The woman in the habit might be a nun and the man a priest.

[6] The king and queen are the next group of interesting people. They are in the mirror, which is to suggest they are present, but they are not as visible as they might be. Velázquez suggests that they are not always at the centre where everyone would expect them to be. *[The writer continues using Notice and Focus plus asking "So what?"; the writer has begun tackling evidence that might conflict with her first interpretation.]*

[7] The last person and the most interesting is Velázquez. He dominates the painting along with the little girl. He takes up the whole left side along with his gigantic easel. But what is he painting? As I previously said, he might be painting the king and queen. But I also think he could be pretending to paint us, the viewers. The easel really gives this portrait an air of mystery because Velázquez knows that we, the viewers, want to know what he is painting. *[The writer starts doing 10 on 1 with her selection of the most significant detail.]*

[8] The appearance of Velázquez is also interesting. His eyes are focused out here. They are not focused on what is going on around him. It is a steady stare. Also interesting is his confident stance. He was confident enough to place himself in the painting of the royal court. <u>I think that Velázquez wants the king to give him the recognition he deserves by including him in the "family."</u> And the symbol on his vest is the symbol given to a painter by the king to <u>show that his status and brilliance have been appreciated by the monarch</u>. It is unknown how it got there. It is unlikely that Velázquez put it there himself. That would be too outright and Velázquez was the type to give his messages subtly. Some say that after Velázquez's death, King Philip IV himself painted it to finally give <u>Velázquez the credit he deserved for being a loyal friend and servant</u>. *[The writer continues doing 10 on 1 and asking "So what?"; she arrives at three tentative theses (underlined).]*

[9] I believe that Velázquez was very ingenious by putting his thoughts and feelings into a painting. He didn't want to offend the king who had done so much for him. It paid off for Velázquez because he did finally get what he

wanted, even if it was after he died. *[The writer concludes and is now ready to redraft in order to tighten links between evidence and claims, formulate a better working thesis, and make this thesis evolve.]*

There are a number of good things about this draft. If you take the time to study it and our observations about it, you can train yourself to turn a more discerning eye toward your own works-in-progress, especially in that all-important early stage where you are writing to discover ideas. As we say at the beginning of this chapter, far and away the biggest problem for student writers when required to produce a thesis-driven paper is that their anxiety about finding a thesis causes them to ignore the evidence and to choose instead to "match" it demonstration-style to the first tenable idea they conjure up. That is, they revert to the pattern we refer to earlier as 1 on 10 (see Chapter 5), wherein one unchanging idea is repeated over and over again about each piece of evidence.

Description to Analysis: The Exploratory Draft

In our chapter on observing (Chapter 1), we argue that most writers do not spend enough time in the data-gathering stage because they rush prematurely to conclusions. In that chapter we suggest some key words and procedures for making the observation stage more systematic. We suggest that the words "interesting," "strange," "revealing," and "significant" are useful for guiding the observation process, as is the tactic of shifting in the observation stage from "What do I think?" to "What do I notice?" The move from description to analysis and interpretation begins at the point when you select certain details in your evidence as more important—more telling—than others and explain why you chose as you did. Study the student's draft for this Notice and Focus (selection) process. The writer has, for example, used the "interesting" prompt to press herself to notice and emphasize particular details in her evidence. In her next draft, she might want to try one or more of the other prompts. Allowing herself to notice things that seem strange in the painting could be a fruitful move. In a final draft, she will want to craft more substantive, less list-like transitions. For an exploratory draft, however, cataloguing and starting to ask "So what?" about interesting detail is a productive tactic.

As you can see, the writer has not wasted time trying for a polished introductory paragraph. There will be time for that later. She has instead crafted an opening that allows her to get started and to start fast—no rambling prefatory material. This introduction, with its overly broad working thesis, does its job. It provides enough direction to guide the writer in her initial examination of evidence, using the artist's intention as her *interpretive context*. The purpose of the exploratory draft is to use writing as a means of arriving at a working thesis that your next draft can more fully evolve. Most writers find that potential theses emerge near the end of the exploratory draft—which is the case in the student draft (see the three claims that are underlined in paragraph 8). We will say more later on about what might happen to this introduction and working thesis in a subsequent draft.

Interpretive Leaps and Complicating Evidence

Notice that as early as paragraphs 3 and 4, the writer has begun to push herself to tentative conclusions (interpretive leaps) about the meaning of selected features of her evidence. What is especially good about the draft is that it reveals the writer's willingness to push on from her first idea (reading the painting as an endorsement of the divine right of kings, expressed by the light shining on the princess) by seeking out *complicating evidence*. The main point of this chapter is that you need to actively seek out evidence that seems not to fit your ideas and use it to make your thesis evolve. As we say in the section of this chapter on the thesis as a camera lens, not only does the thesis direct a writer's way of looking at evidence, but the analysis of evidence should also direct and redirect (bring about revision of) the thesis.

The writer could have settled for the divine-right-of-kings idea, and then simply foregrounded details in the picture that would corroborate this idea, such as the deferential bowing of the *meninas* arranged in a circle with the princess at the centre. But this potential thesis would not have accounted for enough of the evidence, and it would have forced the writer to ignore evidence which clearly doesn't fit, such as the small size and decentring of the king and queen and the large size and foregrounding of the painter himself. Rather than ignoring these potentially troublesome (for her initial idea) details, the writer instead zooms in on them, making the painter's representation of himself and of his employers the "1" for doing 10 on 1 (making a number of observations about a single representative piece of evidence and analyzing it in depth). This analytical move produces a burst of interpretive thinking in the form of three related claims (underlined in the student's draft, paragraph 8), all of which have thesis potential.

Revising the Exploratory Draft

Now what? The writer is ready to rewrite the paper in order to more carefully formulate and evolve her thesis. What could she do better as she reviews her evidence in preparation for starting this next draft?

First, she could make more use of Five-Step Analysis (see Chapter 1), looking for significant patterns of repetition and contrast (exact repetition, strands, and binaries—organizing contrasts). What kinds of exact or nearly *exact repetitions* are there in the picture? Examples: the pictures in the background, the fact that both the dwarf and the painter, each on his own side of the painting, stare confidently and directly at the viewer. What might you select as *strands* (repetition of a similar kind of detail)? Examples: One strand might be details having to do with family. Another might include servants (dwarf, *meninas*, dog? painter?). There are also a number of details having to do with art and the making of art. Where in the painting, and in the student's draft, do you find *organizing contrasts*—binaries? Examples: royalty/commoners; employers/servants; large/small; foreground/background; central (prominent)/marginalized (less prominent).

Along with searching out significant patterns of repetition and opposition in her evidence, the writer also needs to make more aggressive use of the "So what?" question, asking it repeatedly about pieces of evidence and about her own claims, thus pressing herself to arrive at a range of possible answers until she finds the one that seems to best fit the evidence. The key in revision is to ask "So what?" not just of the evidence but also of your own observations. "So what?" is shorthand for questions like the following: Where does this get me? What am I getting at here? What (and what else) might I conclude about this feature of my evidence?

So what that the king and queen are small, but the painter, princess, and dwarf are all large and fairly equal in size and prominence? *So what* that there are size differences in the painting? What might large or small size mean? Here are some possible answers to these "So what?" questions:

- Perhaps the king and queen have been reduced so that Velázquez can showcase their daughter, the princess.
- Perhaps the size and physical prominence of the king and queen are relatively unimportant. In that case, what matters is that they are a presence, always overseeing events (an idea implied but not developed by the writer in paragraph 6).
- Perhaps the relative size and/or prominence of figures in the painting can be read as indicators of their importance or of what the painter wants to say about their importance.

- Perhaps the painter is demonstrating his own ability to make the king and queen any size—any level of importance—he chooses. Although the writer does not overtly say so, the king and queen are among the smallest as well as the least visible figures.

The writer's answers to these "So what?" questions cause her to generate a new set of claims about the painter's intention. The writer has, in other words, made her way through the first five steps of the procedure for making a thesis evolve using complication (see page 153). She is now ready for step 6, which calls first for a return to step 2. Here she will begin again by seeing how well the evolved claims can be made to account for evidence. She will locate evidence that is not yet adequately accounted for and query the significance of the evidence that seems not to fit in order to further evolve the claim (steps 3, 4, and 5).

Testing the Adequacy of the Thesis

As we see, the writer of the *Las Meninas* paper has already begun the process of testing her thesis against evidence that seems not to fit and then using that evidence to reformulate her thesis. The evidence that the writer includes in paragraphs 6 and 7 (the decentring of the king and queen and the prominence and confident stare of the painter) causes her to drop her initial thinking—the idea that the painter's intentions were clear and that the primary intention was to endorse the divine right of kings. The direction that her thinking takes next is not, however, an entirely new idea. The shift she is apparently making (but not yet overtly articulating) is from the painting as showcase of royal power to the painting as showcase of the painter's own power.

Given the answers posed above to the "So what?" question about the size and importance of the king and queen relative to the size and importance of the painter—parallel if not greater in prominence to the princess herself—the writer should probably choose the second of the two potential theses arrived at in paragraph 8. That idea—that the painting is a bid for recognition of the painter's status and brilliance—explains more of the evidence than anything else she has come up with so far. It explains, for example, the painter's prominence and the relative insignificance of the monarchs; the painter, in effect, creates their stature (size, power) in the world through his paintings. Framed in a mirror and appearing to hang on the wall, the king and queen are, arguably, suspended among the painter's paintings, mere reflections of themselves—or, rather, the painter's reflection of them.

We are not going to rewrite the student's draft, but here is how the next draft might go. Having chosen the status-and-brilliance idea as a more satisfactory theory, she would use the first part of her next draft to share with her readers the thinking that got her to the three ideas that emerged at the end of her exploratory draft and caused her to pick one of them. The working thesis of this new draft might be worded using the seems-to-be-about-X formula: the painting *seems* to be about the princess and how all are waiting upon her but may *actually* be more concerned with the painter himself. (Notice that this new working thesis sums up the history of the writer's thinking about the picture in a way that is more specific than her first working thesis but is not so specific that it would leave no room for leading readers through her chain of thought.)

The writer would next utilize steps 2 and 3 of the procedure (pages 153–154, offering first summary and analysis of details in the picture that endorse the centrality of the princess and the power of monarchy, noting potentially conflicting details, and explaining why these details don't fit. Using step 4—asking "So what?" repeatedly of the details that seem not to fit—she would show us how it is possible to arrive at the three claims in paragraph 8 of her first draft. In this way, the paper retraces and shares with readers the evolution of the thesis. This recursive process of trying on, testing, and evolving the thesis continues until you are satisfied that the thesis statement accounts for your evidence as fully and accurately as possible.

Let's see how well the status-and-brilliance idea does in accounting for details in the painting. This thesis seems useful in accounting for the presence of the large dwarf in the right-hand foreground. Positioned in a way that links him with the painter, the dwarf arguably furthers the painting's message and does so, like much else in the painting, in the form of a loaded joke: the small ("dwarfed" by the power of others) are brought forward and made big. What other features of the painting might the thesis account for? How about the various ways that the painting seems to deny viewers' expectations? Both by decentring the monarchs and concealing what is on the easel, the painter again emphasizes his power, in this case, over the viewers (among whom might be the king and queen if their images on the back wall are mirrored reflections of them standing, like us, in front of the painting). He is not bound by anyone's expectations and in fact appears to take a certain pleasure in using viewers' expectations to manipulate them: he can make them wish to see something he has the power to withhold.

Does this mean that the status-and-brilliance thesis is adequately evolved? In this case, as the writer locates additional evidence that the thesis explains, it will continue to evolve but perhaps only slightly. For example, if (as the writer has said) the painter is demonstrating that he can make the members of the royal family any size he wants, then the painting is not only a bid for recognition but also a playful, though not so subtle, threat: be aware of my power and treat me well, or suffer the consequences. As artist, the painter decides how the royal family will be seen. The king and queen depend on the painter—as they do in a different way on the princess, with whom Velázquez makes himself equal in prominence—to extend and perpetuate their power.

Before leaving this example we want to emphasize that the version of the thesis that we have just proposed is not necessarily the "right" answer. Looked at in a different context, the painting might have been explained primarily as a demonstration of the painter's mastery of the tools of his trade—light, for example, and perspective. But our proposed revision of the thesis for the *Las Meninas* paper meets two important criteria for evaluating the adequacy of a thesis statement:

1. It unifies the observations the writer has made.
2. It is capable of accounting for a wide range of evidence.

A plausible thesis in an analytical paper makes a claim about the meaning of features of the evidence that would not have been immediately obvious (not obviously true) to readers.

Remember that the thesis develops through successive complications. Allowing your thesis to run up against potentially conflicting evidence ("But what about this?") enables you to build upon your initial idea, extending the range of evidence it can accurately account for by clarifying and qualifying its key terms. Although throwing out the old thesis and starting over may be what is needed, you should first try to use evidence that is not accounted for by your current thesis as a means of evolving the thesis further.

D. THE THESIS-BUILDER'S BOTTOM LINE

1. A thesis is an idea that you formulate and reformulate about your subject. It should offer a theory about the meaning of evidence that would not have been immediately obvious to your readers.
2. Look for a thesis by focusing on an area of your subject that is open to opposing viewpoints or multiple interpretations. Rather than

attempting to locate a single right answer, search for something that raises questions.

3. Treat your thesis as a hypothesis to be tested rather than an obvious truth.

4. The body of your paper should serve not only to substantiate the thesis by demonstrating its value in selecting and explaining evidence, but also to bring the opening version of the thesis into better focus.

5. Evolve your thesis—move it forward—by seeing the questions that each new formulation of it prompts you to ask.

6. Develop the implications of your evidence and of your observations as fully as you can by repeatedly asking "So what?"

7. When you encounter potentially conflicting evidence (or interpretations of that evidence), don't simply abandon your thesis. Take advantage of the complications to expand, qualify, and refine your thesis until you arrive at the most accurate explanation of the evidence that you can manage.

8. Arrive at the final version of your thesis by returning to your initial formulation—the position you set out to explore—and restating it in the more carefully qualified way that you have arrived at through the body of your paper.

9. To check that your thesis has evolved, locate and compare the various versions of it throughout the draft. Have you done more than demonstrate the general validity of an unqualified claim?

ASSIGNMENT

Earlier in this chapter, a *Try This* exercise encouraged you to track the evolution of Kelly Hannah-Moffat's thesis in her article "Gendering Risk at What Cost: Negotiations of Gender and Risk in Canadian Women's Prisons." That exercise also emphasized the language of her title, which features two of the article's key concepts: gender and risk.

Return to Hannah-Moffat's article and notice that, in addition to a title, it contains three sub-titles, which divide the article into four sections. The following questions, intended for class discussion, provide a means of assessing this four-part development:

1. Using Five-Step Analysis, explain to what degree the repetitions of "gender" and "risk" affect our understanding of those terms. Does Hannah-Moffat create strands (groupings of similar words) that contribute to her evolving thesis?

2. Which section do you think contains the most refined version of the article's thesis?

3. Does the longest section ("Gendered Adaptations of Risk: Practitioners' Ad Hoc Responses") provide evidence that affects the thesis significantly?

4. The fourth section, which is only a single paragraph, presents the article's conclusion. How does it relate, analytically, to the article's first section (the three introductory paragraphs)? Can you find a version of the thesis in those first three paragraphs? If so, which sentences express it? If not, why does Hannah-Moffat delay her thesis?

CHAPTER

7

Recognizing and Fixing Weak
Thesis Statements

It takes time and effort to make a thesis evolve. The path from your working thesis to the final, fully articulated and qualified version of the central claim is usually circuitous—fraught with false starts, dead ends, recursive returns to earlier pieces of evidence and evolutions of the thesis. And in any piece of writing, you can only get so far from the start to the finish. Virtually any thesis can be evolved further—taken in another direction and/or fine-tuned—by adding complicating evidence to broaden or narrow its scope.

Obviously, the farther along you *begin* on the path from your working thesis to its final version, the more efficiently you will proceed and the further you will get. A working thesis that is already partially qualified, in language you have already subjected to reworking, is far more likely to produce a successful paper than an opening claim that is overstated, fuzzy, unsupportable, or otherwise weak.

So it matters a lot what kind of thesis you start with. The point at which inexperienced writers choose a thesis is, as we discuss early in Chapter 5, a chronic problem site. It's at this point in the paper-writing process—as writers turn from preliminary data gathering and analysis to actually composing a draft—that they are most likely to revert to the kinds of weak theses characteristic of five-paragraph-form demonstrations.

The aim of this chapter is to discuss ways of *starting* with an improved claim. Toward that end, the chapter will make you conscious of what weak theses look and sound like, in the hope that you will then be less likely to revert to them. Think of the chapter as a version of habits of mind (Chapter 2) that is specifically addressed to thesis construction. This chapter is organized in problem–solution format. Using actual excerpts from student papers, it will exemplify five kinds of weak thesis statements and show how they can be reworded in ways that will stimulate a thesis to evolve.

A. FIVE KINDS OF WEAK THESES AND HOW TO FIX THEM

A *strong thesis* makes a claim that (1) requires analysis to support and evolve it and (2) offers some point about the significance of your evidence that would not have been immediately obvious to your readers. By contrast, a *weak thesis* either makes no claim or makes a claim that does not need proving. As a quick flash-forward, here are the five kinds of weak thesis statements—ones that

1. make no claim ("This paper will examine the pros and cons of …");
2. are obviously true or a statement of fact ("Exercise is good for you");
3. restate conventional wisdom ("Love conquers all");
4. offer personal conviction as the basis for the claim ("Shopping malls are wonderful places");
5. make an overly broad claim ("Individualism is good").

Weak Thesis Type 1: The Thesis Makes No Claim

The following statements are not productive theses because they do not advance an idea about the topics the papers will explore.

Problem Examples

I'm going to write about Darwin's concerns with evolution in *The Origin of Species*.

This paper will address the characteristics of a good corporate manager.

The problem examples each name a subject and link it to the intention to write about it, but they don't make any claim about the subject. As a result, they direct neither the writer nor the reader toward some position or plan of attack. The second problem example begins to move toward a point of view through the use of the value judgment "good," but this term is too broad to guide the analysis. The statement-of-intention thesis invites a list: one paragraph for each quality the writer chooses to call good. Even if the thesis were rephrased as "This paper will address why a good corporate manager needs to learn to delegate responsibility," the thesis would not adequately suggest why such a claim would need to be argued or defended.

There is, in short, nothing at stake, no issue to be resolved. A writer who produces a thesis of this type is probably unduly controlled by "banking"—that relatively passive, information in/information out approach to learning we discuss in Chapter 2, "Habitual Thinking."

Solution

Raise specific issues for the essay to explore.

Solution Examples

Darwin's concern with survival of the fittest in *The Origin of Species* initially leads him to neglect a potentially conflicting aspect of his theory of evolution—survival as a matter of interdependence.

The very trait that makes for an effective corporate manager—the drive to succeed—can also make the leader domineering and therefore ineffective.

Some disciplines expect writers to offer statements of method and/or intention in their papers' openings. Generally, however, these openings also make a claim: for example, "In this paper I will examine how the sponsorship scandal undermined Prime Minister Martin's attempt to present the Liberal platform during the 2004 federal election campaign," *not* "In this paper I will discuss the Liberal platform during the 2004 federal election campaign." (See Chapter 10, "Introductions and Conclusions," for further discussion of using overt statements of intention.)

✻*TRY THIS:* In the final paragraph of her article's opening section (page 285), Kelly Hannah-Moffat offers a statement of intention and method. Emphasizing that her "discussion is based on interview data," she announces what it is that the "article examines." Does Hannah-Moffat succeed in presenting a working thesis for the analytical discussion that is to follow? Or do you find that the paragraph displays any of the weaknesses mentioned here in Chapter 7? □

Weak Thesis Type 2: The Thesis Is Obviously True or Is a Statement of Fact

The following statements are not productive theses because they do not require proof. A thesis needs to be an assertion with which it would be possible for readers to disagree.

Problem Examples

The jeans industry targets its advertisements to appeal to young adults.

The flight from teaching to research and publishing in higher education is a controversial issue in the academic world. I will show different views and aspects concerning this problem.

If few people would disagree with the claim that a thesis makes, there is no point in writing an analytical paper on it. Though one might deliver an inspirational speech on a position that virtually everyone would support (such as the value of tolerance), endorsements and appreciations don't usually lead to analysis; they merely invite people to feel good about their convictions.

In the second problem example, few readers would disagree with the fact that the issue is "controversial." In the second sentence of that example, the writer has begun to identify a point of view—that the flight from teaching is a "problem"—but her next declaration, that she will "show different views and aspects," is an overly vague statement of intention, not an idea. The phrasing of the claim is noncommittal and so broad that it prevents the writer from formulating a workable thesis. If you find yourself writing theses of this type, review the discussion of the habits of mind presented in Chapter 2: banking, generalizations, and clichés.

Solution

Find some avenue of *inquiry*—a question about the facts or an issue raised by them. Make an assertion with which it would be possible for readers to disagree.

Solution Examples

By inventing new terms, such as "loose fit" and "relaxed fit," the jeans industry has attempted to normalize, even glorify, its product for an older and fatter generation.

The "flight from teaching" to research and publishing in higher education is a controversial issue in the academic world. As I will attempt to show, the controversy is based to a significant degree on a false assumption, that doing research necessarily leads teachers away from the classroom.

Weak Thesis Type 3: The Thesis Restates Conventional Wisdom

Restatement of one of the many clichés that constitute a culture's conventional wisdom is not a productive thesis unless you have something to say about it that hasn't been said many times before.

Problem Examples

An important part of one's college education is learning to better understand others' points of view.

From cartoons in the morning to adventure shows at night, there is too much violence on television.

"I was supposed to bring the coolers; you were supposed to bring the chips!" exclaimed ex-Beatle Ringo Starr, who appeared on TV commercials for Sun County Wine Coolers a few years ago. By using rock music to sell a wide range of products, the advertising agencies, in league with corporate giants such as Pepsi, Michelob, and Ford, have corrupted the spirit of rock and roll.

All of these examples say nothing worth proving because they are clichés. ("Conventional wisdom" is a polite term for cliché.) Most clichés were fresh ideas once, but over time they have become trite, prefabricated forms of nonthinking. Faced with a phenomenon that requires a response, many inexperienced writers rely on a knee-jerk reaction: they resort to a small set of culturally approved "answers." In this sense, clichés resemble statements of fact. So commonly accepted that most people nod to them without thinking, statements of conventional wisdom make people feel a comfortable sense of agreement with one another. The problem with this kind of packaged solution is that because conventional wisdom is so general and so conventional, it doesn't teach anybody—including the writer—anything. Worse, since the cliché masquerades as an idea, it prevents the writer from engaging in a fresh, open-minded exploration of his or her subject.

There is some truth in all of the problem examples above, but none of them *complicates* its position. A thoughtful reader could, for example, respond to the claim that advertising has corrupted the spirit of rock and roll by suggesting that rock and roll was highly commercial long before it colonized the airwaves. The conventional wisdom that rock and roll is somehow pure and honest while advertising is phony and exploitative invites the savvy writer to formulate a thesis that overturns these clichés. As our solution example demonstrates, one could argue that rock actually has improved advertising, not that ads have ruined rock—or, alternatively, that rock has shrewdly marketed idealism to a gullible populace. At the least, a writer deeply committed to the original thesis would do better to examine what it was that Ringo was selling—what he stands for in this particular case—than to discuss rock and advertising in such general terms.

To help you liberate yourself from enslavement to conventional wisdom, take another look at the various discussions in Chapter 2 of how our culture influences us as thinkers and writers. See in particular the preliminary discussion about skepticism and the sections on judging, debate-style argument, and opinions.

Solution

Seek to complicate—see more than one point of view on—your subject. Avoid conventional wisdom unless you can qualify it or introduce a fresh perspective on it.

Solution Examples

While an important part of one's college education is learning to better understand others' points of view, a persistent danger is that the students will simply be required to substitute the teacher's answers for the ones they grew up uncritically believing.

While some might argue that the presence of rock and roll soundtracks in TV commercials has corrupted rock's spirit, this point of view not only falsifies the history of rock but also blinds us to the ways that the music has improved the quality of television advertising.

✯**TRY THIS:** You can learn a lot about writing strong thesis statements by analyzing and rewriting weak ones. Rewrite the following three weak theses. As in the case of our solution examples, revising will require you to add information and thinking to the weak theses. Try, in other words, to come up with some interesting claims that most readers would not already have thought of to develop the subject of television violence. (The third thesis you will recognize as a problem example for which we offered no solution.) ☐

1. In this paper I will discuss police procedures in recent domestic violence cases.
2. The way that the media portrayed the events of April 30, 1975, when Saigon fell, greatly influenced the final perspectives of the American people toward the end result of the Vietnam War.
3. From cartoons in the morning to adventure shows at night, there is too much violence on television.

Weak Thesis Type 4: The Thesis Offers Personal Conviction as the Basis for the Claim

A statement of one's personal convictions or one's likes or dislikes does not alone supply sufficient grounds for a productive thesis.

Problem Examples

The songs of the punk rock group Minor Threat relate to the feelings of individuals who dare to be different. Their songs are just composed of pure emotion. Pure emotion is very important in music, because it serves as a vehicle to convey the important message of individuality. Minor Threat's songs are meaningful to me because I can identify with them.

Sir Thomas More's *Utopia* proposes an unworkable set of solutions to society's problems because, like communist Russia, it suppresses individualism.

Although I agree that environmentalists and business should work together to ensure the ecological future of the world, and that this cooperation is beneficial for both sides, the indisputable fact is that environmental considerations should always be a part of any decision that is made. Any individual, if he looks deeply enough into his soul, knows what is right and what is wrong. The environment should be protected because it is the right thing to do, not because someone is forcing you to do it.

Like conventional wisdom, personal likes and dislikes can lead inexperienced writers into knee-jerk reactions of approval or disapproval, often expressed in a moralistic tone. The writers of the problem examples above assume that their primary job is to judge their subjects, or testify to their worth, not to evaluate them analytically. As a result, such writers lack critical detachment not only from their topics but, crucially, from their own assumptions and biases. They have *taken personal opinions for self-evident truths.* You can test a thesis for this problem by asking if the writer's response to questions about the thesis would be "because I think so."

The most blatant version of this tendency occurs in the third problem example, which asserts, "Any individual, if he looks deeply enough into his soul, knows what is right and what is wrong. The environment should be protected because it is the right thing to do." Translation (only slightly exaggerated): "Any individual who thinks about the subject will obviously agree with me because my feelings and convictions feel right to me and therefore they must be universally and self-evidently true." The problem is that this writer is not distinguishing between his own likes and dislikes (or private convictions) and what he takes to be right, real, or true for everyone else. Testing an idea against your own feelings and experience is not an adequate means of establishing whether something is accurate or true.

Solution

Try on other points of view honestly and dispassionately; *treat your ideas as hypotheses to be tested rather than obvious truths.* In the following solution examples, we have replaced opinions (in the form of self-evident truths) with ideas—theories about the meaning and significance of the subjects that could be supported and qualified with evidence.

Solution Examples

Sir Thomas More's *Utopia* treats individualism as a serious but remediable social problem. His radical treatment of what we might now call "socialization" attempts to redefine the meaning and origin of individual identity.

> While cooperation between environmentalists and business is essential to the eco-
> logical future of the world, what matters most is that pressure be applied to private
> corporations—to ensure that they confront environmental concerns that may not
> benefit them in the short run.

It is fine, of course, to write about what you believe and to consult your feelings as you formulate an idea. But the risk you run in arguing from your unexamined feelings and convictions is that you will prematurely dismiss from consideration anything that is unfamiliar or does not immediately conform to what you already believe. The less willing you are to test these established and habitual convictions, the less chance you will have to refine or expand the ways in which you think. You will continue to play the same small set of tunes in response to everything you hear. And without the ability to think from multiple perspectives, you will be less able to defend your convictions against the ideas that challenge them because you won't really have examined the logic of your own beliefs—you just believe them.

At the root of this problem lurks an anti-analytical bias that predisposes many writers to see any challenge to their habitual ways of thinking as the enemy and to view those who would raise this challenge as cynics who don't believe in anything. Such writers often feel personally attacked, when in fact the conviction they are defending is not really so personal after all. Consider, for example, the first two problem examples above, in which both writers take individualism to be an incontestable value. Where does this conviction come from? Apparently, neither of the writers arrived at the thesis independent of the pervasive American culture to which they were exposed, permeated as it is by the "rugged individualism" of John Wayne and Sylvester Stallone movies.

In other words, "individualism" as an undefined blanket term verges on *cultural cliché*. That it is always good or positive is a piece of conventional wisdom. But part of becoming educated is to take a look at such global and undefined ideas that one has uncritically assimilated. For instance, what Bruce McCall describes as "the quasi-British Canadian idea of modesty and self-restraint" (page 94) is itself a challenge to rugged individualism. From a Canadian perspective, Americans are "jammed permanently in extroverted high gear, confident to the brink of, if not over the edge of, arrogance; strident, take-charge, can-do—fatiguing."

In light of such perspectives, the writers of the first two problem examples would have to question *to what extent* they should attack a book or support a rock band merely on the basis of whether or not each hon-ours individualism. If the author of the second problem example had been willing to explore how Thomas More conceives of and critiques individualism, he or she might have been able to arrive at a revealing analysis of the tension between the individual and the collective rather than merely dismissing the entire book.

This is not to say that the first requirement of analytical writing is that you abandon all conviction or argue for a position in which you do not believe. But we are suggesting that the risk of remaining trapped within a limited set of culturally inherited opinions is greater than the risk that you will run by submerging your personal likes or dislikes and instead honestly and dispassionately trying on different points of view. The energy of analytical writing comes not from rehearsing your convictions but from treating them as hypotheses to be tested, as scientists do—from finding the boundaries of your ideas, reshaping parts of them, seeing connections you have not seen before.

When a writing assignment asks for your ideas about a subject, it is usually not asking for your opinion—what you think *of* the subject—but for your reasoning on *what* and *how* the subject means. As we discuss in Chapter 2, *an idea is not the same thing as an opinion.* The two are closely related, since both, in theory, are based on reasoning. Opinions, however, often take the form of judgments, the reflections of our personal attitudes and beliefs. While having ideas necessarily involves your attitudes and beliefs, it is a more disinterested process than is opinion making. The formulation of ideas, which is one of the primary aims of analysis, involves questioning. By contrast, opinions are often habitual responses, mental reflexes that kick in automatically when an answer seems to be called for. (The sections on personalizing, judging, and opinions in Chapter 2 explain more fully how placing too much emphasis on yourself can interfere with your thinking.)

Weak Thesis Type 5: The Thesis Makes an Overly Broad Claim

An overly general claim is not a productive thesis because it oversimplifies and is too broad to direct development. Such statements usually lead either to say-nothing theses or to reductive either/or thinking.

Problem Examples

Violent revolutions have had both positive and negative results for man.

There are many similarities and differences between the Carolingian and the Burgundian Renaissances.

Othello is a play about love and jealousy.

It is important to understand why leaders act in a leadership role. What is the driving force? Is it an internal drive for the business or group to succeed, or is it an internal drive for the leader to dominate over others?

Overly generalized theses avoid complexity. (See the discussion of generalizing in Chapter 2.) At their worst, as in our first three examples, they settle for assertions broad enough to fit almost any subject and thus say nothing in particular about the subject at hand. A writer in the early stages of his or her drafting process might begin working from a general idea, such as what is positive and negative about violent revolutions or how two historical periods are like and unlike, but these formulations are not specific enough to guide the development of a paper. Such broad categories are likely to generate listing, not thinking. We can, for example, predict that the third thesis will prompt the writer to produce a couple of paragraphs demonstrating that *Othello* is about love and then a couple of paragraphs demonstrating that *Othello* is about jealousy, without analyzing what the play says about either.

Our fourth problem example, inquiring into the motivation of leaders in business, demonstrates how the desire to generalize can drive writers into logical errors. Because this thesis overtly offers readers two possible answers to its central question, it appears to avoid the problem of oversimplifying a complex subject. But this appearance of complexity is deceptive because the writer has reduced the possibilities to only two answers—an either/or choice: Is "the driving force" of leadership a desire for group success or a desire to dominate others? Readers can only be frustrated by being asked to choose between two such options when the more logical answer probably lies somewhere in between or somewhere else altogether. (See the discussion of binaries in Chapter 2.)

The best way to avoid the problem evident in the first three examples is to sensitize yourself to the characteristic phrasing of such theses: "both positive and negative," "many similarities and differences," or "both pros and cons." Virtually everything from meatloaf to taxes can be both positive and negative.

Solution

Convert broad categories and generic (fits anything) claims to more specific, more qualified assertions; find ways to bring out the complexity of your subject.

Solution Examples

Although violent revolutions begin to redress long-standing social inequities, they often do so at the cost of long-term economic dysfunction and the suffering that attends it.

The differences between the Carolingian and Burgundian Renaissances outweigh the similarities.

Although *Othello* appears to attack jealousy, it also supports the skepticism of the jealous characters over the naïveté of the lovers.

B. HOW TO REPHRASE THESIS STATEMENTS: SPECIFY AND SUBORDINATE

Clear symptoms of an overly generalized thesis can be found by looking at its grammar. Each of the first three problem examples on page 185, for example, relies mostly on nouns rather than verbs; the nouns announce a broad heading, but the verbs don't do anything with or to the nouns. In grammatical terms, these thesis statements don't *predicate* (affirm or assert something about the subject of a proposition). Instead, they rely on anemic verbs such as "is" or "are," which function as equal signs that link general nouns with general adjectives rather than specifying more complex relationships.

By replacing the equal sign with a more active verb, you can force yourself to advance some sort of claim, as in one of our solutions; for example, "The differences between the Carolingian and Burgundian Renaissances *outweigh* the similarities." While this reformulation remains quite general, it at least begins to direct the writer along a more particular line of argument. Replacing the "is" or "are" equal signs with stronger verbs will usually impel you to rank ideas in some order of importance and to assert some conceptual relation among them.

In other words, the best way to remedy the problem of overgeneralization is to *move toward specificity in word choice, in sentence structure, and in idea.* If you find yourself writing "The economic situation is bad," consider revising it to "The tax policies of the current government threaten to reduce the tax burden on the middle class by sacrificing education and health care programs for everyone."

Here's the problem/solution in schematic form:

Broad Noun +	**Weak Verb** +	**Vague, Evaluative Modifier**
The economic situation	is	bad

Specific Noun +	**Active Verb** +	**Specific Modifier**
(The) tax policies (of the current government)	threaten to reduce (the tax burden on the middle class)	by sacrificing education health care programs for everyone

By eliminating the weak thesis formula—broad noun plus "is" plus vague evaluative adjective—a writer is compelled to qualify, or define carefully, each of the terms in the original proposition, arriving at a more particular and conceptually rich assertion.

A second way to rephrase overly broad thesis statements, in tandem with adding specificity, is to subordinate one part of the statement to another. The both-positive-and-negative and both-similar-and-different formulas are recipes for say-nothing theses, since they encourage point-less comparisons. Given that it is worthwhile to notice both strengths and weaknesses—that your subject is not all one way or all another—what, then, can you do to convert the thesis from a say-nothing to a say-something claim? Generally, there are two strategies for this purpose that operate together. The first we have already discussed.

1. *Specify*—Replace the overly abstract terms—terms like "positive" and "negative" (or "similar" and "different")—with something specific; *name* something that is positive and something that is negative instead.
2. *Subordinate*—Rank one of the two items in the pairing below the other. When you subordinate, you put the most important, pressing, or revealing side of the comparison in what is known as the main clause and the less important side in what is known as the subordi-nate clause, introducing it with a word like "while" or "although."

Voices Across the Curriculum

Making the Thesis Specific

Good thesis: "While Graham and Wigman seem different, their ideas on inner expression (specifically subjectivism versus objectivism) and the incorporation of their respective countries' surge of nationalism bring them much closer than they appear."

Not so good thesis/question: "What were Humphrey's and Weidman's reasons behind the setting of *With My Red Fires*, and of what importance were the set and costume design to the piece as a whole?"

What I like about the good thesis is that it moves beyond the standard "they are different, but alike" (which can be said about anything) to actually tell the reader what specific areas the paper will explore. I can also tell that the subject is narrow enough for a fairly thorough examination of one small slice of these two major choreographers' work rather than some overgeneralized treatment of these two historic figures. I would prob-ably encourage the writer of the not so good thesis to search for a better thesis with the question: How does the costume design of *With My Red Fires* support this story of young lovers and their revolt against the family matriarch?

—Karen Dearborn, professor of dance

(See Chapter 12 for the definitions—as well as more discussion—of main and subordinate clauses.)

In short, specify to focus the claim, and subordinate to qualify (further focus) the claim still more. This strategy produces the remedies to both the *Othello* and the violent revolution examples in "Weak Thesis Type 5: The Thesis Makes an Overly Broad Claim." As evidence of the refocusing work that fairly simple rephrasing accomplishes, consider the following version of the violent revolution example, in which we merely invert the ranking of the two items in the pair.

> Although violent revolutions often cause long-term economic dysfunction and the suffering that attends it, such revolutions at least begin to redress long-standing social inequities.

This rephrasing has given analytical emphasis to the "long-standing social inequities" by placing that phrase within the sentence's main clause (which follows the comma). At the same time, it has relegated "long-term economic dysfunction and the suffering that attends it" to a supporting role—by making that phrase part of the sentence's subordinate clause (which precedes the comma).

Can a Thesis Be a Question?

The following question is frequently asked about thesis statements: is it okay to phrase a thesis as a question? The answer is both "yes" and "no." Phrasing a thesis as a question makes it more difficult for both the writer and the reader to be sure of the direction the paper will take, because a question doesn't make an overt claim. Questions, however, can clearly imply claims. And many writers, especially in the early, exploratory stages of drafting, will begin with a question. As we note in Chapter 2 in the section called "Ideas Across the Curriculum," an idea answers a question; it explains something that needs to be explained. Also, an idea may result from the discovery of a question where there seemed not to be one. Ideas start with something you want to figure out rather than with something that you and possibly most of your readers already understand.

As a general rule, use thesis questions cautiously, especially in final drafts. While a thesis question often functions well to spark a writer's thinking, it can too often muddy the thinking by leaving the area of consideration too broad. Just make sure that you do not let the thesis-question approach allow you to evade the responsibility of making some kind of claim. Especially in the drafting stage, a question posed overtly by the writer can provide focus, but only if he or she then proceeds to answer it with what would become a first statement of thesis.

❧*TRY THIS:* Learning to diagnose the strengths and weaknesses of thesis statements is a skill that comes in handy as you read the claims of others and revise your own. A good question for diagnosing a thesis is "What does the thesis require the writer to do next?" This question should help you to figure out what the thesis actually wants to claim, which can then direct you to possible rephrasings that would better direct your thinking. Using this question as a prompt, list the strengths and weaknesses of the two thesis statements below, and then rewrite them. In the first statement, just rewrite the last sentence (the other sentences have been included to provide context). ☐

1. Many economists and politicians agree that federal legislation to protect endangered species could damage the Canadian economy. Because of the expense of environmental restrictions on landowners and industry, domestic companies would suffer financially. Others argue, however, that severe regulatory steps must be taken to prevent the extinction of over 350 endangered plants and animals. Despite both legitimate claims, the issue of protecting endangered species while still securing our global competitiveness remains critical.

2. Regarding the promotion of women into executive positions, they are continually losing the race because of a corporate view that women are too compassionate to keep up with the competitiveness of a powerful firm.

C. COMMON LOGICAL ERRORS IN CONSTRUCTING A THESIS

To further provide you with ways of avoiding weak thesis statements, this section will move briefly to the field of logic, which has given us terms that are shorthand for certain common thinking errors. We will treat six errors, all of which involve the root problem of oversimplification in the way the thesis explains the meaning of evidence.

1. Simple cause–complex effect

One of the most common problems of thinking—the fallacy of simple cause–complex effect—involves assigning a simple cause to a complex phenomenon that cannot be so easily explained. A widespread version of this fallacy is seen in arguments that blame individual figures for broad historical events, for example, "Pierre Trudeau caused the death of Quebec's minister of labour by imposing the War Measures Act in October of 1970." This claim ignores the ongoing tensions between provincial politicians and the FLQ, as well as a multitude of cultural and linguistic factors. When you reduce a complex sequence of events to a simple and single cause—or assign a simple effect to a complex cause—you will virtually always be wrong.

2. False cause

Another common cause/effect thinking error, false cause, is produced by assuming that two events are causally connected when such causal connection does not necessarily exist. One of the most common forms of this fallacy—known as *post hoc, ergo propter hoc* (Latin for "after this, therefore because of this")—assumes that because A precedes B in time, A causes B. For example, it was once thought that the sun shining on a pile of garbage caused the garbage to conceive flies.

This error is the stuff that superstition is made of. "I walked under a ladder, and then I got hit by a car" becomes "Because I walked under a ladder, I got hit by a car." Because one action precedes a second one in time, the first action is assumed to be the cause of the second. A more dangerous form of this error goes like this:

Evidence: A new neighbour moved in downstairs on Saturday. My television disappeared on Sunday.

Conclusion: The new neighbour stole my TV.

As the examples illustrate, typically in "false cause," *some significant alternative has not been considered*, such as the presence of flies' eggs in the garbage. Similarly, it does not follow that if a person watches television and then commits a crime, television watching necessarily causes crime; there are other causes to be considered.

Predictably, instances of simple cause–complex effect and false cause are harder to spot when we encounter them in published settings. Consider how the information offered in the following real-life example might be interpreted in terms of cause and effect. A newspaper article on a study conducted at Stanford University about the connection between adolescents' television viewing habits and drinking reports that high school students who watch a lot of television and music videos are more likely to start drinking than are other high school students. In the study of fifteen hundred and fifty-three ninth-graders, with each increase of one hour per day of watching music videos there was a thirty-one percent greater risk of starting to drink. Each hour increase of watching other kinds of television corresponded with a nine percent greater risk. Each hour spent watching movies in a video cassette recorder (VCR) corresponded to an eleven percent *decreased* risk of starting to drink alcohol. Computer and video games had no effect either way, and among those who already drank, watching television and videos made no difference. Because these data were reported in the newspaper in abbreviated form, there was little interpretation of the evidence except for the observations that alcohol is the most common beverage shown on television and that drinking on television is done by attractive people, often in association with sexually suggestive content.

❦*TRY THIS:* Identify possible sites of simple cause–complex effect and false cause in the report (above) on teen drinking. Then, formulate a few alternative explanations one might offer to the theory that television watching is the primary cause of the increased risk of starting drinking. What explanations might there be for the decreased risk of drinking that corresponds with adolescents watching movies on the VCR? □

3. Analogy and false analogy

An analogy is a device for understanding something that is relatively foreign in terms of something that is more familiar. When you argue by analogy, you *infer* that, because two things are alike in some respects, they will be alike in others (as we explained in Chapter 3, inference is the logical process of drawing out implications). One of the most memorable analogies of our modern era was derived by Judith Jarvis Thompson to support a woman's right to abortion; she compared finding yourself pregnant to finding yourself kidnapped and placed back to back in bed with an unconscious violinist, where you were to remain plugged into his circulatory system for nine months because "he has been found to have a fatal kidney ailment, and the Society of Music Lovers has canvassed all the available medical records and found that you alone have the right blood type to help."

The danger that arguing analogically can pose is that an *inaccurate* comparison prevents you from looking carefully at the evidence. Is being a university student analogous to serving time in prison? Well, the comparison may work to a certain point (after all, some classrooms are like cells and some professors are like guards), but the process of inference leads often to oversimplification. In most ways that matter, pursuing higher education is not comparable to spending that same number of years behind bars.

Another way that an analogy can become false is when it becomes *overextended:* there is a point of resemblance at one juncture, but the writer then goes on to assume that the two items being compared necessarily resemble each other in most other respects. To what extent is balancing your chequebook really like juggling? On the other hand, an analogy that first appears overextended may not be. How far, for example, could you reasonably go in comparing a presidential election to a sales campaign or an enclosed shopping mall to a village main street?

Let's examine one more false analogy, from a recent ad campaign: "You choose your federal member of Parliament; why not choose your cable company?" What's wrong with this comparison? For one thing, each of us is not entitled to our choice of MP. If we were, there would be a lot of MPs from the same riding. And, second, the rules and circumstances covering what is best in the nation's communication network are not necessarily the same as the rules and circumstances guiding the structure of our federal government. So the analogy doesn't work very well. What is true for one side of the comparison is not necessarily true for the other side; the differences are greater than the similarities.

When you find yourself reasoning by analogy, ask yourself two questions: (1) are the basic similarities greater and more significant than the obvious differences? and (2) am I overrelying on surface similarities and ignoring more essential differences?

4. Equivocation

Equivocation is the first of three logical errors that deal with matters of phrasing. As shown in Chapters 5 and 6, finding and developing a thesis emphasizes the importance of word choice—of carefully casting and recasting the language with which you categorize and name your ideas.

Equivocation—slipping between two meanings for a single word or phrase—confuses an argument. An example would be: "Only man is capable of religious faith. No woman is a man. Therefore, no woman is capable of religious faith." Here the first use of "man" is generic, intended to be gender neutral, while the second use is decidedly masculine. One specialized form of equivocation results from what are sometimes called *weasel words*. A weasel word is one that has been used so loosely that it ceases to have much of any meaning (the term derives from the weasel's reputed practice of sucking the contents from an egg without destroying the shell). The word "natural," for example, can mean good, pure, and unsullied, but it can also refer to the ways of nature (flora and fauna). Such terms ("love," "reality," "experience," and so forth) invite equivocation because they mean so many different things to different people.

5. Begging the question

To beg the question is to argue in a circle by asking readers to accept without argument a point that is actually at stake. This kind of fallacious argument hides its conclusion among its assumptions. For example, "Robert Crumb's drawings should be banned in Canada as obscene because they feature obscene images" begs the question by presenting as obviously true issues that are actually in question: the definition of obscenity and the assumption that the obscene should be banned because it is obscene.

6. Overgeneralization

An overgeneralization is an inadequately qualified claim. It may be true that some heavy drinkers are alcoholics, but it would not be fair to claim that all heavy drinking is or leads to alcoholism. As a rule, be wary of "totalizing" or making global pronouncements; the bigger the generalization, the more likely it will admit to exceptions. See for examples the process of qualifying a claim we illustrate in the discussion of *Educating Rita* in Chapter 6 and in the solutions in the section "Weak Thesis Type 5" in this chapter.

One particular form of overgeneralization, the *sweeping generalization*, occurs when a writer overextends the reach of the claim. The claim itself may be adequately qualified, but the problem comes in an overly broad application of that generalization, suggesting that it applies in every case when it applies only in some.

When you move prematurely from too little evidence to a broad conclusion, you have fallen into *hasty generalization*. Much of this book addresses ways of avoiding this problem, also known as an unwarranted inductive leap. See the section "Demonstrating the Representativeness of Your Example" in Chapter 5.

There are, of course, other common logical errors that can undermine the construction of valid claims. For one more example, see the section called "Strategy 3: Put Your Sources into Conversation with One Another" in Chapter 8 for a discussion of the problem in argument called *straw man*, in which a writer builds his or her case on a misrepresentation of an opponent's argument.

ASSIGNMENT

Back in Chapter 3 ("Interpreting Your Data") we mentioned Roger Martin's editorial essay "The Wrong Incentive" (pages 420–423). This essay's subtitle—"Executives taking stock will behave like athletes placing bets"—establishes the two sides of its central analogy, namely, the New York Stock Exchange (NYSE) and the National Football League (NFL).

As explained a few pages ago, analogy means inferring that because two things are alike in some respects, they will be alike in others too. Your assignment is to test that inference. Complete the following table by identifying characteristics of the New York Stock Exchange that, according to Roger Martin, align with those of the National Football League. (We've provided two examples to get you started.) Then discuss with your peers whether or not the analogous characteristics combine to present a logical and persuasive argument.

ANALOGY	
SIDE A: New York Stock Exchange	**SIDE B: National Football League**
Analogous Sub-Topics	
manipulating the expectations market :	betting on games
prices on the NYSE :	point spreads in NFL games
:	
:	
:	
:	
:	
:	
:	

8

Writing the Researched Paper

A. SOURCE ANXIETY AND WHAT TO DO ABOUT IT

Too often, inexperienced writers either use secondary sources as "answers"—they let the sources do too much of their thinking—or ignore them altogether as a way of avoiding "losing their own ideas." Both of these approaches are understandable but inadequate. For now let's concentrate on the second problematic approach: ignoring sources altogether.

Confronted with the seasoned views of experts in a discipline, you may well feel that there is nothing left for you to say because it has all been said before or, at least, it has been said by people who greatly outweigh you in reputation and experience. So why not avoid what other people have said? Won't this avoidance ensure that your ideas will be original and that, at the same time, you will be free from the danger of getting brainwashed by some "expert"?

The answer is "no." If you don't consult what others have said, you run at least two risks: you will waste your time reinventing the wheel, and you will undermine your analysis (or at least leave it incomplete) by not considering information or acknowledging positions that are commonly discussed in the field.

By remaining unaware of existing thinking, you choose, in effect, to stand outside of the conversation that others interested in the subject are having. Standing in this sort of intellectual vacuum sometimes appeals to writers who fear that consulting sources will leave them with nothing to say. But it is possible, as this chapter shows, to find *a middle ground* between developing an idea that is entirely independent of what experts have written on a subject and producing a paper that does nothing but repeat other people's ideas. A little research—even if it's only an hour's browse in the reference collection of the library—will virtually always raise the level of what you have to say above what it would have been if you had consulted only the information and opinions that you carry around in your head.

A good rule of thumb for coping with "source anxiety" is to formulate a tentative position on your topic before you consult secondary sources.

Voices Across the Curriculum

Write Up Experiments as They're Done

Most of the students I've supervised in the past thirty-two years have been intimidated by the prospect of writing their theses. Even if they are excellent record keepers in the laboratory, they find the idea of writing about their research quite daunting. So they put it off as long as possible, doing other, "important" activities (such as planning experiments and completing assignments for their course work) that give them a sense of accomplishment. But this does not advance their thesis work. Many wait until six months before their scheduled defence before beginning to write. Naturally, this creates a tremendous amount of pressure and anxiety.

One way to decrease the anxiety—and get the job done in a more comfortable fashion—is to do what scientists do best: break down the task into smaller, more manageable pieces, and tackle the writing one section at a time. This may seem obvious, but even students who use this approach effectively in their research and courses often do not think of applying it to their writing projects.

The best time to write up major experiments is immediately upon completion. This is when everything is freshest in your mind: the relevant literature, what you did, how you interpret the data. It's the time when you've given the experiment the *most* thought. It's also when your bias is probably the highest. But this doesn't matter; what's important is that you've worked out your ideas on paper. You've recorded the methodology, results, and your discussion. And you have a narrative that may very well become one of the building blocks of your thesis. You may learn in later experiments that your initial interpretation was "off." This is a normal part of the discovery process. The greatest problem is not in learning that one's interpretation is wrong; it's in having a flash of insight that has been forgotten—because it was never recorded.

One of the interesting things about *formally* writing up your experiments as you complete them is that the process forces you to critically examine and clarify your thoughts about your research.... Simply *thinking* about your results is just not the same.

—Andrew M. Kropinski, professor of microbiology and immunology

---

In other words, give yourself time to do some preliminary thinking. Try writing informally about your topic, analyzing some piece of pertinent information already at your disposal. That way you will have your initial responses written down to weigh in relation to what others have said. Writing of this sort can also help you to select what to look at in the sources you eventually consult.

And what kinds of sources should you be consulting? Notice that we use the terms *source* and *secondary source* interchangeably to designate ideas and information about your subject that you find in the work of other writers. Secondary sources allow you to gain a richer, more informed, and complex vantage point on your *primary sources*. Here's how primary and secondary sources can be distinguished: if you were writing a paper on the philosopher Nietzsche, his writing would be your primary source, and critical commentaries on his work would be your secondary sources. If, however, you were writing on the poet Yeats, who read and was influenced by Nietzsche, a work of Nietzsche's philosophy would become a secondary source of yours on your primary source, Yeats's poetry.

The Conversation Analogy

Now, let's turn to *the major problem in using sources as answers—a writer leaving the experts he or she cites to speak for themselves*. In this situation, the writer characteristically makes a generalization in his or her own words, juxtaposes it to a quotation or other reference from a secondary source, and assumes that the meaning of the reference will be self-evident. This practice not only leaves the connection between the writer's thinking and his or her source material unstated but also substitutes mere repetition of someone else's viewpoint for a more active interpretation. The source has been allowed to have the final word, with the effect that it stops the discussion, as well as the writer's own thinking.

First and foremost, then, you need to do something with the reading. Clarify the meaning of the material you have quoted, paraphrased, or summarized, and explain its significance in light of your evolving thesis.

It follows that the first step in using sources effectively is to reject the assumption that sources provide final and complete answers. If they did, there would be no reason for others to continue writing on the subject. As in conversation, we raise ideas for others to respond to. Accepting that no source has the final word does not mean, however, that you should shift from unquestioning approval to the opposite pole and necessarily assume an antagonistic position toward all sources. Indeed, a habitually antagonistic response to others' ideas is just as likely to bring your conversation with your sources to a halt as is the habit of always assuming that the source must have the final word.

Most people would probably agree on the attributes of a really good conversation. There is room for agreement and disagreement, for give and take, among a variety of viewpoints. Generally, people don't deliberately misunderstand each other, but a significant amount of the discussion may go into clarifying one's own as well as others' positions. Such conversations construct a genuinely collaborative chain of thinking: Karl builds on what David has said, which induces Naomi to respond to Karl's comment, and so forth.

There are, of course, obvious differences between conversing aloud with friends and conversing on paper with sources. As a writer, you need to construct the chain of thinking, orchestrate the exchange of views with and among your sources, and give the conversation direction. A good place to begin in using sources is to recognize that you need not respond to everything another writer says, nor do you need to come up with an entirely original point of view—one that completely revises or refutes the source. You are using sources analytically, for example, when you note that two experiments (or historical accounts, or whatever) are similar but have different priorities or that they ask similar questions in different ways. Building from this kind of observation, you can then analyze what these differences imply.

There are, in any case, many ways of approaching secondary sources, but these ways generally share a common goal: to use the source as a point of departure. Here is a partial list of ways to do that.

- Make as many points as you can about a single representative passage from your source, and then branch out from this centre to analyze other passages that "speak" to it in some way. (See the section "Analyzing Evidence in Depth: '10 on 1'" in Chapter 5.)
- Use Notice and Focus to identify what you find most strange in the source (see Chapter 1); this will help you cultivate your curiosity about the source and find the critical distance necessary to thinking about it.
- Use Five-Step Analysis to identify the most significant organizing contrast in the source (see Chapter 1); this will help you see what the source itself is wrestling with, what is at stake in it.
- Apply an idea in the source to another subject. (See the section "Applying a Reading as a Lens" in Chapter 4.)

- Uncover the assumptions in the source, and then build upon the source's point of view, extending its implications. (See the section "Uncovering the Assumptions in a Reading" in Chapter 4.)
- Agree with most of what the source says, but take issue with one small part that you want to modify.
- Identify a contradiction in the source, and explore its implications, without necessarily arriving at a solution.

The second chapter of this book, "Habitual Thinking," ends with a brief description of ideas—what they are and especially what they do. We call that section "Ideas Across the Curriculum." We say that it's one thing to acquire knowledge, but you also need to learn how to produce knowledge, to think for yourself. In this chapter we offer ways of using secondary sources to help you arrive at ideas. Sources don't relieve you of the responsibility of thinking for yourself; they "up the stakes," so to speak, and increase the chances of your arriving at better ideas. Here is a repeat of the list from "Ideas Across the Curriculum" that stresses goals and methods you'll find in this chapter:

- An idea may be the discovery of a question where there seemed not to be one.
- An idea usually starts with an observation that is puzzling, with something that you want to figure out rather than with something that you think you already understand.
- An idea may make explicit and explore the meaning of something implicit—an unstated assumption upon which an argument rests or a logical consequence of a given position.
- An idea may connect elements of a subject and explain the significance of that connection.
- An idea often accounts for some *dissonance*—that is, something that seems not to fit together.
- An idea provides the answer to a good question; it explains something that needs to be explained.

Most strong analytical ideas launch you in a process of resolving problems and bringing competing positions into some kind of alignment. They locate you where there is something to negotiate, where you are required not just to list answers but also to ask questions, make choices, and engage in reasoning about the significance of your evidence.

If you quote with the aim of conversing with your sources rather than allowing them to do your thinking for you, you will discover that sources can promote rather than stifle your analysis. In short, think of sources not

Voices Across the Curriculum

Encouraging Students in Times of Stress

Research in chemistry often seems to go in fits and starts, two steps forward followed by one backward, then one forward followed by two in reverse. Over the three years or so of a doctorate program, however, a hardworking graduate student does make progress and, as the time for thesis writing approaches, the various observations begin to make sense, a story unfolds in his or her mind, and it is anticipated that at long last the lab work is almost finished. The experiments have been completed, a hypothesis has been soundly supported, and the results look like they might be well worth the time and effort put in.

At this point, some supervisors suggest "one last experiment," which will ice the cake, as it were. "Do this," he or she may say, "and the whole thing will be wrapped up even more beautifully." Sometimes Father Nature smiles on this final endeavour, and everyone is happy.

Other times, however, the "final experiment" turns out disastrously. It not only does not confirm the picture that had developed over the years, it contradicts what were to have been the major conclusions of the thesis. All of a sudden the student fears that finishing his or her work will require another year, and the experience can be quite devastating.

When this happens to my students, I commiserate briefly, think damn quickly with a focus which is most unlike me, and suggest casually that the result is not a disappointment but an opportunity. Although it is true that our results to date had made a lot of sense, i.e., had been consistent with the prevailing view at the time, in fact if we could fit the new evidence into the body of knowledge at hand, we would in fact contradict the conventional wisdom in a way which would draw a great deal of attention and possibly even praise.

In other words, there is greater glory in meeting and overcoming seemingly insurmountable roadblocks than in confirming the current dogma. And it's true: solving this type of problem certainly gives one a much greater sense of achievement.

—Michael Baird, professor of chemistry

as answers but as voices inviting you into a community of interpretation, discussion, and debate. As the discussion in "Voices Across the Curriculum" demonstrates, this practice is common to different academic disciplines.

B. SIX STRATEGIES FOR ANALYZING SOURCES

Many people never get beyond like/dislike responses with secondary materials. If they agree with what a source says, they say it's "good," and they cut and paste the part they can use as an answer. If the source somehow disagrees with what they already believe, they say it's "bad," and they attack it or—along with readings they find "hard" or "boring"—discard it. As readers they have been conditioned to develop a point of view on a subject without first figuring out the conversation (the various points of view) that their subject attracts. They assume, in other words, that their subject probably has a single meaning—a gist—disclosed by experts, who mostly agree. The six strategies that follow offer ways to avoid this trap.

Strategy 1: Make Your Sources Speak

Quote, paraphrase, or summarize *in order to* analyze—not *in place of* analyzing. Don't assume that either the meaning of the source material or your reason for including it is self-evident. Rid yourself of the habit of just stringing together citations for which you provide little more than conjunctions to connect them. Instead, explain to your readers what the quotation or paraphrase or summary of the source *means*. What elements of it do you find interesting or revealing or strange? Emphasize how those affect your evolving thesis.

In making a source speak, focus on articulating how the source has led to the conclusion you draw from it. Beware of simply putting a generalization and a quotation next to each other (juxtaposing them) without explaining the connection. Instead fill the crucial site between evidence and claim (see Figure 5.2) with your *thinking*. Consider this problem in the following paragraph from a student's paper on political conservatism.

> Edmund Burke's philosophy evolved into contemporary American conservative ideology. There is an important distinction between philosophy and political ideology: philosophy is "the knowledge of general principles that explain facts and existences." Political ideology, on the other hand, is "an overarching conception of society, a stance that is reflected in numerous sectors of social life" (Edwards 22). Therefore, conservatism should be regarded as an ideology rather than a philosophy.

The final sentence offers the writer's conclusion—what the source information has led him to—but how did it get him there? The writer's choice of the word "therefore" indicates to the reader that the idea following it is the result of a process of logical reasoning, but this reasoning has been omitted. Instead, the writer assumes that the reader will be able to connect the quotations with his conclusion. The writer needs to *make the quotation speak* by analyzing its key terms more closely. What is "an overarching conception of society," and how does it differ from "knowledge of general principles"? More important, what is the rationale for categorizing conservatism as either an ideology or a philosophy?

Here, by contrast, is a writer who makes her sources speak. Focus on how she integrates analysis with quotation.

> Stephen Greenblatt uses the phrase "self-fashioning" to refer to an idea he believes developed during the Renaissance—the idea that one's identity is not created or born but rather shaped, both by one's self and by others. The idea of self-fashioning is incorporated into an attitude toward literature that has as its ideal what Greenblatt calls "poetics of culture." A text is examined with three elements in mind: the author's own self, the cultural self-fashioning process that created that self, and the author's reaction to that process. Because our selves, like texts, are "fashioned," an author's life is just as open to interpretation as that of a literary character.

> If this is so, then biography does not provide a repository of unshakeable facts from which to interpret an author's work. Greenblatt criticizes the fact that the methods of literary interpretation are applied just to art and not to life. As he observes, "We wall off literary symbolism from the symbolic structures operative elsewhere, as if art alone were a human creation" (Begley 37). If the line between art and life is indeed blurred, then we need a more complex model for understanding the relationship between the life and work of an author.

In this example, the writer shows us how her thinking has been stimulated by the source. At the end of the first paragraph and the beginning of the second, for example, she not only specifies what she takes to be the meaning of the quotation but also draws a conclusion about its implications (that the facts of an author's life, like his or her art, require interpretation). And this manner of proceeding is habitual: the writer repeats the pattern in the second paragraph, *moving beyond what the quotation says to explore what its logic suggests.*

Strategy 2: Use Your Sources to Ask Questions, Not Just to Provide Answers

Use your selections from sources as a means of raising issues and questions. Avoid the temptation to plug in such selections as answers that require no further commentary or elaboration. You will no doubt find viewpoints you believe to be valid, but it is not enough to drop these answers from the source into your own writing at the appropriate spots. You need to *do* something with the reading, even with those sources that seem to have said what you want to say.

If you consider only the source in isolation, you may not discover much to say about it. Once you begin considering it in other contexts and with other sources, you may begin to see aspects of your subject that your source does not adequately address. Having recognized that the source does not answer all questions, you should not conclude that the source is "wrong"— only that it is limited in some ways. Discovering such limitations is in fact advantageous, because it can lead you to identify a place from which to launch your own analysis.

It does not necessarily follow that your analysis will culminate in an answer to replace those offered by your sources. Often—in fact, far more often than many writers suspect—it is enough to discover issues or problems and raise them clearly. Phrasing *explicitly* the issues and questions that remain *implicit* in a source is an important part of what analytical writers do, especially in cases for which there is no solution, or at least none that can be presented in a relatively short paper. Here, for example, is how the writer on Stephen Greenblatt's concept of self-fashioning concludes her essay:

> It is not only the author whose role is complicated by New Historicism; the critic also is subject to some of the same qualifications and restrictions. According to Adam Begley, "it is the essence of the new-historicist project to uncover the moments at which works of art absorb and refashion social energy, an endless process of circulation and exchange" (39). In other words, the work is both affected by and affects the culture. But if this is so, how then can we decide which elements of culture (and text) are causes and which are effects? If we add the critic to this picture, the process does indeed appear endless. The New Historicists' relationship with their culture infuses itself into their assessment of the Renaissance, and this assessment may in turn become part of their own self-fashioning process, which will affect their interpretations, and so forth....

Notice that this writer *incorporates the quotation into her own chain of thinking*. By paraphrasing the quotation ("In other words"), she arrives at a question ("how then") that follows as a logical consequence of accepting its position ("but if this is so"). Note, however, that she does not then label the quotation right or wrong. Instead, she tries to figure out *to what position it might lead* and to what possible problems.

By contrast, the writer of the following excerpt, from a paper comparing two films aimed at teenagers, settles for plugging in sources as answers and consequently does not pursue the questions implicit in her quotations.

In both films, the adults are one-dimensional caricatures, evil beings whose only goal in life is to make the kids' lives a living hell. In *Risky Business*, director Paul Brickman's solution to all of Joel's problems is to have him hire a prostitute and then turn his house into a whorehouse. Of course, as one critic observes, "the prostitutes who make themselves available to his pimply faced buddies are all centerfold beauties: elegant, svelte, benign and unquestionably healthy (after all, what does V.D. have to do with prostitutes?)" (Gould 41)—not exactly a realistic or legal solution. Allan Moyle, the director of *Pump Up the Volume*, provides an equally unrealistic

---

Voices Across the Curriculum

Bringing Sources Together

Bringing one's sources together is one stage in the multi-stage process of writing a paper. You need to develop a means of note taking that will allow you to sort and re-sort the notes from your sources according to various headings that may be employed in the paper.

As you read, begin to think of what the thesis of the paper will be and what the basic points will be to support the thesis. Take notes on everything that appears to be relevant. Begin to formulate the basic headings or topics that will need to be discussed in the paper. Once you have finished most or all of your reading, reread all your notes. This is the time to make a final decision on the thesis of the paper—and to make a firm outline of all the points that must be made to support the thesis. It is also the time to weigh and use those arguments from your source notes to support the thesis you have developed. You bring your sources together either by showing how they contribute to the evidence supporting your thesis or by showing how, although they make a case against your thesis, you can counter that. Only occasionally and for emphasis do you use the actual words of the sources (direct quotations). Nor do you simply use their sentence structures, changing a few words along the way. Instead, you take what you have understood from their claims and incorporate it into your argument in your own words.

As you write, you can draw on the specifics of the arguments made in the sources you have read. Still, you need to be aware of two opposite pitfalls. The first is the temptation to use a source as though simply the fact that it is in print gives it authority. Every source must be weighed for its credibility and its usefulness for your particular thesis. The second is the temptation to make the sources fit your preconceived point of view. You need to use your sources fairly.

In most cases, the sources are the experts. Experts may disagree. It is your job to weigh varying positions and present a coherent use of the scholarly evidence by making it part of your own argument.

—Pamela Dickey Young, professor of religious studies

---

solution to Mark's problem. According to David Denby, Moyle "offers self-expression as the cure to adolescent funk. Everyone should start his own radio station and talk about his feelings" (59). Like Brickman, Moyle offers solutions that are neither realistic nor legal.

This writer is having a hard time figuring out what to do with sources that offer well-phrased and seemingly accurate answers (such as "self-expression is the cure to adolescent funk"). Her analysis of both quotations leads her to settle for the bland and undeveloped conclusion that films aimed at teenagers are not "realistic"—an observation that most readers would already recognize as true. But, unlike the writer of the previous example, she does not ask herself, "*If this is true, then what follows?*" Had she asked some such version of the "So what?" question, she might have inquired how the illegality of the solutions is related to their unrealistic quality. So what, for example, that the main characters in both films are not marginalized as criminals and made to suffer for their illegal actions, but rather are celebrated as heroes? What different kinds of illegality do the two films apparently condone, and how might these be related to the different decades in which each film was produced? Rather than use her sources to think with, in order to clarify or complicate the issues, the writer has used them only to confirm an obvious generalization.

Strategy 3: Put Your Sources into Conversation with One Another

Rather than limiting yourself to agreeing or disagreeing with your sources, aim for conversation with and among them. Although it is not wrong to agree or disagree with your sources, it is wrong to see these as your only possible moves. You should also understand that, although it is sometimes useful and perhaps even necessary to agree or disagree, these judgments should (1) always be *qualified* and (2) occur only *in certain contexts*.

Selective analytical summarizing of a position with which you essentially agree or disagree, especially if located early in a final draft (after you've figured out what to think in your previous drafts), can be extraordinarily helpful in orienting your readers for the discussion to follow. This practice of *framing the discussion* typically locates you either for or against some well-known point of view or frame of reference; it's a way of sharing your assumptions with the reader. You introduce the source, in other words, to succinctly summarize a position that you plan to develop or challenge in a qualified way. This latter strategy—sometimes known as *straw man*, because you construct a "dummy" position specifically in order to knock it down—

can stimulate you to formulate a point of view, especially if you are not accustomed to responding critically to sources.

As this boxing analogy suggests, however, setting up a straw man can be a dangerous game. If you do not fairly represent and put into context the straw man's argument, you risk encouraging readers to dismiss your counterargument as a cheap shot and to dismiss you for being *reductive*. On the other hand, if you spend a great deal of time detailing the straw man's position, you risk losing momentum in developing your own point of view. In any case, if you are citing a source in order to frame the discussion, the more reasonable move is both to agree *and* disagree with it. First, identify shared premises; give the source some credit. Then distinguish the part of what you have cited that you intend to develop or complicate or dispute. This method of proceeding is obviously less combative than the typically blunt straw man approach; it verges on conversation.

In the following passage from a student's paper on Darwin's theory of evolution, the student clearly recognizes that he needs to do more than summarize what Darwin says, but he seems not to know any way of conversing with his source other than indicating his agreement and disagreement with it.

> The struggle for existence also includes the dependence of one being on another being to survive. Darwin also believes that all organic beings tend to increase. I do not fully agree with Darwin's belief here. I cannot conceive of the fact of all beings increasing in number. Darwin goes on to explain that food, competition, climate, and the location of a certain species contribute to its survival and existence in nature. I believe that this statement is very valid and that it could be very easily understood through experimentation in nature.

This writer's use of the word "here" in his third sentence is revealing. He is tagging summaries of Darwin with what he seems to feel is an obligatory response—a polite shake or nod of the head: "I can't fully agree with you there, Darwin, but here I think you might have a point." The writer's tentative language lets us see how uncomfortable, even embarrassed, he feels about venturing these judgments on a subject that is too complex for this kind of response. It's as though the writer moves along, talking about Darwin's theory for a while, and then says to himself, "Time for a response," and lets a particular summary sentence trigger a "yes/no" switch. Having pressed that switch, which he does periodically, the writer resumes his summary, having registered but not analyzed his own interjections. There is no reasoning in a chain from his own observations, just random insertions of unanalyzed agree/disagree responses.

Here, by contrast, is the introduction of an essay that uses summary to frame the conversation that the writer is preparing to have with her source.

> In *Renaissance Thought: The Classic, Scholastic and Humanist Strains*, Paul Kristeller responds to two problems that he perceives in Renaissance scholarship. The first is the haze of cultural meaning surrounding the word "humanism": he seeks to clarify the word and its origins, as well as to explain the apparent lack of religious concern in humanism. Kristeller also reacts to the notion of humanism as an improvement upon medieval Aristotelian scholasticism.

Rather than leading with her own beliefs about the source, the writer emphasizes the issues and problems she believes are central in it. Although the writer's position on her source is apparently neutral, she is not summarizing passively. In addition to making choices about what is especially significant in the source, she has also located it within the conversation that its author, Kristeller, was having with his own sources—the works of other scholars whose view of humanism he wants to revise ("Kristeller responds to two problems").

As an alternative to formulating your opinion of the sources, try constructing the conversation that you think the author of one of your sources might have with the author of another. *How might they recast each other's ideas, as opposed to merely agreeing or disagreeing with those ideas?* Notice how, further on in the paper, the writer uses this strategy to achieve a clearer picture of Kristeller's point of view:

> Unlike Kristeller, Tillyard [in *The Elizabethan World Picture*] also tries to place the seeds of individualism in the minds of the medievals. "Those who know most about the Middle Ages," he claims, "now assure us that humanism and a belief in the present life were powerful by the 12th century" (30). Kristeller would undoubtedly reply that it was scholasticism, lacking the humanist emphasis on individualism, that was powerful in the Middle Ages. True humanism was not evident in the Middle Ages.
>
> In Kristeller's view, Tillyard's attempts to assign humanism to medievals are not only unwarranted, but also counterproductive. Kristeller ends his chapter on "Humanism and Scholasticism" with an exhortation to "develop a kind of historical pluralism. It is easy to praise everything in the past that appears to resemble certain favorable ideas of our own time, or to ridicule and minimize everything that disagrees with them. This method is neither fair nor helpful" (174). Tillyard, in trying to locate humanism within the medieval world, allows the value of humanism to supersede the worth of medieval scholarship. Kristeller argues that there is inherent

worth in every intellectual movement, not simply in the ones that we find most agreeable.

Kristeller's work is valuable to us primarily for its forthright definition of humanism. Tillyard has cleverly avoided this undertaking: he provides many textual references, usually with the companion comment that "this is an example of Renaissance humanism," but he never overtly and fully formulates the definition in the way that Kristeller does.

As this excerpt makes evident, the writer has found something to say about her source by putting it into conversation with another source with which she believes her source, Kristeller, would disagree ("Kristeller would undoubtedly reply..."). Although it seems obvious that the writer prefers Kristeller to Tillyard, her agreement with him is not the main point of her analysis. She focuses instead on foregrounding the problem that Kristeller is trying to solve and on relating that problem to different attitudes toward history. In so doing, she is deftly orchestrating the conversation between her sources. Her next step would be to distinguish her position from Kristeller's. Having used Kristeller to get perspective on Tillyard, she now needs somehow to get perspective on Kristeller. The next strategy addresses this issue.

Strategy 4: Find Your Own Role in the Conversation

Even in cases in which you find a source's position entirely congenial, it is not enough simply to agree with it. In order to converse with a source, you need to find some way of having a distinct voice in that conversation. This does not mean that you should feel compelled to attack the source but rather that you need to find something of your own to say about it.

In general, you have two options when you find yourself strongly in agreement with a source: (1) you can apply it in another context to qualify or expand its implications or (2) you can seek out other perspectives on the source in order to break the spell it has cast upon you. "To break the spell" means that you will necessarily become somewhat disillusioned but not that you will then need to dismiss everything you previously believed.

How, in the first option, do you take a source somewhere else? Rather than focusing solely on what you believe your source finds most important, *locate a lesser point, not emphasized by the reading, that you find especially interesting and develop it further.* This strategy will lead you to uncover new implications that depend upon your source but lie outside its own governing preoccupations. In the preceding humanism example, the writer might apply Kristeller's principles to new geographic (rather than theoretical) areas, such as Germany instead of Italy.

The second option, researching new perspectives on the source, can also lead to uncovering new implications. Your aim need not be simply to find a source that disagrees with the one that has convinced you and then switch your allegiance, because this move would perpetuate the problem from which you are trying to escape. Instead, you would use additional perspectives to gain some critical distance from your source. An ideal way of sampling possible critical approaches to a source is to consult book reviews on it found in scholarly journals. Once the original source is taken down from the pedestal through additional reading, there is a greater likelihood that you will see how to distinguish your views from those it offers.

You may think, for example, that another source's critique of your original source is partly valid and that both sources miss things that you could point out; in effect, you *referee* the conversation between them. The writer on Kristeller might play this role by asking herself: "So what that subsequent historians have viewed his objective—a disinterested historical pluralism—as not necessarily desirable and in any case impossible? How might Kristeller respond to this charge, and how has he responded already in ways that his critics have failed to notice?" Using additional research in this way can lead you to *situate* your source more fully and fairly, acknowledging its limits as well as its strengths.

In other words, this writer, in using Kristeller to critique Tillyard, has arrived less at a conclusion than at her next point of departure. A good rule to follow, especially when you find a source entirely persuasive, is that if you can't find a perspective on your source, you haven't done enough research.

Strategy 5: Analyze Sources Along the Way (Don't Wait Until the End)

Unless disciplinary conventions dictate otherwise, analyze *as* you quote or paraphrase a source, rather than summarizing everything first and leaving your analysis for the end. A good conversation does not consist of long monologues alternating among the speakers. Participants exchange views, query, and modify what other speakers have said. Similarly, when you orchestrate conversations with and among your sources, you need to *integrate your analysis into your presentation* of them.

In supplying ongoing analysis, you are much more likely to explain how the information in the sources fits into your unfolding presentation, and your readers will be more likely to follow your train of thought and grasp the logic of your organization. You will also prevent yourself from using the sources simply as an answer. A good rule of thumb in this regard is to *force*

Voices Across the Curriculum

Assimilating Prior Research

The most common problem I see in undergraduate papers comes about because writers too often let evidence speak for itself. As a result, these papers consist of a collection of "facts" about the topic at hand. These are not yet essays, but the raw material out of which an essay can be constructed; as such, they represent an excellent start, but a poor finish. An essay needs facts, but facts alone do not make an essay—an essay is an *interpretation* of the facts. No interpretation, no essay; it's as simple as that.

Always remember that facts never speak for themselves—you must speak for them. By themselves, facts contain no meaning; meaning is something that we *assign* to facts. In other words, facts must be converted into *evidence* (and it is essential that you ask yourself, "Evidence of what?"). Take, for example, the (invented) "fact" that 78% of car accidents involve drinking. So what? Is this figure high? Low? Acceptable? Is the percentage increasing? Decreasing? What does this "fact" *mean*? Why have I brought it to your attention? It may be evidence, but evidence of what? Without further comment, this "fact" is, literally, meaningless.

Who, exactly, is this "we" that assigns meaning to facts? In essay writing, this is a critical question. As a writer, you want to convince the reader that your interpretation—the meaning that you assign to the facts that you present—is reasonable, even compelling. This you cannot do with any assurance if you leave your reader free to assign his or her own meaning. The whole point of writing an essay is to present your interpretation, not to encourage your readers to interpret for themselves.

This means that constructing an essay consists of (at least) two separate activities: gathering and presenting the relevant evidence, and telling your reader what this evidence means. Both are essential; without supporting evidence your "essay" will be no more than a statement of unsupported opinion, and without interpretation you will have nothing but a collection of meaningless facts. You must be familiar with the prior research on your topic, but be sure that you use this research to make a point of your own. For every fact that you include, answer the "So what?" question. What does this *mean*? What's my point? In this way, you will *assimilate* this prior research into your own thinking and your own writing.

—Paul Gamache, writing instructor

Where Do My Ideas Fit In?

I struggle to write without backing up anything I say. Maybe it is a science student thing, but I am constantly searching for sources and proving all my points. I sometimes believe that I spend more time researching and backing ideas up than writing. Thus, I find it difficult to answer the question "What do *I* think?" because my ideas have been moulded by so many others, especially people with PhDs.

—Matthew So, fourth-year biology major

yourself to ask and answer "So what?" at the ends of paragraphs. In laying out your analysis, however, take special care to distinguish your voice from the sources'. (For further discussion of integrating analysis into your presentation of sources, see the commentary on the research paper later in this chapter.)

Strategy 6: Watch Your Language When You Paraphrase or Quote

Rather than generalizing broadly about ideas in your sources, you should spell out what you think is significant about their key words. In those disciplines in which it is permissible, *quote sources if the actual language that they use is important to your point.* This practice will help you to represent the view of your source fairly and accurately. In situations where quoting is not allowed—such as in the report format in psychology—you still need to attend carefully to the meaning of key words in order to arrive at a paraphrase that is not overly general. As we have suggested repeatedly, paraphrasing provides an ideal way to begin interpreting, since the act of careful rephrasing usually illuminates attitudes and assumptions implicit in a text. It is almost impossible not to have ideas and not to see the questions when you start paraphrasing.

Another reason that quoting and paraphrasing are important is that your analysis of a source will nearly always benefit from attention to the way the source represents its position (not just from dwelling on the position itself). Although focusing on the manner of presentation matters more with some sources than with others—more with a poem or scholarly article in political science than with a paper in the natural sciences—the information is never wholly separable from how it is expressed. If you are going to quote *Maclean's* on Rwanda, for example, you will be encountering not "the truth" about Canadian involvement in this African nation but rather one particular representation of the situation—in this case, one crafted to meet or shape the expectations of mainstream popular culture. Similarly, if you quote a federal minister on military policy, what probably matters most is that he or she chose particular words to represent—and promote—the government's position. *It is not neutral information.* The person speaking and the kind of source in which his or her words appear usually acquire added significance when you make note of these words rather than just summarizing them.

⚸*TRY THIS:* Let's say that you are preparing a paper on the September 11th terrorist attacks. One of your secondary sources is Erna Paris's article, "What Sort of People Did This?" (pages 101–103). After rereading her article, try doing a passage-based focused freewrite on it. That is, choose a passage from the article in answer to the question "What is the one passage in the source that I need to discuss, that poses a question or a problem or that seems, in some way perhaps difficult to pin down, anomalous or even just unclear?" Copy the passage at the top of the page, and write for twenty minutes. As we discuss in the section entitled "Passage-Based Focused Freewriting" in Chapter 4, try to isolate and paraphrase key terms as you relentlessly ask "So what?" about the details. Also, remember to consider how the passage is representative of broader issues in the source; you may wish to refer to a similar passage for this purpose. □

❦*TRY THIS:* As a variation on the preceding exercise, *apply a brief passage from a secondary source to a brief passage from a primary source.* Your secondary source is Chapter 4 of this book, which deals with reading; select a passage from the chapter that you find particularly interesting, revealing, or problematic. Then locate a passage that interests you from one of the articles that follow Chapter 4. The article will serve as your primary source. Ask yourself how the secondary-source material (from Chapter 4) applies to the primary-source material (the article you've selected). Copy both passages at the top of the page, and then write for twenty minutes. You should probably include paraphrases of key phrases in both, but your primary goal is to think about the two together, to allow them to interact. □

C. MAKING THE RESEARCH PAPER MORE ANALYTICAL: A SAMPLE ESSAY

The following is an example of a typical university research paper. We offer a brief analysis of each paragraph with an eye to diagnosing what typically goes wrong in writing a research paper and how applying a version of the six strategies for analyzing sources can be used to remedy the problems.

The Flight from Teaching

[1] The "flight from teaching" (Smith 6) in higher education is a controversial issue of the academic world. The amount of importance placed on research and publishing is the major cause of this flight. I will show different views and aspects concerning the problem plaguing our colleges and universities, through the authors whom I have consulted.

[The introductory paragraph needs to be revised to eliminate prejudgment. Calling the issue "controversial" implies that there are different points of view on the subject. The writer, however, offers only one and words it in a way that suggests she has already leaped to a premature and oversimplified conclusion. Instead, she needs to better frame the issue and then replace the procedural opening

(see Chapter 10) with a more hypothetical working thesis that will enable her to explore the subject.]

[2] Page Smith takes an in-depth look at the "flight from teaching" in *Killing the Spirit*. Smith's views on this subject are interesting, because he is a professor with tenure at UCLA. Throughout the book, Smith stresses the sentiment of the student being the enemy, as expressed by many of his colleagues. Some professors resent the fact that the students take up their precious time—time that could be better used for research. Smith goes on about how much some of his colleagues go out of their way to avoid their students. They go as far as making strange office hours to avoid contact. Smith disagrees with the hands-off approach being taken by the professors: "There is no decent, adequate, respectable education, in the proper sense of that much-abused word, without personal involvement by a teacher with the needs and concerns, academic and personal, of his/her students. All the rest is 'instruction' or 'information transferral,' 'communication technique,' or some other impersonal and antiseptic phrase, but it is not teaching and the student is not truly learning" (7).

[The writer summarizes and quotes one of her sources but does not analyze or offer any perspective on it.]

[3] Page Smith devotes a chapter to the ideal of "publish or perish," "since teaching is shunned in the name of research." Smith refutes the idea that "research enhances teaching" and that there is a "direct relation-ship between research and teaching" (178). In actuality, research inhibits teaching. The research that is being done, in most cases, is too specialized for the student. As with teaching and research, Smith believes there is not necessarily a relationship between research and publication. Unfortunately those professors who are devoted to teaching find themselves without a job and/or tenure unless they conform to the requirements of publishing. Smith asks, "Is not the atmosphere hopelessly polluted when professors are forced to do research in order to validate themselves, in order to make a living, in order to avoid being humiliated (and terminated)?" (197). Not only are the students and the professors suffering, but also as a whole, "Under the publish-or-perish standard, the university is perishing" (180).

[The writer continues her summary of her source, using language that implies but does not make explicit her apparent agreement with it. She appears to use the source to speak for her but has not clearly distinguished her voice from that of her source. See, for example, the third sentence and the last sentence of the paragraph. Is the writer only reporting what Smith says or appropriating his view as her own?]

[4] Charles J. Sykes looks at the "flight from teaching" in *Profscam: Professors and the Demise of Higher Education*. Sykes cites statistics to

show the results of the reduction of professors' teaching loads enabling them time for more research. The call to research is the cause of many problems. The reduced number of professors actually teaching increases both the size of classes and the likelihood that students will find at registration that their courses are closed. Students will also find they do not have to write papers, and often exams are multiple choice, because of the large classes. Consequently, the effects of the "flight from teaching" have "had dramatic ramifications for the way undergraduates are taught" (40).

[The writer summarizes another of her sources without analysis of its reasoning and again blurs the distinction between the source's position and her own.]

[5] E. Peter Volpe, in his chapter "Teaching, Research, and Service: Union or Coexistence?" in the book *Whose Goals for American Higher Education?*, disagrees strongly that there is an overemphasis on research. Volpe believes that only the research scholar can provide the best form of teaching because "Teaching and research are as inseparable as the two faces of the same coin" (80). The whole idea of education is to increase the student's curiosity. When the enthusiasm of the professor, because of his or her research, is brought into the classroom, it intensifies that curiosity and therefore provides "the deepest kind of intellectual enjoyment" (80). Volpe provides suggestions for solving the rift between students and professors, such as "replacing formal discourse by informal seminars and independent study programs" (81). He feels that this will get students to think for themselves and professors to learn to communicate with students again. Another suggestion is that the government provide funding for "research programs that are related to the education function" (82). This would allow students the opportunity to share in the research. In conclusion, Volpe states his thesis to be, "A professor in any discipline stays alive when he carries his enthusiasm for discovery into the classroom. The professor is academically dead when the spark of inquiry is extinguished within him. It is then that he betrays his student. The student becomes merely an acquirer of knowledge rather than an inquirer into knowledge" (80).

[Here the writer summarizes a source that offers an opposing point of view. It is good that she has begun to represent multiple perspectives, but as with the preceding summaries, there is not yet enough analysis. If she could put Volpe's argument into active conversation with those of Sykes and Smith, she might be able to articulate more clearly the assumptions her sources share and to distinguish their key differences. How, for example, do the three sources differ in their definitions of research and of teaching?]

[6] The "flight from teaching" is certainly a problem in colleges and universities. When beginning to research this topic, I had some very definite opinions. I believed that research and publication should not play any role in

teaching. Through the authors utilized in this paper and other sources, I have determined that there is a need for some "research" but not to the extent that teaching is pushed aside. College and universities exist to provide an education; therefore, their first responsibility is to the student.

[Here the writer begins to offer her opinion of the material, which she does, in effect, by choosing sides. She appears to be compromising—"there is a need for some 'research' but not to the extent that teaching is pushed aside"—but, as her last sentence shows, she has in fact dismissed the way that Volpe complicates the relationship between teaching and research.]

[7] I agree with Smith that research, such as reading in the professor's field, is beneficial to his or her teaching. But requiring research to the extent of publication in order to secure a tenured position is actually denying education to both the professors and their students. I understand that some of the pressure stems from the fact that it is easier to decide tenure by the "tangible" evidence of research and publication. The emphasis on "publish or perish" should revert to "teach or perish" (Smith 6). If more of an effort is required to base tenure upon teaching, then that effort should be made. After all, it is the education of the people of our nation that is at risk.

[The writer continues to align herself with one side of the issue, which she continues to summarize but not to raise questions about.]

[8] In conclusion, I believe that the problem of the "flight from teaching" can and must be addressed. The continuation of the problem will lead to greater damage in the academic community. The leaders of our colleges and universities will need to take the first steps toward a solution.

[The writer concludes with a more strongly worded version of her endorsement of the position of Smith and Sykes on the threat of research to teaching. Notice that the paper has not really evolved from the unanalyzed position it articulated in paragraph 2.]

D. STRATEGIES FOR WRITING AND REVISING RESEARCH PAPERS

Here we offer some general strategies gleaned from and keyed to our analysis of a typical paper, "The Flight from Teaching," that can be applied to any research project.

1. Be sure to make clear who is talking.

When, for example, the writer refers to the professors' concern for their "precious time" in paragraph 2 or when she writes that "In actuality, research inhibits teaching" in paragraph 3, is she simply summarizing Smith or endorsing his position? You can easily clarify who's saying what by inserting attributive tag phrases such as "in Smith's view" or "in response to Smith, one might argue that." Remember that your role is to provide explanation of and perspective on the ideas in your source—not, especially early on, to cheerlead for it or attack it.

2. Analyze as you go along rather than saving analysis for the end (disciplinary conventions permitting).

It is no coincidence that a research paper that summarizes its sources and delays discussing them, as "The Flight from Teaching" does, should have difficulty constructing a logically coherent and analytically revealing point of view. The *organization* of this research paper interferes with the writer's ability to have ideas about her material because the gap is too wide between the presentation and analysis of her sources. As a result, readers are left unsure how to interpret the positions she initially summarizes, and her analysis, by the time she finally gets to it, is too general.

3. Quote *in order to* analyze: make your sources speak.

Even if the language you quote or paraphrase seems clear in what it means to you, the aim of your analysis is to put what you have quoted or paraphrased into some kind of frame or perspective. Quoting is a powerful form of evidence, but recognize that you can quote *very* selectively—a sentence or even a phrase will often suffice. After you quote, you will usually need to paraphrase in order to discover and articulate the implications of the quotation's key terms. *As a general rule, you should not end a discussion with a quotation but rather with some point you want to make about the quotation.*

The following sentence from the second paragraph of "The Flight from Teaching" demonstrates the missed opportunities for analysis that occur when a quotation is allowed to speak for itself.

> Smith disagrees with the hands-off approach being taken by the professors: "There is no decent, adequate, respectable education, in the proper sense of that much-abused word, without personal involvement by a teacher with the needs and concerns, academic and personal, of his/her students" (7).

This sentence is offered as part of a neutral summary of Smith's position, which, the writer informs us, "disagrees with the hands-off approach." But notice how Smith's word choices convey additional information about his point of view. The repetition of "personal" and the quarrelsome tone of "much-abused" suggest that Smith is writing a polemic—that he is so preoccupied with the personal that he wishes to restrict the definition of education to it. The writer may agree with Smith's extreme position, but the point is that if she attends to his actual language, she will be able to characterize that position much more accurately.

By contrast, notice how the writer in the following example quotes *in order to* analyze the implications of the source's language:

> If allegations that top levels of U.S. and British governments acted covertly to shape foreign policy are truthful, then this scandal, according to Friedman, poses serious questions concerning American democracy. Friedman explains, "The government's lack of accountability, either to Congress or to the public, was so egregious as to pose a silent threat to the principles of American democracy" (286). The word "principles" is especially important. In Friedman's view, without fundamental ideals such as a democracy based on rule by elected representatives and the people, where does the average citizen stand? What will happen to faith in the government, Friedman seems to be asking, if elected representatives such as the president sully that respected office?

By emphasizing Friedman's word choice ("principles"), this writer uses quotation not only to convey information but also to frame it, making a point about the source's point of view.

4. Try converting key assertions in the source into questions.

When you are under the spell of a source, its claims sound more final and unquestionably true than they actually are. So a useful habit of mind is to experiment with rewording selected assertions as questions. Consider, for example, what the writer of "The Flight from Teaching" might have discovered had she tried converting the following conclusions (in paragraph 4) drawn from one of her sources into questions.

> The call to research is the cause of many problems. The reduced number of professors actually teaching increases both the size of classes and the likelihood that students will find at registration that their courses are closed. Students will also find they do not have to write papers, and often exams are multiple choice, because of the large classes.

Some questions: Is it only professors' desire to be off doing their own research that explains closed courses, large class sizes, and multiple-choice tests? What about other causes for these problems, such as the cost of hiring additional professors or the pressure universities put on professors to publish in order to increase the status of the institution? We are not suggesting that the writer should have detected these particular problems in the passage but rather that she needs, somewhere in the paper, to *raise questions about the reasoning implicit in her sources.*

By *querying how your sources are defining, implicitly and explicitly, their key terms*, you can gain perspective on the sources, uncovering their assumptions. Consider in this context the writer's own fullest statement of her thesis (in paragraph 6).

> Through the authors utilized in this paper and other sources, I have determined that there is a need for some "research" but not to the extent that teaching is pushed aside. Colleges and universities exist to provide an education; therefore, their first responsibility is to the student.

More questions: What do she and her sources mean by "research" and by "teaching"? To what extent can the writer fairly assume that the primary purpose of universities is and should be "to provide an education"? Can't an education include being mentored in the skills that university teachers practise in their own research? And isn't teaching only one of a variety of contributions that universities make to the cultures they serve?

5. Get your sources to converse with one another, and actively referee the conflicts among them.

By doing so, you will often find the means to reorganize your paper around issues rather than leaving readers to locate these issues for themselves as you move from source to source. Both looking for difference within similarity and looking for similarity despite difference are useful for this purpose (see Chapter 4).

The organizing contrast that drives "The Flight from Teaching" is obviously that between teaching and research, but what if the writer actively sought out an unexpected similarity that spanned this binary? For example, the writer asserts that "research inhibits teaching" (paragraph 3), whereas Volpe contends that "only the research scholar can provide the best form of teaching because 'teaching and research are as inseparable as the two faces of the same coin'" (paragraph 5). But both sides *agree* that educating students is the "first responsibility" of colleges and universities, despite differing radically on how this responsibility is best fulfilled. Given this unexpected similarity, the writer could then explore the significance of the difference—that Smith believes professors' research gets in the way of excellent teaching, whereas Volpe believes research is essential to it. If the writer had brought these sources into dialogue, she could have discovered that the assertion she offers as her conclusion is, in fact, inaccurate, even an evasion.

By way of conclusion, we would like to emphasize that these five strategies share a common aim: to get you off the hot seat of judging the experts when you are not an expert. Most of us are more comfortable in situations in which we can converse amicably rather than judge and be judged. Think of that as you embark on research projects, and you will be far more likely to learn and to have a good time doing it.

E. A CANADIAN RESEARCH PAPER: ASSESSING THE CONVERSATION

We return now to the work of Kelly Hannah-Moffat, whose article on women's prisons appears on page 285–291. The fact that Hannah-Moffat accomplished meaningful research is clear from the list of references at the end: sixteen sources are included therein. Notice that four of those sources bear her own name. Is it possible that Hannah-Moffat is dominating the "conversation" that this chapter recommends every research writer orchestrate?

To answer that question, let's keep in mind the five strategies explained in the preceding section. The first strategy is "to make clear who is talking." While Hannah-Moffat employs the first-person "I" to clarify her research methodology ("I do this by focusing on initial classifications practices and assessments …), she clearly identifies other voices at the beginnings of some sentences: for instance, "Parton notes 'the idiom of risk not only presupposes ideas of choice and calculation, but also responsibility' (2001: 62)." More frequently, however, she chooses to name her sources within parentheses at the ends of sentences. Either way, readers are kept informed about who is talking.

What about the other four strategies? Is Hannah-Moffat analyzing as she goes rather than saving analysis for the end? Is she quoting *in order to* analyze? Is she converting key assertions into questions? And—perhaps most importantly—is she getting her sources to converse with one another (and actively refereeing any conflicts)?

By looking closely at the conclusion of the article, we should be able to answer these important questions—and to decide whether or not Hannah-Moffat is actually conversing with her fellow researchers. Here are the first three sentences of that concluding paragraph:

> The marginalization of gender is not new. However, in this instance, it is coupled with renewed apathy and gender neutrality that appears to negate the 'progress' made in Canadian women's corrections over the past decade. Researchers and policy makers need to be more attentive to how gender and racial and/or cultural differences can be meaningfully integrated into

institutional structures and how systems that resist such diversity can be challenged and held accountable.

Like all true idea-holders, Hannah-Moffat is motivated by something mentioned back in Chapter 2 of this book: the need to account for some *dissonance*—that is, for something that seems not to fit together. As far as she's concerned, there hasn't been enough progress made in Canadian women's corrections; hence, the word itself is placed in quotation marks. Furthermore, researchers have not been sufficiently "attentive to how gender and racial and/or cultural differences can be meaningfully integrated ..." From this dissonant perspective, she proceeds—in the article's conclusion—to quote a source in order to analyze:

> Carlen's recent book posits the questions: 'Is the concept of gendered justice still worth discussing? Is "gendered justice" viable as an organizing principle of sentencing, non-custodial and custodial regimes?' (2002: 11). While notions of gendered justice and gendered risk are fraught with conceptual and operational difficulties, the abandonment and ignorance of gender in penal assessment and classification is bound to entrench existing barriers to programming and create new ones for women prisoners.

While demonstrating the third of our five strategies ("Quote *in order to* analyze: make your sources speak"), Hannah-Moffat appears to reverse the terms of our fourth strategy: rather than converting key assertions into questions, she is converting key questions into assertions. Carlen's two questions stimulate an analytical retort from the writer; Hannah-Moffat asserts the viability of "gendered justice" as an organizing principle for penal assessment and classification. The final two sentences of the conclusion emphasize just how perilous it would be to ignore this principle:

> In Canada, women's correctional systems are obliged to directly address gender and reconcile the incongruity between gender-sensitive policy, law, and correctional practice. In the long run, a failure to understand and respond to gender is inefficient and counter-intuitive in terms of the development of 'best practices for women' particularly if one subscribes to the logic of 'what works.'

With the conclusion of this research article comes an evolved version of an earlier thesis: "In brief, assessment and classification practices fail to recognize the gendered and racialized aspects of social life and experiences of women in conflict with the law." Hannah-Moffat—in conversation with her sources—has articulated the consequences of failing to recognize those gendered and racialized aspects of social life.

As you reread the article, notice how often the word "practitioners" appears throughout the body paragraphs (by doing so, you will be fulfilling Step 1 of Chapter 1's Five-Step Analysis). In addition to conversing with other researchers, Hannah-Moffat is also is talking with—and collecting "interview data" from—numerous federal corrections practitioners. She views these professionals as part of the problem; their lack of training "has resulted in specious links between factors such as a history of victimization and risk to re-offend."

Thus, from the start, Hannah-Moffat's research project involved collaborating with more than fellow researchers. She also took into account the attitudes, as well as the behaviour, of "institutional classification officers, parole board members, probation officers, and case managers." In other words, her "conversation" was multifaceted and complex. So let's not be too surprised to see that our chapter's five strategies are employed by this writer with some degree of flexibility. For example, Hannah-Moffat saves most of her analysis for the end—in the conclusion—rather than analyzing as she goes along. Also (as already mentioned) she turns Carlen's questions into assertions instead of turning assertions into questions. Such modifications are inevitable because no two research writers confront identical circumstances. The bottom line—for Kelly Hannah-Moffat as well as for you—is "to do something with the reading." This phrase is quoted from the beginning of the chapter (on page 199), which goes on to say, "Clarify the meaning of the material you have quoted, paraphrased, or summarized, and explain its significance in light of your evolving thesis."

That amounts to some very important advice, worth repeating (which we just did).

ASSIGNMENT

Back in Chapter 4, you were urged to become "conversant" with material, to actively engage with sources rather than reading passively. This assignment requires conversancy with Michael Posner's "Image World" (pages 110–117) and Mark Kingwell's "The Mirror Stage: Infinite Reflections on the Public Good" (pages 268–276). Each of the following exercises should be accomplished in teams of two; by collaborating with another conversant reader, you will surely enhance your "conversation" with sources.

1. Notice that both Posner (in his introduction) and Kingwell (in his conclusion) refer to "philosopher Guy Debord." To what extent does Debord influence the thesis statements presented by these writers?

2. Among the sources mentioned in Kingwell's "Notes" is the former leader of the Liberal Party, Michael Ignatieff. Posner also uses a source associated with the political activism: Naomi Klein. Which of the two articles do you think is more diverse in its conversation with sources? Does such diversity strengthen the writer's analysis of his topic?

3. In Chapter 6, we cited a passage from Mark Kingwell's article as an example of a deductive argument, one that "draws out the implications . . . of a position you already agree to." Here is a second example, from "Image World." Read it carefully and discuss with your partner how Posner's reasoning moves "inevitably" from assumption to conclusion:

> Images are immediate. They require less judgment, less interpretation. They appeal not to our reason but to our intuition, not to thought but to feeling.
>
> Inevitably, therefore, the ascendancy of the image economy, and the concomitant decline of print culture, means that ever larger percentages of the population are being conditioned to respond emotionally and viscerally to the daily blizzard of images that bombard them.

Writing the Researched Paper: A Final Checklist of Strategies for Success

1. Avoid the temptation to plug in sources as answers. Aim for a *conversation* with them. Think of sources as voices inviting you into a community of interpretation, discussion, and debate.

2. Quote, paraphrase, or summarize *in order to* analyze. Explain what you take the source to mean, showing the reasoning that has led to the conclusion you draw from it.

3. Quote sparingly. You are usually better off centring your analysis on a few quotations, analyzing their key terms, and branching out to aspects of your subject that the quotations illuminate.

4. Don't underestimate the value of close paraphrasing. You will almost invariably begin to interpret a source once you start paraphrasing its key language.

5. Locate and highlight what is at stake in your source. Which of its points does the source find most important? What positions does it want to modify or refute, and why?

6. Attribute sources ("According to Einstein…,") in the text of your paper, not just in parenthetical citations. This practice will distinguish source material from your remarks about it and allow readers to evaluate its credibility up front.

7. Look for ways to develop, modify, or apply what a source has said, rather than simply agreeing or disagreeing with it.

8. If you challenge a position found in a source, be sure to represent it fairly. First, give the source some credit by identifying assumptions you share with it. Then, isolate the part that you intend to complicate or dispute.

9. Look for sources that address your subject from different perspectives. Avoid relying too heavily on any one source.

10. When your sources disagree, consider playing mediator. Instead of immediately agreeing with one or the other, clarify areas of agreement and disagreement among them.

9

Finding and Citing Sources

With this chapter we shift to more practical and technical matters associated with writing the researched paper. After offering advice on finding and evaluating sources in print and electronic format (the first three steps of the research process), we target a chronic problem area for many writers—how to integrate quotations into your own prose—and conclude with a brief discussion of how to cite secondary materials and how to compose abstracts of sources.

Inevitably, this chapter also addresses plagiarism, a topic that always seems to be making headlines. For example, media around the world were abuzz in the spring of 2011 with the fate of Karl-Theodor zu Guttenberg, one of Germany's most popular and capable politicians. He was forced to resign as defence minister after being stripped of his doctoral degree by the University of Bayreuth. It turned out that in 2007 Guttenberg had copied passages—without acknowledgement—from the work of other writers (McGroarty n.p.). His dissertation was built on a foundation of plagiarism. It crumbled.

We begin, though, with the research process itself, which involves working through a series of steps such as those outlined in Table 9.1 (adapted from the Big Six model by Eisenberg and Berkowitz). Of course, these steps need not be sequential and may very well involve "looping back" when actions do not yield useful or appropriate information.

TABLE 9.1

Steps in the Research Process

1. Topic Focus	• Define topic. • Find background information. • What questions need to be answered?
2. Information-Seeking Strategies	• Identify range of suitable resource types. • Determine best tool for accessing resources. • Construct search strategy within tool.
3. Location and Access	• Locate sources whether in print or online. • Find information within sources.
4. Use of Information	• Identify information that is valuable for the topic. • Focus on the specific topic at hand. • Take notes to record information and source. Writing aids personal understanding and interpretation.
5. Synthesis	• Organize/combine information from multiple sources. • Restructure information into a new format. • Cite sources as necessary.
6. Evaluation	• Judge product based on set criteria. • Analyze personal problem-solving style.

Notice that Step 4 emphasizes the advantage of not postponing your writing until the end of the research process. By composing sentences and paragraphs along the way, every researcher will enhance his or her "personal understanding and interpretation" of the material at hand.

A. GETTING STARTED

The problem with doing research in the Information Age is that so much information is available. How do you get an overview of a subject that you don't know much about? How do you know which information is considered respectable in a particular discipline and which isn't? How can you avoid wasting time with source materials that have been effectively refuted and replaced by subsequent thinking? A short answer to these questions is that you should start not in the stacks but in the reference collection of your library or with its electronic equivalent.

If you start with specialized encyclopedias, dictionaries, and handbooks, you can rapidly gain a broad perspective on your subject. Your library's reference room will provide access to a wide variety of encyclopedias, including:

- Canadian Encyclopedia
- Encyclopedia of the Novel
- Encyclopedia of Victoriana
- Encyclopedia of World Environmental History
- Encyclopedia of Religion and Society
- Encyclopedia of Urban Cultures

These reference tools provide background information, identify key issues in an area, and define concepts and terminology that you might not be familiar with. Also consult your class textbook for an overview of the subject area. Given a topic on *television violence*, here is an example of what you find by consulting a related encyclopedia on sociology. The first entry ("aggression cues and") leads to citations for two scholarly articles that analyze research studies on the effects of watching violent television shows.

Encyclopedia of Sociology (2000), 5 vols.

Sample topics under "Television" in the index:

- aggression cues and
- American social effects of
- as attitude influence
- time-spent-viewing survey

As you begin to explore potential resources, continue focusing on the assigned topic. Generating questions is an effective means of discovering what it is you really need to know.

Step 1. Topic Focus

Topic: The effects of television violence on children

Questions to answer:

- How many hours of television on average do children watch?
- How many acts of violence are in a typical cartoon?
- How pervasive is this phenomenon in Canada?
- Are there research studies that have observed children before and after watching a violent program?

Because every university library is different, the effort to become familiar with its special features is crucial. Here are some reliable strategies:

- Go to your library's website and look for the link on how to set up your computer so that you can access library resources from home.
- Look for the link to research guides on different subjects. All academic libraries create these to describe key resources in each discipline, including best indexes, full-text collections, and websites.
- Go to your library's reference desk and speak to a librarian about the specific research tools that are best suited to an assignment you are working on. A half-hour spent with a reference librarian can save you half a day wandering randomly through the stacks.
- Check the library website for classes offered on how to do research. These will orient you to the pathways, tools, and search techniques that enable effective research.

B. SELECTING THE MOST RELIABLE AND HELPFUL SOURCES

With your research questions in hand, you can proceed to use the other tools in the reference collection such as article indexes, abstracts, and bibliographies. Indexes vary in what they include. Some only list citations that provide article author and title information within scholarly journals. Others include abstracts or summaries of what each article is about. Others may provide the full text of all the articles included.

The scope of each index also varies. Some list scholarly articles while others may include any combination of popular magazines, newspapers, government documents, primary sources, statistics, books, book chapters, interviews, literature reviews, dissertations, and conference proceedings. While some indexes are small and include only English-language materials, others are international in scope and include works in multiple languages. Index date coverage also varies; some are historical and cover writing from the earliest centuries while others gather materials from the last six months. The range of index attributes reveals why tool selection is often one of the most difficult steps in undertaking research.

Many students find it difficult to distinguish between scholarly and popular sources. If your instructor requires the use of "peer-reviewed" papers or "scholarly" studies, keep in mind the distinctions described in Table 9.2.

TABLE 9.2

Distinguishing Between Scholarly and Popular Articles

Feature	Scholarly Article	Popular Article
Audience	The intended audience is scholars, researchers, professionals in the field, and students. The language tends to be technical and complex.	The intended audience is the general public. The article is written to entertain and is usually short and in simple language.
Author	Authors are experts in their fields and may be researchers or affiliated with a college or university. Qualifications and title often stated. Articles are usually peer-reviewed—evaluated by other scholars in the field.	Authors are usually journalists or freelance writers. Staff writers don't often sign articles and their credentials are not given.
Content	Content reports on original research or experimentation. Qualitative or quantitative study methods may be described. The journal focuses on articles in the same subject area (e.g., sociology, geography). Has few glossy pictures; may include graphs and charts as illustrations.	Content reports on information second or third hand, usually popular topics and current affairs. The magazine covers a range of general topics rather than one particular subject area. Includes pictures or photographs, and is slick in appearance.
Publisher	The publisher may be a scholarly professional association or university press. The name of the issuing body often appears on the front cover (e.g., Canadian Association of Geographers publishes *The Canadian Geographer*).	The publisher is not a professionally affiliated group or association. Magazines are usually owned by corporations (e.g., *Maclean's* is published through Rogers Communications).
References	Citations within the text, references, footnotes, or a list of sources is always included.	A list of works consulted in the writing of the article is not usually included.

A Closer Look at Indexes

Before attempting to search an index, identify the form of information that will help you answer your proposed questions.

Step 2. Information-Seeking Strategies

What form of information is needed?

- How many hours of television do children watch? Need <u>statistics</u>.
- How pervasive is this phenomenon in Canada?

- Need <u>popular sources</u> such as newspapers or magazines for examples and also statistics from <u>government document</u> or academic source.
- Are there research studies that have observed children before and after watching a violent program?
- Need <u>research study</u> reported in a scholarly article, not just a popular source that presents opinions without citing evidence.

Which tool is best to access the information needed on television violence?

- Statistics: Statistics Canada on the Web
- Government Documents: Federal government Web pages
- Newspapers: Canadian newspaper database
- Magazines and Scholarly Articles: Article index such as *Canadian Business and Current Affairs* with articles from both scholarly (*Canadian Journal of Sociology*) and popular (*Time* and *Maclean's*) magazines
- More Scholarly Articles: Index that lists research studies such as *Social Sciences Index* (small index of 415 journals in English)
- More Scholarly Articles: *Sociological Abstracts* (large index of 2,000 journals in 30 languages from 55 countries)
- Full-text articles: Try JSTOR (Journal Storage) and Ontario Scholar's Portal. Holdings in sociology are limited in these full-text indexes.

Some indexes specialize only in statistics; some list federal, provincial, or municipal documents. Several very specific ones only index reviews—such as *Book Review Digest* and *Book Review Index*. Still others offer scholarly peer-reviewed articles with research studies, such as these academic indexes: *Humanities Index, Social Sciences Index*.

Popular opinion pieces on current topics are indexed in newspaper and magazine indexes such as *Canadian Newsstand* (16 papers across the country) and *Canadian Business and Current Affairs* (750 journals and magazines including *Time* and *Maclean's* and 9 daily newspapers). Many newspapers and popular magazines now index their own publications at individual websites. One example is Montreal's *The Gazette*, whose website offers an "Archives" service and "Search Tools" for locating particular stories. To locate the sites of nearly all newspapers with an online presence, worldwide, visit *News and Newspapers Online* (http://library.uncg.edu/news/), maintained by the library of the University of North Carolina at Greensboro. This site is useful for finding out whether a newspaper offers a free searchable archive.

Given the range and diversity of indexes, it is always a good idea to consult with a professional librarian for assistance (see Table 9.3). Most academic libraries also have subject guides on the Web that describe the content and scope of key information tools for individual disciplines.

Keyword Searches

Once you know which indexes to consult, you can brainstorm for keywords with which to search. Keywords are your words and reflect the main concepts of your topic. The encyclopedia will already have given you some ideas. Let's consider the topic at hand.

TABLE 9.3
How to Choose an Index

Questions to Ask	Information to Consider
What type of information do I need?	Consider the form of information in different resources: books, scholarly or popular articles, newspapers, primary sources, government documents, images, maps, videos, dissertations, book reviews, conference proceedings, and websites.
Do I need primary or secondary sources?	A primary source provides the "data" to be analyzed by a research writer. Here are some examples: diaries, speeches, letters, memoirs, interviews, manuscripts (fiction or non-fiction), and government documents. A secondary source interprets and analyzes primary sources. As a researcher, you examine a primary source of information and, as a writer, you engage in a "conversation" with your secondary sources (as explained in Chapter 8).
What date coverage is suitable for my topic?	Currency varies in different sources: newspapers—daily; magazines—weekly to four months old; journal articles—one to two years old; books—five years old; encyclopedias—seven years old; Web pages—variable. For primary sources, find an index that covers past centuries.
Do I need international information?	Some indexes include only North American sources while others include materials from many countries in a variety of languages.
Does it include full text?	Some indexes provide the complete article while others give only a citation or possibly a summary of the work. If full text is not provided, check your library catalogue by the title of the journal for a paper copy or speak to your interlibrary loans department.

Step 2. Information-Seeking Strategies (continued)

List your concepts and keywords in preparation for searching.

Concept:	television	violence	children	research
Related	media	aggression	youth	articles
Keyword(s):	cartoons	social effects attitudes behaviour	teenagers adolescents	references bibliography (this is something you don't add in an academic index but it can be useful on the Web)

The purpose of this exercise is to maximize your chances of finding information. Electronic indexes are best searched by keywords rather than subject headings. You should be aware that reference sources use agreed-upon subject headings for different topics. Thus, don't be surprised if the keywords you enter initially yield nothing. Keep trying various combinations. Once you identify a useful article, check the subject headings that are listed with it for more searchable terms. For example, consider the subjects used in *Sociological Abstracts* that are discovered on searching the television violence topic.

Sociological Abstracts Search

Search Words	Number of Records Retrieved with Each Search
Keyword search: television and violence and children	62
Subject headings listed and searched:	
mass media violence	203
television viewing	614
mass media effects	2890

The above example gives you some idea why subject headings must be explored. If you don't use them, you may miss some of the best articles on your topic. The television and violence and children search yields 62 possible records, of which the library will carry a small number. However, there are hundreds of other possible articles that can only be found using other subject headings. While there are paper indexes that list subject headings, it's usually easier to identify these by starting with a keyword search in an electronic index and exploring subjects from there.

Unfortunately, it's no good only searching indexes that provide the complete paper online because they may not cover your topic or even your discipline. Let's take an example. Many students have heard that the JSTOR index (Journal Storage) is a good index for everything because it contains full-text articles. What they don't know is that it includes a limited number of journals in different areas and that it lists only those works published up to five years prior to the present day. For example, JSTOR indexes only twenty-nine sociology journals with coverage up to 1999. On the other hand, *Sociological Abstracts* covers 2,000 journals with coverage up to the present. Ontario Scholar's Portal also offers complete full-text articles from 3,369 journals (as of August 2004), but content favours the sciences. Compare the number of hits on the TV violence topic in the chart below.

Search Results in Full-Text vs. Other Indexes

Search	Full-Text Index	Other Indexes
"television" and "violence" and "children"	*JSTOR*: 29 sociology journals covering up to 1999 yields only 1 hit from 1973	*Sociological Abstracts*: 2,000 journals up to the present yields 62 hits from 1960–2004
in abstract	*Ontario Scholar's Portal*: Social sciences journal search yields only 7 hits from 1994–2004	*Social Sciences Index*: 415 journals up to the present yield 41 hits from 1985–2004

This comparison demonstrates that restricting your search to only full-text indexes or collections has its pitfalls. Keep in mind that much of the world's greatest writing is not in electronic format. The most productive approach to information seeking is to search the indexes that specialize in your field, regardless of whether they include full-text articles, and then check your library catalogue to find out if there is an online or paper version available outside the index itself. The library can usually get materials for you (sometimes for a small fee) through a service known as interlibrary loan.

Students often assume that when they search an index in the library (whether paper or online), the library will carry all the titles mentioned in the index. Given the hundreds of thousands of journal titles available, this is not possible. Therefore, the next step in your research strategy is to check the library catalogue to see if it carries a particular journal or book title (see Table 9.4). Searching by journal author or journal article title won't work because library catalogues do not list this level of detail—that is the function of article indexes. A library catalogue lists only book titles and journal titles (among other formats) but not journal article titles.

TABLE 9.4

Locating a Journal Article in the Library

> Many journal indexes list only article citations. Sometimes abstracts or summaries are also included. Below is a citation taken from the *Social Sciences Index*. A citation lists the author, article title, journal title (source), volume, issue, year, and page numbers.
>
> To find out if a library has this article, search by the source name (journal title): *Developmental Psychology* and look for the location of Volume 39.
>
> **Title:** Longitudinal Relations Between Children's Exposure to TV Violence and Their Aggressive and Violent Behavior in Young Adulthood: 1977–1992
>
> **Author:** Huesmann, L. Rowell; Moise-Titus, Jessica; Podolski, Cheryl-Lynn; and Eron, Leonard D.
>
> **Source:** Developmental Psychology v 39 no2 Mar 2003. p. 201–21

Step 3. Location and Access

Locate sources whether in print or online by searching the library catalogue.

- Search by journal title, not article title.
- If there is an electronic copy, follow the link provided.
- Look for the volume number.

At this point it's worth mentioning that you should keep a record of what you've searched and how you searched it (see Table 9.5). Such a research journal helps develop an awareness of the steps in the research process and provides a means for recording effective search strategies. Some instructors require this information as part of research assignments so they can track a student's unique search process and discourage plagiarism.

TABLE 9.5

Tips for Your Research Journal

> Record your questions and your problems.
>
> Track your research strategy. This can be used in your literature review.
>
> What type of content is in each relevant database? Which operators does it use?
>
> Who are key authors in the field?
>
> Which keywords yield the best results?
>
> Write down important citations or copy them to disk for the writing stage.

Searching the Internet

These days, plenty of research can be accomplished in front of your own computer screen and even on your cell phone. Indeed, searching the Internet is the preferred strategy of many analytical writers. Keep in mind, though, that not everything on the Internet is there for the taking. Many databases, indexes, and scholarly journals are restricted to subscribers; the license agreements at your university's library will determine what you may or may not be able to locate online.

In recent years, though, licensing and copyright barriers have been significantly diminished by the trend towards "open access." Along with many other North American student organizations, the Canadian Federation of Students has signed the "Student Statement on the Right to Research" issued by the Right to Research Coalition (www.righttoresearch.org). The goal of the open-access movement is to encourage researchers and other writers to publish their work in ways that will make it freely available on the Internet. This allows for greater dissemination of reputable research materials, including peer-reviewed scholarly journal articles.

So not just the availability of sources should concern you but also their reliability. Both of these criteria are met by Google Scholar, a straightforward interface that allows anyone to search a variety of databases and types of documents. Here is the description of Google Scholar provided by the library website at Queen's University:

Access: Google Scholar

Access restrictions: *Free access*

Summary: Use the Google search engine to locate articles from a wide variety of academic publishers, professional societies, preprint repositories and universities, as well as scholarly articles published on the "open" Web.

Notice that the two key criteria for successful research are front-and-centre: availability ("Free access" on the "open" Web) and reliability ("academic publishers," "scholarly articles"). Of course, any search engine from Google Scholar to Yahoo to WiseNut may have its limitations in terms of retrieving the most recent or relevant material for a specific project. Google Scholar is a good starting point for research but you should never end your search there. Discipline specific databases will provide access to additional reputable research that is not freely available on the Internet. It's always a good idea, therefore, to consult with a reference librarian in order to narrow your search effectively and to make optimal use of your time.

Tᴀʙʟᴇ **9.6**
Web Searching Tips

1. **Learn how to apply your favourite search engine's special operators.**
   Does it use quotation marks for phrases? e.g., "artificial intelligence"
   Can it truncate words to get alternate endings? e.g., adolescen★ (adolescent/s, adolescence)
   Can you use the plus sign to make words mandatory in results? e.g., "online learning" +music
   Does the order of the words change the results?
   Can you limit by date or language?

2. **Check the end of a Web address for clues about who created it.**
   .net = network
   .edu = educational
   .gov = government
   .org = organization
   .com = company
   .ca = Canada
   .uk = United Kingdom

   An aid to reveal authorship or institutional affiliation is to backspace a URL. Place the cursor at the end of the URL, backspace to the last slash, and press Enter. Continue backspacing to each preceding slash, examining each level as you go.

3. **Add keywords that describe the type of material you are looking for.**
   e.g., research "genetically modified wheat"
   e.g., statistics women poverty

4. **Explore various synonyms for the same topic.**
   e.g., nuclear weapons, nuclear arms, mass destruction
   e.g., ethics, ethical issues

5. **Use words that reflect how a factual answer might appear rather than random words.**
   e.g., "The Titanic sank on"

6. **Explore subject directories that select and evaluate scholarly resources.**
   e.g., BUBL at http://bubl.ac.uk/link/

   BUBL LINK is a catalogue of selected Internet resources covering all academic subject areas. Items are selected, evaluated, catalogued, and described. Links are checked and fixed each month. LINK stands for Libraries of Networked Knowledge.

   e.g., Infomine at http://infomine.ucr.edu

   "INFOMINE is a virtual library of Internet resources relevant to faculty, students, and research staff at the university level. It contains useful Internet resources like databases, electronic journals, electronic books, bulletin boards, mailing lists, online library card catalogues, articles, directories of researchers, and many other types of information."

7. **Evaluate sites according to a thorough set of criteria (see Table 9.7 later in this chapter).**

When a search engine is used, specialized search techniques must be applied in order to narrow results and push the most relevant pages to the top of the results list. First, identify a range of important focus words to perform your search. Think of synonyms and related phrases. Write out a series of search strings and test them. Check to see how you force specific words to appear on a page, whether you can ask that words be close together (ten words or so), and how to identify exact phrases. Are there other special options to limit by language or date that might be helpful to you? Web searching is a matching process, so testing different search word combinations will yield quite different results.

Relevancy of results also depends on the size of the search engine and how it processes your words. Each engine determines relevancy of results in unique ways. Consult the help file of each engine to learn about these. In Alta Vista, which was shut down in 2011, document relevancy was calculated according to frequency, hierarchy (closer to the top of the document gets more points), and adjacency (proximity or how close your words are to one another) of search words. In Google, relevancy is determined by how frequently a site is linked to other Web pages as a measure of popularity and presumed usefulness. The more pages that link to a site, the higher that site will appear in your results list. Google is very good at tracking straightforward content because of its size. For fun, take a look at how someone used Google to track down people who had purchased degrees from diploma mills: http:// www.hep.uiuc.edu/home/g-gollin/diploma_mills.pdf. Fascinating reading!

Comparisons of results between engines, given the same keyword search, yield different findings based on search capabilities, size, and updating frequency. Putting words in different orders can also change results. Always put the most important words first. The choice of search tool depends on the nature of your question. Different questions necessitate different types of information to answer them. Are you looking for quick facts, government documents, statistics, pictures, or research papers? Decide which starting point is best for the information you need rather than entering with a search engine each time. Bookmark sites that group useful types of information together, such as encyclopedias for quick facts, dictionaries for definitions, and subject directories that compile and organize academic websites.

Web Page Evaluation

Unlike library resources that are generally peer-reviewed and purchased to support academic research, Web pages can be written by anyone. For this reason, it is best to test websites against set criteria before deciding to use them for a class assignment. There are many examples of sites that appear to be informative on first viewing, but are in fact written by people who are not experts, hold biased opinions, or have a product to sell.

Take as an example the Dihydrogen Monoxide Research Division at http://www.dhmo.org. This purports to be a clearinghouse of information for citizens concerned about dihydrogen monoxide, supposedly present in numerous toxic substances and lethal if inhaled. But there is a much more common name for this "dangerous chemical": water.

Along with such hoax websites exist others that aim to seriously misinform the reader. Consider http://www.martinlutherking.org. While the site is skillfully constructed and claims to include "essays, sermons, speeches & more," it is authored by a white supremacy group called Stormfront (http://www.stormfront.org). Reader beware!

Use Table 9.7 to evaluate websites before you accidentally cite pages written by clever school children, companies doing e-business, or even subversive hate groups.

C. PLAGIARISM AND THE LOGIC OF CITATION

Of course, scholarly writing requires the documentation of all sources that contributed to the ideas in your essay, whether or not they are quoted directly. All types of resources should be included: books, book chapters, newspaper articles, journal articles, government documents, videos, interviews with people, messages on discussion lists, or websites. The purpose of listing resources is to give credit to authors, reveal the depth of your research, and allow readers to consult the original sources. This practice of citation involves listing all key details of a work, such as author's name, title, format (e.g., video, Web page), page numbers, URL, etc.

There are many documentation styles, and it is best to consult your instructor directly on the form that is expected for assignments. Some instructors may wish you to use footnotes at the bottom of each page and a final bibliography. Others may prefer references within the text itself, complemented by a list of works cited. All scholarly journals require precise documentation according to their preferred style.

It is impossible to discuss the rationale for citing sources without reference to plagiarism, even though the primary reason for including citations is *not* to prove that you haven't cheated. It's essential that you give credit where it's due as a courtesy to your readers. Along with educating readers about who has said what, citations enable them to find out more about a

TABLE 9.7

Anatomy of a Web Page

Evaluation Criteria Credibility	Issues to Consider
Who wrote the page? What is the contact information? What is the purpose of the document and why was it produced? Is this person qualified to write this document? What is the evidence of quality control?	Does author provide e-mail or a contact address/phone number? Back up the URL to find the source from which the page is linked. What are the author's credentials? What institution is the author affiliated with? Check the URL or back up the address in the Location Box to find out. Know the distinction between author and webmaster.
Accuracy	
How comprehensive is the document? Is the information popular or scholarly? When was the information produced and last updated? Are the links working?	Who is the target audience: novices or experts on the subject? Does the depth of information match the potential audience? Are references or a bibliography provided? Is the site primarily images without content? Check for the date the page was last updated. Check for broken links.
Reasonableness	
What goals/objectives does this page meet? How detailed is the information? What opinions (if any) are expressed by the author? Is the page associated with some form of advertising? If so, information might be biased.	Does the page state the level of information being provided and the target audience? View any Web page as you would an infomercial on television. Why and for whom was it written? Do messages appear across the screen prompting use of other services?
Support	
Is the information that is presented cited correctly? Are supporting links on the topic pro-vided? Is additional software required to view the site or access its information? Are viewing options recommended or available? Is the information free?	Are references and a bibliography provided? Are the links evaluated and do they complement the document's theme? Is there an option for text only, or frames, or a suggested browser for better viewing? Is supporting software provided? Are there restrictions to accessing the information, such as registrations or fees for service?

Voices Across the Curriculum

Knowledge-Based Writing

The root of scholarly writing is knowledge—indeed, it is the basis for essentially all intelligent human activity. But how do we acquire, store, and retrieve knowledge? Until quite recently, a learned person was one who had read all the "good books" and who knew enough from each to go back quickly to check facts and flesh out ideas. With the explosion of information in all scholarly fields this was no longer possible, and scholars at all levels came to rely on reference works—today, we all use dictionaries and encyclopedias.

A significant step forward in knowledge acquisition and retrieval took place when the *Oxford English Dictionary* was put into digital form in a project at the University of Waterloo in 1992 (its publishers claim that the *OED* is the accepted authority on the evolution of the English language over the last millennium). This allowed search and correlation of items to retrieve connections that the creators of this classic dictionary never knew were there. More and more reference material is becoming available on the Internet every day, and many have come to rely on an Internet search as their first step in searching for and retrieving new knowledge. Although there are many effective search engines, Google (http://www.google.com) is a standard for many people.

Effective as an Internet search can be, it is a crude and blunt instrument. A Google search on "Oxford English Dictionary" returned over 1.5 million items—far too many to review—but fortunately the second item was an authoritative source. The explosion of search results could be contained if all of the "knowledge objects" being searched were described with metadata—that is, data describing the knowledge object. We see simple examples of metadata as the key words provided with a journal article. All of this is central to the new scholarly field of knowledge management—a fast-evolving body of knowledge about how information systems can help individuals and organizations acquire, store, retrieve, and manage knowledge. And, of course, write with authority.

—Tom Calvert, professor of information technology

given position and to pursue other discussions on the subject. Nonetheless, plagiarism is an important issue because academic integrity matters. And, as the dilemma of Karl-Theodor zu Guttenberg illustrates (page 227), the stakes are very high.

In recent years there has been a significant rise in the number of plagiarism cases, both across North America and abroad. For example, the "Plagiarism Advisory Service" issued a report in the summer of 2004 that found one in four British university students to have "copied and pasted material from the Internet into an essay and passed it off as their own work" (Curtis n.p.). While the Internet is blamed by many commentators for the rise in plagiarism, others cite a lack of clarity about what plagiarism is and why it is a serious problem. So, let's start by clarifying.

Most people have some idea of what plagiarism is. You already know that it's against the rules to buy a paper from an Internet "paper mill" or to download others' words verbatim and hand them in as your own thinking. And you probably know that even if you change a few words and rearrange the sentence structure, you still need to acknowledge the source. By way of formal definition, plagiarism (as one handbook puts it) gives "the impression that you have written or thought something that you have in fact borrowed from someone else" (Gibaldi 30). It is a form of theft and fraud. Borrowing from someone else, by the way, also includes taking and not acknowledging words and ideas from your friends or your parents. Put another way, any assignment with your name on it signifies that you are the author—that the words and ideas are yours—with any exceptions indicated by source citations and, if you're quoting, by quotation marks.

Knowing what plagiarism is, however, doesn't guarantee that you'll know how to avoid it. Is it okay, for example, to cobble together a series of summaries and paraphrases in a paragraph, provided you include the authors in a bibliography at the end of the paper? Or what if you insert a single footnote at the end of the paragraph? The answer is that both are still plagiarism, because your reader can't tell where your thinking starts and others' thinking stops. As a basic rule of thumb, *"Readers must be able to tell as they are reading your paper exactly what information came from which source and what information is your contribution to the paper"* (Hult 203). More on this later.

Why Does Plagiarism Matter?

A recent American survey indicated that fifty-three percent of Who's Who High Schoolers thought that plagiarism was no big deal (Cole and Kiss 6). So why should institutions of higher learning care about it? Here are two great reasons:

- Plagiarism poisons the environment. Students who don't cheat get alienated by students who do and get away with it, and faculty can become distrustful of students and even disillusioned about teaching when constantly driven to track down students' sources.

It's a lot easier, by the way, than most students think for faculty to recognize language and ideas that are not the student's own. And now there are all those search engines provided by firms like Turnitin (http://turnitin.com) that have been generated in response to the Internet paper-mill boom. Who wants another Cold War?

- Plagiarism defeats the purpose of going to college or university, which is learning how to think. You can't learn to think by just copying others' ideas; you need to learn to trust your own intelligence. Students' panic about deadlines and their misunderstandings about assignments sometimes spur plagiarism. It's a good bet that your professors would much rather take requests for help and give extra time on assignments than have to go through the anguish of confronting students about plagiarized work.

So plagiarism gets in the way of trust, fairness, intellectual development, and, ultimately, the attitude toward learning that sets the tone for a college or university community.

Frequently Asked Questions (FAQs) About Plagiarism

Is it still plagiarism if I didn't intentionally copy someone else's work and present it as my own; that is, if I plagiarized it by accident?

Yes, it is still plagiarism. Colleges and universities put the burden of responsibility on students for knowing what plagiarism is and then making the effort necessary to avoid it. Leaving out the quotation marks around someone else's words or omitting the attribution after a summary of someone else's theory may be just a mistake—a matter of inadequate documentation—but faculty can judge only what you turn in to them, not what you intended.

If I include a list of works consulted at the end of my paper, doesn't that cover it?

No. A works-cited list (bibliography) tells your readers what you read but leaves them in the dark about how and where this material has been used in your paper. Putting one or more references at the end of a paragraph containing source material is a version of the same problem. The solution is to cite the source at the point that you quote or paraphrase or summarize it. To be even clearer about what comes from where, also use what are called in-text attributions. See the next FAQ on these.

What is the best way to help my readers distinguish between what my sources are saying and what I'm saying?

Be overt. Tell your readers in the text of your paper, not just in citations, when you are drawing on someone else's words, ideas, or information. Do this with phrases like "According to X..." or "As noted in X..."—so-called in-text attributions.

Are there some kinds of information that I do not need to document?

Yes. Common knowledge and facts you can find in almost any encyclopedia or basic reference text generally don't need to be documented (for example, that Pierre Trudeau was Canada's prime minister during the 1970s). This distinction can get a little tricky because it isn't always obvious what is and is not common knowledge. Often you need to spend some time in a discipline before you discover what others take to be known to all. When in doubt, cite the source.

If I put the information from my sources into my own words, do I still need to include citations?

Yes. Sorry, but rewording someone else's idea doesn't make it your idea. Paraphrasing is a useful activity because it helps you to better understand what you are reading, but paraphrases and summaries have to be documented and carefully distinguished from ideas and information you are representing as your own.

If I don't actually know anything about the subject, is it okay to hand in a paper that is taken entirely from various sources?

It's okay if (1) you document the borrowings and (2) the assignment called for summary. Properly documented summarizing is better than plagiarizing, but most assignments call for something more. Often comparing and contrasting your sources will begin to give you ideas, so that you can have something to contribute. If you're really stumped, go see the professor.

You will also reduce the risk of plagiarism if you consult sources after—not before—you have done some preliminary thinking on the subject. If you have become somewhat invested in your own thoughts on the matter, you will be able to use the sources in a more active way, in effect making them part of a dialogue.

Is it plagiarism if I include things in my paper that I thought of with another student or a member of my family?

Most academic behaviour codes, under the category called "collusion," allow for students' cooperative efforts only with the explicit consent of the instructor. The same general rule goes for plagiarizing yourself—that is, for submitting the same paper in more than one class. If you have questions about what constitutes collusion in a particular class, be sure to ask your professor.

Voices Across the Curriculum

Citing Your Sources

The issue of citing one's sources is usually handled negatively by linking it to plagiarism and all of its resulting punishments. I try to approach the issue more positively by appealing to students' sense of scholarly responsibility. Here is what I tell them...

Whether you are aware of it or not, you have joined the Community of Scholars, a community that extends around the world and throughout time. You are joining what I think is the only Brother/Sisterhood that matters. With this membership comes a serious responsibility, however.

Knowledge is difficult to find, but surprisingly easy to lose. Should a book be omitted from a computerized catalogue, no one will thereafter find it; indeed, no one will even look for it because no one will know that it ever existed. In effect, it has disappeared from our collective knowledge. Knowledge is of no use if we do not know of its existence and cannot get to it when it is needed. The world is awash in information, but without directions, much can be lost.

When you cite—fully and accurately—you are helping to conserve humanity's collected knowledge by ensuring that future scholars will know about and will be able to find the sources that you have used. Your citations are, in essence, signposts that will direct others to the same places that you have found useful. In this way, you will be helping scholars yet unborn, just as those who came before helped us by conserving the knowledge that we have inherited. Thus, citing is not just about giving credit where it is due; it is about passing on humanity's intellectual inheritance.

Just as you and I have benefited from the work of those who came before us, those who will follow will benefit from the work that we do. As members of this Brother/Sisterhood, we have the responsibility of helping scholars yet to come. Should we neglect this responsibility and fail to direct future scholars to essential knowledge, we will be contributing to humanity's decline by ensuring that important knowledge is lost, perhaps irrevocably. As science fiction writers are fond of saying, we are only one generation away from the cave.

—Paul Gamache, writing instructor

What about looking at secondary sources when my professor hasn't asked me to? Is this a form of cheating?

It can be a form of cheating if the intent of the assignment was to get you to develop a particular kind of thinking skill. In this case, looking at others' ideas may actually retard your learning process and leave you feeling that you couldn't possibly learn to arrive at ideas on your own.

Professors usually look favourably on students who are willing to take the time to do extra reading on a subject, but it is essential that, even in class discussion, you make it clear that you have consulted outside sources. To conceal that fact is to present others' ideas as your own. Even in class discussion, if you bring up an idea you picked up on the Internet, be sure to say so explicitly.

How to Cite Sources

In general, you will be expected to follow a formalized style of documentation. The two most common styles of documentation are those established by the Modern Language Association (MLA) and the American Psychological Association (APA). MLA style is used for humanities topics while APA is used for those in the social sciences. These associations provide examples of basic citation of electronic and print resources on their websites; you will find the MLA at http://www.mla.org and APA at http://www.apastyle.org. For specific citation examples not given on these websites, you can consult the associations' printed manuals—the *MLA Handbook* or the *Publication Manual of the American Psychological Association*—in their most recent editions. As well, many universities provide online sites that summarize documentation procedures. Two of the most comprehensive are maintained by Purdue University (http://owl .english.purdue.edu) and the University of Toronto (http://www.utoronto .ca/writing).

The various styles differ in the specific ways that they organize the bibliographical information, but all of them share the following characteristics:

1. They place an extended citation for each source, including the author, the title, the date, and the place of publication, at the end of the paper. These end-of-text citations are organized in a list, usually alphabetically.
2. They insert an abbreviated citation within the text, located within parentheses directly following every use of the source. Usually this in-text citation consists of the author's name and either the page

(in MLA) or date (in APA). In-text citations indicate in shorthand form in the body of your paper the source you are using and direct your readers to the complete citation located in a list of references at the end of the paper or report.

3. They distinguish among different kinds of sources—providing slightly differing formulas for citing books, articles, encyclopedias, government documents, interviews, and so forth.

4. They have particular formats for citing electronic sources of various kinds, such as CD-ROMs, the Internet, and online journals and databases. These citations replace the publication information typically provided for text references to printed material with what is called an *availability statement*, which provides the method of accessing the source. This statement should provide the information sufficient to retrieve the source.

You have probably already discovered that some professors are more concerned than others that students obey the particulars of a given documentation style. Virtually all faculty across the curriculum agree, however, that *the most important rule for writers to follow in documenting sources is formal consistency*. That is, all of your in-text citations should follow the same abbreviated format, and all of your end-of-text citations should follow the same extended format.

Once you begin doing most of your writing in a particular discipline, you may want to purchase or access on the Internet the more detailed style guide adhered to by that discipline. Because documentation styles differ not only from discipline to discipline but also even from journal to journal within a discipline, you should consult your professor about which documentation format he or she wishes you to use in a given course.

Here are a few basic examples of in-text and end-of-text citations in both MLA and APA form, followed by a brief discussion of the rules that apply. Keep in mind that "in-text" refers to the parenthetical citations that appear within the paragraphs of your essay. Each of these citations serves as a guide for your reader, indicating where—alphabetically—more detailed information on the source can be found in the "end-of-text" list of sources.

1. Single author, MLA style

In-text citation: The influence of Seamus Heaney on younger poets in Northern Ireland has been widely acknowledged, but Patrick Kavanagh's "plain-speaking, pastoral" influence on him is "less recognized" (Smith 74).

"(Smith 74)" indicates the author's last name and the page number on which the cited passage appears. If the author's name had been mentioned in the sentence—had the sentence begun "According to Smith"—you would include only the page number in the citation. Note that there is no abbreviation for "page," that there is no intervening punctuation between name and page, and that the parentheses precede the period or other punctuation. If the sentence ends with a direct quotation, the parentheses come after the quotation marks but still before the closing period. Also note that no punctuation occurs between the last word of the quotation ("recognized") and the closing quotation mark.

End-of-text book citation: Douglas, Ann. *Terrible Honesty: Mongrel Manhattan in the 1920s*. New York: Farrar, Straus, and Giroux, 1995.

End-of-text article citation: Cressy, David. "Foucault, Stone, Shakespeare and Social History." *English Literary Renaissance* 21 (1991): 121–33.

MLA style stipulates an alphabetical list of references (by author's last name, which keys the reference to the in-text citation). This list is located at the end of the paper on a separate page and entitled "Works Cited."

Each entry in the "Works Cited" list is divided into three parts: author, title, and publication data. Each of these parts is separated by a period from the others. Titles of book-length works are italicized, unless your instructor prefers underlining. (Underlining is a means of indicating italics.) Journal citations differ slightly: article names go inside quotations, no punctuation follows the titles of journals, and a colon precedes the page numbers.

2. Single author, APA style

In-text citation: In both oral and written discourse, clarity is always a two-way street. It can be best understood as "the transition between my mind and yours: if my meaning has not changed when it reaches you, the words that conveyed it were clear" (McCumber, 2003, p. 63).

For both books and articles, include the author's last name, followed by a comma, and then the date of publication. If you are quoting or referring to a specific passage, include the page number as well, separated from the date by a comma and the abbreviation "p." (or "pp."), and followed by a space. If the author's name has been mentioned in the sentence, include only the date in the parentheses immediately following the author's name.

In-text citation:	McCumber (2003) addresses the interplay between speaker or writer, on the one hand, and listener or reader, on the other.
End-of-text book citation:	Tannen, D. (1991). *You just don't understand: Women and men in conversation.* New York: Ballantine Books.
End-of-text article citation:	Baumeister, R. (1987). How the self became a problem: A psychological review of historical research. *Journal of Personality and Psychology, 52,* 163–176.

APA style requires an alphabetical list of references (by author's last name, which keys the reference to the in-text citation). This list is located at the end of the paper on a separate page and entitled "References." Regarding manuscript form, the first line of each reference is not indented, but all subsequent lines are indented three spaces.

In alphabetizing the references list, place entries for a single author before entries that he or she has co-authored, and arrange multiple entries by a single author by beginning with the earliest work. If there are two or more works by the same author in the same year, designate the second with an "a," the third a "b," and so forth, directly after the year. For all subsequent entries by an author after the first, substitute three hyphens followed by a period [---.] for his or her name. For articles by two or more authors, use commas to connect the authors, and precede the last one with a comma and an ampersand [&].

The APA style divides individual entries into the following parts: author (using only initials for first and middle names), year of publication (in parentheses), title, and publication data. Each part is separated by a period from the others. Note that only the first letter of the title and subtitle of books is capitalized (although proper nouns would be capitalized as necessary).

Journal citations differ from those for books in a number of small ways. The title of a journal article is neither italicized (or underlined) nor enclosed in quotation marks, and only the first word in the title and subtitle is capitalized. The name of the journal is italicized (or underlined), however, and the first word and all significant words are capitalized. Also, notice that the volume number (which is separated by a comma from the title of the journal) is italicized (or underlined) to distinguish it from the page reference. Page numbers for the entire article are included, with no "p." or "pp.," and are separated by a comma from the preceding volume number. If the journal does not use volume numbers, then "p." or "pp." is included.

How to Integrate Quotations into Your Paper

An enormous number of writers lose authority and readability because they have never learned how to correctly integrate quotations into their own writing. The following guidelines should help.

1. Acknowledge sources in your text, not just in citations.

When you incorporate material from a source, attribute it to the source explicitly in your text—not just in a citation. In other words, when you introduce the material, frame it with a phrase such as "according to Marsh" or "as Cartelli argues."

Although it is not required, you are usually much better off making the attribution overtly, even if you have also cited the source within parentheses or with a footnote at the end of the last sentence quoted, paraphrased, or summarized. If a passage does not contain an attribution, your readers will not know that it comes from a source until they reach the citation at the end. Attributing up-front clearly distinguishes what one source says from what another says and, perhaps more important, what your sources say from what you say. Useful verbs for introducing attributions include the following: "notes," "observes," "argues," "comments," "writes," "says," "reports," "suggests," and "claims." Generally speaking, by the way, you should cite the author by last name only—as "Cartelli," not as "Thomas Cartelli" or "Mr. Cartelli."

2. Splice quotations onto your own words.

Always attach quotations to some of your own language; don't let them sit in your text as independent sentences with quotation marks around them. You can normally satisfy this rule with an attributive phrase—commonly known as a tag phrase—that introduces the quotation.

> According to Paul McCartney, "All you need is love."

Note that the tag phrase takes a comma before the quote.

Alternatively you can splice quotations into your text with a setup: a statement followed by a colon (as in this sentence and the example to follow).

> Gilles Vigneault's song lyric expresses the inevitable link between nationhood and climate: "Mon pays ce n'est pas un pays, c'est l'hiver.'"

The colon, you should notice, usually comes at the end of an independent clause (that is, a subject plus verb that can stand alone), at the spot where a period normally goes. It would be incorrect to write "Gilles Vigneault is known for:'Mon pays ce n'est pas un pays, c'est l'hiver.'"

The rationale for this guideline is essentially the same as that for the previous one: if you are going to quote, you first need to identify its author so that your readers will be able to put it in context quickly.

Spliced quotations frequently create problems in grammar or punctuation for writers. Whether you include an entire sentence (or passage) of quotation or just a few phrases, you need to integrate them into the grammar of your own sentence.

One of the most common mistaken assumptions is that a comma should always precede a quotation, as in "A spokesperson for the Crown attorney's office demanded, 'an immediate response from the mayor.'" The sentence structure in fact does not call for any punctuation after "demanded."

3. Cite sources after quotations.

Locate citations in parentheses after the quotation and before the final period. The information about the source appears at the end of the sentence, with the final period following the closing parenthesis.

> A recent article on the best selling albums in North America claimed that "Ever since Elvis, it has been pop music's job to challenge the mores of the older generation" (Hornby 168).

Note that there is normally *no punctuation* at the end of the quotation itself, either before or after the closing quotation mark. A quotation that ends either in a question mark or an exclamation mark is an exception to this rule, because the sign is an integral part of the quotation's meaning.

> As Hamlet says to Rosencrantz and Guildenstern, "And yet to me what is this quintessence of dust?" (2.2.304–05).

See the section entitled "How to Cite Sources" earlier in this chapter for the appropriate formats for in-text citations.

4. Use ellipses to shorten quotations.

Add ellipsis points to indicate that you have omitted some of the language from within the quotation. Form ellipses by entering three dots (periods) with spaces in between them, or use four dots to indicate that the deletion continues to the end of the sentence (the last dot becomes the period). Suppose you wanted to shorten the following quotation from a recent article about Radiohead by Alex Ross:

> The album "OK Computer," with titles like "Paranoid Android," "Karma Police," and "Climbing Up the Walls," pictured the onslaught of the information age and a young person's panicky embrace of it (Ross 85).

Using ellipses, you could emphasize the source's claim by omitting the song titles from the middle of the sentence:

> The album "OK Computer" ... pictured the onslaught of the information age and a young person's panicky embrace of it (Ross 85).

In most cases, the gap between quoted passages should be short, and in any case, you should be careful to preserve the sense of the original. The standard joke about ellipses is well worth mentioning here: A reviewer writes that a film "will delight no one and appeal to the intelligence of invertebrates only, but not average viewers." An unethical advertiser cobbles together pieces of the review to say that the film "will delight ... and appeal to the intelligence of ... average viewers."

5. Use square brackets to alter or add information within a quotation.

Sometimes it is necessary to change the wording slightly inside a quotation in order to maintain fluency. Square brackets indicate that you are altering the original quotation. Brackets are also used when you insert explanatory information, such as a definition or example, within a quotation. Here are a few examples that alter the original quotations cited above.

> According to one music critic, the cultural relevance of Radiohead is evident in "the album 'OK Computer'... [which] pictured the onslaught of the information age and a young person's panicky embrace of it" (Ross 85).

> Popular music has always "[challenged] the mores of the older generation," according to Nick Hornby (168).

Note that both examples respect the original sense of the quotation; they have changed the wording only to integrate the quotations gracefully within the writer's own sentence structure.

D. HOW TO PREPARE AN ABSTRACT

There is one more skill essential to research-based writing that we need to discuss: how to prepare an abstract. The aim of the nonevaluative summary of a source known as an abstract is to represent a source's arguments as fairly and accurately as possible, not to critique them. Learning how to compose an abstract according to the conventions of a given discipline is a necessary skill for academic researched writing. Because abstracts differ in format and length among disciplines, you should sample some in the reference section of your library or via the Internet to provide you with models to imitate. Some abstracts, such as those in *Dissertation Abstracts*, are very brief—less than two hundred and fifty words. Others may run as long as two pages.

Despite disciplinary differences, abstracts by and large follow a generalizable format. The abstract should begin with a clear and specific explanation of the work's governing thesis (or argument). In this opening paragraph, you should also define the work's purpose, and possibly include established positions that it tries to refine, qualify, or argue against. What kind of critical approach does it adopt? What are its aims? On what assumptions does it rest? Why did the author feel it necessary to write the work—that is, what does he or she believe the work offers that other sources don't? What shortcomings or misrepresentations in other criticism does the work seek to correct?

You won't be able to produce detailed answers to all of these questions in your opening paragraph, but in trying to answer some of them in your note taking and drafting, you should find it easier to arrive at the kind of concise, substantive, and focused overview that the first paragraph of your abstract should provide. Also, be careful not to settle for bland, all-purpose generalities in this opening paragraph. And if you quote there, keep the selections short, and remember that quotations don't speak for themselves.

In sum, your aim in the first paragraph is to define the source's particular angle of vision and articulate its main point or points, including the definition of key terms used in its title or elsewhere in its argument.

Once you've set up this overview of the source's central position(s), you should devote a paragraph or so to the source's *organization* (how it divides its subject into parts) and its *method* (how it goes about substantiating its argument). What kind of secondary material does the source use? That is, how do its own bibliographic citations cue you to its school of thought, its point of view, its research traditions?

Your concluding paragraph should briefly recount some of the source's conclusions (as related to, but not necessarily the same as, its thesis). In what way does it go about culminating its argument? What kind of significance does it claim for its position? What final qualifications does it raise?

What follows is a representative example of a dissertation abstract. Note that, in this situation, the writer is summarizing his own work. Thus, the requirement to be objective and nonevaluative is especially challenging.

Abstract of "Journey into the World of the School: High School Students' Understanding of Citizenship in British Columbia and Quebec"

by Stephane Levesque

(2001)

Regional, multicultural, and national divergences in Canadian politics and education have contributed to the emergence of different forms of nationalism, identity, and citizenship in Canada. The practice and content of secondary education in B.C. and Québec illustrate this general proposition. Two multi-ethnic high schools, one in Québec and one in B.C. (Vancouver), provide a window into Québec history (grade 10) and B.C. social studies (grade 11) classrooms. These classes are used to examine how students construct and understand their citizenship. Key concepts (citizenship rights, participation, pluralism, collective identity) guided this research.

Using a multiple case study design, this qualitative study employed multiple data collection. In addition to the analysis of the documentary record, I observed and interviewed B.C. and Québec high school students, history and social studies teachers, and finally staff from each school. The study generated findings on citizenship education practice and learning. In both provinces, citizenship education is the *raison d'être* of history and social studies. Despite divergent programs and teaching approaches, teachers at both sites recognize the necessity of preparing students for the exercise of democratic citizenship. Students at both sites accord importance to the key citizenship concepts introduced in their history/social studies classes.

Yet contrasts emerge in the findings between francophone Québecois and anglophone British Columbian students, particularly in terms of collective identity. The findings suggest that theoretical discussions on multicultural and multinational citizenship in political theory do not adequately take into account all the complex views of B.C. and Québecois student informants. This study concludes with further research into the study of students' conceptions of citizenship.*

E. THE ULTIMATE *TRY THIS*

For Part II (Writing the Thesis-Driven Paper), you will be concentrating on a reliable three-step sequence for composing a paper based upon secondary sources: *summary*, *comparative analysis*, and *synthesis*. The following exercises include these steps, as well as some preliminary activities. If you are already

---

* Stephane Levesque. Reprinted by permission from the author.

involved in research for a particular assignment, those activities—such as creating a list of sources—may not be necessary. If you're not yet working on a particular assignment, consider one of the topics addressed by the readings in this book, such as prison reform, communications technology, attention deficit disorder, or racialized power relations. By doing so, the relevant reading could become one of your secondary sources.

1. *Compose a relatively informal prospectus* in which you formulate your initial thinking on a subject before you do more research. Include what you already know about the topic, especially what you find interesting, particularly significant, or strange. This exercise will help to deter you from being overwhelmed by and absorbed into the sources you will later encounter.

2. *Conduct a "what's going on in the field" search, and create a preliminary list of sources.* This exercise is ideal for helping you to find a topic or, if you already have one, to narrow it. The kinds of bibliographic materials you consult for this portion of the research project will depend on the discipline within which you are writing. Whatever the discipline, start in the reference room of your library with specialized indexes, book-review indexes, specialized encyclopedias and dictionaries, and bibliographies (print version or CD-ROM) that will give you an overview of your subject or topic. If you have access to databases through your school or library, you should also search them.

The "what's going on in the field" search has two aims:

- To survey materials in order to identify trends—the kinds of issues and questions that others in the field are talking about (and, thus, find important), and
- To compile a bibliography that includes a range of titles that interest you, that could be relevant to your prospective topic, and that seem to you representative of research trends associated with your subject (or topic).

You will not be committed at this point to pursuing all of these sources but rather to reporting what is being talked about. You might also compose a list of keywords that you have used in conducting your search. If you try this exercise, you will be surprised how much value there is in exploring indexes *just for titles*, to see the kinds of topics people are currently conversing about. And you will almost surely discover how *narrowly* focused most research is (which will get you away from global questions).

Append to your list of sources (which is a very preliminary bibliography) a few paragraphs of informal discussion of how the information you have encountered (the titles, summaries, abstracts, etc.) has affected your thinking and plans for your paper. These paragraphs might respond to the following questions:

a. In what ways has your "what's going on in the field" search led you to narrow or shift direction in or focus your thinking about your subject?
b. How might you use one or more of these sources in your paper?
c. What has this phase of your research suggested you might need to look for next?

3. *Write an abstract—a nonevaluative summary—of an article (or book chapter)* from your "what's going on in the field" exercise that you think you might use in your final paper. Use the procedure offered in this chapter's "How to Prepare an Abstract." Aim for two pages in length. If other members of your class are working on the same or similar subjects, it is often extremely useful for everyone to share copies of their abstracts. Remember that your primary concern should lie with representing the argument and point of view of the source as fairly and accurately as possible.

Append to the end of the abstract a paragraph or two that addresses the question "How has this exercise affected your thinking about your topic?" Objectifying your own research process in this way will help to move you away from the cut-and-paste–provide-only-the-transitions mode of writing research papers.

4. *Write a comparative analysis of two reviews of a single source.* Most writers, before they invest the significant time and energy required to study a book-length source, take the much smaller amount of time and energy required to find out more about the book. Although you should always include in your final paper your own analytical summary of books you consult on your topic, it's extremely useful also to find out what experts in the field have to say about the source.

Select from your "what's going on" list one book-length source that you've discovered is vital to your subject or topic. As a general rule, if a number of your indexes, bibliographies, and so forth, refer you to the same book, it's a good bet that this source merits consulting.

Locate two book reviews on the book, and write an analysis that compares the two reviews. Ideally, you should locate two reviews that diverge in their points of view or in what they choose to emphasize. Depending on the length and complexity of the reviews, your comparative analysis should require two or three pages.

In most cases, you will find that reviews are less neutral in their points of view than are abstracts, but they always do more than simply judge. A good review, like a good abstract, should communicate the essential ideas contained in the source. It is the reviewer's aim also to locate the source in some larger context, by, for example, comparing it to other works on the same subject and to the research tradition the book seeks to extend, modify, and so forth. Thus, your analysis should try to encompass how the book contributes to the ongoing conversation on a given topic in the field.

Append to your comparative analysis a paragraph or two answering the question "How has this exercise affected your thinking about your topic?"

Obviously, you could choose to do a comparative analysis of two articles, two book chapters, and so forth, rather than of two book reviews. But in any event, if you use books in your research, you should always find a means of determining how these books are received in the relevant critical community.

F.   THE FINAL STEP IN THE SEQUENCE: SYNTHESIS

At the beginning of this chapter, we presented six "Steps in the Research Process," and number five was *synthesis*: the assembling of separate parts into a whole. Many research papers begin with an opening paragraph (or more than one) that synthesizes prevailing, perhaps competing, interpretations of the topic being addressed. In other words, a writer's synthesis should demonstrate how ideas and issues raised in the secondary sources complement, contradict, or qualify each other. Few effective research papers consist only of such synthesis, however. Instead, writers use synthesis to frame their ideas and to provide perspective on their own arguments; the synthesis provides a platform or foundation for subsequent analyses.

The natural relationship between synthesis and analysis is recognized in all academic fields. Its importance was underscored at the Civil and Environmental Engineering (CEE) New Millennium Colloquium in the spring of 2000. Ralph Gareth Gray, an architect and structural engineer, made several key observations:

- We arrive on this planet equipped with the ability to synthesize and analyze, full-time.

- Design consists of both synthesis and analysis, a blend, not one or the other.
- One first models the thing being designed (synthesis) and then tests the model (analysis), makes the adjustments, and goes around again.
- The proper balance defines good design.

In designing your research paper, use *synthesis* as a means of making your sources begin to speak. As we discussed in Chapter 8, the ensuing conversation will allow you—the writer—to move forward with *analysis*. The proper balance between these two important procedures will define the quality of your written work.

READINGS FOR PART II

Writing the Thesis-Driven Paper

Laying out a *genuine issue* is an essential part of analytical writing. The readings for Part II do exactly that, beginning with "Japan's Long Nuclear Disaster Film" by **Peter Wynn Kirby**. The Japanese earthquakes and tsunami of 2011 prompt the writer to consider a half century of resiliency within "a human population that is, again and again, boxing above its weight class." Kirby's examination of the evidence is informed and thorough. Logical thoroughness is also featured in **Christine Overall**'s analysis of whether or not "Karla Homolka Has a Right to Study at Queen's." A professor of philosophy, Overall examines the case of a high-profile convict from both moral and legal perspectives. Her thesis evolves, step by step, as she uncovers others' assumptions and tests her own. Another philosopher, **Mark Kingwell**, demonstrates one of the points emphasized in Chapter 7: that "a thesis question often functions well to spark a writer's thinking." Throughout "The Mirror Stage: Infinite Reflections on the Public Good," Kingwell uses questions to push his analysis forward and to thereby hone his thesis.

Leslie Millin authoritatively links evidence to claims in his detailed critique of what he calls our "era of cheap and abundant communication." Drawing on his own career in journalism, Millin applies Francis Bacon's notion of the "Idols of the Tribe" to the issues of technology, editorial responsibility, and plagiarism.

The final two readings are taken from specialized academic journals—in the fields of feminism and psychology. As a consequence, the writers' jargon and scholarly allusions will challenge those of us who do not share their expertise. But close, persistent reading is one of the guiding principles of this book; work hard and you will be rewarded. **Kelly Hannah-Moffat** employs interview data in order to articulate the dilemma of Canada's female prison population. Like many a research writer's, her analytical objective is the one announced early in Chapter 8: "to construct the chain of thinking, orchestrate the exchange of views with and among [her] sources, and give the conversation direction." "Memory in Canadian Courts of Law," by **Elizabeth Loftus**, also engages expert sources in order to establish and develop a thesis. Her use of both personal experience and rhetorical tone differs from that of Hannah-Moffat. By contrasting these readings—as well as others in the book—you will develop analytical skills that can be applied to your own writing.

Japan's Long Nuclear Disaster Film†
Peter Wynn Kirby

OXFORD, England—Peering at the post-tsunami devastation in Japan on miniature YouTube windows or video-streaming displays from Japanese news outlets provokes not only empathy and concern, but an unmistakable feeling of déjà vu. As a scholar focusing on the place of nuclear energy in Japanese culture, I've seen more than my share of nuclear-themed monster movies from the '50s onward, and the scenes of burning refineries, flattened cities, mobilized rescue teams and fleeing civilians recall some surreal highlights of the Japanese disaster film genre.

This B-movie fare is widely mocked, often for good reason. But the early "Godzilla" films were earnest and hard-hitting. They were stridently anti-nuclear: the monster emerges after an atomic explosion. They were also anti-war in a country coming to grips with the consequences of World War II. As the great saurian beast emerges from Tokyo Bay to lay waste to the capital in 1954's "Gojira" ("Godzilla"), the resulting explosions, dead bodies and flood of refugees evoked dire scenes from the final days of the war, images still seared in the memories of Japanese viewers. Far from the heavily edited and jingoistic, shoot'em-up, stomp'em-down flick that moviegoers saw in the United States, Japanese audiences reportedly watched "Gojira" in somber silence, broken by periodic weeping.

Yet it is the film's anti-nuclear message that seems most discordant in present-day Japan, where nearly a third of the nation's electricity is generated by nuclear power. The film was inspired by events that were very real and very controversial. In March 1954, a massive thermonuclear weapon tested by the United States near Bikini Atoll in the Pacific, codenamed "Bravo," detonated with about 2.5 times greater force than anticipated. The unexpectedly vast fallout from the bomb enveloped a distant Japanese tuna trawler named the Lucky Dragon No. 5 in a blizzard of radioactive ash. Crewmembers returned to their home port of Yaizu bearing blackened and blistered skin, acute radiation sickness and a cargo of irradiated tuna. Newspapers reported on the radioactive traces left by the men's bodies as they wandered the city, as well as "atomic tuna" found in fish markets in Osaka and later at Japan's famed Tsukiji Market in Tokyo. The exalted Emperor Hirohito himself was said to have eliminated seafood from his diet.

In a nation fixated on purity, the revulsion against this second nuclear contamination of the homeland was visceral. In late September 1954, the Lucky Dragon's radio operator Aikichi Kuboyama died. "Gojira" appeared in cinemas the following month, breaking the record for opening-day receipts in Tokyo and becoming one of the top-grossing films of the year. During the same month, there was an upsurge in anti-nuclear petitions in response to Kuboyama's death, and the peace movement went national.

Audiences who flocked to "Gojira" were clearly watching more than just a monster movie. The film's opening scenes evoked the nuclear explosion in the Pacific and the damaged Japanese bodies so poignant to domestic viewers. Godzilla—relentless, vengeful, sinister—looms as an overt symbol of science run amok. The creature's every footstep and tail-swipe lay bare the shaky foundations on which Japan's postwar prosperity stood. The great reptilian menace onscreen—actually a man in a 200-pound lizard suit stomping through miniaturized versions of Tokyo neighborhoods—illustrated both Japan's aversion to nuclear radiation and its frustrating impotence in a tense cold war climate.

The bizarre and suggestive menagerie of creatures that followed Godzilla onto the silver screen ranged from the intriguing to the ridiculous. Two pterodactyl-like monsters, both named Rodan, wreak havoc on Japan after being disturbed by Japanese mining operations. Mothra, the giant, pied moth-god of Infant Island—a fictional nuclear testing ground in the South Pacific—unleashes devastation on Japan in one film and actually gets the better of Godzilla in an epic smackdown in another. Other monsters include Gamera, a giant turtle, and the absurd Varan the Unbelievable, a large reptile resembling a flying squirrel. In all the films, Japanese populations alternately mobilize against and cower from the threats that wash up, or lumber onto, Japan's shores.

If there is any thread running through this sprawling bestiary of monster films, it is the "profound vulnerability of Japan," as William Tsutsui writes in his acclaimed book *Godzilla on My Mind*. Japan, relatively powerless in the cold war arena in reality, is able in a fictional world to muster its heavily armed and impressively disciplined Self-Defense Forces to fight against, or occasionally delay or redirect, the colossal rampaging of outlandish threats.

But the films also clearly depict a human population that is, again and again, boxing above its weight class. Over time, Godzilla morphs into a defender of Japan, but dangers begin to materialize within the nation itself.

For example, in addition to the lost moral compass of Japanese developers and other businessmen critiqued in several films, works like "Godzilla vs. the Smog Monster" (1971) gave voice to popular opposition against toxic pollution from Japanese industry and rapacious development that had notoriously poisoned Japanese bodies and defiled the nation's once-famed "Green Archipelago" in a series of environmental debacles worthy of their own horror movie marathon.

If the monster-film genre is less ubiquitous than it once was, the themes it reflected are no less present today, particularly in the 24-hour blanket coverage of last week's earthquakes and tsunami. It shows a Japan that remains visibly beset by large-scale threats that strike without warning. Japan's emergency response teams rescue citizens stranded amid once-thriving cities I have visited in years past that are now little more than sludge and debris. Cars, trucks, trains and large ships lie swept into piles ashore or float in murky water like misshapen bath toys. Buildings implode and fires rage as if ignited by a burst of radioactive breath or a flick of a great creature's tail.

But it also brings back into focus Japan's awkward postwar nuclear predicament that was ambiguously illustrated by the Godzilla series. Japan now has 54 nuclear reactors, ranking third in terms of energy output behind the United States and France. Japan also has an unusually shoddy record for nuclear safety. The long string of occasionally fatal nuclear mismanagement lapses over the past few decades in a nation famed worldwide for manufacturing quality control and high-tech achievement is troubling and almost incomprehensible, to say the least. Part of this story is distinctly Japanese, as lack of transparency, insufficient inspection regimes and a sometimes paralyzing inability to make imperfect but practical decisions can leave an industry vulnerable to the sort of dangerous situations that confront the Fukushima reactors.

What is different this time, however, is that we don't need a disaster film to bring out the nuclear contradictions of Japanese society. The tsunami was but one clear counterargument to the claim that nuclear power is a safe solution to climate change and dwindling oil supplies. As our thoughts remain focused on the plight of tens of thousands of people in harm's way, Japan's flawed nuclear record can help shed revealing light on nuclear power plans in other nations, including the United States, that have to succeed in the real world instead of in a far-fetched film plot.

Karla Homolka Has a Right to Study at Queen's‡
Christine Overall

Almost like a footnote to the Paul Bernardo trial, there has been considerable debate about whether or not Karla Homolka, Bernardo's ex-wife, should be permitted to take courses at Queen's University. While serving 12 years for manslaughter, Homolka is taking correspondence courses in sociology. Some people have argued against permitting her to do this, while others have just as strongly defended what might be called her "right to study."

To take courses in the faculty of arts and science at Queen's, candidates must meet certain academic standards. Presumably, Homolka met those standards. But while the university assesses candidates' educational qualifications, it makes no attempt to measure the moral worthiness of prospective students. Nor should it. There are no reliable methods by which an academic institution could assess the moral integrity of all its future students.

However, those who think Homolka shouldn't take university courses would probably say it is not moral criteria that should be used to assess prospective students, but legal ones. A person convicted of a crime should not be admitted to university.

But if the university were to reject students with criminal records, it would be usurping the role of the legal system. In our democracy, legal punishment is set by the courts. It is not appropriate for universities to add further penalties by excluding people from tertiary education. The university is not an arm of the Corrections Service. There is no justification for punishing people twice.

Instead of advocating the exclusion of all persons with a criminal record, those who wish to bar convicted criminals from Queen's would be on firmer ground if they argued on the basis of the potential danger some persons might pose to members of the university community. Where there is strong evidence that a prospective student has a history of violence, for example, there might be reason for caution about permitting that person access to the Queen's campus.

However, Karla Homolka is not a danger to anyone while she is working on correspondence courses in the confinement of her prison cell.

‡ Christine Overall. *The Kingston Whig-Standard,* 21 August 1995. Reprinted with permission from the author.

However manipulative she may be, she is not able to cause harm from a distance, to instructors, staff, or other students.

What about the question of funding for Homolka's university education? Some people have argued that she should not be given a free education.

In fact, Homolka herself, with the support of her family, is paying for her courses. But even so, some critics have asked why Homolka, after committing heinous crimes, should be earning a university degree at all, when many law-abiding citizens can't afford to do so.

This is a good question. But it's mainly a question about financial privileges and socio-economic class. The issue is the cost of a university education, not the fact that Karla Homolka is taking university courses. Instead of accepting high tuitions, which make university education financially unattainable for growing numbers of people, we should support access to post-secondary education for everyone who qualifies.

Another argument against Homolka's access to university is based on some assumptions about rehabilitation. It's claimed that Homolka should be receiving vocational instruction, not a university education. This argument overlooks the fact that Homolka already has vocational training, as a veterinary assistant. And some of the skills she learned were put to grisly use in the killings in which she participated.

A possible benefit of university courses in the humanities and social sciences is that they may provide Homolka with an opportunity to reflect upon what she did, and acquire moral insight into the origins and context of her actions. Of course, there's no guarantee that someone who takes university courses will acquire these abilities, just as there is no guarantee that any other forms of training will help prisoners lead law-abiding lives.

Some people opposed to Homolka's taking university courses may not want her to engage in activities that are interesting and enjoyable. The feeling may be that she committed horrible atrocities, and she should be punished for doing so—not using her time in prison for reading books and writing essays.

Many students will tell you that taking university courses is not just a matter of enjoyment. Academic study requires hard work, and it can be stressful.

Nonetheless, it's true that post-secondary studies offer the opportunity to learn and to grow. Should Homolka be barred from the university on the grounds that she might enjoy her education?

If so, then the question becomes, how miserable should imprisonment be? And how effective do we think a miserable sentence is?

If we are interested in preventing recidivism, it's not in our interest, as a culture, to send the Homolkas who are now in prison back to the outside world feeling bored, alienated, angry, or asocial. For the sake of reducing violence, it's in our interest to try to ensure that inmates leave prison with something more in mind than criminal activities.

I have no idea whether allowing Homolka access to correspondence courses will make any difference to her future. But I think the arguments against allowing her access to a university education are insufficient to justify making her an exception—an exception to the principle that everyone with sufficient academic qualifications should have access to university studies.

The Mirror Stage: Infinite Reflections on the Public Good§

Mark Kingwell

Socrates, that great hero of public discourse, remarks somewhere in one of Plato's dialogues that "an excess of precision is a mark of ill-breeding." Maybe it is in the *Theaetetus*. Or maybe in one of those works nobody actually reads, like the *Charmides* or the *Lesser Hippias*. I could tell you, but I won't: bad manners. And of course it is possible Socrates was just kidding anyway. Precision is God's gift to philosophers, after all, and if a taste for it, once acquired, occasionally leads them to spend whole afternoons discussing the logically modal differences between the ordinary language conditionals "if it was" and "if it were," well then, so be it. It keeps them happy and off the streets, where they might do damage to somebody innocent. I could begin by suggesting that more philosophers should get back on the streets, and that people on the streets should perhaps get more philosophy, but I want to begin instead by applying what I trust is only a well-bred modicum of precision to our chosen topic.

Before we can say what *the* public good is, or even whether there is one, we have to ask what *a* public good might be. And before we can talk about *public* goods, it is probably a good idea for us to specify the class of things we are modifying with that adjective. That is, before there can be *public goods* there must be *goods* in general. What are they?

A good is, first of all, something both desirable and worth desiring, something (as we say) that is choice worthy. In the early parts of Plato's *Republic* Socrates remarks that goods come in basically three flavours, which he rank-orders from lowest to highest: those desired because, although not necessarily pleasant in themselves, they achieve an end we wish for (think of going to the dentist or working out at the gym); those desired not because they realize any end at all but because they are inherently pleasant (like taking a stroll or whistling a tune); and those desired because they are both good in themselves and contribute to something beyond themselves. His paradigm example of the last kind of good is personal integrity, the sort of harmony in the soul that is both intrinsically enjoyable and directed toward the greater ends of justice.

Now of course Plato was able to think this way in part because he was convinced that there was really one Good, with a capital G, that structured all

§ Mark Kingwell. *Queen's Quarterly,* 106/1 (Spring 1999): 51-61. Reprinted with permission from the author.

of reality. Good acts and good people, good qualities and good thought—not to mention good knives and good horses and good looks—were all related to this Form of the Good as reflections are related to that which they reflect. The Form of the Good is eternal and unchanging; any actually experienced good thing or person is but imitation of that divine reality.

For various compelling reasons, we have abandoned this robustly metaphysical notion of the Good. Aristotle, Plato's otherwise devoted pupil, advanced ten separate arguments against the theory of the Forms in his *Nicomachean Ethics*. We cannot actually demonstrate that all things we call "good" share in some single property of Goodness. Things are good in different ways, and it is not simply a matter of people disagreeing in particular cases to judge meaningfully what makes a good society, it just does not help us much to know what makes a good knife. We may speak of functionality and the virtues that make for it, as Plato did—as sharpness is to the knife, so justice is to the city, the excellence that makes an activity possible—but beyond a certain elementary kind of analogical generality, we are in murky waters. And putting capital letters on the words does not help.

Goods are choice worthy, then, but probably not because they all share some overarching quality; or, anyway, this is not a quality we can expect to get our hands on in general or before-the-fact terms. Goods are choice worthy, rather, because they serve some local or contingent end, like cutting the bread or riding into town.

Where does that leave us with respect to the subset of goods we choose to call public? What, exactly, makes a good a public one? Well, we have to say what a public undertaking is for, what purpose it has. The roots of the word provide one kind of clue here. *Public* comes from the Latin *publicus*, which in turn is rooted in *pubes*, or adult. Thus Cicero's famous work *De re publica* is not best translated as "of the shared thing" but rather as "of the grown-up thing." (Who would have thought that the old typographical joke, keying in "pubic" when you mean "public," was actually a sign of deeper meaning?) If the public is the community of adults, then public goods are presumably ones that serve that community's interests.

Fine: in public we are all supposed to be grown-ups. But leaving behind Plato's Forms—or any other lofty account of higher-order goodness, for that matter—saddles us with a special problem with respect to the idea of public goods. We can say, perhaps, that public goods are those that contribute to the functional success of the society, but how do we conceive and measure that success? Where do we base our judgments that a whole *society* is good or not?

The modern answer has been that the source of public goods is the democratic will of the people, and the point of public goods is, by the same token, their happiness—even if their happiness is, in the event, much confused and subject to distortions or manipulations that only a very reckless philosopher would try to untangle in, say, a 400-page book called, of all things, *Better Living*. I will not try to assess, here, whether this modern democratic answer is the best one possible because it is, like it or not, the answer we now have. And as with most modern things, it's been a mixed blessing, but one on the whole we rightly celebrate.

One immediate consequence of the democratic answer is that we can no longer continue to speak of "*the* public good," as if there were one, even a very complex one, which could embrace all the needs, desires, and wills of the people in a society. In other words, a primary cost of surrendering the Platonic metanarrative, or any other grand story of capital-R reality, capital-T truth, is accepting that there is a multiplicity of goods, and no possibility of final agreement on the nature of them. No metalanguage of philosophy or politics can translate all our individual claims into a smooth transcript—not even, as some philosophers still maintain, the allegedly pure language of reason itself.

This notion of reason's triumph is an intoxicating dream, to be sure, and one rooted not in the eternal ether but in ourselves. Yet we must recognize that any ideal of perfect rational consensus, realized via an extraordinary public discourse in which fractious citizens hammer all their differences into a kind of uniform political purée, a single ringing language of legitimation, is a fiction. Such transcendental consensus may be an intermittently *useful* fiction, as ideals sometimes are when they serve to regulate and direct our less-than-ideal actions; but, taken too literally, it has as many dangers as the frankly otherworldly metaphysics of the Forms. It denies the deep otherness that marks genuine political encounters, the face-to-face confrontation of stranger with stranger which is the moment of truth in any social web of relations.[1] It denies, too, the residue of otherness that must persist in democratic societies even after all our best efforts at reconciliation.

It is in the nature of politics today, then (and by "today" I mean, as philosophers usually do, the period roughly since the democratic revolutions, in thought and deed, of the seventeenth and eighteenth centuries) that we can no longer be seduced by the idea of a unitary public good. The multiplicity of goods is a fact that politics must address, not with some kind of final settlement, but with a flexibility and tolerance that forever postpones the impossible task of reconciling all competing claims. *In social life conflict is endemic; more than that, it is ineliminable.*

This may sound worse than it is. Many of the goods we pursue are not public ones at all, and therefore potential conflicts simply do not arise as actual problems. Suppose I privately despise opera, while you spend thousands of hours and dollars on your unhealthy obsession with the up-and-down career of troubled diva Anna Moffo. Well, who cares? We agree to disagree, or we simply don't speak of it. Now music may seem a trivial matter—though I confess it is not to me—but could we imagine performing the same abstraction on more serious matters, like sexual mores, or the work ethic? This, indeed, is the aspiration of some forms of liberalism: that all deep conflicts should be placed somewhere off the public agenda, leaving just a basic agreement about fundamental social and economic structures that allows us as individuals to go about our private business in peace.

We know, however, that this vision of a bright line between public and private cannot be so easily realized: it is itself a source of deep conflict. Is child-rearing a public or a private undertaking? What about work? Or marriage? Or death? Is what you do with your garbage merely a private affair? Is a lack of literacy skills? In fact, the distinction between public and private realms is one that must be publicly debated.[2] And that means that the most important of the specifically public goods, the thing that serves the ends of society as a key enabling condition, is the public discussion of where, if anywhere, a line can be drawn separating public from private.

This idea not only emphasizes the discursive elements of public life for us democrats—the incessant political debate that is our birthright and our burden—but also begins from the important assumption that no claim to privacy can be made except in public. It is never enough to say to a fellow citizen, "It's a private thing. You wouldn't understand." We have to justify claims to privacy, not simply assert them. All claims, if they really are claims, are made on the basis of reason; and a reason is only truly a reason if it can be publicly defended. You may not always actually articulate your justifications to somebody else; but it is essential that you should be *able* to do so, if called upon. That requires wit and goodwill, civility and tolerance, forthrightness and sensitivity—all the workaday virtues of citizens.

I should jump in right here and forestall some obvious, if misdirected, criticism of this position. I am not suggesting that there is no privacy, that everything is public, that society should be dedicated to panoptic surveillance, or any of the other bugbears that haunt the febrile imaginations of various right-wing libertarians (and some left-wing ones). For one thing, as much as our bland, arrogant elected leaders appear to believe so, the public sphere cannot simply be reduced to the state, nor the public good to the will of the state. The state, if it is legitimate, serves the public good; it never determines it. Nor is it the case that there is no private realm remaining merely because, as we sometimes say on the left, everything is political. Everything is political because every piece of private property, every lawsuit, every relatively secure personal space, is the result of an ongoing negotiation that must be seen as always provisional, fractious, and open-ended. Social relations and the distribution of goods are—must be—always up for grabs. Those of us who enjoy privileges in this world do so not by any divine grace or natural right but by convention, as the result of a complex history of argument and settlement, of challenge and reply.

That does not mean, however, that the public good is always somehow over or against us, or just something that we confront passively. Rather, a genuine public sphere of goods demands active participation. Some public goods, like clean water or fresh air, call for no particular degree of participation, as long as we don't hamper their availability for others. But others, like the maintenance of vibrant public discourse or a distinct civic culture, are participatory as well as public. That is, they are goods that, as my colleague Denise Réaume once put it, "involve activities that not only require many in order to produce the good, but are valuable only because of the joint involvement of many."[3] Even if goods are only ever enjoyed by individuals, in other words, it is not the case that all goods are enjoyed individually. Participation is part of what makes the good a good in the first place. That's why non-participants or free-riders, whether disaffected or distracted or just apathetic, are actively bad for the overall health of the public good. Like party-goers who won't join in the game, they bring the rest of us down: they reduce the goods in play; they don't just leave them neutral.

So, distinctively public goods must be plural, discursive, moderately rational, and participatory. They must be oriented to the success of the social project, a success whose measurement lies, however unclearly for now, in the happiness of its participants. The public goods are not fixed or unchanging, but rather the result of ongoing debates, sometimes vexations, between citizens who perforce share a stake in their society.

What, now, is the role of reflection? There are three difficulties we face immediately in answering that question, all derived from important criticisms of the social democratic conception of the public good I have been defending. One: *are we sufficiently stable as subjects to engage in public discourse*, or is it rather the case that our much-scored and fluid status as concatenations of interest and power makes citizenship an impossible role to take up? Two: *where should we go to engage in public reflection*, given that the public sphere sometimes seems to be little more than a kind of "phantom" space, and the contemporary political landscape a ruin of isolated communities and jagged self-interest, governed only by the cash nexus and the mass media?[4] And three: even assuming it is possible for us, and we can find places to do it, *what exactly are we trying to achieve when we engage in public discourse?*

These are deep challenges, but not unanswerable ones. It is true that our contemporary selves are fragile social and narrative constructions. It is true that there is no obvious marketplace of ideas to walk to, the way Socrates could prowl the *agora* of ancient Athens. It's true that we do not always know what we are up to, in some final transcendent sense, when we engage in halting attempts at public utterance. It is true, in short, that we are never completely transparent to ourselves, neither as individuals nor as a society. Indeed, it may feel at times that the public good is opaque and unknowable, and we ourselves no more than brute clots of interest and conflict that neither reason nor God could make clear.

But I want to say: full transparency is the wrong criterion of success in public discourse anyway. We do not need to be entirely clear to ourselves in order to get on with the business of citizenship. Indeed, there is a better metaphor for social relations, though it is also a more challenging one. It is a metaphor that has exercised the imaginations of thinkers as diverse as Joseph Addison, Norbert Elias, Sigmund Freud, and Jacques Lacan. It is the image of consciousness as a kind of mirror: not Plato's mirror, reflecting some realm of true reality, but, rather, something like what psychoanalysts call the mirror-stage of self, which achieves consciousness only through being reflected by an Other—an Other who may well be perceived now and then as a threat to me and my private interests.

Democratic society thus resembles an infinite hall of mirrors, forever bouncing and refracting its light like that scene from *Last Year at Marienbad*. We shine only in the presence of others, and they help define us as who we are: reflection is the first activity, and first duty, of citizens. The public sphere always houses a kind of generalized Other for each of us. It is the place where we confront that which is enduringly alien and try to come to terms with it, and with ourselves as we do so. And in this complex of reflections, the intricate cross-references and input-output protocols that define us as citizens, the public good emerges as that which makes private interest and personal comfort insufficient standards of justification. It is not enough that I and my family are financially secure if the gap between our household and the majority yawns ever wider. It is not enough that I am educated and literate if the majority lack the basic skills of citizenship—reading and writing. It is not enough that I am happy if the majority is not. The public good is something both greater than, and reflective of, myself—something with which, as an ideal forever approached but never fully achieved, I identify as I identify with the image of myself in many mirrors.

The danger lately, of course, is that this complex hall of mirrors has become a sort of mad funhouse, with distorting surfaces and devious curves that create spectacle—but not, as good mirrors should, speculation. Nowadays the play of images is so pervasive, indeed, that we seem to have reached a condition, as the philosopher Guy Debord expressed it in *The Society of the Spectacle*, in which "the image has become the final form of commodity reification." That is, we inhabit a culture in which images are produced and consumed so relentlessly that substance drains from both the public sphere and private life at once, leaving us, at an extreme, in the position of consuming not products and services but the act of consumption itself: going shopping, using technology, or ingesting media product as ends in themselves, precluding any real or discursive forms of social interaction.[5] In this pathological condition, we become distracted with the play of light rather than what light should illuminate; we lose track of the wisdom acquired through interpersonal relations—wisdom concerning the never-ending task of citizenship. For, like the series of doorways that extends into the infinite mirrored distance, our obligations to our fellow citizens are unending.

But to what purpose? What is the point of this or any kind of reflection on the public good? Well, the point of any society is *justice*. And justice, like happiness or wisdom, is both demanding and elusive. It is not a state to get to and then call it a day, the political equivalent of "Miller Time." There is no final goal here, no position we can reach where all our obligations will be realized, so that we can finally relax. In fact, this desire to pass beyond obligation by meeting obligation is really an evasion of responsibility—the same sort of evasion you can hear in those who claim that paying taxes and voting absolves them of any further, more participatory, duties to society.

Now, you may want to say: *But there are only so many hours in a day. There is only so much one person can do. You're suggesting that nothing we do is ever enough.* Indeed I am. It is an obligation I put on myself as well as on you, and which I fail to meet as much as anyone. Because when it comes to the public good, there is no "enough"; there is always more to do. That is the nature of being a citizen. The late Canadian critic Bill Readings once compared citizenship to Freud's notion of adulthood. There is no template for complete adulthood.[6] Likewise, and for the same reasons, there is no template for complete citizenship. No citizen *models* the public good in the way ancient republicans demanded, because there is no higher-order reality to be modeled. There is only the lower-order world of our multiple and provisional reflections, down here where we live with each other, with people who are somewhat—enough—like us to argue with now and then. We do not reflect an ideal city; we only reflect ourselves.

If we recall the very adult roots of the word *public*, which got us started on these reflections, these intricate turnings-towards and bouncings-back, then we see the point. When do we finish becoming just? When do we finish becoming good citizens? When do we finish realizing the public good? Well, ask yourself: when do we finish growing up?

Notes

1. Bruce Ackerman calls this the basic fact of political life, usually a confrontation between someone who has and someone who has not. See his *Social Justice in the Liberal State* (New Haven: Yale University Press, 1980). Michael Ignatieff's compelling discussion of what we owe the strangers who share our social spaces is *The Needs of Strangers* (London: Chatto & Windus, 1984).

2. This point has been made by numerous political theorists, especially those recently associated with the idea of "deliberative democracy." On the whole I align myself with this school of what might be called late-model liberalism, though with some reservations. My defence of *civility* as the first virtue of public discourse is found in Kingwell, *A Civil Tongue: Justice, Dialogue, and the Politics of Pluralism* (University Park: Penn State University Press, 1995).

3. See Denise Réaume, "Individuals, Groups, and Rights to Public Goods," *University of Toronto Law Journal,* 38 (1988), 1–27; see p. 10. "The publicity of production itself is part of what is valued—the good *is* the participation," she continues. "[M]y argument depends not on what kind of entities there are but on how the goods are enjoyed. Whether or not all goods are enjoyed by individuals, not all are individually enjoyed" (pp. 10–11). Moreover: "It is not enough that people go through the motions of enjoying the artifacts of culture; they must really do so in order to make the required contribution to creating and developing the culture" (p. 13).

   Réaume's argument is made in the context of group rights within liberal societies, but her point has a larger relevance for the very idea of "pure jointness" in any group. "In such cases the right cannot be an individual one because it is a claim to a participatory good," she says, "and it is a group right because it is a claim to a public good which applies only to a segment of society and must be claimed against the rest.... [T]here is good reason for separating such rights from the usual sorts of individual rights. Although the group can be treated as an individual, it cannot be treated as an individual human being would be. The interests of the group, because they are interests in the maintenance and development of a participatory good, cannot be reduced to a set of individualized interests" (p. 24).

4. See, for statements of this critical position, *The Phantom Public Sphere,* ed. Bruce Robbins (Minneapolis: University of Minnesota Press, 1993).

5. See Guy Debord, *The Society of the Spectacle* (Detroit: Black & Red, 1983). Writes the postmodern socialist critic Fredric Jameson of this spectacular implosion: "We must therefore also posit another type of consumption [in late capitalism]: consumption of the very process of consumption itself, above and beyond its content and the immediate commercial products. It is necessary to speak of a kind of technological bonus of pleasure afforded by the new machinery and, as it were, symbolically re-enacted and ritually devoured at each session of official media consumption itself." From "Postmodernism and the Market," ch. 8 of *Postmodernism, or, The Cultural Logic of Late Capitalism* (Durham: Duke University Press, 1991), p. 276. In "The Precession of Simulacra," Jean Baudrillard takes issue with Debord and argues that our society is not spectacular but *simulacral:* when the medium decisively becomes the message, then there is no mediation left, and no spectacle. There is only a play of simulations whose logic destroys the very idea of the real. See Baudrillard, *Simulations* (New York: Semiotext(e), 1983), p. 54.

6. Bill Readings, *The University in Ruins* (Cambridge, MA: Harvard University Press, 1996), p. 189.

Idols of the Tribe[1]
Leslie Millin

> The Idols of the Tribe have their foundation in human nature itself....
> And the human understanding is like a false mirror, which receiving
> rays irregularly, distorts and discolours the nature of things by ming-
> ling its own nature with it. (Francis Bacon, Novum Organum, 1620)

Thirty-six years ago, as the sun sank over that riot-torn centre of Detroit,
I was upside down in a glass telephone booth attempting to kick out
the ceiling light fixture while sweet-talking the AT&T operator into
placing a collect long distance call to the Toronto newsroom of *The Globe
and Mail*. The operator needed persuading because all telephone lines out of
that unhappy city were supposed to be reserved for military or emergency
use. The light fixture had to go because as dusk fell its cheery beams would
reveal me to be a white man in a business suit, and thus an obvious target
for ill-disposed rifle-bearing folk in the immediate vicinity who most defin-
itely were not white men wearing business suits. A wire cage protected the
light fixture from my hands, hence the need to use my feet while hoping
the AT&T operator would assume she was hearing just the usual riot background—the paint and linoleum store across the street was certainly burning
merrily—while I used my best blend of mid-Atlantic accent, calm authority
and blatant flattery to assure her that the safety of the United States and her
own dear family would not be jeopardized if she let me talk for ten minutes
to a rewrite man at *The Globe*. Fortunately, she agreed.

This image, long forgotten, came back when—after a sojourn on a remote
Mexican mountaintop, insulated from modern news media—I started digging
through the coverage of the build-up to and then commencement of the military incursion into Iraq. North American reporters back in the 1960s tended
to think of the Vietnam war as their benchmark for covering violent, difficult
situations. While working through the Iraq stuff, listening to the radio and
watching the television news channels, it was instantly clear that war coverage
in 2003 was remarkably different from such coverage in 1967, and that most of
the difference was due—directly or indirectly—to technology.

We have become so accustomed to rapid changes in computer-based
technology—which these days means practically all technology—that we

[1] Leslie Millin. *Queen's Quarterly*, 110/3 (Fall 2003): 391–403. Reprinted with permission from
the author.

don't much reflect on how slowly communications technology changed before it became computer-enhanced. When the news organizations of North America set forth to cover the war in Vietnam, their planning was little different from that of their forebears during the First World War. Quite arguably, the news communications practices of the First World War had evolved very little from those pioneered in the American Civil War, which was probably the first human war to be initiated, fought, lost, won and reported on the basis of industrial technology.[1] Coverage was difficult, expensive, and depended almost absolutely on mastery of the telegraph cable and, where possible, physical movement of materials by available transportation systems.

Today, we are in an era of cheap and abundant communication: so cheap, so abundant, that the traditional gatekeeping function of the editor—a quality-control function—is quite clearly being swamped. Particularly when it comes to events of high news interest that require no specialized content knowledge on the part of reporters, editors are being swirled downstream by the torrents of words dumped on them electronically by folk in the field with little to limit their prolixity but sheer exhaustion. In turn, the editors are clearly letting the words flow by until the available space is filled, with little attempt to reconcile conflicting accounts or to allocate space or prominence according to some rational choice based on a consideration of importance or even probability. Nor is this necessarily an unconsidered choice, nor an unfortunate consequence of limited resources: the recent debacle at *The New York Times* resulted at least in part from the deliberate adoption of a "flood the scene" doctrine of news gathering, and no one can say of the *Times* that its adoption of such doctrine stems from thoughtlessness or shortage of funds.

When Samuel F.B. Morse patented the first successful electric telegraph in the United States in 1844, he was, like most inventors, seeking to do more quickly and cheaply what was already being done by a more primitive system: transmitting information reliably over long distances. Visual telegraph systems—sequential arrays of various shapes (by day) or, less reliably, of lanterns (by night) had come into their own during the Napoleonic wars, when both sides used them to transmit urgent information over distances of a hundred miles and more. Such systems in turn derived from the flag signals used in the navies of that day and their immediate predecessors, and of course relied on line-of-sight: clear sight. What the ingenious Morse and his competitors sought was a system that was faster, cheaper, immune to normal weather, and less labour-intensive. The railway systems of Europe could rely on visual systems—indeed, did so in some cases well into the twentieth century—because distances were short and manpower was cheap. North America's comparatively enormous distances and relatively high rates of pay demanded the new technology if railways were to become practical.

Virtually all new technologies have unintended consequences. Morse succeeded in making North American railways practical, but he also inadvertently created the modern news editor.

Railway companies accepted the high infrastructure cost of building the electric telegraph systems, but of course they sought immediately to find ways of recovering at least some of that cost. A system built for the service of a railway company inevitably had a great deal of idle time, since essential traffic messages might take up no more than a very few minutes per hour, especially after the adoption of standard letter groups to represent much longer routine messages. The system had to be manned at all times, in case of emergency; fine, the telegraphers could earn their pay (and the company much more) if they were kept busy sending messages for paying customers.[2] Inevitably, financial corporations were the first to avail themselves of such services (and the first to develop codes for confidentiality), but other business customers came along quickly, as well as private individuals with urgent requirements, and in due course—often reluctantly—major news organizations. Some of the reluctance was aesthetic—quite correctly, it was foreseen that the very nature of gathering and writing news would change drastically—but much of it was economic. Newspaper owners in an era of enormous competition, however, had little option: they grumbled and paid.

But they insisted on several things: wire messages must be as terse as possible; as many as possible of the facts of a story must be at its very beginning; and where possible the story should be sent in packets rather than as a continuous transmission—this last was probably a concession to telegraph owners, but also served the needs of the newspapers. Terseness, never previously seen as a virtue, saved money. Stacking the facts towards the beginning, and sending in packets, were a basic hedge against failure of service. Taken together, the impacts were considerable.

Reporters came to be esteemed for recognizing the heart of a story and describing it clearly and concisely, rather than for eloquence or style. In pre-wire days, a correspondent might have written something like this:

> In a rarely granted reencounter last evening with His Majesty's Lord Chancellor, that most gracious Lord Bilgewater, he condescended to acquaint me, and thus the readership of this journal,

of some of the most important affairs occupying the attention of Government....[3]

Now, due to the new technology, the preferred style would be:

Capitol Hill sources confirmed snight Whouse seeks new whiskey tax, vow won't pass.

Telegraph messages, of course, had to be put into a more readable form, hence the rise of the rewrite man, who became an even larger cog in the machine when telephones arrived. But more important was the news editor, who had to understand the meaning of a story—what, if anything, was needed to fill it out; what instructions to give to a rewrite man; who would copy-edit the eventual text; how it would fit within the day's presentation of news; whether some further packet of news might be forthcoming (the North American convention of ending a packet with "more" derived from the need to advise the editor of that probability, whereas "30"[4] signified the end of transmission); what sort of headline was indicated; and a great many other matters. Telegraphic messages meant that the editor was under constant bombardment with new material up until the last moment technically possible, leading in turn to a revolution in new judgement: reflective consideration yielded to the ability to choose swiftly and accurately amid a host of competing and sometimes conflicting options. Those who could do so, and do it well, were very rightly esteemed.

In all of this, we may discern the expression of a principle: what is scarce is valuable; what is valuable is costly. The function of the news editor and his trusty sidekick, the rewrite man, was to keep the costs down and the value high. The reader, working through the main story on the front page of the newspaper, could be reasonably assured that what was being offered was a digest and summary of the best information available. Ultimately, the news editor controlled quality, however defined by the news organization. The news editor embodied the compact between news consumer and news supplier. This tradition carried on into the North American broadcast news media, most of whose original eminences had a newspaper background. The tradition faded away as the various media evolved in their various ways, yet the iron laws of communications scarcity—absence of bandwidth, and the cost of overcoming that absence—continued to dictate a style and doctrine of news gathering and reporting where the concept of the key story and thus the pre-eminence of the news editor absolutely prevailed, and the compact between news consumer and news supplier stood, in principle, inviolate.

That compact is gone. Comparing the front pages of *The New York Times* and *The Globe and Mail* for three key news events is instructive. The three selected are: the Tet offensive in the Vietnam war, the ground offensive in the first Gulf war, and the incursion into Iraq. Both newspapers consider themselves exemplars of journalism; both dispose of ample funds. In all three cases, managers had plenty of time to make their plans, since the military actions involved were foregone decisions with no more than a week or so of possible variation in timing. Neither newspaper was short of human or financial resources; neither was taken by surprise. Both would consider themselves the pride of the profession.

In each case, both treated the action at hand in the same way. For the first two actions, each ran a major story giving a summarized account of the situation, ascribing it to an individual correspondent but clearly drawing on supplementary files. Each major story was backed up with subsidiary stories—"sidebars" in the jargon—offering supplementary *but clearly subordinated* information or insights. Bylines—"By William Jones"—were rare. In contrast, the front pages following the Iraq incursion were a riot of individual stories, all bylined and sprayed across the page with no apparent logic or design. In effect, the editors of each of these newspapers had turned the editing function over to the readers: "This is what we have received. Make of it what you will." Inconsistencies among the various accounts passed without notice, let alone comment. Where in previous years a rewrite man might have noted "However, a report from the Grand Voix news agency contains a flat denial that…" we had in 2003 in effect an editorial shrug— "All the news that fits, we print." You choose.

At the root of this is a simple and ever cheaper device: the global satellite telephone. This is a handheld machine that can transmit voice, text and images[5] from anywhere to anywhere. Cost to acquire and use it is by no means insignificant, but in the overall scheme of newsgathering budgets, it is no great thing. And, in accordance with Moore's Law, the cost drops sharply every year.

Thus it becomes quite practical to put a dozen correspondents into a situation where managers of the past would have thought very carefully about committing one, given the costs of transmitting the product. If only one can be sent, then it is your best (or most willing), in the model of William Howard Russell, the legendary war correspondent of London's *The Times*, who single-handedly created the tradition of his craft. If the same constraints had prevailed when Iraq was invaded, *The New York Times* would have relied solely on John F. Burns, their ace war correspondent and the true linear heir of the Russell tradition. That is: he seeks to give a balanced and, so far as possible, neutral account of what he has seen and heard, allowing for the necessary risks of second and third-hand information, and making his account as inclusive and comprehensive as possible. Working through the *Times* pages recounting the inexorable incursion, one sees his contributions as in great contrast to the daily garnishings of correspondents—some embedded,[6] some not—colleagues who described, one hopes accurately, what they saw within their various spheres of observation, with no attempt to distil a clear overview or even resolve internal contradictions.

One consequence was a failure of perspective. The embedded reporter whose armoured personnel carrier had its progress blocked for an hour or two filed a story that suggested that the entire progress of the column to which it belonged had been blocked, and thus the advance on Baghdad or wherever was stalled. No effort was made back in the newsroom to set these individual perceptions into any kind of perspective: clearly each bylined piece stood as received—none of the traditional tooling marks of the rewrite man blemished these works. Nor was there any sense that these correspondents were particularly well informed of the situation, or the people or history or geography of the country they would invade. They looked through the tiny glazed slot of the ACP in which they were embedded, and said what they saw. Such an approach to news gathering is only possible where bandwidth has effectively become infinite, and thus without cost.

In such an information world, each person acts as personal editor. Yet the skills of an editor, the knowledge and the instincts, are not given to us all. Even if we sought to acquire them, we each have only a limited time every day. The filtering and quality control that are the value a professional editor adds to the news reporting process are true value. Without them, even the product of as respected a news agency as *The New York Times* is little more than a particularly rich seam in the intellectual landfill of the Internet.

Then, just to grind everyone's face into it, came Jayson Blair. Many thousands of words have been written about how this young man almost single-handedly destroyed the credibility of *The New York Times*, ultimately forcing the resignations of its top two editors. Yet nowhere has there been commentary on the fact that his remarkable career of intellectual embezzlement, theft, fraud and perjury was made possible by the communications technology whose instruments his employers placed in his hands, and which he duly mastered. Even twenty years ago, such a career was impossible. To create a false history that would stand more than routine scrutiny would take financial and human resources on a government scale—for example, creating credible but false identification papers was highly skilled work, and thus highly paid. He could not have plagiarized easily from regional newspapers, because he could not have had timely access to them, even in New York. He could not have treated long-distance telephone calls as casual and inexpensive: they were neither. He could not have manufactured supporting documents through a customer-friendly computer program in the comfort of his home, if that's indeed what he did. Today, teenagers with access to a superior copying machine can produce forged currency (especially US dollars) that will pass muster in a dark bar, especially once stained with beer.

Like baffled adults driven to beseech their children to set up the home video equipment, the senior *Times* managers succumbed to a most impressive display of technical virtuosity—what in the world of the bull ring is called *tremendismo*—and ultimately paid the price. New technologies demand new operating systems.

Blair was not the first nor will he be the last of news reporters who betray their trust. At least two national Canadian journalists active today produce work I read for amusement rather than information—the memory of their padding actual stories with invented material, back when we worked together, remains. But Blair's capacity to subvert the news process exceeded anything they had in those days by many, many orders of magnitude, not because he was any more treacherous or ingenious, but simply because he was better tooled up.

As consumers of news, we can—however reluctantly—take on as best we may the roles and responsibilities that once we assumed were the work of the news editors in the organizations whose news we buy. But against the guns of Jayson the Kid we are lightly armed indeed. Looking around for the town marshal is not just a waste of time—he rode away in the night quite a while ago—but it could just give The Kid time to get off another shot. We must think of something better.

What?

Notes

1. The war arose because of deep social and economic conflicts arising from technology. Introduction of the automatic spinning machine made possible the mass production of cloth from short-staple cotton, which could only be cultivated economically through slavery combined with the drain of capital to the much

more lucrative slave-based economy to create armed conflict. The Union states won, despite inferior public morale and vastly inferior military leadership, because of their superior strength in miles of railway track, the communications advantage of the signalling systems required by the rail systems, and the mass production of standardized weapons, especially small arms. War correspondents learned to use the railway-based communications systems to expedite their dispatches, and in the process developed the distinctively North American newspaper reporting style which is only starting to change today. The Confederate states lost not least because they could not mass-manufacture standardized ammunition for their largely artisan-produced small arms.

2. Non-essential traffic could be interrupted in case of an emergency by overriding it with a "bulletin bell," a practice that survived in newspaper wire services at least into the 1970s.

3. If you think I'm making this up, try reading today's dispatches in quite respectable French or Spanish daily newspapers, where the normative influence of the wire service has never penetrated. You will find articles not so very far from this imaginary specimen.

4. The origins of this code have been the fodder for journalistic folk etymology for aeons. A common story is that it was an instruction to printers for 30 em-dashes, the horizontal line denoting the end of the text of a story on a newspaper page. This is unlikely. Most probably it is simply a relic of the system of two-digit codes by which telegraphers sent compressed messages. For example, a priority message used the designation "95" which has no meaning whatever, except that—like "30"—the digits are far apart on the standard keyboard and thus unlikely to be combined accidentally.

5. Images also proliferated. Pages full or almost full of coloured photographs were common in Iraq coverage, in contrast with the rare, monochrome images of the previous conflicts. Yet, judging by how the images were presented, there was remarkable consensus on which shots were best. The secondary and tertiary images were offered, clearly, simply because they could be—not because the photo editors held them in high regard.

6. Worth noting is that every device used to control news reporting of the Iraq incursion, including "embedding," was used by the Japanese authorities in the Russo-Japanese War of 1904. Willard Straight, an AP stringer, described poignantly how the assiduous attentions of the Japanese authorities combined to "deaden the sense of duty" of otherwise tough correspondents.

Gendering Risk at What Cost: Negotiations of Gender and Risk in Canadian Women's Prisons**
Kelly Hannah-Moffat

A major turning point in Canadian federal[1] women's corrections occurred nearly 14 years ago when the federal government accepted the report of The Taskforce on Federally Sentenced Women (TTFSW, 1990). This report mandated a new women-centered and culturally sensitive approach to the management and organization of federal women's prisons. Yet many of the difficulties identified by the taskforce still exist (Hannah-Moffat and Shaw, 2001) and are subject to ongoing evaluation by state and non-state agencies, including the Auditor General (Auditor General of Canada, 2003) and the Canadian Human Rights Commission.[2] A major concern for Canadian researchers is the potential for systematic discrimination resulting from gender-neutral risk assessment practices that ineffectively account for gender and cultural differences (see also Van Voorhis and Presser, 2001, for the USA context).

Risk tools have an intuitive appeal to practitioners because they ground decisions in statistical (thus objective) relationships (Feeley and Simon, 1992). Strategically, such tools are used to inform service rationalization and to increase professionals' accountability in decision making in the named efficient and just management of a range of risks (recidivism, suicide, self-harm, violence, escape). Whilst risk assessments may be considered by some practitioners (institutional classification officers, parole board members, probation officers and case managers) as a "matter of common sense," such a discourse is not persuasive in court or at inquests, so a standardized risk assessment ensures a decision is defensible should something go wrong: "they back you up if something goes wrong—you can demonstrate that you used a standardized approach that his empirically based."[3]

This article examines how the Canadian penal system attempts to reconcile this risk emphasis with its commitments to gender-sensitive corrections. I do this by focusing on initial classifications practices and assessments of recidivism that are connected to program and release planning. This abridged discussion is based on interview data (N = 90) obtained in three semi-structured interview-based studies (Hannah-Moffat and Shaw, 2001; Hannah-Moffat, 2002a; Hannah-Moffat and Maurutto, 2003). In each of

** Hannah-Moffat, Kelly. "Gendering Risk at What Cost: Negotiations of Gender and Risk in Canadian Women's Prisons." *Feminism & Psychology* 14(2): 243–49. © 2004 by Sage Publications Ltd. Reprinted by Permission of SAGE.

these studies, practitioners were asked if , and how, gender is relevant to the assessment of risk/need, and how women's risk is assessed in the absence of clear gender-sensitive operational guidelines and assessment tools.

Acknowledging Gender Differences

For over 30 years, North American research has demonstrated that crime is gendered and that gender matters in shaping criminal justice responses to women and in the differential effects of policies (Carlen, 2002). Evidence clearly shows women's demographic characteristics—motivations for offending, patterns of offending, types of offenses, substance use, prison adjustment, and level of community support—are different from men's. Even when offences are similar (assault, fraud, or murder), the context of offending and the relationship to the victim tend to be different between men and women. There is also evidence to suggest that woman's responses to, and experiences of, incarceration are different from men's, that women do not have equitable access to resources in the community upon release and that the issues they face in terms of reintegration are often contextually different from men's—even though the problems may have the same labels (addiction, homelessness, unemployment, and housing). Finally, research suggests correctional staff tend to respond differently to men and women in custody and, more often than not, these responses evoke gender or racialized stereotypes (Hannah-Moffat and Shaw, 2001).

Interviews with practitioners revealed that they generally perceived women (and minority ethnic) prisoners as having different needs and experiences that were relevant to assessing risk. In turn, practitioners believed different methods of assessing recidivism were required for women and minority ethnic populations to capture the complexity and stability of women's relationships and their personal emotional issues. Some argued that risk tools contained vague criteria defined in accordance with male norms (i.e. sexual behavior, and employment criteria) that did not fit women prisoners. Further, concerns were expressed about the exclusion of information deemed relevant to women's risk, including the value of intimate relationships, the lack of social support, victimization, and parent issues (Hannah-Moffat and Shaw, 2001).

In brief, assessment and classification practices fail to recognize the gendered and racialized aspects of social life and experiences of women in conflict with the law. However, attempts to incorporate gendered criteria into assessment and classification practices have encountered institutional resistance[4] even though Canadian correctional legislation[5] mandates gender-sensitivity. Currently, there are no attempts to begin from "ground zero" to develop a managerial model for women, using women's differences as a starting point. Further, there are no policy directives on how to use existing tools to assess women's risk. Generic tools and categorizations of risk/need factors persist because they characterize problems and define solutions in ways that fit with the dominant correctional culture and the power structure that narrowly and instrumentally defines risk and need.[6] Canada's small female prison population and the lack of centralized, independent line of authority over the five federal prisons for women further complicate the problem. In the following sections, I examine how practitioners working with women prisoners have responded to the absence of gender- and "race"-sensitive risk/need assessment tools.

Gendered Adaptations of Risk: Practitioners' Ad Hoc Responses

The absence of research, best practice guidelines and clear organizational direction as to how to assess women's risk has contributed to the emergence of various ad hoc attempts to modify risk to reflect the gendered nature of women's experiences. The practitioners interviewed have three typical responses to this dilemma: "Gender Neutrality," "Caution" and "Appendage." The first response discounts gender differences, and applies the same risk tools and criteria to women on the assumption that criteria established for men are relevant for women or are "better than nothing." This approach negates the relevance of gender and fails to see how risk/need criteria can produce systemic biases and/or inaccurate readings of women's risk.

"Caution" results in more intense scrutinizing of women's files and self-reports and is associated with more conservative decisions. One-third of practitioners admitted to being *more rigorous* and careful when making decisions about women's risk of re-offending (particularly when women were perpetrators of violence) *because* of "uncertainty" associated with the absence of gender relevant actuarial assessments:

> I am much more inclined to look at what information I do not have for high risk offenders such as a good risk assessment that includes a PCL-R and the VRAG or the HCR-20. Knowing that I don't have these tools to guide me, means that I have to be much more cautious.[7]

In a social-political climate in which there is an expectation of identifying degrees of risk and increased public accountability of practitioners, the uncertainty created in the absence of relevant actuarial data combined with wider structural impediments to release that are magnified for women (absence of community resources, programs and housing), have specific effects. For example, a woman may not be released because it cannot be said with certainty that she is a "manageable" risk: "there is no backup if things go wrong—you're out there on a limb—so I am more careful."[8]

A third more systematic approach is to supplement or append risk assessment with information acquired through gender-sensitivity training. Such training generally includes summaries of current research, descriptive characteristics of the female offender population (self-reported needs and experiences) and information about women's gendered experiences such as a history of abuse and maternal status. It is implied that if women's needs are targeted and addressed, then risk will be reduced (Bloom, 2003). While not sufficiently empirically established as risk factors, the "need facts" have been used strategically. Most practitioners interviewed believed it was critical to place women's offending in a broader context of their past victimization, and so routinely asked women about intimate relationships during parole hearings—identifying these as criminogenic factors. Some practitioners rejected the relevance of victimization as a mitigating factor, and five argued that the relationship between women's victimization was overstated and that an offender's emphasis on her victim status indicated her failure to take responsibility for her offending.

This practice of augmenting risk assessment with perceptions of women's needs is complicated by the fact that in Canada definitions of risk and need are conflated (Hannah-Moffact, 2002b). When asked the difference between risk and need, nearly two-thirds of the 90 interviewees hesitated before stating that needs were dynamic risk factors. This focus on "needs" inadvertently associates assessment of recidivism with unmet need in relation to, for example, trauma and abuse, self-esteem, assertiveness, employment skills, mental health, medical care, parenting, and relationships.

Attempts by practitioners to be gender-sensitive also reinforced gender stereotypes:

> I think we judge risk (for women) in large measure based on who they live with, or the quality of their relationships in the community. For men we see them as more independent and judge them as if they were independent (emotionally).[9]

> [When dealing with women who commit violent or sexual offences]—you know you have a tough case 'cause women are not by nature violent or sexually aggressive.[10]

Institutional practices like gender-sensitivity training are intended to heighten decision makers' awareness of, and sensitivity to gender (similarly with cultural information). Practitioners, however, are not directed on *how* to use this knowledge to modify their understandings of policy (or what

Carlen, 1998, calls "woman-wise" decisions). This absence generates inconsistencies and confusion, so that the inclusion of gender information is left to the discretion of individual practitioners who can either choose to use (sometimes inappropriately) or ignore it. The combination of practitioners' need for risk information and training that does not meaningfully structure gender information such as experience of victimization has resulted in specious links between factors such as a history of victimization and risk to re-offend which shift the focus onto women's past and future relationships. It attributes to women a degree of responsibility for their victimization, a position that is inconsistent with the original intent of gender-sensitive policy.

Parton notes "the idiom of risk not only presupposes ideas of choice and calculation, but also responsibility" (2001: 62). By default, victimization becomes an informal measure of risk, and women are expected to "deal with their victimization" in order to show that they have "gained insight" into their offending and are willing to take responsibility for their actions. Taking responsibility for offending is tacitly connected to risk minimization and is central to evaluations of future risk—ironically not of victimization but offending. Here freedom (the capacity to choose one's actions without external constraints) and agency (the power to act) are conflated, producing a "new form of institutional licensing" (Culpitt, 1990: 50). Women's gendered experiences are transformed into potentially forseeable risks that someone is accountable for and therefore open to sanctions (Rose, 1998). Such practices contribute to the continued marginalization of women who are already at the "correctional fringe."

Conclusion

The marginalization of gender is not new. However, in this instance, it is coupled with renewed apathy and gender neutrality that appears to negate the "progress" made in Canadian women's corrections over the past decade. Researchers and policy makers need to be more attentive to how gender and racial and/or cultural differences can be meaningfully integrated into institutional structures and how systems that resist such diversity can be challenged and held accountable. Carlen's recent book posits the questions: "Is the concept of gendered justice still worth discussing? Is 'gendered justice' viable as an organizing principle of sentencing, non-custodial and custodial regimes?" (2002: 11). While notions of gendered justice and gendered risk are fraught with conceptual and operational difficulties, the abandonment and ignorance of gender in penal assessment and classification is bound to entrench existing barriers to programming and create new ones for women prisoners. In Canada, women's correctional systems are obliged to directly address gender and reconcile the incongruity between gender-sensitivity policy, law, and correctional practice. In the long run, a failure to understand and respond to gender is inefficient and counter-intuitive in terms of the development of "best practices for women" particularly if one subscribes to the logic of what works."

Notes

1 A federal term of imprisonment has to be two years or more, and is managed by The Correctional Service of Canada in federal institutions.
2. See Canadian Association of Elizabeth Fry Societies (CAEFS) (2002).
3. Interview YJ007
4. Attempts to develop separate assessment tools for use in women's facilities were superseded by the generic male-based Offender Intake Assessment (OIA) in 1994.
5. See the Canadian Corrections and Conditional Release Act as well as the Charter of Rights and Freedoms.
6. See Andrews and Bonta, 1998, for a discussion of the logic and research informing this paradigm.
7. Interview S10
8. Interview S20
9. Interview S4
10. Interview DJ013

References

Andrews, D. and Bonta, J. (1998) *Psychology of Criminal Conduct*. Cincinnati, OH: Anderson Publishing.

Auditor General of Canada (2003) *Report of the Auditor General of Canada to the House of Commons*. Ottawa: Office of the Auditor General of Canada.

Bloom, B. (2003) *Gendered Justice: Addressing Female Offenders*. Durham, NC: Carolina Academic Press.

Canadian Association of Elizabeth Fry Societies (CAEFS) (2002) "Response to the Canadian Human Rights Commission's Consultation Paper for the Special Report On the Situation of Federally Sentenced Women." Available at: http://www.Elizabethfry.ca/sentence.

Carlen, P. (1998) *Sledgehammer: Women's Imprisonment at the Millennium*. London: Macmillan.

———. (2002) *Women and Punishment: The Struggle for Justice*. London: Willan Publishing.

Culpitt, I. (1999) *Risk and Social Policy*. Thousand Oaks, CA: Sage.

Feeley, M., and Simon, J. (1992) "New Penology: Notes On The Emerging Strategy Of Corrections And Its Innplications," *Criminology* 30(4): 449–74.

Hannah-Moffat, K. (2002a) "Summary Results of a Survey of Parole Board Members," paper presented to the National Parole Board, Ottawa, Canada.

————. (2002b) "The Transformative Risk Subject: The Hybridizations Of Risk/ Need in Penality," paper presented at the British Society of Criminology annual meeting, Keele.

Hannah-Moffat, K., and Maurutto, P. (2003) *Youth Risk/Needs Assessment: An Overview of Issues and Practices*. Ottawa: Department of Justice.

Hannah-Moffat. K., and Shaw, M. (2001) *Ideal Prison: Critical Essays on Women's Imprisonment in Canada*. Halifax: Fernwood Publishing.

Parton, N. (2001) "Risk and Professional Judgment," in L. Cull and J. Roche (eds) *The Law and Social Work: Contemporary Issues for Practice*, pp. 99–114. Milton Keynes: The Open University Press.

Rose, N. (1998) "Governing Risky Individuals: The Role of Psychiatry in New Regimes of Control," *Psychiatry, Psychology And The Law* 5(2): 177-95.

Taskforce on Federally Sentenced Women (TTFSW). (1990) *Creating Choices: Report of the Taskforce on Federally Sentenced Women*. Ottawa: Correctional Service of Canada. Available: http:/lwww.csc-scc.gc.ca/text/prgnn/fsw/cboices.

Van Voorhis, P., and Presser, L. (2001) *Classification of Woman Offenders: National Assessment of Current Practices*. Washington, DC: National Institute of Corrections.

Memory in Canadian Courts of Law††
Elizabeth Loftus

Abstract

Thousands of people have found themselves facing criminal or civil litigation as a result of questionable memories. Sometimes these involve faulty memory of eyewitnesses to crimes. Psychological science has informed the legal system about memory and enabled productive changes in the handling of eyewitness evidence. The chances of wrongful convictions hopefully go down in the process. But sometimes the questionable memories involve allegations of massive repression of horrible brutalization. In these cases, there is enormous controversy, and downright skepticism, over whether such massive repression even occurs. Unless or until better proof becomes available for these types of claims, a reasonable argument exists for keeping these dubious claims out of the courtroom altogether.

Canada has seen its share of problematic, if not downright dangerous, memories being introduced into legal cases. I had a chance to play a role in two such cases. One of them involved the mistaken identification of Thomas Sophonow, described in detail by Yarmey (2003). The other involved dubious allegations of repressed memories that forced teacher Michael Kliman to endure three trials before his ultimate acquittal, a case that should probably be considered when evaluating the conclusions drawn by Porter, Campbell, Birt, and Woodworth (2003). In both of these cases, witnesses came to court to testify based on their memories, and in both cases false or highly dubious memories were accepted by Canadian jurors. For centuries now, we have had experience with people who come to court to testify, and they take the familiar solemn oath. In light of what psychological science has taught us about human memory, I recently proposed that witnesses probably ought to be taking a more realistic oath: "Do you swear to tell the truth, the whole truth, or whatever it is you think you remember?" (Loftus, 2002).

Thomas Sophonow was accused of murdering a young waitress who worked in a donut shop in Winnipeg, Manitoba. Several eyewitnesses testified against Sophonow but there were problems with each one. For example, the photo array shown to a number of witnesses contained a picture of Sophonow,

†† *Canadian Psychology*, 44:3, August 2003, pp 207–12. Reprinted with permission from the author.

which was significantly different than the other men in the array. For one thing, Sophonow's picture was taken outdoors while the rest of the men were photographed inside. Sophonow is shown wearing a cowboy hat, unlike most of the other possible suspects. Sophonow was also the only man who was depicted in both the photo and the physical lineup, making it possible witnesses chose him because they had seen his picture before. Moreover, Sophonow was the tallest man shown to witnesses, and the killer had been described as a tall man.

Despite these and other problems with the eyewitness testimony, Sophonow was convicted of murder and spent nearly four years in prison. Eventually, he was declared factually innocent. An official inquiry was established to investigate what went wrong, to determine just compensation for Mr. Sophonow, and to make recommendations about future cases. Commissioner Peter Cory was eloquent in his description of the suffering of this one man, falsely accused:

> What has he suffered? … He is psychologically scarred for life. He will always suffer from the core symptoms of post-traumatic stress disorder. As well, he will always suffer from paranoia, depression and the obsessive desire to clear his name. His reputation as a murderer has affected him in every aspect of his life, from work to family relations. The community in which he lived believed him to be the murderer of a young woman, and that the crime had intimations of sexual assault. The damage to his reputation could not be greater.… His reputation as a murderer will follow him wherever he goes. There will always be someone to whisper a false innuendo.… In the mind of Thomas Sophonow, he will always believe that people are talking about him and his implication in the murder.

Commissioner Cory was particularly affected by one illustrative incident in Sophonow's life. Co-workers were uncomfortable with the hiring of Sophonow since they believed that he was a murderer who had gotten off on a technicality. During this time, Sophonow went to a Christmas party with his wife and two of his children. Not a single co-worker would sit with them. This "cruel treatment" illustrated for the Commissioner the tragic consequences flowing from Sophonow's reputation as a murderer.

Commissioner Cory awarded damages exceeding $2 million. It was not the largest award given to a wrongfully convicted Canadian citizen. Several years earlier David Milgaard was awarded $10 million (nearly U.S. $7 million) after serving 23 years in prison for a murder he didn't commit (*New York Times*, 1999). The tax-free payments were made by both the Federal and the Saskatchewan governments, and prompted this comment from the justice minister: "It's very difficult to come up with any amount to deal with 23 years in prison for a crime you didn't commit" (p. A5).

Commissioner Cory made a number of recommendations designed to minimize future miscarriages of justice. Citing relevant psychological research, the inquiry report calls for more care in conducting line-ups (e.g., use of unbiased instructions, sequential presentation, and blind testing). In several respects the recommendations go beyond those recommended by the U.S. Department of Justice (Technical Working Group, 1999, hereafter, The Guide), which had stopped short of recommending blind testing or sequential presentation of photos when presented for identification. The Guide did comment on sequential line-ups, acknowledging the psychological research in the area:

> Scientific research indicates that identification procedures such as line-ups and photo arrays produce more reliable evidence when the individual line-up members or photographs are shown to witnesses sequentially—one at a time—rather than simultaneously. Although some police agencies currently use sequential methods of presentation, there is not a consensus on any particular method or methods of sequential presentation that can be recommended as a preferred procedure; although sequential procedures are included in the Guide, it does not indicate a preference for sequential procedures (p. 9).

The Guide also commented on blind testing:

> … unintentional cues (e.g., body language, tone of voice) may negatively impact the reliability of eyewitness evidence. Psychology researchers have noted that such influences could be avoided if "blind" identification procedures were employed (i.e., procedures conducted by investigators who do not know the identity of the actual suspect). However, blind procedures, which are used in science to prevent inadvertent contamination of research results, may be impractical for some jurisdictions to implement. Blind procedures are not included in the Guide but are identified as a direction for future exploration and field testing (p. 9).

Just two years later, Commissioner Cory would urge these procedural innovations on law enforcement in Canada. The very first recommendation for conducting line-ups: "The third officer who is present with the prospective eyewitness should have no knowledge of the case or whether the suspect is contained in the line-up." And, with regard to the photo arrays, he said "The photo pack must be presented sequentially and not as a package" (see: http://www.gov.mb.ca/justice/ sophonow/eyewitness/ recommend.html).

And the same year that Commissioner Cory gave his blessing to sequential line-ups and blind testing, the State of New Jersey began requiring sequential line-ups and recommended blind testing. As the *New York Times* reported (Kolata & Peterson, 2001), New Jersey became the first state in the U.S. to give up the familiar mug shot books and adopt the new techniques after being required to do so by John Farmer, Jr., New Jersey's attorney general. While the exact method of conducting the sequential test has varied in the research studies, New Jersey adopted a specific approach:

> Under the new system, victims and other eyewitnesses would be shown pictures one after the other. They would not be allowed to browse. If they wanted a second look, they would have to view all the photos a second time, in a new sequence. Also, the pictures would usually be shown by a person who would not know who the real suspect was (Kolata & Peterson, 2001).

What is heartwarming to psychologists who have toiled in the research fields all these years is the acknowledgment that these recommendations grew out of a quarter-century of psychological research. While a number of psychologists have worked on these specific procedural innovations, the primary work has been done by Gary Wells, who spent many years at the University of Alberta and is now at Iowa State University, and by Rod Lindsay, from Queen's University.

The Sophonow Inquiry report also encourages judges to emphasize to juries the frailties of memory, the tragedies of wrongful convictions, and to readily admit expert testimony on the subject of memory. As for expert testimony on the subject of memory, Yarmey (2003) is correct that psychologists are still occasionally excluded from testifying as experts on the subject of eyewitness identification, both in Canadian and American courts. But progress is being made. A recent United States court case contains some especially promising language embracing the eyewitness expert (*Newsome v. McCabe et al.*, 2003). Newsome arose out of a murder that occurred at Cohen's grocery store in Chicago. Three eyewitnesses testified that they saw Newsome in the store, or fleeing. Fifteen years after his conviction, Newsome was pardoned on the ground of innocence. He sued the officers involved in assisting the witnesses to falsely accuse him, and the City of Chicago. An eyewitness expert testified in support of the claim that the misidentifications of Newsome were more likely attributable to deliberate manipulation rather than chance. A jury found that by concealing evidence favourable to the defence, Newsome's constitutional rights had been violated. They awarded $15 million. The City of Chicago appealed the case claiming the expert should not have been admitted. But the appellate court concluded that it was not an abuse of discretion to admit the expert testimony. Moreover, the Court went further in asserting that the expert testimony "was not a distraction in this civil proceeding but went to an important ingredient of the plaintiff's claim." The best lines in this opinion will probably be cited in many future court cases:

> Jurors, however, tend to think that witnesses' memories are reliable … and this gap between the actual error rate and the jurors' heavy reliance on eyewitness testimony sets the stage for erroneous convictions when (as in Newsome's prosecution), everything depends on uncorroborated eyewitness testimony by people who do not know the accused. This is why it is vital that evidence about how photo spreads, showups and lineups are conducted be provided to defense counsel and the court. The constitutional violation justifying an award of damages is not the conduct of the lineups, but the concealing of evidence about them.

The expert witness in Newsome, who happened to be Gary Wells, is clearly one of the preeminent experts in the field in eyewitness identification. It is worth knowing that his views are shared by most experts in the field, as evidenced by surveys of eyewitness experts that have been published over the last decade (see Kassin et al., 1989; Kassin et al., 2001). These articles documenting the consensus of experts (even if not universal) have been important for individual experts to use in showing the courts that their views are reasonably widely held in the field. They have assisted in helping attorneys and their clients gain greater acceptance of psychological expert testimony.

So, all in all, the contemporary picture with respect to eyewitness testimony is good and getting better all the time—for the accused, for the legal system, for psychological researchers, and the public. The DNA exonerations helped to bring about the newly acquired appreciation of the problem of wrongful convictions, and to reveal faulty eyewitness memory as the major cause. This set the stage for the legal system to recognize the value of relevant psychological science, as it had not quite done before. As psychologists we can all proudly share in the success story, and hold it high when we are asked "What have you done for us lately?"

Allegedly Repressed Memories

The story is somewhat different for the legal landscape touched in the article by Porter et al. (2003). A counterpart to the Thomas Sophonow affair is the criminal prosecutions of Michael Kliman, who was a teacher at James McKinney Elementary School in Richmond, B.C. (see Brook, 1998, for a lengthy article about this case). Kliman had taught since receiving his education degree at the University of British Columbia, and was making a rather decent salary as vice-principal. He was even on the short list for principal. His world came crashing down when he was accused of molesting a sixth grade student some 20 years earlier, a student who "recovered" her memories 17 years after the abuse allegedly happened. According to an article in the *Vancouver Sun* (Brook, 1999): "In 1992, after years of psychiatric treatment, she 'recovered' long-lost memories of a year-long series of assaults by Kliman and, encouraged by the Richmond RCMP, laid charges."

Amongst the woman's many claims was the "pointer incident." Kliman had allegedly taken her into the "prep" room for innumerable acts of sexual torture, including one incident in which he pulled down her underpants and thrust the pointer into her vagina. A second student was also dredged up who, after initially saying she had no recollection of any abuse by Kliman, later said she too was regularly abused by him (Brook, 1998, p. 26). Never mind the fact that other teachers talked about making regular use of the "prep" room, which was steps from the cloakroom, washrooms, a water fountain, and the principal's office. Never mind the fact that no one seemed to notice a student and teacher being gone 15 to 20 minutes, two to three times a week, from September to June of that year. Never mind that the two complainants were friends and talked about how much they hated their teacher. Never mind that another Richmond teacher had sued the investigating officer, and the judge was critical of the methods of questioning in that case. Never mind that the investigating officer's superiors had to apologize to yet one more Richmond teacher for biased handling of a recovered memory investigation. Despite the dubious recovered memory testimony, Kliman was convicted of sexual assault in Trial 1 (in 1994), prompting one commentator to remark "it speaks volumes about the susceptibility of juries to trendy thinking" (Brook, 1999). Fortunately for Kliman, his conviction was overturned on appeal; he had a hung jury in Trial 2 (in 1996), and was eventually acquitted in Trial 3 (in 1997). This was one of the most painful and almost certainly egregious prosecutions I have seen in my quarter-century of involvement with the legal system. So moved was I by his plight, that I cancelled any outstanding bills after

Kliman's final acquittal; after all, he had already spent hundreds of thousands of dollars on top of his years of untold anguish.

As Commissioner Cory recognized with Sophonow, there are many for whom a declaration of innocence or even acquittal for that matter, carries little or no weight. Kliman too knows that there are people who see him and ask themselves, "Did he do it?" (Brook, 1998, p. 29).

Porter, Campbell, Birt, and Woodworth (2003) review some psychological science that might help us think about cases like that of Kliman. Then they go on to make recommendations that might help in cases such as these. Unfortunately, we do not have quite the same success story to tell when we delve into this "repressed memory" area as we did in the case of eyewitness testimony.

Reading the Porter et al. article made me feel like I was on a seesaw. That is, while strongly agreeing with some of their conclusions, I disagreed with others. Here is why. Porter et al. reiterate the widely cited studies that have been used to salvage the repressed memory concept, but give only minimal attention to the highly critical analyses of these studies. They point to the "best-known study cited as evidence," namely, the Williams (1994) study that showed that over a third of women failed to mention the documented episodes of sexual abuse when interviewed 20 years later. (Actually it was 17 years, but more importantly some of these individuals were under the age of three at the time of the "abuse." This is one of many reasons why the abuse might not have been mentioned.) Porter et al. might be interested to know that a more recent study (Goodman et al.) interviewed "abused" individuals who were ages 4 to 17 at the time they were first studied. When interviewed 13 years later, on three occasions, only 8% failed to mention the documented abuse. Less severe abuse was less likely to be disclosed. Given that abuse in this study could include exhibitionism or kissing (as well as rape or intercourse), there may be numerous reasons why even the 8% failed to disclose. One notable conclusion from this study: "These findings do not support the existence of special memory mechanisms unique to traumatic events, but instead imply that normal cognitive operations underlie long-term memory for CSA (child sexual abuse)" (p. 117).

Porter et al. acknowledge that theoretical basis of repression is weak and unconvincing. Moreover, they rightfully assert that the unconscious processes involved in retaining a repressed memory and the potential recoverability of the original memory have not been validated. But they then go on to suggest that the questionable validity of the concept of repression does not negate the possibility that an individual can have a delayed memory in which the cause of the delay is unknown or poorly understood. True enough but should the Mike Klimans of the Canadian world, and their families, have to endure the kind of agony that they did based on a concept of "questionable validity."

Porter et al. suggest that expert testimony about relevant findings would prove useful in legal cases involving delayed memory. This may be true, but keep in mind that surveys along the lines of those done by Kassin and colleagues have not been done. Given the divisiveness in this area, one thing seems clear: Who responds to the survey will strongly influence what gets concluded. Prominent psychiatrist Paul McHugh, long-time chair of the prestigious Johns Hopkins Psychiatry Department, recently concluded that "The Memory Wars are over" (McHugh, 2003). Why ended? According to McHugh,

> The wars are ending for several reasons. The memories reported by many patients became absurd. Satanic cults were imagined, and even alien abduction. Many psychiatrists were rebuked for malpractice—sometimes professionally, sometimes in civil court. And most importantly, patients after discharge gradually began to doubt their memories, recanting their accusations and rejoining their parents.

The wars may be winding down in the U.S., but if more Michael Klimans are prosecuted in Canada, the wars will continue for some time to come.

Porter et al. propose that when the repressed memory cases get into the courts, a number of guidelines might be followed. For example, they suggest that the use of suggestive techniques to recover memories should raise suspicions about the validity of the allegations, and that therapy notes and police interview notes would be useful in this assessment. I agree. However, this suggestion will be met with opposition when one thinks for a minute about the long-simmering debate over how to protect the privacy rights of victims of sex crimes while upholding the rights of the accused to a fair trial. My colleagues and I considered this issue extensively and recommended that at the very least an in-camera inspection of those materials should be allowed (Loftus, Paddock, & Guernsey, 1996).

Porter et al. also hint that various guides to assessing the credibility of the content of a report might be used in these cases. This is a dangerous idea at the present time. We are so far away from being able to take a single memory and reliably classify it as real versus unreal that any efforts to do this before a trial of fact are sure to lead to miscarriages of justice. Although it might be true that statistically speaking real memories are more vivid or detailed or emotional than false ones, we know that false memories, especially with repetition, can be vivid, detailed, and expressed with great emotion. Recent work by Richard McNally from Harvard shows that even memories for alien abduction can be described with confident, vivid details, and expressed with an emotion that is equivalent to that felt by those who are describing true traumas.

One place where Porter et al. make good sense is on their emphasis on corroboration. "Corroboration will add credibility to the memory and lack of it may raise doubts about the allegations," they assert. For years, experts have been pointing out that without independent corroboration, there is virtually no way to reliably distinguish a real memory from one that is a product of imagination, suggestion, or some other process. But law enforcement in the Kliman case managed to find something that on the surface of it looked like "corroboration"; however, it came in the form of a second dubious memory. Should this count as corroboration?

In thinking about Porter et al.'s review of the literature, and guidelines for the legal system, perhaps we should be contemplating a slightly different question. Assume, as I do, that Goodman et al. are right that there is no special memory mechanism for child sexual abuse. Assume, as I think the evidence warrants, that normal cognitive operations underlie memory for sexual abuse, as they also underlie memory for other unpleasant or even traumatic experiences. What would happen if the accuser of Kliman came forth and said, "22 years ago you repeatedly stole money from me" or "Two decades ago, you week after week slapped me, and I have now recovered the memories." If Mike Kliman had been the object of such accusations, would we subject him to three criminal trials to have the claims judged? One might be tempted to say that the question is not fair. That sex abuse is different from other crimes like theft, or repeated physical abuse. There is one important way in which this is true, as Pulitzer Prize winner Dorothy Rabinowitz recently noted in the *Wall Street Journal*. Rabinowitz has been covering dubious sex abuse prosecutions for many years, and has repeatedly faced a line of hostile questioning that implied that she fails to recognize that child sex abuse exists and is a serious problem. She found this hostile questioning to be quite strange: "The discussion of no other crime would require such a disclaimer. Journalists who have written about false murder charges are seldom asked to provide reassurance that they know murder is a bad thing, and it really happens" (Rabinowitz, 2003). Society ought to be thinking, then, about why we treat one criminal accusation differently from others, and whether doing so is truly justified by psychological science or any other evidence.

Final Remarks

Probably the best thing about thinking about psychological studies of memory in the context of legal cases, is that new research ideas have been spawned in the process. Many exciting studies of memory have been conceived and published, including studies by the authors of these two articles. We know much more about how memories get distorted, how false beliefs and memories are created, and who might be more susceptible to memory contamination than we ever knew before. Our work in this area can and does make a difference to important societal concerns. But as legal controversies come and go, these research results have even more than their applied impact. They will live on as contributions to the field of psychological science. It is something in which we can all feel pride of accomplishment.

References

Brook, P. (1998, September). The trials of Mike K. *Saturday Night*, pp. 22–29.

Brook, P. (1999, December 15). Accused falls victim to a legal nightmare. *The Vancouver Sun*, p. A19.

Canada to pay highest award to exonerated ex-prisoner. (1999, May 18). *New York Times*, p. A5.

Cory, Honourable Peter deC. (2001, September). *The inquiry regarding Thomas Sophonow*. Available at: http://www.gov.mb.ca/justice/sophonow/toc.html.

Goodman, G. S., Ghetti, S., Quas, J. A., Edelstein, R. S., Alexander, K. W., Redlich, A. D., Cordon, I. M., & Jones, D. P. H. (2003). A prospective study of memory for child sexual abuse: New findings relevant to the repressed-memory controversy. *Psychological Science, 14*, 113–118.

Kassin, S. M., Ellsworth, P. C., & Smith, V. L. (1989). The "general acceptance" of psychological research on eyewitness testimony: A survey of the experts. *American Psychologist, 44*, 1089–1098.

Kassin, S. M., Tubb, V. A., Hosch, H. M., & Memon, A. (2001). On the "general acceptance" of eyewitness testimony research: A new survey of the expert. *American Psychologist, 56*, 405–416.

Kolata, G., & Peterson, I. (2001, July 21). New way to insure eyewitnesses can ID the right bad guy. *New York Times*. Available at: http://www.nytimes.com/2001/07/21/nyregion/21WITN.html.

Loftus, E. F. (2002). Memory faults and fixes. *Issues in Science and Technology* (Publication of the National Academies of Science), 18 (4), 41–50.

Loftus, E. F., Paddock, J. R., & Guernsey, T. F. (1996). Patient-psychotherapist privilege: Access to clinical records in the tangled web of repressed memory litigation. *University of Richmond Law Review, 30*, 109–154.

McHugh, P. (2003, March 2). Ending the "Memory Wars" does not redeem the victims. *The Baltimore Sun*.

Newsome v. McCabe et al. (2003). 319 F.3d 301. United States Court of Appeals for the Seventh Circuit.

Porter, S., Campbell, M. A., Birt, A., & Woodworth, M. T. (2003). He said, she said. *Canadian Psychology, 44,* 190–206.

Rabinowitz, D. (2003, March 27). The Amiraults, Snowden and other innocents. *The Wall Street Journal.*

Technical Working Group for Eyewitness Evidence. (1999). *Eyewitness evidence: A guide for law enforcement.* Washington, DC: United States Department of Justice, Office of Justice programs. Available at: www.ojp.usdoj.gov.

Yarmey, A. D. (2003). Eyewitness identification: Guidelines and recommendations for identification procedures in the United States and in Canada. *Canadian Psychology, 44,* 181–189.

PART III

Organization and Style

CHAPTER

10

Everything in Order

A. HARMONIZED PARAGRAPHS

Back in Chapter 5, you were cautioned about pitfalls of the five-paragraph form, which "invites writers to list rather than analyze, to plug supporting examples into categories without examining the examples or how they are related." Clearly, we weren't recommending it as the most effective way to organize your thoughts.

Improving on the five-paragraph form means paying more attention to the potential of paragraphs themselves. In the end, every strong writer depends on paragraphs to represent the logical pathway of his or her thinking. Take, for example, the one on page 271 (by Mark Kingwell) that begins "This may sound worse than it is." Look closely and you will see that this paragraph appears in the middle of "The Mirror Stage: Infinite Reflections on the Public Good." Reread it in context and you will realize that the paragraph also answers several key questions for Kingwell's audience:

1. What is it that may sound worse than it is? (Answer: the fact that "in social life conflict is endemic")
2. Why isn't it worse than it is? (Answer: because "potential conflicts simply do not arise as actual problems")
3. What's a good example of potential conflict? (Answer: opera)
4. What are some more serious examples of potential conflict? (Answer: sexual mores and the work ethic)
5. Why are these examples meaningful? (Answer: because they inform us about "fundamental social and economic structures")

As an experienced academic writer, Kingwell creates paragraphs that harmonize with each other. Each new one connects to its predecessor while at the same time advancing the essay's thesis. In the example cited above, the paragraph's topic—the fact that "[m]any of the goods we pursue are not public ones at all"—certainly advances Kingwell's thesis. And a connection to the preceding paragraph is furnished by the lead sentence ("This may sound worse than it is"), whose first word establishes a *transition* from one point to the next.

The Shaping Force of Transitions

The linkage between where you've been and where you're going is usually a point in your writing at which thinking is taking place. Often this kind of transitional thinking will require you to concentrate on articulating *how* what has preceded connects to what will follow—the logical links. This is especially the case in the evolving, rather than static, model of thesis development, wherein the writer needs to keep updating the thesis as it moves through evidence. And so it follows that *thinking tends to occur at points of transition*. If it doesn't, you're far more likely to run into problems in organization.

The first step toward improving your use of transitions (and thereby, the organization of your writing) is to become *conscious* of them. To see how the transitions work as a skeleton for something you are reading, actively search out words that function as directional indicators, especially at the beginnings of but also within paragraphs. "And," for example, is a plus sign. It indicates that the writer will add something, essentially continuing in the same direction. The words "but," "yet," "nevertheless," and "however" are among the many transitional words that alert readers to changes in the direction of the writer's thinking. They might indicate, for example, the introduction of a qualification, a potentially contradictory piece of evidence, an alternative point of view, and so forth. Note as well that some additive transitions do more work than "also" or "another." The word "moreover" is an additive transition, but it adds emphasis to the added point. The transitional sequence "not only… but also" restates and then adds information in a way that clarifies what has gone before.

❦*TRY THIS:* You can learn much about the shape of a writer's thinking and his or her method of connecting and advancing ideas by tracking the transitions. Take, for instance, the final two paragraphs of Mark Kingwell's "The Mirror Stage: Infinite Reflections on the Public Good" (pages 268–276).

Reread those paragraphs carefully. Then consider—in an open-ended class discussion—each of these questions: □

- How effectively do transition words prepare Kingwell's readers for the four questions that conclude his essay?
- Can you locate an example of subordination (this grammatical concept was introduced in Chapter 7)? Does the subordinate clause create a transition from one point to the next?
- How does the implication of the transition word "Now" differ from that of the transition word "Indeed"?

B. PRESCRIBED FORMATS

Academic disciplines differ in their use of prescribed organizational schemes—or formats—to which the members of the discipline must conform. In biology and psychology, for example, formal papers and reports generally follow an explicitly prescribed pattern of presentation. Some other disciplines are less uniform and less explicit about their reliance on formats, but writers in these fields—economics, for example, or political science—usually operate within fairly established forms as well. Thus, we also use the term "format" for organizational schemes that, although not rigidly discipline-specific, are often treated as formats in writing assignments, laying out the form of prospective papers in a series of steps.

Predictably, given the disciplinary emphasis in this chapter, there are a substantial number of "Voices Across the Curriculum" boxes that provide advice from faculty members in the natural and social sciences. But these voices will also serve to reveal the significant underlying similarities among the various disciplinary formats, for, ultimately, this chapter is less concerned with teaching you particular formats than with teaching you ways of thinking about and putting to the best use whatever formats you are asked to write in.

The Two Functions of Formats: Product and Process

The first step in learning to use formats productively is to recognize that they have two related but separate functions: product and process.

- *As sets of rules for organizing a final product,* formats make communication among members of a discipline easier and more efficient. By standardizing the means of displaying thinking in a discipline, the format enables readers to compare more readily one writer's work to that of others in the field, because readers will know where to look for particular kinds of information—the writer's methodology, for example, or his or her hypothesis or conclusions.

• *As guides and stimulants to the writing process*, formats offer writers a means of finding and exploring ideas. The procedures that formats contain seek to guide the writer's thinking process in a disciplined manner, prompting systematic and efficient examination of a subject. The notion of formats functioning as aids to invention—idea generation—goes back at least as far as Aristotle, whose *Rhetoric* defined twenty-eight general "topics" (such as considering causes and effects or dividing a subject into parts) that speakers might pursue in order to invent arguments.

Most of the writing (and thinking) we do is generated by some kind of format, even if we are not aware of it. Writers virtually never write in the absence of instructions. Accordingly, you should not regard most of the formats that you encounter simply as *prescriptive* (that is, strictly required) sets of artificial rules. Rather, think of them as descriptive accounts of the various *heuristics*—sets of questions and categories—that humans typically use to guide and stimulate their thinking.

Perhaps the biggest problem that formats can create for writers is a *premature emphasis on product*—on the form of the finished paper at the expense of process. In effect, the format can rush the writer through the successive steps, inhibiting his or her ways of generating the thinking that the finished product will present. In other words, the concept of formats as lines of inquiry (what Aristotle and other classical rhetoricians called the *topics of invention*) has become partially lost in the concept of formats as methods of arranging a finished piece of writing—imposing shape on a final product.

The Relation Between Writing and Genre

Of course, when your professors hand out assignments, they do more than prescribe formulaic structures for writing. They also invite you to participate in a social exchange. In other words, your essay (or lab report or memorandum) is a combination of *format* and *action*: what researchers in the field of composition and discourse call a *genre*. Genre studies emphasize the fact that written texts do not exist autonomously; they are always part of social interactions that occur in the university—or, for professionals, in the workplace. The more you observe the range of social interactions around you—in the classroom, during office-hour consultations, at the writing centre—the better prepared you will be to work effectively within the assigned format.

The primary goal in the first half of this chapter is to suggest the heuristic potential of formats. The conventional format of the scientific paper, for example, stimulates rather than merely contains thought. By stipulating the inclusion of a review of prior research, for instance, this format induces the writer to arrive at thoughtful connections between his or her work and earlier experiments. Nor is the process aspect of formats limited to the sciences. Poets, for example, have continued to write sonnets, one of the most highly structured poetic formats, for hundreds of years because the form has heuristic value. It guides the writer down certain pathways that provoke thought. The sonnet form itself—typically fourteen lines of rhymed iambic pentameter, moving in one logical and/or emotional direction for eight lines and then shifting direction in the final six—lends itself to the production of certain kinds of thinking, such as putting ideas into dialogue with each other, establishing complex logical relationships.

Clearly, formats can both stimulate the writing process and organize the final product, but not when writers think of formats primarily as packaging and thus concern themselves with rigid adherence to form at the expense of more thoughtful exploration of content. At its worst, this "slot-filler approach" to formats can mislead writers into being more concerned with merely filling the slots than with analyzing the material they are filling them with. This is the primary problem we diagnose in our critique of five-paragraph form at the beginning of Chapter 5. (Typically, this format has a three-part thesis, an example supporting each part, and a concluding paragraph that repeats the thesis from the introduction practically verbatim.)

Unlike five-paragraph form, most of the formats encountered in university are roomier. They are not as rigidly overspecified, and they usually leave the writer space for more complex development of ideas. Generally speaking, formats provide a logic for dividing a subject into manageable parts and a logical order for dealing with each of these parts. To develop ideas in depth, writers need some means of deciding what to talk about and when. Unlike more mechanical organizational schemes, good formats help you to order your thinking sequentially, according to relatively distinct phases.

Using Formats Heuristically: An Example

As we observe in our discussion of formats as process and product, it is possible to lose sight of the heuristic value of formats and instead become concerned with formats primarily as disciplinary etiquette. The solution to this problem probably sounds easier than it is: you need to *find the space in a format that will allow it to work as a heuristic.* Consider how you might go about using even a highly specified organizational scheme like the following:

1. State the problem.
2. Develop criteria of adequacy for a solution.
3. Explore at least two inadequate solutions.
4. Explicate the proposed solution.
5. Evaluate the proposed solution.
6. Reply to anticipated criticisms.

The comforting feature of this format is that it appears to tell you exactly what to do. Thinking, however, especially in the early stages of the writing process, is rarely as linear as the six numbered steps in this example imply. Only by testing the adequacy of various solutions (step 3) is one likely to arrive at a clear statement of the problem (step 1), for example. And what if the problem has no solution or has several possible solutions, depending on the details of the problem? And couldn't the exploration of inadequate solutions (step 3) be the best means of discovering criteria of adequacy (standards for determining the acceptability of a solution) in step 2?

Our questions about the format, however, also reveal your best means of using one like it:

• In the early stages of drafting, allow yourself to move freely among the steps in the order that best sparks your thinking. There will be time later to reassemble your results in the required order.
• Recognize that few formats insist on the writer's devoting exactly the same amount of space and attention to each of its steps or phases. If, for example, the relative inadequacy of any solution seems to you the most pressing thing you have to say, you should be able to place your emphasis accordingly.

This advice doesn't mean that you can select from the format the steps you wish to attend to and ignore the others. You can, however, lean more heavily on one of the steps and build your paper around it.

The best reason not to ignore any of the six steps in this problem/solution format we've been looking at is that *the format does have a logic,* although it leaves that logic unstated. The purpose of including at least two inadequate solutions (step 3), for example, is to protect the writer against moving to a conclusion too quickly on the basis of too little evidence. The requirements that the writer evaluate the solution and reply to criticisms (steps 5 and 6) are there to press the writer toward complexity, to prevent a one-sided and uncritical answer. In short, heuristic value in the format is there for a writer to use if he or she doesn't allow a premature concern with matters of form to take precedence over thinking.

C. INTRODUCTIONS AND CONCLUSIONS

The study of rhetoric is primarily concerned with the various means at a writer's (or speaker's) disposal for influencing the views of an audience. For ancient Greek and Roman writers, a key component of rhetoric was *ethos*, which has to do with the character of the speaker or writer. If, let's say, an audience perceives a speaker to be ethical and rational, it will be inclined to perceive her or his argument as ethical and rational too. Thus, writers attend to the kind of *persona* they become on the page, the personality conveyed by the words and the tone of the words (more on this topic in Chapter 11).

In classical orations—the grandparent of virtually all speech and essay formats—the first section was always allotted to particular means of establishing an appealing persona, one that an audience would want to listen to and believe. The same holds true today. Take, for example, the introduction to Mark Kingwell's essay (page 268), whose direct address to the reader—"I could tell you, but I won't"—creates a personal contact that is renewed in the essay's final sentence ("Well, ask yourself: when do we finish growing up?").

At both ends of every academic text, a lot is at stake. The introduction gives the reader his or her first impression, and we all know how indelible that can be. The conclusion leaves the reader with a last—and potentially lasting—impression of the written world you have constructed.

Most of the difficulties in composing introductions and conclusions will arise in deciding how you should deal with theses. How much of a thesis should you put into the introduction? Should your conclusion summarize the thesis or extend it? The model of organization we recommend—of evolving a thesis through successive encounters with evidence—requires a different kind of introduction and conclusion than those you may have been taught to write. It assumes, for example, that the introduction should not and cannot preview a paper's entire interpretation or argument.

As was discussed in Chapter 6, a fully evolved thesis is usually too complex and too dependent on the various reshapings that have preceded it to be stated succinctly but still coherently at the outset. But readers do need to know early on what your paper is attempting to resolve or negotiate.

(See two sections of Chapter 6, "Locating the Evolving Thesis in the Final Draft" and "The Evolving Thesis and Introductory and Concluding Paragraphs.")

To an extent, the conventions of a particular academic discipline may arbitrate such questions. In regard to introductions, for example, a philosophy paper usually locates the thesis in the paper's first sentence and explains in the rest of the opening paragraph how the claim will be proved. Yet, even this model of beginning, which is strictly deductive and conclusion-oriented, normally devotes more space to showing readers the issues that the rest of the paper will address than to dwelling on the answers.

As with other aspects of writing analytically, there are no absolute rules for writing introductions and conclusions, but there does seem to be a consensus across the disciplines that *introductions should raise issues rather than settle them* and *conclusions should go beyond merely restating what has already been said*. Put another way, insofar as disciplinary conventions permit, *in introductions, play an ace but not your whole hand*; and *in conclusions, don't just summarize—culminate*.

D. THE FUNCTION OF INTRODUCTIONS

As the Latin roots of the word suggest—*intro*, meaning "within," and *ducere*, meaning "to lead or bring"—an introduction brings the reader into a subject. Its length varies, depending on the scope of the writing project. An introduction may take a paragraph, a few paragraphs, a few pages, a chapter, or even a book. In most academic writing that you will do, one or two paragraphs is a standard length. In that space you should try to accomplish some or all of the following objectives:

- Define your topic—the issue, question, or problem—and say why it matters.
- Indicate your method of approach to the topic.
- Provide necessary background or context.
- Offer the working thesis (hypothesis) that your paper will develop.

An objective missing from this list that you might expect to find there is the admonition to engage the reader. Clearly, all introductions need to engage the reader, but this admonition is too often misinterpreted as a directive to be entertaining or cute. In academic writing, you don't need a gimmick to engage your readers; you can assume they care about the subject. You will engage them if you can articulate why your topic matters, doing so in terms of existing thinking in the field.

Especially in a first draft, the objectives just listed are not so easily achieved, which is why many writers defer writing the polished version of the introduction until they have completed at least one draft of the paper. At that point, you will usually have a clearer notion of why your subject matters and which aspect of your thesis to place first. Often the conclusion of a first draft becomes the introduction to the second draft. Other writers find that they can't proceed on a draft until they have arrived at an introduction that clearly defines the question or problem they plan to write about and its significance. For these writers, crafting an approach to the topic in the introduction is a key part of the planning phase, even though they also expect to revise the introduction based on what happens in the initial draft.

One of the most common metaphors used to describe an introduction is the *funnel*. It starts wide, providing background and generalization, and then narrows the subject to a particular issue or topic. Here is a typical example from a student paper.

> People have a way of making the most important obligations perfunctory, even trivial, by the steps they take to observe them. For many people traditions and rituals become actuality; the form overshadows the substance. They lose sight of the underlying truths and what these should mean in their lives, and they tend to believe that observing the formalities fulfills their obligation. This is true of professional ethics as they relate to the practice of examining and reporting on financial data—the primary role of the auditor.

The paragraph begins with a generalization in the first sentence (about making even important obligations perfunctory) and funnels down in the last sentence to a working thesis (about the ethics of an auditor's report on financial data).

Putting an Issue or Question in Context

In the accompanying "Voices Across the Curriculum" boxes, notice that professors do not always agree on the wisdom of constructing a *funnel* or on how much material to preview in the introduction. As we've already conceded, there are no absolute rules. What matters most is clear communication with your intended audience, based upon the expectations of that audience.

Although the various models we offer here differ in small ways from discipline to discipline, the essential characteristics that they share suggest that most professors across the curriculum want the same things in an

Voices Across the Curriculum

Providing an Introductory Context

There is no formula for writing a good introduction, since different disciplines and different topics require different approaches. In general, however, it can be said that your introduction should define the scope of the issue and the approach you intend to take. Do not resort to dictionary definitions of terms, which are another form of pomposity and condescension to your reader. Explain why the topic is important and how you intend to approach it, but *do not summarize what you will subsequently say*. A effective introduction could be framed as follows:

> Virginia Woolf's *To the Lighthouse* uses a small group of people—the Ramsays and some of their friends—to show how intelligent people in the years before and after the Great War dealt with the perennial problems of instability, change, and death. Reflecting the decline of religion among the intelligentsia, the characters in Woolf's novel find new ways of imposing order on the world around them. By looking at how Woolf portrays her principal characters, we can understand her analysis of the historical and social forces which shape us; in looking at the contrasts between men and women, and between different generations, we can see how some characters are able to create freer, more meaningful lives for themselves.

This introduction suggests, through the word "perennial," that attitudes towards change and death are a feature of all societies, but it avoids the vague and windy generalization that can occur with the *funnel* approach. It defines the specific approach it will take—the examination of how characters are portrayed and contrasted—but avoids the *preview* approach of giving away the details of what is to come; it does not, for example, mention individuals. It makes clear that the topic is an important one, but leaves the discussion of its implications to the conclusion, where such discussion belongs.

—Edward Lobb, professor of English

I think it is important to understand that an introduction is not simply the statement of a thesis but also the place where the student needs to set a context, a framework that makes such a thesis statement interesting, timely, or in some other way important. It is common to see papers in political science begin by pointing out a discrepancy between conventional wisdom (what the pundits say) and recent political developments, between popular opinion and empirical evidence, or between theoretical frameworks and particular test cases. Papers, in other words, often begin by presenting anomalies.

(continued)

I encourage students to write opening paragraphs that attempt to elucidate such anomalies by:

1. Stating the specific point of departure: are they taking issue with a bit of conventional wisdom? Popular opinions? A theoretical perspective? This provides the context in which a student is able to "frame" a particular problem, issue, and so forth. Students then need to indicate:

2. Why the wisdom/opinion/theory has become problematic or controversial by focusing on a particular issue, event, test case, or empirical evidence. (Here the students' choice of topic becomes important, because topics must be both relevant to the specific point of departure as well as to some degree controversial.) I would also expect in the opening paragraph(s):

3. A brief statement of the tentative thesis/position to be pursued in the paper. This can take several forms, including the revising of conventional wisdom/theory/opinion, discarding it in favour of alternative conceptions, or calling for redefinition of an issue and question. In papers directed toward current political practices (for instance, an analysis of a particular environmental policy or of a proposal to reform political parties), the thesis statement may be stated by indicating (a) hidden or flawed assumptions in current practices or (b) alternative reforms and/or policy proposals.

—Jack Gambino, professor of political science

introduction: *the locating of a problem or question within a context that provides background and rationale, culminating in a working thesis.*

Using Procedural Openings

In the interests of clear organization, some professors require students to include in the introduction an explanation of how the paper will proceed. Such a general statement of method and/or intention is known as a *procedural opening.* Among the disciplines in which you are most likely to find this format are philosophy, political science, and sociology.

As the professor of political science observes, the procedural opening is particularly useful in longer papers, where it can provide a condensed version of what's to come as a guide for readers. Also note that he advises placing it early in the essay but not in the first paragraph, which he reserves for "presenting anomalies." In other words, he seems to value the introduction primarily as a site for the writer's idea, for "stating the specific point of departure" and, that taken care of, only secondarily as a place for forecasting the plan of the paper. These priorities bear mentioning because they imply *a potential danger in relying too heavily on procedural openings: that the writer will avoid making a claim at all.*

The statement of a paper's plan is not the same thing as its thesis. As Chapter 7 discusses, one kind of weak thesis offers a general plan *in place of* supplying an idea about the topic that the paper will explore and defend. Consider the deficiencies of the following procedural opening.

> In this paper I will first discuss the strong points and weak points in America's treatment of the elderly. Then I will compare this treatment with that in other industrial nations in the West. Finally, I will evaluate the various proposals for reform that have been advanced here and abroad.

Voices Across the Curriculum

Procedural Openings

My first piece of advice is to treat your introduction as the first in what should be a series of signposts throughout your paper that let the reader understand clearly what you want to show.

You may have been told that the most important function of an introduction is to catch the reader's interest. That's certainly one function, but not the most important one in an academic paper. The most important function is to alert the reader to your main claim, idea, or thesis in the paper. An academic paper is not a detective story. You shouldn't keep the reader guessing or engaged in detective work to figure out what your paper is about. It's a matter of courtesy to your readers to let them know, near the beginning, the topic of your paper and your approach to it. It also makes sense to clearly state these things in the introduction, because then the reader is much more likely to be able to follow the exposition or argument in the rest of the paper. Don't be afraid to be somewhat mechanical. You can use sentences that begin, "In this paper I will argue . . ." or "The purpose of this essay is to show. . . ." The important thing is to tell the reader clearly what your paper is about. You can then add more to the introduction to indicate why the topic is interesting and to encourage your reader to read on.

My second piece of advice is to write the introduction last. It may seem counter-intuitive to do so; it may seem that you ought to write your paper in the order in which it will be read. But it's much harder to write an introduction and then make the rest of your paper fit it, than to write a paper and then create an introduction that fits the paper. You can certainly produce a rough version of the introduction early on in writing the paper, but it is only when you have at least a complete draft of your paper that you will clearly know what the paper is about and how you have developed it. Then you are in a good position to produce an introduction that will prepare the reader for the rest of the paper.

—Christine Overall, professor of philosophy

This paragraph does not fare well in fulfilling the four functional objectives of an introduction listed at the beginning of this chapter. It identifies the subject, but it neither addresses why the subject matters nor suggests the writer's approach. Nor does it provide background to the topic or suggest a hypothesis that the paper will pursue. Even though a procedural opening is built into the conventions of report writing, these conventions also stipulate that the writer include some clear statement of the hypothesis, which counteracts the danger that the writer won't make any claim at all.

E. HOW MUCH TO INTRODUCE UP FRONT

Introductions need to do a lot in a limited space. To specify a thesis and locate it within a larger context, to suggest the plan or outline of the entire paper, and to negotiate first relations with a reader—that's plenty to pack into a paragraph or two. In deciding how much to introduce up front, you must make a series of difficult choices. We list some of these choices next, phrased as questions you can ask yourself:

- How much can I assume my readers know about my subject?
- Which parts of the research and/or the background are sufficiently pertinent to warrant inclusion?
- How much of my thesis do I include, and which particular part or parts should I begin with?
- What is the proper balance between background and foreground?
- Which are the essential parts of my plan or road map to include?

Typical Problems That Are Symptoms of Doing Too Much

If you ponder the preceding questions, you can avoid writing introductions that try to turn an introduction into a miniature essay. Consider the three problems discussed next as symptoms of *overcompression*, telltale signs that you need to reconceive, and probably reduce, your introduction.

Digression   *Digression* results when you try to include too much background. If, for example, you plan to write about a recent innovation in video technology, you'll need to monitor the amount and kind of technical information you include in your opening paragraphs. You'll also want to avoid starting at a point that is too far away from your immediate concerns, as in "From the beginning of time humans have needed to communicate." Such sweeping declarations result from the writer's use of a gaping funnel: "Unless the appeal to history is specific—telling a story from the past, for example—the comment that something has happened 'throughout recorded history' or 'from the beginning of history' is throat clearing. The writer is getting ready to say something. Far better to get right to the point" (Marius 223).

The standardized formats that govern procedural openings in some disciplines can help you to avoid digressing endlessly. There is a given sequence of steps to follow for a psychology report of an empirical study, for instance. Nonetheless, these disciplinary conventions leave plenty of room for you to lose your focus. You still need to be selective about which contexts are sufficiently relevant to be included up front.

In disciplines that do not stipulate a specific format for contextualizing, the number of choices is greater, and so is the danger that you will get sidetracked into paragraphs of background that bury your thesis and frustrate your readers. One reason that many writers fall into this kind of digression in introductions is that they misjudge how much their audience needs to know. As a general rule in academic writing, *don't assume that your readers know little or nothing about the subject.* Instead, use the social potential of the introduction to negotiate your audience, setting up your relationship with your readers and making clear what you are assuming they do and do not know.

Incoherence   *Incoherence* results when you try to preview too much of your paper's conclusion. Incoherent introductions move in too many directions at once, usually because the writer is trying to conclude before going through the discussion that will make the conclusion comprehensible. The language you are compelled to use in such cases tends to be too dense, and the connections between the sentences tend to get left out, because there isn't enough room to include them. After having read the entire paper, your readers may be able to make sense of the introduction, but in that case, the introduction has not done its job.

The following introductory paragraph is incoherent, primarily because it tries to include too much. It neither adequately connects its ideas nor defines its terms.

> Twinship is a symbol in many religious traditions. The significance of twinship will be discussed and explored in the Native American, Japanese Shinto, and Christian religions. Twinship can be either in opposing or common forces in the form of deities or mortals. There are several forms of twinship that show duality of order versus chaos, good versus evil, and creation versus destruction. The significance of twinship is to set moral codes for society and to explain the inexplicable.

Note that the dominant verb in this paragraph is the verb *to be* ("is," "will be," "can be," "are," "is"). The writer is preoccupied with telling the reader how it *is*—instead of introducing an issue, question, or problem.

Prejudgment *Prejudgment* results when you appear to have already settled the question to be pursued in the rest of the paper. The problem here is logical. In the effort to preview your paper's conclusion at the outset, you risk appearing to assume something as true that your paper will in fact need to test. In most papers in the humanities and social sciences, where the thesis evolves in specificity and complexity between the introduction and conclusion, writers and readers can find such assumptions prejudicial. Opening in this way, at any event, can make the rest of the paper seem redundant. Even in the sciences, where a concise statement of objectives, plan of attack, and hypothesis are usually required up front, a separate "Discussion" section is reserved for the conclusion.

The following introductory paragraph *prejudges*: it offers a series of conclusions already assumed to be true without introducing the necessary background issues and questions that would allow the writer to adequately explore these conclusions.

> Field hockey is a sport that can be played by either men or women. All sports should be made available for members of both sexes. As long as women are allowed to participate on male teams in sports such as football and wrestling, men should be allowed to participate on female teams in sports such as field hockey and lacrosse. If women press for and receive equal opportunity in all sports, then it is only fair that men be given the same opportunity. If women object to this type of equal opportunity, then they are promoting reverse discrimination.

Like incoherence, prejudgment results from writing that's in too much of a hurry to reach the finish line. In place of method and context, such writing depends upon a cluster of declarations that are connected, loosely, by a common theme. Unfortunately, the indispensable connection—precise logic—is missing.

❦*TRY THIS:* Working in groups of three, carefully read and assess the two introductory paragraphs of "Female Eavesdropping on Male Song Contests in Songbirds" (page 427). Try to articulate (1) what the authors assume their audience knows, and (2) to what extent their assumptions seem to influence how material is presented in this scientific article. ☐

Voices Across the Curriculum

Misunderstanding Introductions and Conclusions

Many apprentice writers of exposition seem to believe that everything has to be said three times—first in the introduction, then in the body of the paper, then in the conclusion. This idea, summarized in the cynical advice "Tell them what you're going to tell them, then tell them, then tell them that you've told them," shows contempt for the intelligence of one's readers; it also reveals a misunderstanding of both introductions and conclusions.

—Edward Lobb, professor of English

Avoiding Strong Claims in the Introduction

I might be careful about the role tentative conclusions should play in the opening paragraph, because this can easily slide into a prejudging of the question at hand. I would be more comfortable with a clear statement of the prevailing views held by others. For example, a student could write on the question, "Was Franklin Delano Roosevelt a Keynesian?" What purpose would it serve in an opening paragraph to reveal without any supporting discussion that FDR was or was not a Keynesian? What might be better would be to say that in the public mind FDR is regarded as the original big spender, that some people commonly associate New Deal policies with general conceptions of Keynesianism, but that there may be some surprises in store as that common notion is examined.

In sum, I would discourage students from making strong claims at or near the beginning of a paper. Let's see the evidence first. We should all have respect for the evidence. Strong assertions, bordering on conclusions, too early on are inappropriate.

—James Marshall, professor of economics

F. OPENING GAMBITS: FIVE GOOD WAYS TO BEGIN

The primary challenge in writing introductions, it should now be evident, lies in occupying the middle ground between overassertive prejudgment and avoidance of taking a position. There are a number of fairly common opening gambits that can help you to stake out an effective middle ground. An opening gambit in games such as chess is the initial move—not an announcement of the entire game plan.

Gambit 1: Challenge a Commonly Held View

One of the best opening gambits is to challenge a commonly held view. This is what the economics professor advises when he suggests that rather than announcing up front the answer to the question at which the paper arrives, you convey that "there may be some surprises in store as that common notion is examined." This move has several advantages. Most important, it provides you with a framework *against* which to reply; it allows you to begin by reacting. Moreover, because you are responding to a known position, you have a ready way of integrating context into your paper. As the economics professor notes of the FDR example, until we understand why it matters whether or not FDR was a Keynesian, it is pointless to answer the question.

Gambit 2: Begin with a Definition

In the case of the FDR example, a writer would probably include another common introductory gambit, *defining* "Keynesianism." Beginning with a definition is a reliable way to introduce a topic, so long as that definition has some significance for the discussion to follow. If the definition doesn't do any conceptual work in the introduction, the definition gambit becomes a pointless cliché or—as the English professor points out at the beginning of this chapter—a form of pomposity and condescension.

You are most likely to avoid a cliché if you cite a source other than a standard dictionary for your definition. The reference collection of any academic library contains a range of discipline-specific lexicons that provide more precise and authoritative definitions than Webster ever could. A useful alternative is to quote a particular author's definition of a key term (such as Keynesianism) because you want to make a point about his or her particular definition: for example, "Although the *Dictionary of Economics* defines Keynesianism as XYZ, Smith treats only X and Y (or substitutes A for Z, and so forth)."

Gambit 3: Offer a Working Hypothesis

But, you may be wondering, where is the thesis in the FDR example? As the economics professor proposes, you are often better off introducing a working hypothesis—an opening claim that stimulates the analytical process—instead of offering some full declaration of the conclusion. The introduction he envisions, for example, would first suggest that the question of FDR's Keynesianism is not as simple as is commonly thought and then imply further that the common association of "New Deal policies with general conceptions of Keynesianism" is, to some extent, false.

Gambit 4: Lead with Your Second-Best Example

Another versatile opening gambit, where disciplinary conventions allow, is to use your *second-best example* to set up the issue or question that you later develop in depth with your best example. This gambit is especially useful in papers that proceed inductively on the strength of representative examples. As you are assembling evidence in the outlining and prewriting stage, in many cases you will accumulate a number of examples that illustrate the same basic point. For example, several battles might illustrate a particular general's military strategy; several election debates might exemplify how a particular candidate tailors his or her speeches to appeal to conservative values; several scenes might show how a particular playwright romanticizes the working class; and so on.

Save the best example to receive the most analytical attention in your paper. If you were to present this example in the introduction, you would risk making the rest of the essay vaguely repetitive. A quick close-up of another example will strengthen your argument or interpretation. By using a different example to raise the issues, you suggest that the phenomenon exemplified is not an isolated case and that the major example you will eventually concentrate upon is indeed representative.

What kind of example should you choose? By calling it second best, we mean to suggest only that it should be another resonant instance of whatever issue or question you have chosen to focus upon. Given its location up front and its function to introduce the larger issues to which it points, you should handle it more simply than subsequent examples. That way your readers can get their bearings before you take them into a more in–depth analysis—a 10 on 1—of your best example in the body of your paper.

Gambit 5: Exemplify the Topic with a Narrative

A common gambit in the humanities and social sciences, the narrative opening introduces a short, pertinent, and vivid story or anecdote that exemplifies a key aspect of a topic. Although generally not permissible in the formal reports assigned in the natural and social sciences, narrative openings turn up in virtually all other kinds of writing across the curriculum. Here is an example from a provocative article written in 1991 by Mordecai Richler:

> On a perfect summer day last year in Montreal, local raspberries in season, two tickets to that night's ballgame riding in my breast pocket, I went to meet some friends at a downtown bar I favoured at the time: Woody's Pub, on Bishop Street. As I arrived, a solemn middle-aged man was taking photographs of the blackboard mounted on the outside steps. He was intent on a notice scrawled in chalk on the board:
>
> TODAY'S SPECIAL
>
> PLOUGHMAN'S LUNCH

The notice happened to be a blatant violation of Québec's Bill 178, which prohibits exterior signs in any language but French, and the photographer was one of a number of self-appointed vigilantes who, on lazy summer days off work, do not head for the countryside to cool off in the woods or fish: instead they dutifully search the downtown streets for English-language or bilingual commercial signs that are an affront to Montreal's *visage linguistique*—"HIYA! VERMONT BASEBALL FANS WELCOME HERE," say, or "HAPPY HOUR 5 to 7."*

As this introduction gives way to increasingly analytical prose, the readers receive a graphic sense of the issue—Quebec politics—that Richler will now develop nonnarratively. Such nonnarrative treatment is usually necessary because by itself anecdotal evidence can be seen as merely personal. Storytelling is suggestive but usually does not constitute sufficient proof; it needs to be corroborated.

Like challenging a commonly held view or using a second-best example, a narrative opening will also help to safeguard you from trying to do too much up front. All three of these gambits enable you to play an ace, establishing your authority with your readers, without having to play your whole hand. They offer a starting position rather than a miniaturized version of the entire paper. As a general rule (disciplinary conventions permitting), use your introduction to pose one problem and offer one suggestive example—seeking in some way to engage readers in the thought process that you are beginning to unfold. Raise the issue; don't settle it.

⚘*TRY THIS:* Revisit the article that was featured in the assignment at the end of Chapter 6: "Image World" by Michael Posner (pages 113–120). What do you think the writer accomplishes in his two introductory paragraphs and his two concluding paragraphs? Does Posner use any of the techniques—or follow any of the advice—from this chapter? How effectively do the introductory and concluding paragraphs complement each other? Compose a few paragraphs of your own that respond to one or more of these questions. Then exchange papers with a colleague. After having read each other's paragraphs, discuss the ways in which your assessments of "Image World" converge or diverge. ☐

G. THE FUNCTION OF CONCLUSIONS

Like the introduction, the conclusion has a key social function: it escorts the readers out of the paper, just as the introduction has escorted them in.

---

*From "Outside/Inside" by Mordecai Richler, *The New Yorker*, Sept. 23, 1991, page 40.
(c) Mordecai Richler Productions Inc.

What do readers want as they leave the textual world you have taken them through? Although the form and length of the conclusion depend on the purpose and disciplinary conventions of the particular paper, it is possible to generalize a set of shared expectations for the conclusion across the curriculum. In some combination most readers want three things: a judgment, a culmination, and a send-off.

Judgment—The conclusion is the site for final judgment on whatever question or issue or problem the paper has focused upon. In most cases, this judgment occurs in overt connection with the introduction, often repeating some of its key terms. The conclusion normally reconsiders the issue raised by the opening hypothesis and amends that hypothesis, based upon the evidence presented. It also explicitly revisits the introductory claim for why the topic matters.

Culmination—More than simply summarizing what has preceded or reasserting your main point, the conclusion needs to culminate. The word "culminate" is derived from the Latin *columen*, meaning "top or summit." To culminate is to reach the highest point, and it implies a mountain (in this case, of information and analysis) that you have scaled. When you culminate a paper in a conclusion, you bring things together and ascend to one final statement of your thinking.

Send-Off—The climactic effects of judgment and culmination provide the basis for the send-off. The send-off is both social and conceptual, a final opening outward of the topic that leads the reader out of the paper with something further to think about. As is suggested by most of the professors in the accompanying "Voices Across the Curriculum" boxes, the conclusion needs to move beyond the close analysis of data that has occupied the body of the paper into a kind of speculation that the writer has earned the right to formulate.

Here is an example of a conclusion that contains a final judgment, a culmination, and a send-off. The paper, a student's account of what she learned about science from doing research in biology, opens by claiming that, to the apprentice, "science assumes an impressive air of complete reliability, especially to its distant human acquaintances." Having been attracted to science by the popular view that it proceeds infallibly, she arrives at quite a different final assessment:

All I truly know from my research is that the infinite number of factors that can cause an experiment to go wrong make tinkering a lab skill just as necessary as reading a buret. A scientist can eventually figure out a way to collect the data she wants if she has the patience to repeatedly recombine her materials and tools in slightly different ways. A researcher's success, then, often depends largely on her being lucky enough to locate, among all the possibilities, the one procedure that works.

Aided more by persistence and fortune than by formal training, I evolved a method that produced credible results. But, like the tests from which it derived, the success of that method is probably also highly specific to a certain experimental environment and so is valid only for research involving borosilicate melts treated with hydrofluoric and boric acids. I've discovered a principle, but it's hardly a universal one: reality is too complex to allow much scientific generalization. Science may appear to sit firmly on all-encompassing truths, but the bulk of its weight actually rests on countless little rules tailored for particular situations.

This writer deftly interweaves the original claim from her introduction—that "science assumes an impressive air of complete reliability"—into a final *judgment* of her topic, delivered in the last sentence. This judgment is also a *culmination*, as it moves from her account of doing borosilicate melts to the small but acute generalization that "little rules tailored for particular situations" rather than "all-encompassing truths" provide the mainstay of scientific research. Notice that *a culmination does not need to make a grand claim in order to be effective*. In fact, the relative smallness of the final claim, especially in contrast to the sweeping introductory position about scientific infallibility, ultimately provides a *send-off* made effective by its unexpected understatement.

Ways of Concluding

The two professors quoted next both advise some version of the judgment/culmination/send-off combination. The first professor stresses the send-off.

Voices Across the Curriculum

Expanding Possibilities in the Conclusion

I tell my students that too many papers "just end," as if the last page or so were missing. I tell them the importance of ending a work. One could summarize main points, but I tell them this is not heavy lifting. They could raise issues not addressed (but hinted at) in the main body: "given this, one could consider that." I tell them that a good place for reflection might be a concluding section in which they take the ball and run: react, critique, agree, disagree, recommend, suggest, or predict.

(continued)

I help them by asking, "Where does the paper seem to go after it ends on paper?" That is, I want the paper to live on even though the five pages are filled. I don't want to suddenly stop thinking or reacting just because I've read the last word on the bottom of page five. I want an experience, as if the paper is still with me.

I believe the ending should be an expansion on or explosion of possibilities, sort of like an introduction to some much larger "mental" paper out there. I sometimes encourage students to see the concluding section as an option to introduce ideas that can't be dealt with now. Sort of a "Having done this, I would want to explore boom, boom, boom if I were to continue further." Here the students can critique and recommend ("Having seen 'this,' one wonders 'that'").

—Frederick Norling, professor of business

Limiting Claims in the Conclusion

In the professional journals, conclusions typically appear as a refined version of a paper's thesis—that is, as a more qualified statement of the main claim. An author might take pains to point out how this claim is limited or problematic, given the adequacy of available evidence (particularly in the case of papers dependent on current empirical research, opinion polls, etc.). The conclusion also may indicate the implications of current or new evidence on conventional wisdom/theory—how the theory needs to be revised, discarded, and so forth. Conclusions of papers that deal with contemporary issues or trends usually consider the practical consequences or the expectations for the future.

The conclusion does not appear simply as a restatement of a thesis, but rather as an attempt to draw out its implications and significance (the "So what?"). This is what I usually try to impress upon students. For instance, if a student is writing on a particular proposal for party reform, I would expect the concluding paragraph to consider both the significance of the reform and its practicality.

I should note that professional papers often indicate the tentativeness of their conclusions by stressing the need for future research and indicating what these research needs might be. Although I haven't tried this, maybe it would be useful to have students conclude papers with a section entitled "For Further Consideration" in which they would indicate those things that they would have liked to have known but couldn't, given their time constraints, the availability of information, and lack of methodological sophistication. This would serve as a reminder of the tentativeness of conclusions and the need to revisit and revise arguments in the future (which, after all, is a good scholarly habit).

—Jack Gambino, professor of political science

Although it is true that the conclusion is the place for "broader ramifications," this phrase should not be understood as a call for a global generalization. As the professor in the above "Voices Across the Curriculum" box suggests, often the culmination represents a final limiting of a paper's original claim.

Three Strategies for Writing Effective Conclusions

There is striking overlap in the advice offered in the cross-disciplinary "voices." They caution that the conclusion should provide more than a restatement of what you've already said. They suggest that the conclusion should, in effect, serve as the introduction to some "larger 'mental' paper out there" (as one professor puts it) beyond the confines of your own paper. By consensus, the professors make three recommendations for conclusions:

1. *Pursue implications.* Reason inductively from your particular study to consider broader issues, such as the study's practical consequences or applications, or future-oriented issues, such as avenues for further research. To unfold implications in this way is to broaden the view from the here and now of your paper by looking outward to the wider world and forward to the future.
2. *Come full circle.* Unify your paper by interpreting the results of your analysis in light of the context you established in your introduction.
3. *Identify limitations.* Acknowledge restrictions of method or focus in your analysis, and qualify your conclusion (and its implications) accordingly.

❧ *TRY THIS:* Read carefully the final three paragraphs of Linda McQuaig's "A Matter of Will" (page 108). Which of the "recommendations for conclusions" (listed above) does McQuaig employ? How effectively does her conclusion complement the argument presented in the essay's opening paragraphs? Discuss your answers to these questions in small groups. Also discuss to what degree the thesis of this article, which was published in 1999, remains relevant today. □

H. SOLVING TYPICAL PROBLEMS IN CONCLUSIONS

The primary challenge in writing conclusions, it should now be evident, lies in finding a way to culminate your analysis without claiming either too little or too much. There are a number of fairly common problems to guard against if you are to avoid either of these two extremes.

Redundancy

In Chapter 5, we lampooned an exaggerated example of the five-paragraph form for constructing its conclusion by stating "Thus, we see" and then repeating the introduction verbatim. The result is *redundancy*. As you've seen, it's a good idea to refer back to the opening, but it's a bad idea just to reinsert it mechanically. Instead, re-evaluate what you said there in light of where you've ended up, repeating only key words or phrases from the introduction. This kind of *selective repetition* is a desirable way of achieving unity and will keep you from making one of two opposite mistakes—either repeating too much or bringing up a totally new point in the conclusion.

Raising a Totally New Point

Raising a totally new point can distract or bewilder a reader. This problem often arises out of a writer's praiseworthy desire to avoid repetition. As a rule, you can guard against the problem by making sure that you have clearly expressed the conceptual link between your central conclusion and any implications you may draw. *An implication is not a totally new point but rather one that follows from the position you have been analyzing.*

Similarly, although a capping judgment or send-off may appear for the first time in your concluding paragraph, it should have been *anticipated* by the body of your paper. Conclusions often indicate where you think you (or an interested reader) may need to go next, but you don't actually go there. In a paper on the economist Milton Friedman, for example, if you think that another economist offers a useful way of critiquing him, you probably should not introduce this person for the first time in your conclusion.

Overstatement

Many writers are confused over how much they should claim in the conclusion. Out of the understandable (but mistaken) desire for a grand (rather than a modest and qualified) culmination, writers sometimes *overstate* the case. That is, they assert more than their evidence has proven or even suggested. Must a conclusion arrive at some comprehensive and final answer to the question that your paper has analyzed? Depending on the question and the disciplinary conventions, you may need to come down exclusively on one side or another. In a great many cases, however, the answers with which you conclude can be more moderate. Especially in the humanities, good analytical writing seeks to unfold successive layers of implication, so it's not even reasonable for you to expect neat closure. In such cases, you are usually better off qualifying your final judgments, drawing the line at points of relative stability.

Anticlimax

It makes a difference precisely where in the final paragraph(s) you qualify your concluding claim. The end of the conclusion is a "charged" site, because it gives the reader a last impression of your paper. As the next chapter on formats will discuss in more detail, if you end with a concession—an acknowledgment of a rival position at odds with your thesis—you risk leaving the reader unsettled and possibly confused. The term for this kind of letdown from the significant to the inconsequential is "anticlimax." In most cases, you will flub the send-off if you depart the paper on an anticlimax.

There are many forms of anticlimax besides ending with a concession. If your conclusion peters out in a random list or an apparent afterthought or a last-minute qualification of your claims, the effect is anticlimactic. And for many readers, *if your final answer comes from quoting an authority in place of establishing your own, that, too, is an anticlimax.*

At the beginning of this section we suggested that a useful rule for the introduction is to play an ace but not your whole hand. In the context of this card-game analogy, it is similarly effective to *save an ace for the conclusion.* In most cases, this high card will provide an answer to some culminating "So what?" question—a last view of the implications or consequences of your analysis.

I.   SCIENTIFIC FORMAT: INTRODUCTIONS AND CONCLUSIONS

Formats control fairly strictly the form of standard writing projects in the natural sciences and psychology. They should not, however, be thought of as academic straitjackets. Far from imposing some mindless formula, they offer a *rhetorical pattern*: "When you master a rhetorical pattern, you have more than a formula for writing, even more than a rhetorical device for addressing readers in a way they understand. You also have a tool for thinking" (Booth, Colomb, and Williams 244).

Introductions of Reports in the Sciences

The professors quoted in the "Voices Across the Curriculum" boxes in the remainder of this chapter emphasize the importance of isolating a specific question or issue and locating it within a wider context. Notice, as you read these "voices," how *little* the model for an introduction changes in moving from a social science (psychology) to the natural sciences of biology and physics.

In the sciences, the introduction is an especially important and also somewhat challenging section of the report to compose because it requires a writer *not merely to assemble but also to assimilate* the background of

---

Voices Across the Curriculum

Introductions in the Sciences

A paper usually starts by making some general observation or a description of known phenomena and by providing the reader with some background information. The first paragraphs should illustrate an understanding of the issues at hand and should present an argument for why the research should be done. In other words, a context or framework is established for the entire paper. This background information must lead to a clear statement of the objectives of the paper and the hypothesis that will be experimentally tested. This movement from broad ideas and observations to a specific question or test starts the deductive scientific process.

—Richard Niesenbaum, professor of biology

Assimilating Prior Research

The introduction is one of the hardest sections to write. In the introduction, students must summarize, analyze, and integrate the work of numerous other authors and use that to build their own argument.

Students frequently have trouble writing the introduction. They tend to just list the conclusions of previous authors. So-and-So said this, and So-and-So said this, and on and on in a list format. Usually, they *quote* the concluding statements from an article. But the task is really to read the article and *summarize* it in your own words. The key is to analyze rather than just repeat material from the articles so as to make clear the connections among them. (It is important to note that experimental psychologists almost never use direct quotes in their writing. Many of my students have been trained to use direct quotation for their other classes, and so I have to spend time explaining how to summarize without directly quoting or plagiarizing the work that they have read.)

Finally, in the introduction the students must show explicitly how the articles they have summarized lead to the hypothesis they have devised. Many times the students see the connection as implicitly obvious, but I require that they explicitly state the relationships between what they read and what they plan to do.

—Laura Snodgrass, professor of psychology

---

information and ideas that frame his or her hypothesis. Like the researcher's use of synthesis, which is explained at the end of Chapter 9, the report writer's use of assimilation ensures that his or her reader will appreciate the context of the analysis.

Discussion Sections of Reports in the Sciences

As is the case with introductions, the conclusions of reports written in the natural sciences and psychology are regulated by formalized disciplinary formats. Conclusions, for example, occur in a section entitled "Discussion." As the accompanying comments in "Voices Across the Curriculum" demonstrate, the organization and contents of discussion sections vary little

---

Voices Across the Curriculum

Writing Conclusions in the Sciences

The conclusion occurs in a section labelled "Discussion" and, as quoted from the *Publication Manual of the American Psychological Association* (4th ed., Washington, DC, 1994), is guided by the following questions:

- What have I contributed here?
- How has my study helped to resolve the original problem?
- What conclusions and theoretical implications can I draw from my study? (19)

In a broad sense, one particular research report should be seen as but one moment in a broader research tradition that *preceded* the particular study being written about and that will *continue after* this study is published. And so the conclusion should tie this particular study into both previous research considering implications for the theory guiding this study and (when applicable) practical implications of this study. One of the great challenges of writing a research report is thus to place this particular study within that broader research tradition. That's an analytical task.

—Alan Tjeltveit, professor of psychology

In the "Discussion" section, students must critically evaluate the extent to which the empirical evidence they have collected supports the hypothesis they put forth in the introduction. If the data does not support their hypothesis, they need to explain why. The reasons typically are either that there was something wrong with the hypothesis or something wrong with the experiment. Interestingly, students usually find it easier to write the "Discussion" section if their hypothesis was not supported than if it was—to guess what went wrong—because it is difficult to integrate new results into existing theory.

—Laura Snodgrass, professor of psychology

---

from discipline to discipline. For that matter, the imperatives that guide discussion sections in the sciences are—in essence—the same as those that guide conclusions in the humanities.

ASSIGNMENT: INFERRING THE FORMAT OF A PUBLISHED ARTICLE

Often the format governing the organization of a published piece is not immediately evident. That is, it is not subdivided according to conventional disciplinary categories that are obeyed by all members of a given discourse community. Especially if you are studying a discipline in which the writing does not follow an explicitly prescribed format, such as history, literature, or economics, you may find it illuminating to examine representative articles or essays in that discipline, looking for an implicit format. In other words, you can usually discern some underlying pattern of organization: the formal conventions, the rules that are being followed even when these are not highlighted.

The following assignment works well whether you tackle it individually or in small groups. It can lead to a paper, an oral report, or both.

Among the six readings that follow Chapter 13 is "MSN Spoken Here" by Charles Foran (pages 424–426). It comes from the third issue of the second volume of *The Walrus*, a magazine advertised as offering "thoughtful, provocative, entertaining discussion of the issues that matter."

Using "MSN Spoken Here" as your evidence, describe the format that seems to govern the organization of articles in *The Walrus*. Consider the likely discourse community (those who seek "thoughtful, provocative, entertaining discussion"). Look carefully at Foran's three-paragraph introduction. Identify organizational techniques that the writer applies to the body of the article and to its conclusion.

Finally, think about the connection between journalistic writing and academic writing. Like the writers of the six pieces following Chapter 4, Foran would not describe himself as an academic. Nevertheless, his article's implicit format is connected to those of many scholarly publications.

CHAPTER

11

The Language of Clarity

A. SELECTING AND ARRANGING WORDS

In 1834, a British adventurer and scholar travelled to the island of Crete, which at the time was part of the Ottoman Empire. A fellow of Trinity College, Cambridge, Robert Pashley Esq. was intent on conducting field research into various sites of Crete's rich, troubled history. Once back in England, he published two volumes of his *Travels in Crete*, which contain many long, complicated sentences. Here is an example: "After this our counterpanes were spread on the floor, for the monastery is not yet sufficiently recovered from the effects of the revolution to possess beds or sheets, and we were soon in that happy state of utter unconsciousness which speedily follows a long day's ride, and an hospitable reception" (228).

Pashley's research required a lot of walking, and on that particular evening, after a hearty meal, he was relieved to get to sleep. And while his 50-word sentence communicates that relief, it also shows its age: the word choice and word order seem characteristic of a bygone era.

Much of any writer's stylistic clarity boils down to his or her handling of word choice (diction) and word order (syntax). These important components of writing style are addressed in the next two chapters, alongside two others—tone of voice and rhythm. We will also look closely at punctuation and grammar, indispensable allies of any competent stylist, whether a nineteenth-century British scholar or a twenty-first-century Canadian one.

It is commonly assumed that "getting the style right" is a task that begins at the *editing stage* of the writing process, as part of polishing the final draft. This assumption is only partly true. You probably should delay a *full-fledged* stylistic revision until a late stage of drafting, but that doesn't mean that you should totally ignore stylistic questions as you draft, because the decisions you make about how to phrase your meaning inevitably exert a powerful influence on the meaning you make.

Keep in mind that style is not just icing on the cake—not just a cosmetic sweetening of the surface. Broadly defined, *style refers to all of a writer's decisions in selecting, arranging, and expressing what he or she has to say.* Many factors affect your style: your purpose and sense of audience, the methods of developing your topic, and the kinds of evidence you select.

Thus, revising for clarity is much more than proofreading for errors in grammar and punctuation. Such proofreading occurs in the relatively codified linguistic world of correct and incorrect usage. Stylistic decisions, by contrast, occur in the more creative realm of *making choices* among the myriad ways of formulating and communicating your meaning.

In this sense, style is personal. The foundations of your style emerge in the dialogue you have with yourself about your topic. When you revise for style, you consciously reorient yourself toward communicating the results of that dialogue to your audience. Stylistic decisions, then, are a mix of the unconscious and conscious, of chance and choice. You don't simply impose style onto your prose; it's not merely a mask you don to impress your readers. Revising for style is more like sculpting. As a sculptor uses a chisel to "bring out" a shape from a block of walnut or marble, a writer uses style to "bring out" the shape of the conceptual connections in a draft of an essay. As the examples that follow suggest, this "bringing out" demands a certain *detachment from your own language.* It requires that you *become aware of your words and sentences as tangible materials of discourse and self-expression.*

If stylistic considerations are not merely cosmetic, then it follows that rethinking the way you have said something can lead you to rethink the substance of what you have said. This point is sufficiently important to illustrate, here at the outset, for both diction and syntax—the two most crucial components of stylistic clarity.

How does the difference in sentence structure affect the meaning of the following two sentences?

Draft: The history of Indochina is marked by colonial exploitation as well as international cooperation.

Revision: The history of Indochina, although marked by colonial exploitation, testifies to the possibility of international cooperation.

In the draft, the claim that Indochina has experienced colonial exploitation is equal in weight to the claim that it has also experienced international cooperation. But the revision ranks the two claims. The "although" clause makes the claim of exploitation secondary to the claim of cooperation. The first version of the sentence would probably lead you to a broad survey of foreign intervention in Indochina. The result would likely be a static list in which you judged some interventions to be "beneficial" and others "not beneficial." The revised sentence redirects your thinking, tightens your paper's focus to prioritize evidence of cooperation, and presses you to make decisions, such as whether the positive consequences of cooperation outweigh the negative consequences of colonialism. In short, revision of the sentence's syntax leads you to examine the dynamic relations between your two initial claims.

Our use of the word "clause" in the preceding paragraph illustrates the inevitable overlap of style and grammar. If that grammatical concept (or any other one) seems confusing, you should make a point of shuttling back and forth between this chapter and Chapter 13, which concludes with a "Glossary of Grammatical Terms."

Rethinking what you mean is just as likely to occur when you attend to diction. Notice how the change of a single word in the following sentences could alter the entire paper.

> **Draft:**   The premier's attitude toward health care spending is ambiguous.
>
> **Revision:**   The premier's attitude toward health care spending is ambivalent.

In the draft, the use of the word "ambiguous" (meaning "open to many interpretations") would likely lead to a paper on ways that the premier's decisions are unclear. The choice of "ambiguous" might also signal that the writer and not the premier is unclear on what the premier's actions could be taken to mean. If the premier's policies aren't unclear—hard to interpret—but are divided—conflicted over competing ways of thinking—then the writer would want the word "ambivalent." This recognition would lead not only to reorganizing the final draft but also to refocusing the argument, building to the significance of this ambivalence (that the premier is torn between adopting one of two stances) rather than to the previous conclusion (that provincial policy is simply incoherent).

B. ATTITUDE AND PACE

Tone is the *implied attitude* of a piece of language toward its subject and audience. Whenever you revise for style, your choices in diction and syntax will affect the tone. There are no hard and fast rules to govern matters of tone, and your control of it will depend upon your sensitivity to the particular context—your understanding of your own intentions and your readers' expectations.

Let's consider, for example, the tonal implications of the warning signs in the subways of London and New York.

London: Leaning out of the window may cause harm.

New York: Do not lean out of the window.

Initially, you may find the English injunction laughably indirect and verbose in comparison with the shoot-from-the-hip clarity of the American sign. But that is to ignore the very thing we are calling *style*. The American version appeals to authority, commanding readers what not to do without telling them why. The English version, by contrast, appeals to logic; it is more collegial toward its readers and assumes they are rational beings rather than children prone to misbehave.

In revising for tone, you need to ask yourself if the attitude suggested by your language is appropriate to the aim of your message and to your audience. Your goal is to keep the tone consistent with your rhetorical intentions. The following paragraph, from a university catalogue, offers a classic mismatch between the overtly stated aim and the tonal implications:

> The student affairs staff believes that the university years provide a growth and development process for students. Students need to learn about themselves and others and to learn how to relate to individuals and groups of individuals with vastly different backgrounds, interests, attitudes and values. Not only is the tolerance of differences expected, but also an appreciation and a celebration of these differences must be an outcome of the student's experience. In addition, the student must progress toward self-reliance and independence tempered by a concern for the social order.

The explicit content of this passage—*what* it says—concerns tolerance. The professed point of view is student-friendly, asserting that the university exists to allow students "to learn about themselves and others" and to support the individual in accord with the "appreciation… of… differences."

But note that the implicit tone—*how* the passage goes about saying *what* it says—is condescending and intolerant. Look at the verbs. An imperious authority lectures students about what they "*need* to learn," that tolerance is "*expected*," that "celebration… *must* be an outcome," and that "the student *must* progress" along these lines. Presumably, the paragraph does not intend to adopt this high-handed manner, but its insensitivity to tone subverts its desired meaning.

We return now to the writing of Robert Pashley, whose attitude towards authority is less than respectful: "The Archbishop is a tall and handsome man: his beard is long and his manner dignified. I had the misfortune of finding out, before I left his Holiness, that he is even more ignorant than is usually the case with individuals of his profession in these parts of the world." Pashley's sarcastic tone is sharpened by the leisurely rhythm of all that precedes the charge of ignorance. For example, the colon in his first sentence slows the pace, encouraging readers to dwell for a moment on the Archbishop's dignified manner. And the clause that interrupts his second sentence ("before I left his Holiness") creates yet another pause, one that heightens the contrast ("dignified"/"ignorant") of Pashley's diction.

Of course, most academic writing deliberately avoids displaying emotional tones of voice. As stated in Chapter 4, "overpersonalizing substitutes merely reacting for thinking." While personal commitment to your ideas is certainly a good thing, the crux of strong analysis is the dispassionate logic of thesis and evidence. Likewise, the rhythm of your sentences should not dominate the spotlight: this component of style contributes most to clarity when it works in a supporting role. As we discuss in Chapter 12, your grammatical decisions will dictate the lengths of your sentences, which in turn will dictate the pace of your writing. Work to achieve grammatical diversity and you will inevitably enhance the rhythm of your sentences.

TRY THIS: Look around for examples of the rhetorical use of tone in daily life. Such examples may be found in magazine advertising, newspaper editorials (like Erna Paris's, on pages 101–103), administrative memorandums from a university dean, or even appeals for money that appear in your mailbox. Type or photocopy one of the passages that you find and bring it to class. In small-group discussion, compare passages with three or four other people. As a group, decide which passage is most noteworthy—either in terms of its effectiveness or ineffectiveness. Then designate one member of the group to present your findings to the entire class. There should be time for five-minute presentations from each group. □

C. LEVELS OF STYLE: HOW FORMAL IS *TOO* FORMAL?

How you say something is always a significant part of *what* you say. To look at words carefully is to focus on the *how* as well as the *what*. Imagine that you call your friend on the phone, and a voice you don't recognize answers. You ask to speak with your friend, and the voice responds, "With whom have I the pleasure of speaking?" By contrast, what if the voice instead responds, "Who's this?" What information do these two versions of the question convey, beyond the obvious request for your name?

The first response—"With whom have I the pleasure of speaking?"—tells you that the speaker is formal and polite. He is also probably fastidiously well educated: he not only knows the difference between "who" and "whom" but also obeys the etiquette that outlaws ending a sentence with a preposition ("Whom have I the pleasure of speaking *with?*"). The very formality of the utterance, however, might lead you to label the speaker pretentious. His assumption that conversing with you is a "pleasure" suggests empty flattery. On the other hand, the second version—"Who's this?"—while also grammatically correct, is less formal. It is more direct but also terse to a fault; the speaker does not seem particularly interested in treating you politely.

The two hypothetical responses represent two different levels of style. Formal English obeys the basic conventions of standard written prose, and most academic writing is fairly formal. An informal style—one that is conversational and full of slang—can have severe limitations in an academic setting. The syntax and vocabulary of written prose aren't the same as those of speech, and attempts to import the language of speech into academic writing can result in your communicating less meaning with less precision.

Let's take one brief example:

> Internecine quarrels within the corporation destroyed morale and sent the value of the stock plummeting.

The phrase "internecine quarrels" may strike some readers as a pretentious display of formal language, but consider how difficult it is to communicate this concept economically. "Fights that go on between people related to each other" is awkward; "brother against brother" is sexist and a cliché; and "mutually destructive disputes" is acceptable but long-winded.

It is arguably a part of North American culture to value the simple and the direct as more genuine and democratic than the sophisticated, which is supposedly more aristocratic and pretentious. Then again, Bruce McCall writes about "the quasi-British Canadian idea of modesty and self-restraint" (page 94). Do Canadian writers favour a "plain-speaking" style? If so, can that style hinder the ability to develop and communicate ideas? In the case of "internecine," the more formal word choice actually communicates more, and does so more effectively, than the less formal equivalents. As with all decisions of diction, though, this one depends upon both the writer's intention and the readers' responsiveness.

When in doubt about how your readers will respond to the formality or informality of your style, you are usually better off opting for some version of "With whom have I the pleasure of speaking?" rather than "Who's this?" The best solution will usually lie somewhere in between: "May I ask who's calling?" would protect you against the imputation of either priggishness or piggishness.

What generalizations about style do the preceding examples suggest?

- There are many ways of conveying a message.
- The way you phrase a message constitutes a significant part of its meaning.
- Your phrasing gives your reader cues that suggest your attitude and your ways of thinking.
- All stylistic decisions depend on your sensitivity to context—who's talking to whom about what subject and with what aims.

The last of these generalizations concerns what is called the *rhetorical situation*. As we pointed out in Chapter 10, *rhetoric* deals with how writers behave in given situations and, more specifically, how they can generate language that produces the effects they desire on a particular audience. Obviously, as you make stylistic choices, you need to be aware of the possible consequences of making certain statements to a certain audience in a certain fashion.

Managing Personal Pronouns

"The person question"—one that involves not only style but also grammar—concerns which of the three basic forms of the pronoun to use when you write. Here are the three forms, with brief examples.

First person: I believe Heraclitus is an underrated philosopher.

Second person: You believe that Heraclitus is an underrated philosopher.

Third person: He or she believes that Heraclitus is an underrated philosopher.

Which person to use is a stylistic concern because it involves a writer's *choices* about level of formality, the varying expectations of different audiences, and overall tone.

As a general rule, in academic writing you should discuss your subject matter in the third person and avoid the first and second persons. There is logic to this rule: most academic analysis focuses on the subject matter rather than on you as you respond to it (of course, if "you" were the writer, you would be referring to yourself as "I"—in the first person!). The standard solution in academic writing is to use a third-person perspective *without* employing any personal pronouns: *Heraclitus is an underrated philosopher.* Keep the attention where it belongs: on the subject under analysis.

Speaking of philosophers, though, we have already heard from one who does not hesitate to write in the first person: Christine Overall explains, in Chapter 4, that the use of "I" is, in some academic contexts, "much clearer, simpler, and more honest." As a writer, your decision must be guided by strategic consideration of your audience's expectations (as George Lovell points out below).

Many writers use the first person in the drafting stage, in order to bring their own points of view to the forefront. In this situation, the "I" becomes

---

Voices Across the Curriculum

Deploying "I" Strategically

"Professor Lovell—am I allowed to use the first person in this assignment?" the student asked warily.

"By all means," I replied. "But just make sure...."

It's taken me 25 years of teaching, and many more as a writer, to feel confident that I can come up with something to finish that sentence satisfactorily. There are no guarantees, but here are four points to consider when putting "me/myself/I" in academic writing:

1. CHOOSE THE FORUM CAREFULLY. First person works better in some scholarly media than in others, so don't think of it as a panacea. An essay may lend itself more to first person, for instance, than a book review or a methodological critique. Creative non-fiction is an ideal genre in which to experiment with first person.

2. DEPLOY YOURSELF STRATEGICALLY. The use of first person should establish or enhance your credibility as a reliable source of information. The idea is to promote a sense of confidence, to convince readers that they can trust you. Do that by thinking critically about what you have to say before you put pen to paper.

3. DON'T OVERDO IT. Some writers are so present in their texts that they get in the way of the story they are trying to tell. Try not to give readers the impression that nothing would have happened were you not there to record and bear witness. Inflated use of the first person can turn readers off.

4. REALIZE YOUR LIMITS, PLAY TO YOUR STRENGTHS. Conveying what you thought, felt, or saw in first person implies that you have had some valuable experience that the reader has not. Stick to what you know best. Relay what strikes you as close and pertinent, not remote and irrelevant, far from your genuine interests. Write about what moves you.

—George Lovell, professor of geography

---

a strategy for loosening up and saying what you really think about a subject rather than adopting conventional and faceless positions. Most final drafts of analytical prose, though, emphasize precision and objectivity by relying on a third-person delivery. By cutting "I am convinced that" from the beginning of an important claim, what is lost in personal conviction will be gained in concision and directness—by keeping the focus on the main idea.

Although a majority of professors may prefer the first-person "I think" to the more awkward "the writer (or 'one') thinks," we would point out that, with the aim of reducing wordiness, you can often avoid both options. For example, in certain contexts and disciplines, the first-person-plural "we" is acceptable usage: "Before we can say what *the* public good is, or even whether there is one, we have to ask what *a* public good might be" (page 268). By employing "we," Mark Kingwell is able to underscore the fact that those interested in philosophy—both writers and readers—constitute a community of scholars.

As for the second person, proceed with caution. Using "you" is a fairly assertive gesture. Many readers will be annoyed, for example, by a paper about advertising that states, "When you read about a sale at the mall, you know it's hard to resist." Most readers resent having a writer airily making assumptions about them or telling them what to do. Some rhetorical situations, however, call for the use of "you." Textbooks, for example, often use "you" because it creates a more direct relationship between authors and readers. (Look back at the Introduction to this book and you'll see that we addressed "you" in the very first paragraph.)

The readiest alternative to "you" is the imperative mood, which requires careful handling for similar reasons. The *imperative mood* of a verb expresses a direct request or command, leaving "you" understood, as in the following transitional sentence from Michael Posner's "Image World" (page 113): "Consider, for a moment, pornography." Such a sentence, though, runs the same kind of risk as one that features direct address: some readers might resent being told what to do. On the other hand, Posner is politely soliciting his readers' attention—less obtrusively than he would by inserting an awkward "you should" or "one should" before the verb.

The conventional argument for using the first and second person is that "I" and "you" are personal and engage readers. It is not necessarily the case, however, that the third person is therefore *impersonal*. Just as film directors put their stamps on films by the way they organize the images, move among camera viewpoints, and orchestrate the soundtracks, so writers, even when writing in the third person, have a wide variety of resources at their disposal for making the writing more personal and accessible for their audiences. See, for example, the discussion of the passive voice in the next chapter.

D. SHADES OF MEANING: CHOOSING THE BEST WORD

The nineteenth-century English statesman Benjamin Disraeli once differentiated between "misfortune" and "calamity" by commenting on his political rival William Gladstone: "If Mr. Gladstone fell into the Thames, it would be a misfortune; but if someone dragged him out, it would be a calamity." "Misfortune" and "calamity" might to some people mean the same thing, but in fact the two words allow a careful writer to discriminate fine shades of meaning.

One of the best ways to get yourself to pay attention to diction is to practise making subtle distinctions among related words. The "right" word contributes accuracy and precision to your meaning. The "wrong" word, it follows, is inaccurate or imprecise. The most reliable guide to choosing the right word and avoiding the wrong word is a dictionary that includes not only concise definitions but also the origin of words (known as their *etymology*). A dicey alternative is a thesaurus (a dictionary of synonyms, now included in most word-processing software): it can offer you a host of choices, but you run a fairly high risk of choosing an inappropriate word.

The Globe and Mail, May 1, 1993. Reprinted with permission from The Globe and Mail.

If you go the thesaurus route, also check in the dictionary for the word you select. The most thorough dictionary for the job, by the way, is the *Oxford English Dictionary*, which commonly goes by its initials, *OED*. Available in every library reference collection and usually online at universities and colleges as well, it provides historical examples of how every word has been used over time.

Frankly, many of the most common diction errors are caused by ignorance. The writer has not learned the difference between similar terms that actually have different meanings. If you confuse "then" and "than," or "infer" and "imply," you will not convey the meaning that you intend, and you will probably confuse your readers and invite them to question your control of language. Getting the wrong word is, of course, not limited to pairs of words that are spelled similarly. A *notorious* figure is widely but unfavourably known, whereas a *famous* person is usually recognized for accomplishments that are praiseworthy. Referring to a famous person as notorious—a rather comic error—could be an embarrassing mistake. Take the time to learn the differences among seemingly similar words.

A slightly less severe version of using the wrong word occurs when a writer uses a word with a shade of meaning that is inappropriate or inaccurate in a particular context. Take, for example, the words "assertive" and "aggressive." Often used interchangeably, they don't really mean the same thing—and the difference matters. Loosely defined, both terms mean "forceful." But "assertive" suggests being "bold and self-confident," whereas "aggressive" suggests being "eager to attack." In most cases, you compliment the person you call assertive but raise doubts about the person you call aggressive (whether you are giving a compliment depends on the situation: "aggressive" is a term of praise on the football field but less so if used to describe an acquaintance's behaviour during conversation at the dinner table).

One particularly charged context in which shades of meaning matter to many readers involves the potentially sexist implications of using one term for women and another for men. If, for example, in describing a woman and a man up for the same job, we referred to the woman as *aggressive* but the man as *assertive*, our diction would deservedly be considered sexist. It would reveal that what is perceived as poised and a sign of leadership potential in a man is being construed as unseemly belligerence in a woman.

In choosing the right shade of meaning, you will get a sharper sense for the word by knowing its etymological history—the word or words from which it evolved. In the preceding example, "aggressive" derives from the Latin *aggressus*, meaning "to go to or approach"; and *aggressus* is itself a combination of *ad*, a prefix expressing motion, and *gradus*, meaning "a step." An aggressive person, then, is "coming at you." "Assertive," on the other hand, comes from the Latin *asserere*, combining *ad* and *serere*, meaning "to join or bind together." An assertive person is "coming to build or put things together"—certainly not to threaten.

ℱ*TRY THIS:* One of the best ways to get yourself to pay attention to words as words is to practise making fine distinctions among related words, as we did with "aggressive" and "assertive." The following exercise will not only increase your vocabulary but also acquaint you with that indispensable reference work for etymology, the *Oxford English Dictionary (OED)*. Look up one of the following pairs of words in the *OED*. Write down the etymology of each word in the pair, and then, in a paragraph for each, summarize its linguistic histories—how their meanings have evolved across time. (The *OED's* dated examples of how the word has been used will be helpful here.)

ordinal/ordinary   explicate/implicate

tenacious/stubborn   induce/conducive

enthusiasm/ecstasy   adhere/inhere

monarchy/oligarchy   overt/covert

Alternatively, select a pair of similar words or, for that matter, any key words from your reading for a course, and submit them to this exercise. There's no better way to learn about—and remember—a word. □

What's Bad About "Good" and "Bad" (and Other Broad, Judgmental Terms)

Vague evaluative terms such as "good" and "bad" can seduce you into stopping your thinking while it is still too general and ill-defined—a matter discussed at length in Chapter 2 in the section entitled "Judging." If you train yourself to select more precise words whenever you encounter these words in your drafts, not only will your prose become clearer but also the search for new words will probably start you thinking again, sharpening your ideas. If, for example, you find yourself writing a sentence such as "The subcommittee made a *bad* decision," ask yourself *why* you called it a bad decision. A revision to "The subcommittee made a short-sighted decision" indicates what in fact is bad about the decision and sets you up to discuss why the decision was myopic, further developing the idea.

Be aware that often these evaluative terms are disguised as neutrally descriptive ones—"natural," for instance, and "realistic." Realistic according to whom and defined by what criteria? Something is natural according to a given idea about nature—an assumption—and the same goes for "moral." These are terms whose meanings depend on personal opinion or personal ideology (that is, an assumed hierarchy of value). Similarly, in a sentence such as "Society disapproves of interracial marriage," the broad and apparently neutral term "society" can blind you to a host of important distinctions about social class, about a particular culture, and so on.

Controlling Verbal Cotton Wool

At its best, effective analytical prose uses both concrete and abstract words. Simply defined, *concrete diction evokes*: it brings things to life by offering your readers words that they can use their senses upon. "Telephone," "eggshell," "crystalline," "azure," "striped," "kneel," "flare," and "burp" are examples of concrete diction. In academic writing, there is no substitute for concrete language whenever you are describing what happens or what something looks like—in a laboratory experiment, in a military action, in a painting or film sequence. In short, the language of evidence and of detail usually consists of concrete diction.

By contrast, *abstract diction* refers to words that designate concepts and categories. "Virility," "ideology," "love," "definitive," "desultory," "conscientious," "classify," and "ameliorate" are examples of abstract diction. So are "democracy," "fascism," "benevolence," and "sentimentality." In academic writing, by and large, this is the language of ideas. Often such language is difficult to comprehend, not because the writer is mediocre but because the ideas themselves are subtle and multifaceted. Examples from the readings in this book include "visual imperative" (Michael Posner) and "analogical generality" (Mark Kingwell). We cannot do without abstract terms, and yet writing made up only of such words loses contact with experience, with the world that we can comprehend through our senses.

The line between abstract and concrete is not always as clear as these examples may suggest. You may recall the concept of the ladder of abstraction that we discuss in the section entitled "Generalizing" in the second chapter. There we propose that abstract and concrete are not hard-and-fast categories so much as a continuum, a sliding scale. Word A (for example, "machine") may be more abstract than word B ("computer") but more concrete than word C ("technology").

Just as evidence needs to be organized by a thesis and a thesis needs to be developed by evidence, so do *concrete and abstract diction depend upon each other.* Use concrete diction to illustrate and anchor the generalizations that abstract diction expresses. Note the concrete language used to define the abstraction "provinciality" in this example.

> There is no cure for *provinciality* like traveling abroad. In America the waiter who fails to bring the check promptly at the end of the meal we rightly convict for not being watchful. But in England, after waiting interminably for the check and becoming increasingly irate, we learn that only an ill-mannered waiter would bring it without being asked. We have been rude, not he.

In the following example, the abstract terms "causality," "fiction," and "conjunction" are integrated with concrete diction in the second sentence.

> According to the philosopher David Hume, *causality* is a kind of *fiction* that we ascribe to what he called "the constant *conjunction* of observed events." If a person gets hit in the eye and a black semicircle develops underneath it, that does not necessarily mean the blow caused the black eye.

A style that omits concrete language can leave readers lost in a fog of abstraction that only tangible details can illuminate. The concrete language helps readers see what you mean, by supplying specific images or examples that bring your ideas to life. Without the shaping power of abstract diction, however, concrete evocation can leave you with a list of graphic but ultimately pointless facts. The best academic writing integrates concrete and abstract diction.

❦*TRY THIS:* Turn to page 95 and reread the paragraph that begins, "Reminders were as plentiful as the comparisons that inevitably followed." Bruce McCall uses abstract diction—"reminders," "comparisons"—to establish the paragraph's topic. How well does he use concrete diction to illuminate those abstractions? Make a list of words and phrases that you consider to be most effective. Also analyze your list in terms of McCall's stylistic techniques (metaphor, tone, etc.) and grammatical parts of speech (noun, adjective, verb, etc.). In class discussion, compare your list with those of other readers. Try to assess, as a group, the degree to which McCall's diction complements his rhetorical intentions. □

Latinate Diction

One of the best ways to sensitize yourself to the difference between abstract and concrete diction is to understand that many abstract words are examples of what is known as Latinate diction. This term describes words in English that derive from Latin roots, words with such endings as "–tion," "–ive," "–ity," "–ate," and "–ent." (Such words will be designated by an *L* in the etymological section of dictionary definitions.) Taken to an extreme, Latinate diction can leave your meaning vague and your readers confused. Note how impenetrable the Latinate terms make the following example:

> The examination of different perspectives on the representations of sociopolitical anarchy in media coverage of revolutions can be revelatory of the invisible biases that afflict television news.

This sentence actually makes sense, but the demands it makes upon readers will surely drive off most of them before they have gotten through it. Reducing the amount of Latinate diction can make it more readable.

> Because we tend to believe what we see, the political biases that afflict television news coverage of revolutions are largely invisible. We can begin to see these biases when we focus on how the medium reports events, studying the kinds of footage used, for example, or finding facts from other sources that the news has left out.

Although the preceding revision retains a lot of Latinate words, it provides a ballast of concrete, sensory details that allows readers to follow the idea. Although many textbooks on writing argue against using Latinate terms where shorter, concrete terms (usually of Anglo-Saxon origin) might be used instead, such an argument seems needlessly limiting in comparison with the advantages offered by a thorough mixture of the two levels of diction. It's fine to use Latinate diction; just don't make it the sole staple of your verbal diet.

✶TRY THIS: Select a paragraph or two from one of your papers and identify the Latin and Anglo-Saxon diction. Actually mark the draft—with an *L* or an *A*, or with a circle around one kind of word and a square around the other. Then find as many Anglo-Saxon substitutes for Latinate terms and as many Latinate substitutes for Anglo-Saxon terms as you can (with the help of a dictionary and perhaps a thesaurus). Ideally, you might then do a final revision in which you synthesize the best from both paragraphs to arrive at a consummate revision of your original paragraph. □

Using and Avoiding Jargon

Many people assume that all jargon—the specialized vocabulary of a particular group—is bad: pretentious language designed to make most readers feel inferior. Many writing textbooks attack jargon in similar terms, calling it either polysyllabic balderdash or a specialized, gatekeeping language designed by an in-group to keep others out.

Yet, in many academic contexts, jargon is downright essential. It is a conceptual shorthand, a technical vocabulary that allows the members of a group (or a discipline) to converse with one another more clearly and efficiently. Certain words that may seem odd to outsiders in fact function as connective tissue for a way of thought shared by insiders. The following sentence, for example, although full of botanical jargon, is also admirably cogent:

> In angiosperm reproduction, if the number of pollen grains deposited on the stigma exceeds the number of ovules in the ovary, then pollen tubes may compete for access to ovules, which results in fertilization by the fastest growing pollen tubes.

We would label this use of jargon acceptable, because it is written, clearly, *by* insiders *for* fellow insiders. The same can be said for the scholarly diction in this book: "gender-neutral risk assessment practices" (Hannah-Moffatt, page 285); "microsatellite paternity analysis" (Mennill et al., page 427). For those of us outside the fields of psychology and biology, such jargon is intimidating; nevertheless, skillful writers will establish enough of a context to make it intelligible.

The problem with jargon comes when this insiders' language is ostensibly directed at outsiders as well. The language of contracts offers a prime example of such jargon at work.

> The Author hereby indemnifies and agrees to hold the Publisher, its licensees, and any seller of the Work harmless from any liability, damage, cost, and expense, including reasonable attorney's fees and costs of settlement, for or in connection with any claim, action, or proceeding inconsistent with the Author's warranties or representations herein, or based upon or arising out of any contribution of the Author to the Work.

Run for the lawyer! What does it mean to "hold the Publisher... harmless"? To what do "the Author's warranties or representations" refer? What exactly is the author being asked to do here—release the publisher from all possible lawsuits that the author might bring? We might label this use of jargon *obfuscating*: although it may aim at precision, it leaves most readers bewildered. Average readers are asked to sign these, yet such documents are really written by lawyers for other lawyers.

As these examples demonstrate, the line between *acceptable* and *obfuscating* jargon has far more to do with the audience to whom the words are addressed than with the actual content of the language. Because most academic writing is addressed to insiders, students studying a particular area need to learn its jargon. Using the technical language of the discipline is a necessary skill for conversing with others in that discipline. Moreover, by

---

Voices Across the Curriculum

Fighting Clutter

"Fighting clutter is like fighting weeds—the writer is always slightly behind," remarks William Zinsser in his classic writer's guide, *On Writing Well* (1985). Clutter, says Zinsser, is a kind of disease of modern writing; in an age of spokespersons and spin doctors we have glorified the inflated prose, the rhetoric of political double-speak, the empty words that fill our sentences. "Clutter" is a broad term for unnecessary words and phrases that take up space in our sentences—or for inflated ways of making a point that could be rendered more simply and concisely.

Clutter is the lengthy word or phrase that is preferred over the short word that means the same thing. Must you "facilitate" or "implement" a plan of action? What is wrong with simply doing it? Why write "at this point in time" when a brief "now" will do? In the languages of business and academia and politics, we have grown so accustomed to longwindedness that we may not be aware of all the unnecessary words that take up space on the page. Do your reader a favour and cut the clutter words and phrases from your sentences.

—Irwin Streight, professor of English

---

demonstrating that you can "talk the talk," you will validate your authority to pronounce an opinion on matters in the discipline.

Here are two guidelines that can help you in your use of jargon: (1) when addressing *insiders*, use jargon accurately ("talk the talk"), and (2) when addressing *outsiders*—the general public or members of another discipline—either define the jargon carefully or replace it with a more generally known term, preferably one operating at the same level of formality (which is to say that you would not substitute "gut" for "abdominal cavity").

The Politics of Language

Lake Shore

by Billy Collins

"The cliché is your enemy."
—from a handbook on writing

It is not easy to admit this on paper,
but the surface of the lake
is sparkling very much like diamonds,

and I hesitate to say the wind is whispering,

but it seems to be doing something

very close to that this morning.

And if these clouds

do not look like fluffy balls of cotton,

I am not sure what they look like.

On the other hand,

the large, newly drilled hole

halfway up this maple tree

is where a woodpecker

must have worked half a day

just banging away at the good wood,

wings tucked in,

gripping the rough bark,

eyes beady with determination,

his red helmet on

and his metal lunch pail

hanging from a nearby branch.★

We cannot leave the domain of style without reflecting on its place in what we label—in Chapter 1—the culture of inattention and cliché that surrounds us. To make this move is to acknowledge that style has political and ethical implications. The famous essay quoted at the beginning of Chapter 2, "Politics and the English Language," warns against the "invasion of one's mind by ready-made phrases… [which] can only be prevented if one is constantly on guard against them." According to its author, George Orwell, the worst modern writing "consists in gumming together long strips of words which have already been set in order by someone else, making the results presentable by sheer humbug."

For writers of university-level papers, Orwell's warning suggests a paradox: experience on the job isn't always a good thing. The more exposure you have to academic language, the greater the chance that academic language will invade your mind. So a practised composer of

---

*Billy Collins. July/August 2004 edition of *The Walrus* magazine, p. 47. Reprinted with permission of the author.

introductory paragraphs may simply operate on automatic pilot, thereby generating Orwellian humbug: "There are several intriguing aspects and numerous key components that must be investigated when investigating the issue of...." Such wordiness and cliché will best be resisted by those who work *carefully* at selecting their words—and who then question *carefully* their own selection of words.

Orwell's famous novel, *1984*, is mentioned by Charles Foran in his article, "MSN Spoken Here" (pages 424–426). Writing about "neologisms" and "argots," Foran is concerned with what he calls the "sinister" potential of language. It is certainly true that words do not simply reflect a neutral world that is out there in some objective, self-evident manner. As our English language evolves, the possibility for distortion and manipulation of meaning evolves too. Orwell's concern with the politics of language is recognition of this fact.

Earlier in this chapter we noted, for example, that the decision to call a woman "aggressive" as opposed to "assertive" matters. There are examples all around you of language creating rather than merely reflecting reality. Start looking for these on the front page of your newspaper, in political speeches, in advertising, even in everyday conversation. Does it matter, for instance, that there are no equivalents to the words "spinster" or "whore" for men? Does it change things to refer to a bombing mission as a "containment effort" or, by way of contrast, to call an enthusiastic person "a fanatic"?

A cogent article in *Foreign Affairs* by Peter van Ham (October 2001) offers one last dispatch from the frontier of the culture of inattention and cliché. The article is about the rise of the so-called brand state—about how nations market themselves not only to consumers but to other nations. A brand, defined as "a customer's idea about a product," is a powerful tool to replace what a thing is with what other people, for reasons of their own, would have you think it is. This is the world we inhabit, and style can be its adversary or its accomplice. In the last analysis, that's what's at stake in choosing to care about style.

ASSIGNMENT: STYLE ANALYSIS

One of the readings in this book is written by someone who never graduated from high school, let alone from university: Robert Fulford. We might expect, therefore, that his style would be anything but "academic."

What do you think?

Reread "My Life as a High School Dropout" (pages 98–100) and take notes (as you read) on Fulford's stylistic decisions. Based on his choice of words and his tone of voice, would you say that this successful journalist is writing in a "journalistic" style? If so, so what? If not, why not?

Keep in mind the definition that begins this chapter: *style refers to all of a writer's decisions in selecting, arranging, and expressing what he or she has to say.* You will have to take into account not only word choice but also the sequencing of information and the degree of detail in presenting that information.

Write up the findings of your stylistic analysis in a brief paper (no more than two pages). During class, several volunteers should read their papers aloud. Class discussion may then focus on the consensus—or lack of one—represented by those papers.

CHAPTER

12

Shaping Up Your Sentences

When you write, you build. Writing, after all, is also known as composition—from the Latin *compositio*, meaning "made up of parts." We speak of *constructing* sentences and paragraphs and essays. The fundamental unit of composition is the sentence. *Every sentence has a shape, and learning to see that shape is essential to editing for style.* Once you can recognize the shape of a sentence, you can recast its *syntax* to make it more graceful or logical or emphatic.

When revising your sentences, your goal is not to prettify your language but rather to reveal the organization of your thought, clarify your meaning, and deliver it more accessibly to your readers. Because meanings are rarely simple themselves, clarifying often does not involve simplifying. Meanings usually involve complex relationships, placing two or more items in balance or elevating one over the others. These relationships can be built into the structure of your sentences. A series of short sentences that breaks up items belonging together will make your prose less readable than a long sentence that overtly makes the connections for your readers. Note the choppiness of the following passage:

> Interactive computer games teach children skills. The games introduce kids to computers. The games enact power fantasies of destroying enemies. These power fantasies are potentially disturbing.

Compare that to the following revision:

> Although interactive computer games teach children certain skills, they also encourage certain potentially disturbing power fantasies.

Because this version connects the items with tighter logic, it generates more forward momentum and is easier to comprehend than the first version, even though the sentence structure is more complex.

If you can approach editing with an eye towards logical precision, then determining how to revise your sentences will become less vague and undirected. If something sounds awkward, but you don't know why, or if you want to make a passage more forceful, but you don't know how, there are fairly standard ways of assessing your grammatical options in order to communicate more effectively.

A. THE ESSENTIAL INGREDIENTS OF EFFECTIVE SENTENCES

Nobody sits down to write and thinks, "I guess I'll begin with a participial phrase." The fact is that grammatical concepts have never inspired great prose. Nevertheless, the moment you compose two words, you're making a decision of syntax—of word order—and you're beginning to construct the grammar of your sentence. Such decisions are inevitable, and knowledge of grammar will make you a better stylist in the end: at the *redrafting stage*, when it's time to revise and edit for clarity and emphasis.

Every sentence is built upon the skeleton of its *independent clause*, the subject and verb combination that can stand alone as a complete idea. Consider the following three sentences:

He confided his troubles.

Six months later, he confided his troubles to a friend.

Six months later, he confided his troubles to a friend—a firefighter who had witnessed similar horrors.

Certainly these three sentences become progressively longer, and the information they contain becomes increasingly detailed, but each version contains the essential ingredient of all sentences: an independent clause (he confided). Without that subject and verb combination, able to stand on its own, a group of words cannot claim the status of "sentence."

You will find the third sentence, which identifies "a firefighter," in the introductory section of Jerome Groopman's "The Grief Industry" (pages 440–449). Dr. Groopman, professor of medicine at the Harvard Medical School, is a prolific and experienced writer. We will be using his sentences throughout this chapter, not only to illustrate principles of syntax and grammar but also to emphasize that no writer can possibly work without such principles.

In short sentences, locating the independent clause is not difficult. Here are two examples, each with its subject and verb highlighted:

Then the woman is told to repeat the story.

Foa's method has begun to find some adherents.

However, most of Groopman's sentences are not as simple as these. He often uses more complex syntax in order to convey more complex and detailed meaning. One of his grammatical options is to place two independent clauses in the same sentence (here again, the subject–verb combinations are highlighted):

The crowd pushed behind him, and he began to struggle for air.

He uses a comma and a coordinating conjunction ("and") to successfully join the independent clauses. Another option, exemplified in the first paragraph of Groopman's article, is to use a semicolon and to forgo the conjunction:

Some were dispatched by charitable and religious organizations; many others worked for private companies that provide services to businesses following catastrophes.

Of course, not all clauses are independent. Despite having subjects and verbs (as all clauses do), some are unable to stand on their own. These are called *subordinate clauses*—or *dependent clauses*, since they depend on others for support. We've already encountered a few in the sentences quoted from Groopman's article:

who had witnessed similar horrors

that provide services to businesses following catastrophes

The words that serve as subjects for dependent clauses—such as the pronouns *who* and *that*—are not always easy to spot. In order to revise and edit with confidence, though, you need to practise locating dependent clauses. Many sentences that employ them tend to be quite long and complex, so the risk of grammatical error increases accordingly.

❦*TRY THIS:* Underline every subject–verb combination in each of the following sentences by Jerome Groopman. Then determine which clauses are independent and which ones are dependent. As a class, compare your views on the clarity and effectiveness of Groopman's sentences.

- The travel agent sat in a conference room with co-workers from the Liberty Street branch who had witnessed the collapse of the World Trade Center and had been evacuated from the building.
- At the end of the session, the two counsellors gave telephone numbers to the workers and encouraged them to call if they felt distressed.
- He had been in the subway when the towers collapsed, but after considerable difficulty he made it home safely. □

B. COORDINATION, SUBORDINATION, AND EMPHASIS

The syntax of a sentence can give your readers cues about whether the information in one clause is equal or subordinate to the information in another clause. In this context, grammar operates as a form of implicit logic, defining relationships among the clauses in a sentence according to the

---

Voices Across the Curriculum

Sentence Variety

Have you ever lived in a subdivision or housing complex where lot after lot, block after block, row upon row, the dwellings all look the same? Or maybe you have worked in an office space designed with uniform cubicles holding identical office chairs, the same style of desk, computer, filing cabinet, and stapler—a cube farm. You know deep in your soul what a deadening effect this has on the human psyche. The mind and spirit crave newness, otherness, variety.

This innate need for variety is especially applicable to written prose. The reader can easily become bored and lose interest if the writing is dull and uninviting. If every sentence you write has a similar shape and rhythm and length, your writing will be a fit habitation for your ideas, stand solid enough, but overall have a look and feel like one of those subdivisions that appears to have been formed by a giant cookie cutter.

Varying sentence length is one simple way to create variety. Most of us tend to pack too much into a sentence. Don't make your reader wander too long down the path of a single sentence lest he or she lose the trail of your thought. Sometimes breaking a long sentence in two is good advice. Likewise, trudging the same distance along each sentence can become tedious for your reader. Allow some short hikes—short sentences that vary the pace of your prose. Short sentences are particularly effective when you want to emphasize a point.

—Irwin Streight, professor of English

---

choices that you make about coordination, subordination, and the order of clauses. In revising your sentences, think of coordination and subordination as tools of logic and emphasis, helping to rank your meanings.

Coordination

Coordination uses grammatically equivalent constructions to link ideas. These ideas should carry roughly equal weight as well. Sentences that use coordination connect clauses with coordinating conjunctions (such as "and," "but," and "or"). Here are two examples.

> Historians organize the past, and they can never do so with absolute neutrality.

> Homegrown corn is incredibly sweet, and it is very difficult to grow.

If you ponder these sentences, you may begin to detect the danger of the word "and." It does not specify a precise logical relationship between the things it connects but instead simply adds them. Of course, simple addition is sometimes sufficient, as in Groopman's sentence expressing two successive actions: "The crowd pushed behind him, and he began to struggle for air."

The exemplary sentences above become more precise, though, if we substitute "but" for "and":

> Historians organize the past, but they can never do so with absolute neutrality.

> Homegrown corn is incredibly sweet, but it is very difficult to grow.

These sentences are still coordinate in structure, but they achieve more emphasis than the "and" versions. In both cases, the "but" clause carries more weight, because "but" always introduces information that qualifies or contradicts what precedes it.

Reversing the Order of Coordinate Clauses

In both the "and" and "but" examples, the second clause tends to be stressed. The reason is simple: *the end is usually a position of emphasis.*

You can see the effect of *clause order* more starkly if we reverse the clauses in our examples.

> Historians are never absolutely neutral, but they organize the past.

> Homegrown corn is very difficult to grow, but it is incredibly sweet.

Note how the meanings have changed in these versions by our emphasizing what now comes last. Rather than simply having their objectivity undermined ("Historians are never absolutely neutral"), historians are now credited with at least providing organization ("they organize the past"). Similarly, whereas the previous version of the sentence about corn was likely to dissuade a gardener from trying to grow it ("it is very difficult to grow"), the new sentence is more likely to lure him or her to nurture corn ("it is incredibly sweet").

Nonetheless, all of these sentences are examples of coordination because the clauses are grammatically equal. As you revise, notice when you use coordinate syntax, and think about whether you really intend to give the ideas equal weight. Consider as well whether reversing the order of clauses will more accurately convey your desired emphasis to your readers.

Subordination

In sentences that contain *subordination*, there are two "levels" of grammar and meaning: the main (independent) clause and the subordinate (dependent) clause. When you put something in a main clause, you emphasize its significance. When you put something in a subordinate clause, you make it less prominent than what is in the main clause.

Of course, matters of significance and prominence are decided by readers as well as writers. All that someone like Jerome Groopman can do is employ subordination to emphasize and clarify relationships between his clauses:

> When it was the agent's turn, he revealed to the group that, at the time of the attacks, he had been sitting in a subway car, just short of the Fulton Street station.

The subject and verb of Groopman's independent clause—he revealed—is able to stand alone, but its prominence isn't really enough; it needs those other, subordinated clauses in order to make full sense. One of the subordinate (dependent) clauses describes *what* he revealed: "that … he had been sitting in a subway car." This is known as a *noun subordinate clause*, because it describes the thing that was revealed. Instead of using a single noun ("he revealed his experience"), Groopman uses a noun subordinate clause.

The other subordinate clause describes the time frame of the revelation: "When it was the agent's turn." Because it relates to the verb of the main clause ("revealed"), this one is known as an *adverb subordinate clause*. Just as Groopman could have opted for a single noun, here he could have opted for a single adverb: "Slowly, he revealed…."

A third type of subordinate clause is the *adjective subordinate clause*, which—as you might expect—functions in place of a single adjective. When Groopman writes "a firefighter who had witnessed similar horrors," he is deciding not to write "a horrified firefighter." The subject and verb of the clause—who had witnessed—relate clearly to the firefighter while giving Groopman room to add more vivid details than he would otherwise have been able to do.

❡*TRY THIS:* Combine the following sentences into a single, grammatically whole sentence. Use subordination. Also try to use the fewest total words possible without sacrificing what you consider to be the essential meaning of the original sentences. Finally, identify any subordinate clauses in your sentence in terms of their grammatical function (noun, adverb, or adjective).

- There is a government-sponsored program.
- The program is called Project Liberty.
- April Naturale is a social worker.
- Her social work is in the field of psychiatry.
- April Naturale is the head of Project Liberty.
- Project Liberty coordinates responses.
- It was established to do so.
- The responses are therapeutic.
- The responses are to September 11th. □

Once you have compared sentences with a few colleagues, turn to the "solution": Jerome Groopman's sentence on page 444.

Reversing Main and Subordinate Clauses

Unlike the situation with coordinate clauses, the emphasis in sentences that use subordination virtually always rests on the main clause, regardless of the clause order. Nevertheless, the principle of end-position emphasis still applies, though to a lesser extent than among coordinate clauses. Let's compare two versions of the same sentence.

Although the art of the people was crude, it was original.

The art of the people was original, although it was crude.

Both sentences emphasize the idea in the main clause ("original"). Because the second version locates the "although" clause at the end, however, the subordinated idea ("crude") has more emphasis than it does in the first version.

You can experiment with the meaning and style of virtually any sentence you write by reversing the clauses:

If the shoe fits, you should wear it.

You should wear the shoe, if it fits.

TABLE 12.1

Types of Subordinate (Dependent) Clauses

Noun Subordinate Clause

- Within a sentence, it functions in place of a single noun, as either a subject or object
- Like all clauses, it has its own grammatical subject and verb
- Its most common lead words (subordinating conjunctions) are "that" and "what"

"Each participant is asked to divulge ***what he was thinking during the event.***"
[the noun subordinate clause functions as the object of the verb "divulge"]

"When it was the agent's turn, he revealed ***that he had been sitting in a subway car.***"
[the noun subordinate clause functions as the object of the verb "revealed"]

Adverb Subordinate Clause

- Within a sentence, it functions in place of a single adverb
- Like all clauses, it has its own grammatical subject and verb
- Its most common lead words (subordinating conjunctions) are "when," "whenever," "as," "although," "since," "because," "if," "unless"

"***When it was the agent's turn***, he revealed that he had been sitting in a subway car."
[the adverb subordinate clause modifies the verb "revealed"]

"They showed a very low incidence of P.T.S.D.—presumably ***because pilots are screened for psychological health.***" [the adverb subordinate clause modifies the verb "showed"]

Adjective Subordinate Clause

- Within a sentence, it functions in place of a single adjective
- Like all clauses, it has its own grammatical subject and verb
- Unlike other subordinate clauses, its lead word often functions as its own grammatical subject
- Its most common lead words are "who" (to modify a person or people) and "that" or "which" (to modify an inanimate object or concept)

"Project Liberty is a program ***that was established*** to coordinate the therapeutic response to September 11th." [the adjective subordinate clause modifies the noun "program']

"Someone ***who witnessed the fall of the towers from afar*** is not as likely to develop the disorder." [the adjective subordinate clause modifies the noun "Someone']

[The exemplary sentences are modified versions of ones by Jerome Groopman.]

You can also experiment with the relative lengths of your clauses:

> If the burgundy shoe with the multicoloured laces and genuine leather soles fits, you and you alone should wear it and flaunt it.

Indeed, Groopman seems to deliberately offset the advantageous end position of his main clause by beginning the following sentence with a long—and therefore more noticeable—subordinate clause:

> If the tone occurs without the shock being given and is repeated on multiple occasions, the rats no longer respond with these anxiety symptoms.

Parallel Structure

One of the most important and useful devices for shaping sentences is *parallel structure* or, as it is also known, *parallelism*. Parallelism is a form of symmetry: it involves placing sentence elements that correspond in some way into the same (that is, parallel) grammatical form. Consider the following examples, in which the parallel items are underlined:

> The three kinds of partners in a law firm who receive money from a case are popularly known as <u>finders</u>, <u>binders</u>, and <u>grinders</u>.

> The Beatles acknowledged their musical debts <u>to American rhythm and blues</u>, <u>to English music hall ballads and ditties</u>, and later <u>to classical Indian ragas</u>.

> In the entertainment industry, the money that <u>goes out</u> to hire film stars or sports stars <u>comes back</u> in increased ticket sales and video or television rights.

As all of these examples illustrate, at the core of parallelism lies repetition—of a word, a phrase, or a grammatical structure. *Parallelism uses repetition to organize and emphasize certain elements in a sentence, so that readers can perceive more clearly the shape of your thought.* In the Beatles example, each of the prepositional phrases beginning with "to" contains a musical debt. In the following sentence from "The Grief Industry," Jerome Groopman clarifies his comparison of two people by deliberately repeating a pronoun and verb tense:

> <u>Someone who witnessed</u> the fall of the towers from afar is not as likely to develop the disorder as <u>someone who worked</u> on the fiftieth floor of Tower One and only narrowly escaped.

Parallelism has the added advantage of *economy*: each of the musical debts in the Beatles example might have had its own sentence, but in that case the prose would have been wordier and the relationships among the parallel items more obscure. Along with this economy come *balance* and *emphasis*. The trio of rhyming words ("finders," "binders," and "grinders") that concludes the law-firm example gives each item equal weight; in the entertainment-industry example, "comes back" answers "goes out" in a way that accentuates their symmetry.

❧*TRY THIS:* List all of the parallelisms in the following famous passage from the beginning of the U.S. Declaration of Independence:

> We hold these truths to be self-evident: that all men are created equal; that they are endowed by their Creator with certain inalienable rights; that, among these, are life, liberty, and the pursuit of happiness.

Which type of subordinate clause is used to anchor the sense of parallelism and rhetorical repetition? ☐

One particularly useful form of balance that parallel structure accommodates is known as *antithesis* (from the Greek word for "opposition"), a conjoining of contrasting ideas. Here the pattern sets one thing against another thing, as in the following example:

> Where bravura failed to settle the negotiations, tact and patience succeeded.

"Failed" is balanced antithetically against "succeeded," as is "bravura" against "tact and patience." Antithesis commonly takes the form of "if not X, at least Y" or "not X, but Y."

When you employ parallelism in revising for style, there is one grammatical rule you should obey. It is important to avoid what is known as *faulty parallelism*, which occurs when the items that are parallel in content are not placed in the same grammatical form.

Faulty:	<u>To study hard</u> for four years and then <u>getting ignored</u> once they enter the job market is a hard thing for many recent college graduates to accept.
Revised:	<u>To study hard</u> for four years and then <u>to get ignored</u> once they enter the job market is a hard thing for many recent college graduates to accept.

As you revise your draft for style, search for opportunities to place sentence elements in parallel structure. Try this consciously: include and underline three uses of it in a draft of your next writing assignment. Remember that parallelism can occur with *clauses*, *phrases*, and *prepositional phrases*. Often the parallels will be hidden in the sentences of your draft, but they can be brought out with a minimum of labour. After you've acquired the habit of casting your thinking in parallel structures, they will rapidly become a staple of your stylistic repertoire, making your prose more graceful, clear, and logically connected.

❦*TRY THIS:* Rewrite the following examples of faulty parallelism. In order to read Jerome Groopman's version of the third sentence, turn to page 440.

1. Venus likes to play tennis and also watching baseball games.
2. In the 1960s the use of drugs and being a hippie was a way for some people to let society know their political views and that they were alienated from the mainstream.
3. In a typical debriefing session, crisis counsellors introduce themselves and provide basic information about common stress reactions—when you can't sleep, getting a headache, if someone's irritable—as well as more debilitating symptoms, like flashbacks and people who suffer from delusions. □

C. PERIODIC AND CUMULATIVE SENTENCES

As should be clear by now, the shape of a sentence governs the way it delivers information. The order of clauses, especially the placement of the main clause, affects what and how the sentence means. There are two common sentence shapes defined by the location of their main clauses; these are known as *periodic* and *cumulative* sentences.

The Periodic Sentence: Snapping Shut

The main clause in a periodic sentence builds to a climax that is not completed until the end. Often, a piece of the main clause (such as the subject) is located early in the sentence, as in the following example from "The Grief Industry."

> Clinical trials of individual psychological debriefings versus no intervention after a major trauma, such as a fire or a motor-vehicle accident, have had discouraging results.

We have placed the subject and verb of the main clause in bold type in order to clarify how various modifiers interrupt them. The effect is suspenseful: not until the final phrase does the sentence consummate its fundamental idea. Pieces of the main clause are spread out across the sentence. (The term *periodic* originates in classical rhetoric to refer to the length of such units within a sentence.)

Another version of the periodic sentence locates the entire main clause toward the end, after introductory modifiers.

> Although there are no published studies on P.T.S.D. among rescue workers at Ground Zero, Corrigan, who has assessed many of these individuals, says it is relatively low.

As was previously discussed, the end of a sentence normally receives emphasis. When you use a periodic construction, the pressure on the end intensifies because the sentence needs the end to complete its grammatical sense. In both of the preceding examples, the sentences "snap shut." They string readers along, delaying *grammatical closure*—the point at which the sentences can stand alone independently—until they arrive at climactic ends. (Periodic sentences are also known as *climactic sentences*.)

You should be aware of one risk that accompanies periodic constructions. If the delay lasts too long because there are too many "interrupters" before the main clause gets completed, your readers may forget the subject that is being predicated:

> If the level of competition is extreme, Simon Whitfield, who proved himself at the Olympic Games in 2000, exhibiting what many observers would call not only

determination but also the ability to adapt to race conditions on a given day, though at the time few track-and-field insiders were expecting him to win the gold medal, will prevail.

Arguably, the additions (the "who" and "though" clauses after the subject) push the sentence into incoherence. The main clause has been stretched past the breaking point. If readers don't get lost in such a sentence, they are at least likely to get irritated and wish the writer would finally get to the point.

Nonetheless, with a little care, periodic sentences can be extraordinarily useful in giving emphasis. *If you are revising and want to underscore some point, try letting the sentence snap shut upon it.* Often the periodic *potential* will already be present in the draft, and stylistic editing can bring it out more forcefully. Note how minor the revisions are in the following example:

> **Draft:**   The novelist Virginia Woolf suffered from acute anxieties for most of her life. She had several breakdowns and finally committed suicide on the eve of World War II.
>
> **Revision:**   Suffering from acute anxieties for most of her life, the novelist Virginia *Woolf not only had* several *breakdowns but*, finally, on the eve of World War II, *committed suicide.*

This revision has made two primary changes. It has combined two short sentences into a longer sentence, and it has made the sentence periodic by stringing out the main clause (italicized). What is the effect of this revision? Stylistically speaking, the revision radiates a greater sense of its writer's authority. The information has been arranged for us. Following the opening dependent clause ("Suffering ..."), the subject of the main clause ("Woolf") is introduced, and the predicate is protracted in a *not only/but* parallelism. The interrupters that follow "had several breakdowns" ("finally, on the eve of World War II") increase the suspense, before the sentence snaps shut with "committed suicide." In general, when you construct a periodic sentence with care, you can give readers the sense that you are in control of your material. You do not seem to be writing off the top of your head but, rather, from a position of greater detachment, rationally composing your meaning.

The Cumulative Sentence: Starting Fast

The cumulative sentence is in many respects the opposite of the periodic. Rather than delaying the main clause or its final piece, the cumulative sentence begins by presenting the independent clause as a foundation and then *accumulates* a number of modifications and qualifications. As the following example illustrates, the independent clause provides quick grammatical closure, freeing the rest of the sentence to amplify and develop the main idea.

> The travel agent sat in a conference room with co-workers from the Liberty Street branch who had witnessed the collapse of the World Trade Center and had been evacuated from the building.

Anchored by the main clause, a cumulative sentence moves serially through one thing and another thing and the next thing, close to the associative manner in which people think. To an extent, then, cumulative sentences can convey more immediacy and a more conversational tone than can other sentence shapes. Look at the following example:

> The film version of *Lady Chatterley's Lover* changed D.H. Lawrence's famous novel a lot, omitting the heroine's adolescent experience in Germany, making her husband much older than she, leaving out her father and sister, including a lot more lovemaking, and virtually eliminating all of the philosophizing about sex and marriage.

Here we get the impression of a mind in the act of thinking. Using the generalization of changes in the film as a base, the sentence then appends a series of parallel participial phrases ("omitting," "making," "leaving," "including," "eliminating") that moves forward associatively, gathering a range of information and laying out possibilities. Cumulative sentences perform this outlining and prospecting function very effectively. On the other hand, if we were to add four or five more changes to the sentence, readers would likely find it tedious, or worse, directionless. As with periodic sentences, overloading the shape can short-circuit its desired effect.

If you consciously practise using periodic and cumulative constructions, you will quickly learn to produce their respective effects (where appropriate) in your own writing. As you go over your drafts, look for opportunities to bring out these shapes, for you can assume that they are already present in some unrefined way in the sentence shapes you normally compose. Try including at least one of each in the next paper you write. Here is an example using the simple sentence "James Joyce was a gifted singer."

Periodic: Although known primarily as one of the greatest novelists of the twentieth century, James Joyce, the son of a local political functionary who loved to tip a few too many at the pub, was also a gifted—and prize-winning—singer.

Cumulative: James Joyce was a gifted singer, having listened at his father's knee to the ballads sung in the pubs, having won an all-Ireland prize in his early teens, and having possessed a miraculous ear for the inflections of common speech that was to serve him throughout the career for which he is justly famous, that of a novelist.

❧*TRY THIS:* Your class should divide into three equal groups. Each group will then be assigned one of the following short sentences. Working collaboratively with the other members of your group, construct two extended variations of your sentence—one periodic and one cumulative. The instructor of your class will call on one member of each group to read its revised sentences aloud. The instructor will then declare the winning group, based upon the sentences' rhetorical strength. Respectful disagreement with your instructor's decision may be voiced in follow-up discussion.

Canadian weather changes unexpectedly.

Life goes on.

I became an intrepid traveller. □

D. CUTTING THE FAT

If you can reduce verbiage, your prose will communicate more directly and effectively. In cutting the fat, you need to consider both the diction and the syntax. As regards diction, the way to eliminate superfluous words is deceptively simple: ask yourself if you need all of the words you've included in order to say what you want to say. Such revision requires an aggressive attitude. *Expect* to find unnecessary restatements or intensifiers such as "quite" and "very" that add words but not significance.

As regards syntax, there are a few technical operations that you can perform— particularly on the *verbs* in your sentences—to reduce the number of words. The remainder of the chapter discusses these matters in more depth, but here's a preview.

- Edit carefully all sentences that employ the passive voice, in order to confirm their clarity and effectiveness (discussed in more detail later in this chapter). Writing "He read the book" (active voice) reduces by a third the version "The book was read by him" (passive voice), and eliminating the prepositional phrase ("by him"), sharpens the relationships within the sentence. While the passive voice can be useful in many analytical contexts, its natural wordiness must be controlled.
- Replace anemic forms of the verb "to be" with vigorous verbs and direct subject–verb–object syntax. Often you will find such verbs lurking in the original sentence, and once you've recognized them, conversion is easy: "The Watergate *scandal was* an event whose effects were felt across the United States" becomes "Watergate *scandalized* people across the United States."

- Avoid unnecessary subordination. Unless rhetorical emphasis is appropriate, avoid writing, "*It is true that* more government services mean higher taxes." Simply state your position—"More government services mean higher taxes"—without muffling your meaning in a subordinate "that" clause.

Beyond these technical operations, perhaps the most useful way to cut the fat is to have confidence in your position on a subject and state it clearly in your paper. A lot of fat in essays consists of "throat clearings," attempts to avoid stating a position. Move quickly to an example that raises the question or issue you wish to analyze.

Expletive Constructions

The syntactic pattern for "It is true *that* more government services mean higher taxes" is known as an *expletive* construction. The term "expletive" comes from a Latin word that means "serving to fill out." The most common expletives are "it" and "there." Consider how such expletives function in the following example:

> It is obvious that there are several prototypes for the artificial heart.

Eliminating the expletives is quick and easy:

> The artificial heart has several prototypes.

As the revision demonstrates, getting rid of expletive constructions encourages conciseness. The "It is obvious" opening, for example, causes the grammar of the sentence to subordinate its real emphasis. In some cases, however, an expletive can provide a useful way of emphasizing material, as in the following examples from Groopman's article:

> It may be that debriefing, by encouraging patients to open their wounds at a vulnerable moment, augments distress rather than lessens it.

> Although there are no published studies on P.T.S.D. among rescue workers at Ground Zero, Corrigan, who has assessed many of these individuals, says it is relatively low.

The second of these two examples should look familiar; we highlighted it a few pages back as an example of a periodic sentence. Clearly, it also uses an expletive construction—"there are"—in order to add force to the introductory subordinate clause. The first example appears at a crucial point in the article: Groopman is presenting his evolving thesis, simultaneously emphasizing it (by way of the expletive) and softening it (by use of the word "may").

Static (Intransitive) Versus Active (Transitive) Verbs: "To Be" or "Not to Be"

Verbs energize a sentence. They do the work, connecting the parts of the sentence with each other. In a sentence of the subject–verb–direct object pattern, the verb—known as a *transitive verb*—functions as a kind of engine, driving the subject into the predicate, as in the following examples.

> These therapists recently *treated* thirty soldiers who had severe P.T.S.D.

> The night after the explosion, a blizzard *descended* on Halifax, hindering the relief effort, and many people whose homes had been destroyed froze to death.

By contrast, "is" and other forms of the verb "to be" provide an equal sign between the subject and the predicate but otherwise tell us nothing about the relationship between them. "To be" is an *intransitive* verb; it cannot take a direct object. Compare the two preceding transitive examples with the following revisions of Groopman's sentences using forms of the verb "to be."

> The therapists' recent effort *was* the treatment of thirty soldiers who had severe P.T.S.D.

> The night after the explosion, an additional problem *was* the arrival in Halifax of a blizzard that hindered the relief effort and caused many people whose homes had been destroyed to freeze to death.

Rather than making things happen through an active transitive verb, these sentences let everything just hang around in a state of being. In the first version, the therapists did something—*treated* thirty soldiers—but in the second their effort just *is* (or *was*, as past tense), and the energy of the original verb has been siphoned into an abstract noun, "treatment." The revised Halifax example suffers from a similar lack of momentum compared with the original version: the syntax doesn't help the sentence get anywhere. Yet, because the forms of "to be" are so easy to use, writers tend to place them everywhere, habitually, producing relatively static and wordy sentences.

Certain situations, however, dictate the use of forms of "to be." For definitions in particular, in which a term does in fact equal some meaning, "is" works well. For instance, "Organic gardening *is* a method of growing crops without using synthetic fertilizers or pesticides." Other appropriate situations are illustrated by Jerome Groopman: to identify professional occupations ("April Naturale *is* a psychiatric social worker"); to underscore, with a bit of periodic suspense, a key concept ("Another concern that leads companies to hire debriefing services *is* the fear of litigation"). As with

TABLE 12.2

Static and Active Verbs

Action Hidden in Nouns and "To Be" Verbs	Action Emphasized in Verbs
The <u>cost</u> of the book *is* ten dollars.	The book *costs* ten dollars.
The <u>acknowledgment</u> of the fact *is* increasingly widespread that television *is* a <u>replacement</u> for reading in today's culture.	People increasingly *acknowledge* that television *has replaced* reading in today's culture.
A computer *is* ostensibly a labour-<u>saving</u> device—until the hard disk *is* the victim of a <u>crash</u>.	A computer ostensibly *saves* labour— until the hard disk *crashes*.
In the <u>laying</u> of a flagstone patio, the important preliminary steps to remember *are* the <u>excavating</u> and the <u>levelling</u> of the area and then the <u>filling</u> of it with a fine grade of gravel.	To *lay* a flagstone patio, first *excavate* and *level* the area and then *fill* it with a fine grade of gravel.

choosing between active and passive voices, the decision to use "to be" or not should be just that—a conscious decision on your part.

If you can train yourself to eliminate every unnecessary use of "to be" in a draft, you will make your prose more vital and direct. In Table 12.2, each of the examples in the left-hand column uses a form of "to be" for its verb (italicized) and contains a potentially strong active verb lurking in the sentence in the form of a noun or gerund (underlined). These "lurkers" have been converted into active verbs (italicized) in the revisions in the right-hand column.

Clearly, the examples in the left-hand column have problems other than their reliance on forms of "to be"—notably wordiness. "To be" syntax tends to encourage this circumlocution and verbosity.

❦*TRY THIS:* Take a paper you've written, and circle the sentences that rely on forms of "to be." Then, examine the other words in these sentences, looking for "lurkers." Rewrite the sentences, converting the lurkers into vigorous verbs. You will probably discover many lurkers, and your revisions will acquire more energy and directness. Of course, you may also discover uses of "to be" that are both necessary and effective. □

Active and Passive Voices: Doing and Being Done To

In the *active voice*, the grammatical subject acts; in the *passive voice*, the subject is acted upon. Here are two examples.

Active:	Marshall McLuhan coined the expression "The medium is the message" in 1967.
Passive:	The expression "The medium is the message" was coined by Marshall McLuhan in 1967.

The two sentences convey identical information, but the emphasis differs—the first focuses on the author, the second on the expression. As the example illustrates, using the passive normally results in a longer sentence than using the active. If we consider how to convert the passive into the active, you can see why. In the passive, the verb requires a form of "to be" plus a past participle (for more on participles, see the "Glossary of Grammatical Terms" in Chapter 13). In this case, the active "coined" becomes the passive "was coined," the subject ("McLuhan") becomes the object of the preposition "by," and the direct object ("the expression 'The medium is the message'") becomes the grammatical subject.

Consider the activity being described in the two versions of the preceding example about Marshall McLuhan: a man coined an expression. The grammar of the active version captures that action most clearly: the grammatical subject ("McLuhan") performs the action, and the direct object ("the expression 'The medium is the message'") receives it. By contrast, the passive version alters the close link between the syntax and the event: the object of the action ("the expression 'The medium is the message'") has become the grammatical subject, whereas the doer ("McLuhan") has become the grammatical object of a prepositional phrase.

Note, too, that the passive would allow us to omit "McLuhan" altogether: "the expression 'The medium is the message' was coined in 1967." A reader who desired to know more and was not aware of the author would not appreciate this sentence. More troubling, the passive can also be used to avoid naming the doer of an action—not "I made a mistake" (active) but rather "A mistake was made" (passive).

In sum, there are three legitimate reasons for avoiding the passive voice: (1) it requires more words than the active voice, (2) its syntax tends to dilute the interaction of subject and object, and (3) it can easily omit the performer responsible for the action.

On the other hand, sometimes there are good reasons for using the passive. The performer of an action may be understood from the context, as these two sentences from "The Grief Industry" illustrate:

In most circumstances, employees are required to attend a debriefing session.

Peacekeeping forces there were exposed to sniper fire and mine explosions, and discovered mass graves.

Groopman also uses the passive voice to stress the importance of those acted upon: "experts predicted that one out of five New Yorkers—some one and a half million people—would be traumatized by the tragedy."

Especially in the natural sciences, the use of the passive voice is a standard practice. There are sound reasons for this disciplinary convention: *science tends to focus on what happens to something in a given experiment, rather than on the performer of the experiment.* Compare the following sentences.

> **Passive:** Separation of the protein was achieved by using an electrophoretic gel.
>
> **Active:** The researcher used an electrophoretic gel to separate the protein.

If you opted for the active version, the emphasis would then rest, *inappropriately*, on the agent of the action (the researcher) rather than on what happened and how (electrophoretic separation of the protein).

More generally, the passive voice can provide a way to avoid using the pronoun "I," whether for reasons of convention, as indicated earlier, or for other reasons. For example, the following passive sentence begins a business memo from a supervisor to the staff in her office.

> The Inventory and Reprint departments have recently been restructured and merged.

Like many passive sentences, this one names no actor; we do not know for sure who did the restructuring and merging, though we might imagine that the author of the memo is the responsible party. The supervisor might, then, have written the sentence in the active voice.

> I have recently restructured and merged the Inventory and Reprint departments.

But the active version is less satisfactory than the passive one for two reasons: one of practical emphasis and one of sensitivity to the audience (tone). First, the fact of the changes is more important for the memo's readers than is the announcement of who made the changes. The passive sentence appropriately emphasizes the changes; the active sentence inappropriately emphasizes the person who made the changes. Second, the emphasis of the active sentence on "I" (the supervisor) risks alienating the readers by taking an autocratic tone and by seeming to exclude all others from possible credit for the presumably worthwhile reorganization.

On balance, "consider" is the operative term when you choose between passive and active as you revise the syntax of your drafts. What matters is that you recognize there is a choice—in emphasis, in relative directness, and in economy. All things being equal and disciplinary conventions permitting, the active is often the better choice.

❦*TRY THIS:* Analyze Jerome Groopman's use of voice (passive or active) in the next-to-last paragraph of his article, beginning with "At the same time...." Begin by writing down all the verbs (some of the six sentences contain just one verb while others contain more). Then decide which of the verbs are in the passive voice. Ask yourself, in each instance, whether or not the writer's use of the passive is effective. What appears to be his rationale? Similarly, try to justify his use of verbs in the active voice. Throughout this exercise, remember that *voice* is not synonymous with *tense*. Groopman employs more than two verb tenses, but his grammatical voices are limited to two. □

E. EXPERIMENT!

A key idea of this chapter is that choices are not necessarily right and wrong when it comes to sentence style but instead better and best for particular situations. The from-the-hip plain style of a memo or a set of operating instructions for your lawn mower is very likely not the best style choice for a good-bye letter to a best friend, a diplomatic talk on a sensitive political situation, or an analysis of guitar styles in contemporary jazz. Is style a function of character and personality? Is it, in short, personal—and thus something to be preserved in the face of would-be meddlers carrying style manuals and grammar guides? Well, as you might guess at this point in the book, the answer is "yes" and "no." We all need to find ways of using words that do not succumb to the mind-numbing environment of verbal cliché in which we dwell. But effective style is not inborn and is not hurt by experimentation. Staying locked into one way of writing because that is "your style" is as limiting as remaining locked into only one way of thinking.

This chapter has presented some terms and techniques for experimenting with sentence styles. Equipped with these, you now need to read and listen for style. Find models. When a style appeals to you, figure out what makes it work. Copy sentences you like. Try imitating them, knowing, by the way, that imitation will not erase your own style: it will allow you to experiment with new moves, new shapes into which to cast your words.

ASSIGNMENTS: STYLISTIC AND GRAMMATICAL ANALYSIS

1. Analyze the writing style of Roger Martin, Dean of the Rotman School of Management at the University of Toronto. His editorial commentary, "The Wrong Incentive," appears on pages 420–423.

Remember our definition of style (page 334): *all of a writer's decisions in selecting, arranging, and expressing what he or she has to say.*

As you read, think about the specific criteria of style mentioned in the last two chapters: diction, syntax, tone, rhetorical intentions, first-person and second-person pronouns, abstraction, jargon, subordination, transitive and intransitive verbs, and voice.

Do you think that Martin's style is appropriate for his intended discourse community? Compose a paper (750–1000 words) that addresses this question and provides detailed evidence to support your point of view.

2. You have already had a taste—in Chapter 11—of Robert Pashley's writing from 1834. Here is another one of his long sentences (we recommend reading it aloud several times):

> But, since I write as a traveller, and nothing more remains to be examined at Makro-Teikho, I shall at once bid farewell to this capital city of ancient Crete, which, even after the Roman conquest, remained for some time a considerable city, but, under the Venetian and Turkish rule, has dwindled down into this miserable hamlet, and the few shapeless heaps of masonry, which alone recal to the remembrance of the passing traveller its ancient and bygone splendour (209).

(a) In composing this sentence, Pashley has combined four clauses. Identify all four, along with their subjects and verbs.

(b) Determine which of the four clauses is the sentence's independent clause.

(c) Identify the types of subordinate clauses represented by the other three (use Table 12.1 as a guide).

13

Nine Basic Writing Errors
and How to Fix Them

A. HOW MUCH DOES "CORRECTNESS" MATTER?

This chapter addresses the issue of grammatical correctness and offers ways of recognizing and fixing (or avoiding) the most important errors. At the outset, though, we need to clarify just what we mean by "correctness." After all, the first reading in this book—Bruce McCall's "The Scavenger of Highway #3"—begins with a sentence fragment, which we identify as the first of nine basic writing errors. What good are rules if professional writers are free to break them? How much does "correctness" really matter?

The answer is twofold. First, every practised writer knows that our language is changing continuously. What used to be obvious mistakes—such as splitting infinitives ("to strongly criticize") and ending sentences with prepositions ("That was the decision he argued against.")—have become generally accepted syntax. Second, a practised writer like Bruce McCall is well aware of both his discourse community and his rhetorical purpose; if he breaks a rule, he has a clear reason for doing so. The point is that, while SWE (Standard Written English) may be flexible and adaptable, it nonetheless requires of its writers a precise knowledge of grammatical rules. If you want to communicate effectively with the vast majority of educated readers, you must put aside personal idioms and national or ethnic dialects. Scottish writer Tom Leonard knows that Glasgow's lovely English can be transcribed to paper ("jist sitn doonin writn"), but he also knows that it won't be clear for most readers.

The first guideline in editing for correctness is to *wait* to do it until you have arrived at a reasonably complete conceptual draft. We have delayed until the end of the book our consideration of technical revisions precisely because if you get too focused on producing polished copy right up front, you may never explore the subject enough to learn how to have ideas about it. In other words, it doesn't make sense for you to let your worries about proper form or persuasive phrasing prematurely distract you from the more important matter of having something substantial to polish in the first place. Writers need a stage in which they are allowed to make mistakes and to use writing as a means of discovering what they want to say. But at the appropriate time—the later stages of the writing process—editing for correctness becomes very important.

Correctness matters, in the end, because your prose may be unreadable without it. If your prose is ungrammatical, not only will you risk incoherence (in which case your readers will not be able to follow what you are saying) but also you will inadvertently invite readers to dismiss you. Is it fair of readers to reject your ideas because of the way you've phrased them?

Voices Across the Curriculum

Writing That Bleeds

Why can't I just be recognized for the improvements I've made in my writing? At least say something constructive. Don't just say, "Oh, it's very good," "It's O.K.," "You need to make some improvements." Just ask me what I'm trying to say in my writing and then try to understand what I said. Then look at my actual writing and explain what could be changed, modified, adjusted—or whatever needs to improve.

It's the only way I can improve my writing—not by learning how to memorize the methodical parts of grammar. "I say, you say, he says, she says, we say, you say, they say." This is just like learning all the French verbs in chart form.

What it takes is to keep writing and keep writing. Practice makes perfect. That'll only happen when constructive criticism is given. I went to the Writing Centre earlier this school year. The person essentially asked what was the question and then started to read and correct my essay, the one I thought I did well on. I felt like she had murdered it, and I could see her pen dashes throughout the paper and the ink soaking through the paper like blood.

So often they say that I understand the resource materials but don't show it very well in the writing. That's the biggest concern I have.

—Jonathan Nicoll, first-year geography/economics major

Perhaps not, but the fact is they often will. A great many readers regard technical errors as an inattention to detail that also signals sloppiness at more important levels of thinking. If you produce writing that contains such errors, you risk not only distracting readers from your message but also *undermining your authority* to deliver the message in the first place.

B. THE CONCEPT OF BASIC WRITING ERRORS (BWEs)

You get a paper back, and it's a sea of red ink. But if you look more closely, you'll often find that you haven't made a million mistakes—you've made only a few, but over and over in various forms. This phenomenon is what the rhetorician Mina Shaughnessy addressed in creating the category of "basic writing errors," or BWEs. Shaughnessy argues that to improve your writing for style and correctness, you need to do two things:

- Look for a *pattern of error*, which will require you to understand your own logic in the mistakes you typically make.
- Recognize that not all errors are created equal. This means that you need to *address errors in some order of importance*—beginning with those most likely to interfere with your readers' understanding.

The following BWE guide, "Nine Basic Writing Errors and How to Fix Them," reflects Shaughnessy's view. First, it aims to teach you how to recognize and correct the basic kinds of errors that are potentially the most damaging to the clarity of your writing and to your credibility with readers. Second, the discussions in the guide seek to help you become aware of the patterns of error in your writing and discover the logic that has misled you into making them. If you can learn to see the pattern and then look for it in your editing and proofreading—expecting to find it—you will get in the habit of avoiding the error. In short, you will learn that your problem is not that you can't write correctly but simply that you have to remember, for example, to check for possessive apostrophes.

Our BWE guide does not, as we've mentioned, cover *all* of the rules of grammar, punctuation, diction, and usage, such as where to place the comma or period when you close a quotation or whether or not to write out numerals. For comprehensive coverage of the conventions of standard written English, you can consult one of the many handbooks available for this purpose. Our purpose is to provide a short guide to grammar—one that identifies the most common errors, provides remedies, and offers the logic that underlies them. This chapter's coverage of nine basic writing errors and how to fix them will help you eliminate most of the problems that routinely occur. We have arranged the error types in a hierarchy, moving in descending order of severity (from most to least problematic).

What Punctuation Marks Signify: A Short Guide

These little road signs really aren't that hard to use correctly. A few of them will be treated in more specific contexts in the upcoming discussion of BWEs, but here are the basic rules of punctuation for the five basic signs. Our exemplary sentences come from Bruce McCall's article; he may break the occasional rule, but he's mastered each and every one of them.

The **period** [.] marks the end of a sentence. Make sure that what precedes it is an independent clause, that is, a subject plus verb that can stand alone. *Essentially*, the period is a mark of closure.

> Example: So let them gibe and rant and call me a turncoat. Give me the shoulder of Highway #3 any day.

The **comma** [,] separates the main (independent) clause from dependent elements that modify the main clause. It also separates two main clauses joined by a conjunction, items in a list, and appositives (see "Voices Across the Curriculum" for an explanation of the appositive). *Essentially*, the comma subdivides a sentence into its constituent parts.

> Example: Most he casts aside after a cursory look, but a few go into a pocket of his short pants, which he then fondly pats each time, as if it were money in there, or jewels.

> Example: It was superficial, but my handful of empirical evidence was all I needed to decide that whatever their failings in the dour Canadian view, the Yanks seemed to be doing things bigger, bolder, better, and reaping the rewards by way of a richer and more exciting life than anybody north of the 49th Parallel could ever hope to live.

> Example: Donald's sons, chips off the old soldier, made almost an avocation of Yankee-potting in the early 1800s, in the course of defending local settlements from marauding intruders in the skirmishing that preceded the all-out Canadian–American War of 1812–14.

The **semicolon** [;] separates two independent clauses that are not joined by a conjunction. Secondarily, the semicolon can separate two independent clauses that are joined by a conjunction if either of the clauses already contains commas. In either case, the semicolon both shows a close relationship between the two independent clauses that it connects and distinguishes where one ends and the other begins. It also provides an easy solution to a comma splice (see BWE 2 on page 383). *Essentially*, the semicolon has the power of a period, but instead of marking closure it marks connection.

> **Example:**   The Bakelite model of the Empire State Building on the desk of Dr. Sihler, the family dentist, had transfixed me from about the age of five; I now realized why.

The **colon** [:] provides a frame, pointing beyond itself, like a spotlight. It usually operates with dramatic force—announcing a detailed description or a list to follow, separating cause and effect, or dividing a brief claim from a more expanded version of the claim. The language on at least one side of the colon must be an independent clause, though both sides can be. *Essentially*, the colon signals an important piece of information to follow.

> **Example:**   Meanwhile, a carton of freshly printed books has arrived at the Eva Brook Donly Museum on Norfolk Street near the center of town: the first copies of *The Genealogy and History of the Norfolk McCall Family and Associate Descendants, 1796–1946*, compiled by Delbert T. McCall, a distant relation.

The **dash** [—] provides an informal alternative to the colon for adding information to a sentence. Its effect is sudden, of the moment—what springs up impulsively to disrupt and extend in some new way the ongoing train of thought. A **pair of dashes** provides an invaluable resource to writers for inserting information within a sentence. In this usage, the rule is that the sentence must read coherently if the inserted information is left out. (Note that to type a dash, type two hyphens with no space between, before, or after. This distinguishes the dash from a hyphen [-], which is the mark used for connecting two words into one.) *Essentially*, the dash allows writers to interrupt themselves or repeat themselves, in the interest of sharpening their messages.

> **Example:**   He was a prototypical United Empire Loyalist—a kind of inverted but non-gender-specific member of the Canadian version of the Daughters of the American Revolution—and as such a superpatriot and founding Canadian.

> **Example:**   Delbert's history records McCalls, generation after generation, clustering there in Norfolk County—farmers working the fertile land, lumbermen, millwrights, storekeepers, innkeepers.

Nine Basic Writing Errors and How to Fix Them

If you're unsure about some of the terms you encounter in the discussions of BWEs, see the "Glossary of Grammatical Terms" at the end of this

---

Voices Across the Curriculum

Picking Up the Pace with an Appositive

You can pick up the pace of your sentences by using appositives. An *appositive* is a word or phrase that is *apposed* to, that is, positioned next to, a noun to describe or to define it in some way. We most commonly use appositive phrases when we are introducing someone:

> Jonathan Cheechoo, an Aboriginal Canadian from Sioux Lookout, Ontario, was the second-highest scorer in his NHL rookie year.

The underlined appositive phrase efficiently provides defining detail about Jonathan Cheechoo. It acts somewhat like an adjective clause, but without the pronoun and verb (the *"who is"*). Fewer words make it a faster kind of modifying phrase.

Appositive words and phrases are often set off with dashes, a form of punctuation that heightens the effect of the appositive as providing quick and concise detail that supports the main point of the sentence:

> In two seasons with the San Jose Sharks' developmental teams—first in Kentucky and then Cleveland—Cheechoo scored 53 goals and added 59 assists in 128 games.

Appositive phrases are a tidy way of adding information about the subject of a sentence or of defining a particular person, word, or idea without greatly interrupting the flow of thought. Fast, full, and informative sentences use appositives to good effect. Be cautioned though not to become dash-happy and overuse appositives in that way. Too many dashed sentences and your reader will get the feeling that you've written the rhetorical equivalent of a McDonald's Happy Meal.

—Irwin Streight, professor of English

---

chapter. You'll also find brief sections called "Test Yourself" interspersed throughout this section. Do them: it's easy to conclude that you understand a problem when you are shown the correction, but understanding is not the same thing as actively practising. An appendix to this chapter contains answers to these sections, along with explanations.

BWE 1: Sentence Fragments

The most basic of writing errors, a *sentence fragment*, is a group of words punctuated like a complete sentence but lacking the necessary structure: it is only part of a sentence. Typically, a sentence fragment occurs when the group of words in question (1) lacks a subject, (2) lacks a verb, or (3) has both a subject and a verb *but* is a subordinate (or dependent) clause.

To fix a sentence fragment, either turn it into an independent clause by providing whatever is missing—a subject or a verb—or attach it to an independent clause upon which it can depend.

Verbal as a Fragment

Falling into debt for the fourth consecutive year.

"Falling" is not a verb, even though it indicates an action. Instead, it is a *verbal*, which we define in our "Glossary of Grammatical Terms" as a word derived from a verb that can function as either a noun, adjective, or adverb. In order to correct this error, a writer must provide a verb, or both a subject and a verb.

Corrections

The company was falling into debt for the fourth consecutive year. *[subject and helping verb added]*

Falling into debt for the fourth consecutive year led the company to consider relocating. *[verb added]*

Falling into debt for the fourth consecutive year, the company considered relocating. *[subject and verb added]*

In the first correction, the addition of a subject and the helping verb "was" converts the fragment into a sentence. The second correction turns the fragment into a gerund phrase functioning as the subject of a new sentence. The third correction converts the fragment into a participial phrase attached to a new independent clause. (See the glossary for definitions of "gerund" and "participle.")

Subordinate Clause as a Fragment

A world where imagination takes over and sorrow is left behind.

I had an appointment for 11:00 and was still waiting at 11:30. Although I did get to see the dean before lunch.

The first fragment is not a sentence but rather a subject ("world") attached to an adjective subordinate clause. While the subordinate clause has its own subject and verb ("imagination takes over"), there is no verb for the main subject ("world").

In the second example, a complete sentence is followed by a fragment, which begins with a subordinating conjunction ("although") that calls for some kind of completion. Like "if," "when," "because," "whereas," and other subordinating conjunctions (see the "Glossary of

Grammatical Terms"), "although" *always* makes the clause that it introduces dependent.

Corrections

A world arose where imagination takes over and sorrow is left behind. *[verb added]*

She entered a world where imagination takes over and sorrow is left behind. *[subject added, along with a verb]*

The first correction adds a new verb ("arose"). The second introduces a new subject and verb, thereby converting "world" into the direct object of "entered."

I had an appointment for 11:00 and was still waiting at 11:30, although I did get to see the dean before lunch. *[fragment attached to preceding sentence]*

As this correction demonstrates, the remedy lies in attaching the fragment to an independent clause on which it can depend.

Sometimes writers use sentence fragments deliberately, usually for rhythm and emphasis or to create a conversational tone (for example, the first sentence of Bruce McCall's article, page 91). In less formal contexts, they are generally permissible, but you run the risk that the fragment will not be perceived as intentional. In formal writing assignments, it is safer to avoid intentional fragments.

Test Yourself: Fragments

There are fragments in each of the following three examples, probably the result of their proximity to legitimate sentences. What's the problem in each case, and how would you fix it?

1. Like many other anthropologists, Margaret Mead studied non-Western cultures in such works as *Coming of Age in Samoa*. And influenced theories of childhood development in America.
2. The catastrophe resulted from an engineering flaw. Because the bridge lacked sufficient support.
3. In the 1840s the potato famine decimated Ireland. It being a country with poor soil and antiquated methods of agriculture.

A Further Note on Dashes and Colons

One way to correct a fragment is to replace the period with a dash: "The campaign required commitment. Not just money." becomes "The campaign required commitment—not just money." The dash offers you one way of attaching a phrase or dependent clause to a sentence without having to construct another independent clause. In short, it's succinct. (Compare the correction that uses the dash with another possible correction: "The campaign required commitment. It also required money.") Moreover, with the air of sudden interruption that the dash conveys, it can capture the informality and immediacy that the intentional fragment offers a writer.

You should be wary of overusing the dash in this way, as the slightly more presentable cousin of the intentional fragment. The energy it carries can clash with the decorum of formal writing contexts; for some readers, its staccato effect quickly becomes too much of a good thing.

One alternative to this usage of the dash is the colon. It can substitute because it also can be followed by a phrase, a list, or a clause. As with the dash, it must be preceded by an independent clause. And it, too, carries dramatic force because it abruptly halts the flow of the sentence.

The colon, however, does not convey informality. In place of a slapdash effect, it offers a *spotlight* on what is to follow it. Hence, as in this sentence you are reading, it is especially appropriate for setting up certain kinds of information: explanations, lists, or results.

BWE 2: *Comma Splices and Fused (or Run-On) Sentences*

A comma splice consists of two independent clauses connected ("spliced") with a comma but no conjunction; a fused (or run-on) sentence combines two such clauses with no conjunction or punctuation. The solutions for both comma splices and fused sentences are the same.

1. Place a conjunction (such as "and" or "because") between the clauses.
2. Place a semicolon between the clauses.
3. Make the clauses into separate sentences.

All of these solutions solve the same logical problem: they clarify the boundaries of the independent clauses for your readers.

Comma Splice

He disliked discipline, he avoided anything demanding.

Correction

Because he disliked discipline, he avoided anything demanding. *[subordinating conjunction added]*

Comma Splice

Today most TV programs are violent, almost every program is about cops and detectives.

Correction

Today most TV programs are violent; almost every program is about cops and detectives. *[semicolon replaces comma]*

Because the two independent clauses in the first example are connected logically in terms of cause and effect, the most effective of the three comma-splice solutions is to add a subordinating conjunction ("because") to the first clause, making it depend on the second. In the second example, a semicolon is inserted to emphasize the close conceptual link (claim/ evidence) between the two independent clauses.

The best cures for the perpetual comma splicer are to learn to recognize the difference between independent and dependent clauses and to get rid of the "pause theory" of punctuation. All of the clauses in our two examples are independent. As written, each of these should be punctuated not with a comma but rather with a period or a semicolon. Instead, the perpetual comma splicer acts on the "pause theory": because the ideas in the independent clauses are closely connected, the writer hesitates to separate them with a period. And so the writer inserts what he or she takes to be a shorter pause—the comma. But a comma is not a "breath" mark, although that is often how it is first explained in early grammar lessons; it provides readers with specific grammatical information. In each of these cases (erroneously), the comma suggests that there is only one independent clause separated by the comma from modifying information. In the corrections, by contrast, the semicolon sends the appropriate signal to the reader: the message that it is joining two associated but independent statements. (Adding a coordinating conjunction such as "and" would also be grammatically correct, though possibly awkward.)

Fused Sentence

The Indo-European language family includes many groups most languages in Europe belong to it.

Correction

The Indo-European language family includes many groups. Most languages in Europe belong to it. *[period inserted after first independent clause]*

You could also fix this fused sentence with a semicolon, or a comma plus the coordinating conjunction "and." Alternatively, you might condense the whole into a single independent clause.

Most languages in Europe belong to the Indo-European language family.

Comma Splices with Conjunctive Adverbs

Quantitative methods of data collection show broad trends, however, they ignore specific cases.

Sociobiology poses a threat to traditional ethics, for example, it asserts that human behaviour is genetically motivated by the "selfish gene" to perpetuate itself.

Corrections

Quantitative methods of data collection show broad trends; however, they ignore specific cases. *[semicolon replaces comma before "however"]*

Sociobiology poses a threat to traditional ethics; for example, it asserts that human behaviour is genetically motivated by the "selfish gene" to perpetuate itself. *[semicolon replaces comma before "for example"]*

Both of these examples contain one of the most common forms of comma splices. Both of them are compound sentences—that is, they contain two independent clauses. Normally, connecting the clauses with a comma and a conjunction would be correct; for example, "Most hawks hunt alone, but osprey hunt in pairs." In the preceding two comma splices, however, the independent clauses are joined by transitional expressions known as conjunctive adverbs (see the "Glossary of Grammatical Terms"). When a conjunctive adverb is used to link two independent clauses, it *always* requires a semicolon. By contrast, when a coordinating conjunction links the two clauses of a compound sentence, it is *always* preceded by a comma (unless each of the two clauses is brief).

In most cases, depending on the sense of the sentence, the semicolon precedes the conjunctive adverb and has the effect of clarifying the division between the two clauses. There are exceptions to this general rule, though, as in the following sentence:

The lazy boy did finally read a book, however; it was the least he could do.

Here "however" is a part of the first independent clause and qualifies its claim. The sentence thus suggests that the boy was not totally lazy, because he did get around to reading a book. Note how the meaning changes when "however" becomes the introductory word for the second independent clause.

The lazy boy did finally read a book; however, it was the least he could do.

Here the restricting force of "however" suggests that reading the book was not much of an accomplishment.

Test Yourself: Comma Splices

What makes each of the following sentences a comma splice? Determine the best way to fix each one and why, and then make the correction.

1. "Virtual reality" is a new buzzword, so is "hyperspace."
2. Many popular cures for cancer have been discredited, nevertheless, many people continue to buy them.
3. Elvis Presley's home, Graceland, attracts many musicians as a kind of shrine, even Paul Simon has been there.
4. She didn't play well with others, she sat on the bench and watched.

BWE 3: Errors in Subject–Verb Agreement

The subject and the verb must agree in number, a singular subject taking a singular verb and a plural subject taking a plural verb. Errors in subject–verb agreement usually occur when a writer misidentifies the subject or verb of a clause.

Agreement Problem

Various kinds of vandalism has been rapidly increasing.

Correction

Various kinds of vandalism *have* been rapidly increasing. *[verb made plural to match "kinds"]*

When you isolate the grammatical subject ("kinds") and the verb ("has") of the original sentence, you can tell that they do not agree. Although "vandalism" might seem to be the subject because it is closest to the verb, it is actually the object of the preposition "of." The majority of agreement problems arise from mistaking the object of a preposition for the actual subject of a sentence. If you habitually make this mistake, you can begin to remedy it by familiarizing yourself with the most common prepositions. (See the "Glossary of Grammatical Terms," which contains a list of these.)

Agreement Problem

Another aspect of territoriality that differentiates humans from animals are their possession of ideas and objects.

Correction

Another aspect of territoriality that differentiates humans from animals *is* their possession of ideas and objects. *[verb made singular to match subject "aspect"]*

The subject of the sentence is "aspect." The two plural nouns ("humans" and "animals") probably encourage the mistake of using a plural verb ("are"), but "humans" is part of the "that" clause modifying "aspect," and "animals" is the object of the preposition "from." "Territoriality" is the object of the preposition "of."

Agreement Problem

The Liberal and the Conservative both believe in doing what's best for Canada, but each believe that the other doesn't understand what's best.

Correction

The Liberal and the Conservative both believe in doing what's best for Canada, but each *believes* that the other doesn't understand what's best. *[verb made singular to agree with subject "each"]*

The word "each" is *always* singular, so the verb ("believes") must be singular as well. The presence of a plural subject and verb in the sentence's first independent clause ("the Liberal and the Conservative both believe") has probably encouraged the error.

Test Yourself: Subject–Verb Agreement

Diagnose and correct any errors in the following examples.

1. The most pressing issues to be addressed at the Conference on Mideast Security is not only what should be done about Israel's settlements in the Gaza Strip but also how to discourage suicide attacks.
2. One of the nicest couples we know, Fred and Irene Stamatakos, have just been added to the guest list.

BWE 4: Shifts in Sentence Structure (Faulty Predication)

This error involves an illogical mismatch between subject and verb. If you continually run afoul of faulty predication, you might use the exercises in a handbook to drill yourself on isolating the grammatical subjects and verbs of sentences, because that is the first move you need to make in fixing the problem.

Shift

In 1987, the release of more information became available.

Correction

In 1987, more information became available for release. *[new subject]*

It was the "information," not the "release," that "became available." The correction relocates "information" from its position as object of the preposition "of" to the subject position in the sentence; it also moves "release" into a prepositional phrase.

Shift

The busing controversy was intended to rectify the inequality of educational opportunities.

Correction

Busing was intended to rectify the inequality of educational opportunities. *[new subject formulated to match verb]*

The controversy wasn't "intended to rectify the inequality," but busing was.

Test Yourself: Faulty Predication

Identify and correct the faulty predication in this example:

1. As Robert Fulford points out, the sharp increase in cases of attention deficit disorder (ADD) has become "a suspiciously fashionable diagnosis."

BWE 5: Errors in Pronoun Reference

There are at least three forms of this problem. All of them involve a lack of clarity about whom or what a pronoun (a word that substitutes for a noun) refers to. The surest way to avoid difficulties is to make certain that the pronoun relates back unambiguously to a specific word, known as the antecedent. In the sentence "Appliances don't last as long as they once did," the noun "appliances" is the antecedent of the pronoun "they."

Pronoun–Antecedent Agreement

A pronoun must agree in number (and gender) with the noun or noun phrase that it refers to.

Pronoun Error

It can be dangerous if a child, after watching TV, decides to practise what they saw.

Corrections

It can be dangerous if children, after watching TV, decide to practise what they saw. *[antecedent (and verb) made plural to agree with pronouns]*

It can be dangerous if a child, after watching TV, decides to practise what he or she saw. *[singular pronouns substituted to match singular antecedent "child"]*

The error occurs because "child" is singular, while the pronoun, "they," is plural. The first correction makes both plural; the second makes both singular. You might also observe in the first word of the example— the impersonal "it"—an exception to the rule that pronouns must have antecedents.

Despite the importance of pronoun–antecedent agreement, keep in mind that some capable editors allow exceptions. In other words, you may encounter published writing with the occasional sentence whose singular noun (such as "child") is followed by a plural pronoun (such as "they"). Such amendments to prescribed grammatical correctness result from the ever-porous boundary between oral and written discourse.

Test Yourself: Pronoun–Antecedent Agreement

What is wrong with the following sentence, and how would you fix it?

1. Every dog has its day, but all too often when that day happens, they can be found barking up the wrong tree.

Ambiguous Reference

A pronoun should have only one possible antecedent. The possibility of two or more confuses relationships within the sentence.

Pronoun Error
Children like comedians because they have a sense of humour.

Corrections
Because children have a sense of humour, they like comedians. *[subordinate "because" clause placed first, and relationship between noun "children" and pronoun "they" tightened]*

Children like comedians because comedians have a sense of humour. *[pronoun eliminated and replaced by repetition of noun]*

Does "they" in the original example refer to "children" or "comedians"? The rule in such cases of ambiguity is that the pronoun refers to the nearest possible antecedent, so here "comedians" possess the sense of humour, regardless of what the writer may intend. As the corrections demonstrate, either reordering the sentence or repeating the noun can remove the ambiguity.

Test Yourself: Ambiguous Reference

As you proofread, it's a good idea to target your pronouns to make sure that they cannot conceivably refer to more than one noun. What's wrong with the following sentences?

1. Alexander the Great's father, Philip of Macedon, died when he was twenty-six.
2. The committee could not look into the problem because it was too involved.

Broad Reference

Broad reference occurs when a pronoun refers loosely to a number of ideas expressed in preceding clauses or sentences. It causes confusion because the reader cannot be sure which of the ideas the pronoun refers to.

Pronoun Error

As a number of scholars have noted, Sigmund Freud and Karl Marx offered competing but also at times complementary critiques of the dehumanizing tendencies of Western capitalist society. We see this in Christopher Lasch's analysis of conspicuous consumption in *The Culture of Narcissism.*

Correction

As a number of scholars have noted, Sigmund Freud and Karl Marx offered competing but also at times complementary critiques of the dehumanizing tendencies of Western capitalist society. We see *this complementary view* in Christopher Lasch's analysis of conspicuous consumption in *The Culture of Narcissism.* **[broad pronoun reference clarified by addition of noun phrase]**

The word "this" in the second sentence of the uncorrected example could refer to the fact that "a number of scholars have noted" the relationship between Freud and Marx, to the competition between Freud's and Marx's critiques of capitalism, or to the complementary nature of the two men's critiques.

Beware of "this" as a pronoun: it's the most common source of broad reference. The remedy is generally to avoid using the word as a pronoun. Instead, convert "this" into an adjective, and let it modify some noun that more clearly specifies the referent: "this complementary view," as in the correction or, alternatively, "this competition" or "this scholarly perspective."

Test Yourself: Broad Reference

Locate the errors in the following examples, and provide a remedy for each.

1. Regardless of whether the film is foreign or domestic, they can be found in your neighbourhood video store.
2. Many experts now claim that dogs and other higher mammals dream, despite their limited brain capacities; for those who don't own such pets, this is often difficult to believe.

A Note on Sexism and Pronoun Usage

Errors in pronoun reference sometimes occur because of a writer's praise-worthy desire to avoid sexism. In most circles, the following correction of the preceding example would be considered sexist.

> It can be dangerous if a child, after watching TV, decides to practise what he saw.

Though the writer of such a sentence may intend "he" to function as a gender-neutral impersonal pronoun, it in fact excludes girls on the basis of gender. Implicitly, it also conveys sexual stereotypes (for example, that only boys are violent, or perhaps stupid, enough to confuse TV with reality).

TINY TIM'S POLITICALLY CORRECT CHRISTMAS

The Globe and Mail, December 21, 1991. Reprinted with permission from The Globe and Mail.

The easiest way to avoid the problem of sexism in pronoun usage usually lies in putting things into the plural form, because plural pronouns ("we," "you," "they") have no gender. (See the use of "children" in the first correction of the pronoun–antecedent agreement example.) Alternatively, you can use the phrase "he or she." Many readers, however, find this phrase and its variants, "s/he" or "he/she," to be awkward constructions. Another remedy lies in rewriting the sentence to avoid pronouns altogether, as in the following revision.

> It can be dangerous if a child, after watching TV, decides to practise some violent activity portrayed on the screen.

BWE 6: Misplaced Modifiers and Dangling Participles

Modifiers are words or groups of words used to qualify, limit, intensify, or explain some other element in a sentence. A *misplaced modifier* is a word or phrase that appears to modify the wrong word or words.

Misplaced Modifier

At the age of three he caught a fish with a broken arm.

Correction

At the age of three the boy with a broken arm caught a fish. *[noun replaces pronoun; prepositional phrase revised and relocated]*

The original sentence mistakenly implies that the fish had a broken arm. Modification errors often occur in sentences with one or more prepositional phrases, as in this case.

Misplaced Modifier

An injured hiker, trapped in an abandoned mine shaft for almost three years, was rescued over the weekend after she lit a fire to attract the attention of passers-by.

Correction

An injured hiker, trapped in a mineshaft that had been abandoned for almost three years, was rescued over the weekend after she lit a fire to attract the attention of passers-by.

As a general rule, you can avoid misplacing a modifier by keeping it *as close as possible to what it modifies*. Thus, the correction removes the implication that the hiker was stuck in the mineshaft for three years.

A *dangling participle* creates a particular kind of problem in modification: the noun or pronoun that the writer intends the participial phrase to modify is not actually present in the sentence. Thus, we have the name dangling participle: the participle has been left dangling because the word or phrase it is meant to modify is not there.

Dangling Participle

After debating the issue of tax credits for the elderly, the bill passed in a close vote.

Correction

After debating the issue of tax credits for the elderly, legislators passed the bill in a close vote. *[appropriate noun added for participle to modify]*

The bill did not debate the issue, as the original example implies. As the correction demonstrates, fixing a dangling participle involves tightening the link between the activity implied by the participle ("debating") and the entity performing that activity ("the legislators").

Test Yourself: Modification Errors

Find the modification errors in the following examples and correct them.

1. After eating their sandwiches, the steamboat filled with passengers left the dock.
2. The bank approves loans to reliable and financially sound individuals of any size.
3. Rounding a tight curve, a flashing light warned the cyclists of dangerous conditions ahead.

BWE 7: Errors in Using Possessive Apostrophes

Adding "'s" to most singular nouns will make them show possession, for example, the plant's roots, the accountant's ledger. If a plural noun already ends in "s," you can remove the second "s" so the apostrophe ends the word: the flowers' fragrances, the ships' berths. For plural nouns that do not end in "s"—for example, *children*—simply add "'s".

Apostrophe Error

The loyal opposition scorned the committees decisions.

Corrections

The loyal opposition scorned the committee's decisions. *[possessive apostrophe added for singular noun]*

The loyal opposition scorned the committees' decisions. *[possessive apostrophe added for plural noun]*

The first correction assumes there was one committee; the second assumes there were two or more.

Apostrophe Error

The advisory board swiftly transacted it's business.

Correction

The advisory board swiftly transacted *its* business. *[apostrophe dropped]*

Unlike possessive nouns, possessive pronouns ("my," "your," "yours," "her," "hers," "his," "its," "our," "ours," "their," "theirs") *never* take an apostrophe. By far the most common error involves the misuse of "it's," which is a contraction for "it is." Remember: (1) the correct possessive form is "its"; (2) "its'" (apostrophe following the "s") does not exist.

Test Yourself: Possessive Apostrophes

Find and correct any errors in the following sentences.

1. The womens movement has been misunderstood by many of its detractors.
2. All of the petitioners signatures were collected and delivered to the prime ministers office.

BWE 8: Comma Errors

As with other rules of punctuation and grammar, the many that pertain to comma usage share an underlying aim: to clarify the relationships among the parts of a sentence. Commas separate the parts of a sentence grammatically. One of their primary uses, then, is to help your readers distinguish the main clause from dependent elements, such as subordinate clauses, introductory phrases, and nonrestrictive phrases and clauses.

Comma Error

After eating the couple went home.

Correction

After eating, the couple went home. *[comma added before independent clause]*

The comma after "eating" is needed to keep the main clause "visible" or separate; it marks the point at which the prepositional phrase ends and the independent clause begins. Without this separation, readers would be invited to contemplate cannibalism as they move across the sentence.

Comma Error

In the absence of rhetoric study teachers and students lack a vocabulary for talking about their prose.

Correction

In the absence of rhetoric study, teachers and students lack a vocabulary for talking about their prose. *[comma added to separate prepositional phrase from main clause]*

Without the comma, readers would have to read the sentence twice to find out where the prepositional phrase ends—with "study"—in order to figure out where the main clause begins.

Comma Error

Dog owners, despite their many objections will have to obey the new law.

Correction

Dog owners, despite their many objections, will have to obey the new law. *[single comma converted to a pair of commas]*

A comma is needed after "objections" in order to isolate the phrase in the middle of the sentence ("despite their many objections") from the main clause. The phrase needs to be set off with commas because it contains additional information that is *not essential* to the meaning of what it modifies. (Dog owners must obey the law whether they object or not.) Phrases and clauses that function in this way are called *nonrestrictive*.

The test of nonrestrictive phrases and clauses is to see if they can be omitted without substantially changing the message that a sentence conveys ("Dog owners will have to obey the new law," for example). Nonrestrictive elements always take two commas—a comma "sandwich"—to set them off. Using only one comma illogically separates the sentence's subject ("dog owners") from its predicate ("will have to obey"). This problem is easier to see in a shorter sentence. You wouldn't, for example, write "I, fell down." As a rule, commas virtually never separate the subject from the verb of a sentence. (An exception occurs when an appositive follows the subject: "Ms. Taloora, a high-fashion model, watches her diet scrupulously." For another apparent exception, look closely at the long sentence—by Robert Pashley—that is featured in the ULTIMATE *TRY THIS* later in the chapter).

Comma Error

Most people regardless of age like to spend money.

Correction

Most people, regardless of age, like to spend money. *[comma sandwich added]*

Here commas enclose the nonrestrictive elements; you could omit this information without significantly affecting the sense. Such is not the case in the following two examples.

Comma Error

People, who live in glass houses, should not throw stones.

Correction

People who live in glass houses should not throw stones. *[commas omitted]*

Comma Error

Please return the library book, that I left on the table.

Correction

Please return the library book that I left on the table. *[comma omitted]*

It is incorrect to place commas around "who live in glass houses" or a comma before "that I left on the table." Each of these is a *restrictive adjective clause*—that is, it contains information that is an essential part of the noun it modifies. In the first sentence, for example, if "who live in glass houses" is left out, the fundamental meaning of the sentence is lost, and becomes: "People should not throw stones." You could also infer from the first sentence that *all* people live in glass houses, since the modifying information is specified as "not essential" to identify *which* people are being written about. The nonrestrictive use of "who" in the sentence suggests a reading of the sentence as "People (who, by the way, live in glass houses) shouldn't throw stones." So the word "who" is defined by restricting it to only those "people" in the category of glass-house dwellers. Similarly, in the second example the "that" clause contributes an essential meaning to "book"; the sentence is referring not to just any book but to a particular one, the one "on the table."

So remember the general rule: if the information in a phrase or clause can be omitted—if it is nonessential and therefore nonrestrictive—it needs to be separated by commas from the rest of the sentence. Moreover, note that nonrestrictive adjective clauses are generally introduced by the word "which," so a "which" clause interpolated into a sentence takes a comma sandwich. By contrast, a restrictive clause is usually introduced by the word "that" and takes no commas. (Although "that" is to be used *only* for restrictive clauses, some grammar handbooks suggest "which" can be used for either restrictive or nonrestrictive clauses, with the punctuation indicating the particular usage in the sentence.) One final note: selecting "who" (instead of "which" or "that") means that punctuation alone will determine whether the clause is restrictive or nonrestrictive; the word "who" is used in both situations.

Test Yourself: Comma Errors

Consider the following examples as a pair. Punctuate them as necessary, and then briefly articulate how the meanings of the two sentences differ.

1. The book which I read yesterday contained a lot of outdated data.
2. The book that I read yesterday contained a lot of outdated data.

BWE 9: Spelling/Diction Errors That Interfere with Meaning

Misspellings are always a problem in a final draft, insofar as they undermine your authority by inviting readers to perceive you as careless (at best). If you make a habit of using the spellchecker of a word processor, you will take care of most misspellings. But the problems that a spellchecker won't catch are the ones that can often hurt you most. These are actually diction errors—incorrect word choices in which you have confused one word with another that it closely resembles. In such cases, you have spelled the word correctly, but it's the wrong word. Because it means something other than what you've intended, you end up misleading your readers. (See the section "Shades of Meaning: Choosing the Best Word" in Chapter 11.)

The best way to avoid this problem is to memorize the differences between pairs of words that are commonly confused with each other but that have distinct meanings. The following examples illustrate a few of the most common and serious of these errors. Most handbooks contain a glossary of usage that *cites* more of these *sites* of confusion.

Spelling/Diction Error: "Their" Versus "There" Versus "They're"

Their are ways of learning about the cuisine of northern India besides going their to watch the master chefs and learn there secrets—assuming their willing to share them.

Correction

There are ways of learning about the cuisine of northern India besides going *there* to watch the master chefs and learn *their* secrets—assuming *they're* willing to share them. *[expletive "there," adverb "there," possessive pronoun "their," and con-traction "they're" inserted appropriately]*

"There" as an adverb normally refers to a place; "there" can also be used as an expletive to introduce a clause, as in the first usage of the correction.

(See the discussion of expletives under "Cutting the Fat" in Chapter 12.) "Their" is a possessive pronoun meaning "belonging to them.""They're" is a contraction for "they are."

Spelling/Diction Error: "Then" Versus "Than"

If a person would rather break a law then obey it, than he or she must be willing to face the consequences.

Correction

If a person would rather break a law *than* obey it, *then* he or she will be willing to face the consequences. *[comparative "than" distinguished from temporal "then"]*

"Than" is a conjunction used with a comparison, for example, "rather X than Y.""Then" is an adverb used to indicate what comes next in relation to time, for example, "first X, then Y."

Spelling/Diction Error: "Effect" Versus "Affect"

BWEs adversely effect the way that readers judge what a writer has to say. It follows that writers who include lots of BWEs in their prose may not have calculated the disastrous affects of these mistakes.

Correction

BWEs adversely *affect* the way that readers judge what a writer has to say. It follows that writers who include lots of BWEs in their prose may not have calculated the disastrous *effects* of these mistakes. *[verb "affect" and noun "effects" inserted appropriately]*

In their most common usages, *"affect" is a verb* meaning "to influence," and *"effect" is a noun* meaning "the result of an action or cause." The confusion of "affect" and "effect" is enlarged by the fact that both of these words have secondary meanings: the verb "to effect" means "to cause or bring about"; the noun "affect" is used in psychology to mean "emotion or feeling." Thus, if you confuse these two words, you will inadvertently make a meaning radically different from the one you intend. Consider the following two sentences:

Last evening's walk in the rain affected Mariana's illness.

Last evening's walk in the rain effected Mariana's illness.

Neither one is incorrect, but each carries a distinct meaning. The first sentence implies that Mariana was ill before she took the walk. The second sentence implies that the walk caused her illness.

Test Yourself: Spelling/Diction Errors

Make corrections as necessary in the following paragraph.

1. Its not sufficiently acknowledged that the behaviour of public officials is not just an ethical issue but one that effects the sale of newspapers and commercial bytes in television news. When public officials don't do what their supposed to do, than their sure to face the affects of public opinion—if they get caught—because there are dollars to be made. Its that simple: money more then morality is calling the tune in the way that the press treats it's superstars.

C. THE ULTIMATE *TRY THIS*

For Part III (Organization and Style), the key concepts highlighted in this exercise are stylistic and grammatical ones: *syntax, diction, tone, clauses, voice,* and *punctuation.*

We return to Robert Pashley, the nineteenth-century writer featured in Chapters 11 and 12. Read carefully the following description of Pashley's Cretan meal (a 71-word sentence) and then analyze his stylistic and grammatical decisions, responding to the questions listed below. Remember that the "Glossary of Grammatical Terms" (pages 400–405) provides concise definitions of stylistic and grammatical terms.

> Mutton from their own flock, turkey, which, after a day's ride among these mountains, one cannot but think tenderer and more delicious than was ever tasted in civilized Europe, pilav, milk, salad, olives in oil, cheese, and almonds, formed the various dishes of a meal, which seemed to us luxurious; and which, since we were now lodged with the regular clergy, failed not to be accompanied by plenty of excellent wine (228).

- What is the grammatical subject (more than one word) of this sentence's independent clause?
- What is the verb (one word) of the independent clause?
- Do you think that this sentence is periodic or cumulative?
- The sentence contains three adjective subordinate clauses, each beginning with the word "which." In terms of the clauses' subjects and verbs, how does the first one differ from the other two?
- Which of the "which" clauses is interrupted by an adverb subordinate clause?
- Look closely at the syntax of two phrases: *one cannot but think* and *failed not to be accompanied.* How does Pashley's phrasing affect his tone of voice?

- Identify the nine prepositional phrases that appear in this sentence. Each one not only contains a noun (the object of the preposition) but also relates logically to a word that precedes the phrase itself. For the majority of the nine prepositional phrases, is that logical relationship adjectival or adverbial? How can you tell?
- Pashley employs the passive voice on three occasions. In each case, do you think he has a good reason for doing so?
- At the beginning of this chapter, we provide "A Short Guide" to punctuation. Pashley's sole usage of a semicolon does not match either of the two rationales on page 378. How does his usage differ?
- The sentence contains 14 commas. In addition to separating items in a list, what other functions are served by these commas?

D. GLOSSARY OF GRAMMATICAL TERMS

adjective   An adjective is a part of speech that usually modifies a noun or pronoun, for example, "blue," "boring," "boisterous."

adverb   An adverb is a part of speech that modifies an adjective, adverb, or verb, for example, "heavily," "habitually," "very." The adverbial form generally differs from the adjectival form via the addition of the ending "–ly"; for example, "happy" is an adjective, and "happily" is an adverb.

appositive   An appositive is a word or phrase, set off by a comma sandwich or by dashes, that renames or explains the noun that precedes it. For example:

> Charlie, the master of proverbial sayings, will now address the crowd.

case   Case refers to the way in which a noun or pronoun functions in a sentence: as a subject (nominative or subjective case); as a direct or indirect object (accusative or objective case); as a possessive (possessive case). Nouns in English do not change their endings, except for the addition of an apostrophe for the possessive case form. Personal pronouns do, however, change their forms—for example, "he" (nominative), "him" (accusative), and "his" (possessive).

clause (independent and dependent)   A clause is any group of words that contains both a **subject** and a **verb**. An **independent clause** (also known as a **main clause**) can stand alone as a sentence. For example:

> The most famous revolutionaries of this century have all, in one way or another, offered a vision of a classless society.

The subject of this independent clause is "revolutionaries," the verb is "have offered," and the direct object is "vision." By contrast, a **dependent** (or **subordinate**) **clause** is any group of words containing a subject and verb that cannot stand alone as a separate sentence because it depends on an independent clause to complete its meaning. The following sentence adds two dependent clauses to our previous example:

> The most famous revolutionaries of this century have all, in one way or another, offered a vision of a classless society, although most historians would agree that this ideal has never been achieved.

The origin of the word "depend" is "to hang": a dependent clause literally hangs on the independent clause. In the preceding example, neither "although most historians would agree" nor "that this ideal has never been achieved" can stand independently. The "that" clause relies on the "although" clause, which in turn relies on the main clause. "That" and "although" function as **subordinating conjunctions**; by eliminating them, we could rewrite the sentence to contain three independent clauses:

> The most famous revolutionaries of this century have all, in one way or another, offered a vision of a classless society. Most historians would agree on one judgment about this vision: it has never been achieved.

comma splice   A comma splice consists of two independent clauses incorrectly connected (spliced) with a comma. (See BWE 2 in this chapter.)

conjunction (coordinating and subordinating)   A conjunction is a part of speech that connects words, phrases, or clauses, for example, "and," "but," "although." The conjunction in some way defines that connection: for example, "and" links; "but" separates. All conjunctions define connections in one of two basic ways. **Coordinating conjunctions** connect words or groups of words that have equal grammatical importance. The coordinating conjunctions are "and," "but," "or," "nor," "for," "so," and "yet." **Subordinating conjunctions** introduce a dependent clause and connect it to a main clause. Here is a partial list of the most common subordinating conjunctions: "after," "although," "as," "as if," "as long as," "because," "before," "if," "rather than," "since," "than," "that," "though," "unless," "until," "what," "when," "where," "whether," "while," and "who."

conjunctive adverb   A conjunctive adverb is a word that links two independent clauses (as a conjunction) but that also modifies the clause it introduces (as an adverb). Some of the most common conjunctive adverbs are "consequently," "furthermore," "however," "moreover," "nevertheless," "similarly," "therefore," and "thus." Phrases can also serve this function, such as "for example" and "on the other hand." When conjunctive adverbs are used to link two independent clauses, they always require a semicolon:

Many pharmaceutical chains now offer their own generic versions of common drugs; however, many consumers continue to spend more for name brands that contain the same active ingredients as the generics.

When conjunctive adverbs occur within an independent clause, however, they are enclosed in a pair of commas, as is the case with the use of "however" earlier in this sentence.

coordination   Coordination refers to grammatically equal words, phrases, or clauses. Coordinate constructions are used to give elements in a sentence equal weight or importance. In the sentence "The tall, thin lawyer badgered the witness, but the judge interceded," the clauses "The tall, thin lawyer badgered the witness" and "but the judge interceded" are coordinate clauses; "tall" and "thin" are coordinate adjectives.

dependent clause (see clause)

direct object   The direct object is a noun or pronoun that receives the action carried by the verb and performed by the subject. In the sentence, "Certain mushrooms can kill you," "you" is the direct object.

fused (or run-on) sentence   A fused sentence incorrectly combines two independent clauses with no conjunction or punctuation. (See BWE 2 in this chapter.)

gerund (see verbal)

independent clause (see clause)

infinitive (see verbal)

main clause (see clause)

mood   Grammatical moods (not to be confused with emotional ones) express a sentence's reason for existing: to state a fact (indicative); to pose a question (interrogative); to issue a command (imperative); to speculate (subjunctive). The vast majority of sentences are written in the indicative mood. The trickiest of moods is the subjunctive, which is formed in two ways:

If I *were* rich, I *would* purchase a Ferrari. *[two clauses—one dependent and one independent—using "were" and "would"]*

It is imperative that each student *submit* his or her work on time. *[unlike the indicative mood, for which a third-person singular verb takes an "s" (e.g., "each student submits"), the subjunctive mood eliminates the "s" ("each student submit")]*.

noun   A noun is a part of speech that names a person ("woman"), place ("town"), thing ("book"), idea ("justice"), quality ("irony"), or action ("betrayal"). Proper nouns are capitalized ("CN Tower," "Saskatchewan," "Christmas," "John Smith").

object of the preposition (see preposition)

participle and participial phrase (see verbal)

phrase   A phrase is any group of words. It may or may not contain either a subject or a verb; if it contains both, it becomes a clause. Phrases function in sentences as adjectives, adverbs, nouns, or verbs. They are customarily classified according to the part of speech of their key word: "over the mountain" is a **prepositional phrase**; "running for office" is a **participial phrase** or a **gerund phrase**; "had been disciplined" is a **verb phrase**; "desktop graphics" is a **noun phrase**; and so forth.

preposition, prepositional phrase   A preposition is a part of speech that links a noun or pronoun to some other word in the sentence. Prepositions usually express a relationship of time ("after") or location ("under") or direction ("toward"). The noun to which the preposition is attached is known as the object of the preposition. A preposition, its object, and any modifiers comprise a prepositional phrase. "*With* love *from* me *to* you" strings together three prepositional phrases. Here is a partial list of the most common prepositions: "about," "above," "across," "after," "among," "at," "before," "behind," "between," "by," "during," "for," "from," "in," "into," "like," "of," "on," "out," "over," "since," "through," "to," "toward," "under," "until," "up," "upon," "with," "within," and "without."

pronoun   A pronoun is a part of speech that substitutes for a noun. The principal types are personal pronouns ("I," "you," "he," "she," "it," "we," "they"), relative pronouns ("who," "that," "which"), demonstrative pronouns ("this," "that," "those," "these"), and indefinite pronouns ("any," "everybody," "many," "no one," "both," "something," "neither").

run-on (or fused) sentence   A run-on sentence incorrectly combines two independent clauses with no conjunction or punctuation. (See BWE 2 in this chapter.)

sentence   A sentence is a unit of expression that can stand independently. It contains two parts, a subject and a verb. The shortest sentence in the Bible, for example, is "Jesus wept." "Jesus" is the subject; "wept" is the verb.

sentence fragment   A sentence fragment is a group of words incorrectly punctuated like a complete sentence but lacking the necessary structure; it is only a part of a sentence. "Walking down the road" and "The origin of the problem" are both fragments because neither contains a **verb**. (See BWE 1 in this chapter.)

subject   The subject, in most cases a noun or pronoun, names the doer of the action in a sentence or identifies what the verb is about. The subject of both this and the previous sentence, for example, is "subject."

subordination, subordinating conjunction   "Subordination" refers to the placement of certain grammatical units, particularly phrases and clauses, at a lower, less important structural level than other elements. As with coordination, the grammatical ranking carries conceptual significance as well: whatever is grammatically subordinated appears less important than the information carried in the main clause. In the following example, the clause containing "486-based personal computers" is subordinated both grammatically and conceptually to that containing "Pentium-based PC systems":

> Although 486-based personal computers continue to improve in speed, the new Pentium-based PC systems have thoroughly outclassed them.

Here "although" is a **subordinating conjunction** that introduces a subordinate clause, also known as a **dependent clause**.

verb   A verb is a part of speech that describes an action ("goes"), states how something was affected by an action ("became angered"), or expresses a state of being ("is").

verbal (participles, gerunds, and infinitives)   Verbals are words derived from verbs. They are verb forms that look like verbs but, as determined by the structure of the sentence in which they appear, they function as nouns, adjectives, or adverbs. There are three forms of verbals.

An **infinitive**—composed of the root form of a verb plus "to" ("to be," "to vote")—becomes a verbal when it is used as a noun ("*To eat* is essential"), an adjective ("These are the books *to read*"), or an adverb ("He was too sick *to walk*").

Similarly, a **participle**—usually composed of the root form of a verb plus "–ing" (present participle) or "–ed" (past participle)—becomes a verbal when used as an adjective. It can occur as a single word, modifying a noun, as in "faltering negotiations" or "finished business." But it also can occur in a participial phrase, consisting of the participle, its object, and any modifiers. Here are two examples:

Having been tried and convicted, the criminal was sentenced to life imprisonment.

Following the path of most resistance, the masochist took deep pleasure in his frustration.

"Having been tried and convicted" is a participial phrase that modifies "criminal"; "Following the path of most resistance" is a participial phrase that modifies "masochist." In each case, the participial phrase functions as an adjective.

The third form of verbal, the **gerund**, resembles the participle. Like the participle, it is formed by adding "–ing" to the root form of the verb, but unlike the participle, it is used as a noun. In the sentence "Swimming is extraordinarily aerobic," the gerund "swimming" functions as the subject. Again like participles, gerunds can occur in phrases. The gerund phrases are italicized in the following example:

Watching a film adaptation takes less effort than *reading the book* from which it was made.

When using a verbal, remember that although it resembles a verb, it cannot function alone as the verb in a sentence: "Being a military genius" is a fragment, not a sentence.

E. REVISING FOR CORRECTNESS: THE BOTTOM LINE

1. In correcting grammar, seek to discover the patterns of error in your writing, and unlearn the logic that has led you to make certain kinds of errors recurrently.

2. Check the draft for errors that obscure the boundaries of sentences: fragments, comma splices, and run-ons. Begin by isolating the simple subject and verb in the main clause(s) of every sentence (to make sure they exist); this check will also help you to spot faulty predication and errors in subject–verb agreement. Then, check to see that each independent clause is separated from others by a period, a comma plus coordinating conjunction, or a semicolon.

3. Check your sentences for ambiguity (the potential of being read in more than one way) by deliberately trying to misread them. If your sentence can be read to mean something other than what you intended, the most common causes are misplaced and dangling modifiers and errors in pronoun reference.

4. Fix errors in pronoun reference and misplaced modifiers by making sure that every pronoun has only one clear antecedent and that every

modifying word or phrase is placed as close as possible to the part of the sentence it modifies.

5. Avoid dangling modifiers by being sure that the noun or pronoun being modified is actually present in the sentence. Avoid broad reference by adding the appropriate noun or noun phrase after the pronoun "this." (You can greatly improve the clarity of your prose just by avoiding use of the vague "this," especially at the beginnings of sentences.)

6. Check that commas are separating dependent clauses, introductory phrases, or other modifying elements from the main clause. A comma is not merely a pause; its function is to help readers locate your sentence's main (independent) clause(s).

7. Enclose nonrestrictive modifiers placed between the subject and predicate of a sentence in a pair of commas or—for more emphasis—in a pair of dashes. A nonrestrictive modifier is a phrase, often beginning with "which," that can be deleted from the sentence without changing the sentence's essential meaning.

ASSIGNMENT: GRAMMAR AND STYLE QUIZ

Here is an error-laden paragraph to rewrite and correct by making changes in grammar and punctuation as necessary. You may need to add, drop, or rearrange words, but do not add any periods. That way, you will be able to test yourself on your ability to use the various road signs of punctuation rather than avoid these options by separating each independent clause into a simple sentence. The quiz also contains a few stylistic problems addressed in Chapters 11 and 12. A discussion of the errors and how to fix them can be found in the appendix to this chapter.

[1] Its an important and undeniable fact that weather channels inform viewers,
[2] however there anchormen should take mandatory charisma enhancement
[3] classes. Watching television last Saturday evening one of them bored me to
[4] tears. I sat their listening to her ramble on about the affects of summer hail on
[5] edmonton alberta which is known for it's bizarre climate. Although, I have
[6] never visited. Three characteristics of these weather channels anchormen are
[7] especially sleep inducing, there always frowning; to much makeup; and when
[8] meteorological theory is expounded by a monotonous voice. Because viewers
[9] are always drawn to television personalities, they have a natural advantage.
[10] But this should not be taken for granted. After all each one of us can simply

[11] turn off the set; walk out into their backyard look up at the sky—and forecast

[12] by yourself weather it will be sunny or cloudy tomorrow. It is because of

[13] this that I would claim that the quality of information transfer between

[14] weather channel anchormen and we television viewers must be improved.

[15] The sooner the better.

Chapter 13 Appendix
Answer Key (with Discussion)

TEST YOURSELF SECTIONS

Test Yourself: Fragments

Original example: Like many other anthropologists, Margaret Mead studied non-Western cultures in such works as *Coming of Age in Samoa*. And influenced theories of childhood development in America.

Problem: The second sentence is actually a fragment; it has no subject for its verb "influenced."

Possible correction: Like many other anthropologists, Margaret Mead studied non-Western cultures (in such works as *Coming of Age in Samoa*) in ways that influenced theories of childhood development in America.

Comment: There are many ways to fix this example, but its original form leaves ambiguous whether the fragment refers only to "Mead" or to "many other anthropologists" as well. The correction offered includes the other anthropologists in the referent and diminishes the emphasis on Mead's book by placing it within parentheses. Although the correction uses a subordinating "that" to incorporate the fragment into the first sentence, it keeps this information in an emphatic position at the end of the sentence.

Original example: The catastrophe resulted from an engineering flaw. Because the bridge lacked sufficient support.

Problem: The second sentence is actually a dependent adverb clause; "because" always subordinates.

Possible correction: The catastrophe resulted from an engineering flaw: the bridge lacked sufficient support.

Comment: Because the colon has causal force, this is an ideal spot to use one, identifying the "flaw."

Original example: In the 1840s the potato famine decimated Ireland. It being a country with poor soil and antiquated methods of agriculture.

Problem: The second sentence is actually a fragment, a subject plus a long participial phrase.

Possible correction: In the 1840s the potato famine decimated Ireland, a country with poor and antiquated methods of agriculture.

Comment: The cause of this kind of fragment is usually that the writer mistakenly believes that "being" is a verb rather than a participle introducing a long phrase (modifying "Ireland" in this case). Our correction turns the fragment into an appositive, which is connected to the noun it describes by a comma.

Test Yourself: Comma Splices

Original example: "Virtual reality" is a new buzzword, so is "hyperspace."

Problem: This is a comma splice—both clauses are independent, yet they are joined with a comma.

Possible correction: "Virtual reality" is a new buzzword; so is "hyperspace."

Comment: Because the clauses are linked by association—both naming buzzwords—a semicolon would show that association. A writer could also condense the clauses into a simple sentence with a compound subject, for example, "Both 'virtual reality' and 'hyperspace' are new buzzwords."

Original example: Many popular cures for cancer have been discredited, nevertheless, many people continue to buy them.

Problem: A comma splice results from the incorrectly punctuated conjunctive adverb "nevertheless."

Possible correction: Many popular cures for cancer have been discredited; nevertheless, many people continue to buy them.

Comment: Without the semicolon to separate the independent clauses, the conjunctive adverb could conceivably modify either the preceding or the following clause. This problem is usually worse with "however."

Original example: Elvis Presley's home, Graceland, attracts many musicians as a kind of shrine, even Paul Simon has been there.

Problem: This is a comma splice—the two independent clauses are linked by a comma without a conjunction. The problem is exacerbated by the number of commas in the sentence; the reader cannot easily tell which one is used to separate the clauses.

Possible correction: Elvis Presley's home, Graceland, attracts many musicians as a kind of shrine—even Paul Simon has been there.

Comment: Although one could justly use a semicolon here, the dash conveys the impromptu effect of an afterthought.

Original example: She didn't play well with others, she sat on the bench and watched.

Problem: Because the second clause develops the first one, a writer might think that it is dependent on the first; conceptually, yes, but grammatically, no.

Possible correction: She didn't play well with others; she sat on the bench and watched.

Comment: If the writer wanted to link the two clauses more tightly, a colon would be appropriate instead of the semicolon.

Test Yourself: Subject–Verb Agreement

Original example: The most pressing issues to be addressed at the Conference on Mideast Security is not only what should be done about Israel's settlements in the Gaza Strip but also how to discourage suicide attacks.

Problem: The grammatical subject of the main clause ("issues") is plural; the verb ("is") is singular.

Possible correction: The most pressing issues to be addressed at the Conference on Mideast Security *are* what to do about Israel's settlements in the Gaza Strip and how to discourage suicide attacks.

Comment: An error of this kind is encouraged by the distance of the verb from the subject—due to the presence of intervening prepositional phrases. In addition to adding a plural verb, our correction creates parallelism by using the infinitive form of "to do" and "to discourage."

Original example: One of the nicest couples we know, Fred and Irene Stamatakos, have just been added to the guest list.

Problem: While both "couples" (the object of a preposition) and "Fred and Irene Stamatakos" (an appositive) are plural, the grammatical subject of the sentence ("One") is a singular pronoun. So the verb should also be singular.

Possible correction: One of the nicest couples we know has just been added to the guest list: Fred and Irene Stamatakos.

Comment: Removing the appositive and employing a colon lessens the dominance of plurals at the beginning of the sentence. Thus, the singular verb "has been added" takes its rightful place more easily.

Test Yourself: Faulty Predication

Original example: As Robert Fulford points out, the sharp increase in cases of attention deficit disorder (ADD) has become "a suspiciously fashionable diagnosis."

Problem: It is the disease itself, not the increase in cases, that has become a fashionable diagnosis.

Possible correction: Noting the sharp increase in cases, Robert Fulford points out that attention deficit disorder (ADD) has become "a suspiciously fashionable diagnosis."

Comment: Adding an introductory participial phrase allows "attention deficit disorder" to become the subject of a subordinate clause (beginning with "that") whose verb is "has become."

Test Yourself: Pronoun–Antecedent Agreement

Original example: Every dog has its day, but all too often when that day happens, they can be found barking up the wrong tree.

Problem: The plural pronoun "they" that is the grammatical subject of the second clause does not have a plural antecedent in the sentence.

Possible correction: Every dog has its day, but all too often when that day happens, the dog can be found barking up the wrong tree.

Comment: If a writer vigilantly checks all pronouns, he or she will identify the intended antecedent of the pronoun "they" to be the singular "dog" and revise accordingly. The sentence would still be incorrect if the pronoun "it" were used instead of the repeated "dog," because "it" could refer to the nearest preceding noun, "day."

Test Yourself: Ambiguous Reference

Original example: Alexander the Great's father, Philip of Macedon, died when he was twenty-six.

Problem: A reader can't be sure whether "he" refers to Alexander or to Philip.

Possible correction: Alexander the Great's father, Philip of Macedon, died at the age of twenty-six.

Comment: The correction rewords to remove the ambiguous pronoun. This solution is less awkward than repeating "Philip" in place of "he," though that would also be correct.

Original example: The committee could not look into the problem because it was too involved.

Problem: A reader can't be sure whether "it" refers to "the committee" or to "the problem."

Possible correction: The committee was too involved with other matters to look into the problem.

Comment: As with the previous example, rewording to eliminate the ambiguous pronoun is usually the best solution.

Test Yourself: Broad Reference

Original example: Regardless of whether the film is foreign or domestic, they can be found in your neighbourhood video store.

Problem: The plural pronoun "they" does not have a plural antecedent in the sentence.

Possible correction: Regardless of whether the film is foreign or domestic, it can be found in your neighbourhood video store.

Comment: Although the sentence offers two options for films, the word "film" is singular and so, as antecedent, requires a singular pronoun ("it"). Note that "it" would still be correct even if the original sentence began, "Regardless of whether the film is a foreign film or a domestic film." The rule for compound subjects that use an either/or construction is as follows: the number (singular or plural) of the noun or pronoun that follows the word "or" determines the number of the verb. Compare the following two examples: "Either several of his aides or the *candidate is* going to speak" and "Either the candidate or *several* of his aides *are* going to speak."

Original example: Many experts now claim that dogs and other higher mammals dream, despite their limited brain capacities; for those who don't own such pets, this is often difficult to believe.

Problem: The referent of the pronoun "this" is unclear. Precisely what is "difficult to believe"—that mammals dream, that they have limited brain capacities, or that experts would make such a claim?

Possible correction: Many experts now claim that, despite their limited brain capacities, dogs and other higher mammals dream; for those who don't own such pets, this claim is often difficult to believe.

Comment: Often the best way to fix a problem with broad reference produced by use of "this" as a pronoun is to convert "this" to an adjective—a strategy that will require a writer to provide a specifying noun for "this" to modify. As a rule, when you find an isolated "this" in your draft, ask and answer the question "This what?"

Test Yourself: Modification Errors

Original example: After eating their sandwiches, the steamboat filled with passengers left the dock.

Problem: This is a dangling participle—the grammar of the sentence conveys that the steamboat ate the sandwiches.

Corrections: After the passengers ate their sandwiches, the steamboat left the dock. Or, After eating their sandwiches, the passengers boarded the steamboat, and it left the dock.

Comment: The two corrections model the two ways of remedying most dangling participles. Both provide an antecedent ("the passengers") for the pronoun "their." The first correction eliminates the participial phrase and substitutes a subordinate adverb clause (beginning with "After"). The second correction adds to the existing main clause ("steamboat left") another one ("passengers boarded") for the participial phrase ("After eating…") to modify appropriately. Note that in the first correction, "After" is a subordinating conjunction introducing a (dependent) clause, whereas in the second correction, "After" is a preposition, and the gerund "eating" is the object of that preposition.

Original example: The bank approves loans to reliable and financially sound individuals of any size.

Problem: A misplaced modifier creates the problem in this sentence, which implies that "any size" refers to the individuals who apply for bank loans. The problem exemplified here is one of syntax: the object of a long prepositional phrase ("individuals") sits beside another phrase ("of any size") and thereby steals it away from its intended antecedent ("loans").

Possible correction: The bank approves loans of any size to reliable and financially sound individuals.

Comment: By adjusting word order, the phrase "of any size" is placed beside its intended antecedent.

Original example: Rounding a tight curve, a flashing light warned the cyclists of dangerous conditions ahead.

Problem: The dangling participle ("Rounding a tight curve") does not have a likely word to modify in the sentence. The sentence suggests that the flashing light was rounding a curve.

Possible correction: Rounding a tight curve, the cyclists were warned by a flashing light of dangerous conditions ahead.

Comment: The noun modified by the participial phrase is now in the subject position. Changing the sentence's verb to the passive voice ("were warned") facilitates this syntactical correction.

Test Yourself: Possessive Apostrophes

Original example: The womens movement has been misunderstood by many of its detractors.

Problem: The possessive apostrophe for "womens" is missing. The trickiness here in inserting the apostrophe is that this irregular noun is already plural.

Possible correction: The women's movement has been misunderstood by many of its detractors.

Comment: Because the word is already plural, it takes a simple "–'s" to indicate a movement belonging to women, not "–s'" (womens').

Original example: All of the petitioners signatures were collected and delivered to the prime ministers office.

Problem: Here again, the possessive apostrophe is missing—for both "petitioners" and "prime ministers."

Possible correction: All of the petitioners' signatures were collected and delivered to the prime minister's office.

Comment: The plural noun takes an apostrophe after the "s" and the singular noun takes an apostrophe before the "s."

Test Yourself: Comma Errors

Original paired examples: The book which I read yesterday contained a lot of outdated data.

The book that I read yesterday contained a lot of outdated data.

Problem: In the first example, the modifying clause "which I read yesterday" is nonrestrictive: it could be omitted without changing the essential meaning of the sentence. The nonrestrictive use suggests that the reader knows which book is being discussed without the modifying information; perhaps it was identified in a previous sentence. Therefore, the clause needs to be enclosed in commas—as the "which" signals.

Possible correction: The book, which I read yesterday, contained a lot of outdated data.

Comment: The second example in the pair is correct as it stands. The restrictive clause, "that I read yesterday," does not take commas around it because the information it gives readers is an essential part of the meaning of "book." That is, the book containing outdated data has to be specifically identified to the reader as the one read "yesterday." Without that modifying information, the reader doesn't know what book is being referred to (that is, it's the one read yesterday, as opposed to the one being read today, or read the week before, and so forth).

Test Yourself: Spelling/Diction Errors

Original example: Its not sufficiently acknowledged that the behaviour of public officials is not just an ethical issue but one that effects the sale of newspapers and commercial bytes in television news. When public officials don't do what their supposed to do, than their sure to face the affects of public opinion—if they get caught—because there are dollars to be made. Its that simple: money more then morality is calling the tune in the way that the press treats it's superstars.

Problems: The paragraph confuses the paired terms discussed under BWE 7 and BWE 9. It mistakes

"its" for "it's" before "not sufficiently."

"effects" for "affects" before "the sale."

"their" for "they're" before "supposed."

"than" for "then" before "their sure."

"their" for "they're" before "sure."

"affects" for "effects" before "of public opinion."

"its" for "it's" before "that simple."

"then" for "than" before "morality."

"it's" for "its" before "superstars."

Possible correction: It's not sufficiently acknowledged that the behaviour of public officials is not just an ethical issue but one that affects the sale of newspapers and commercial bytes in television news. When public officials don't do what they're supposed to do, then they're sure to face the effects of public opinion—if they get caught—because there are dollars to be made. It's that simple: money more than morality is calling the tune in the way that the press treats its superstars.

Comment: If you confuse similar words, the only solution is to memorize the differences and consciously check your drafts for any problems until habit takes hold.

GRAMMAR AND STYLE QUIZ ANSWERS

The answers offered here are not the only ways to correct the problems. In some cases, we have offered various satisfactory remedies and, as previously noted, a few of the suggested revisions—marked by a bullet—address editing for style (Chapters 11 and 12) rather than editing for correctness.

Line 1

- The paragraph should begin with the contraction "It's" instead of the possessive form "Its."
- The lead expletive ("It's an important and undeniable fact") is unnecessarily wordy.

Line 2

- A comma splice exists between "viewers" (Line 1) and the conjunctive adverb "however": insert a semicolon as the preferred option, and follow "however" with a comma.
- Replace the adverb "there" with the possessive pronoun "their."
- The noun "anchormen" is sexist: replace with a gender-neutral term such as "anchorpersons."
- The two-word adjective—"charisma-enhancement"—needs a hyphen.

Line 3

- The participial phrase that begins the sentence is a misplaced modifier. It should be followed by a comma, then the pronoun "I."

Line 4

- Replace the possessive pronoun "their" with the adverb "there."
- The noun "affects" (meaning "feelings") is inappropriate in this context. Replace it with "effects."

Line 5

- Add capitalization for the proper nouns "Edmonton" and "Alberta," each of which should be followed by a comma.
- The contraction "it's" must be replaced by the possessive pronoun "its."
- "Although" begins a subordinate adverb clause, which cannot stand alone as a sentence; and as a subordinating conjunction, "although" cannot be followed by a comma.

Line 6

- Eliminate the "s" in channels and create a two-word adjective by adding a hyphen between "weather" and "channel."

- As in Line 2, replace the sexist "anchormen" with the gender-neutral "anchorpersons."

Line 7

- Another two-word adjective in need of a hyphen is "sleep-inducing."
- The list that begins after the word "sleep-inducing" requires a colon instead of a comma.
- The adverb "there" must be replaced by the contraction "they're."
- The preposition "to" must be replaced by the adverb "too."
- Fix faulty parallelism: each of the three items in the list should share the same grammatical structure.

Line 8

- The third item in the list is unnecessarily wordy.

Line 9

- The pronoun "they" is ambiguous because it has more than one possible antecedent.

Line 10

- Fix the broad reference of the pronoun "this," which refers loosely to more than one idea in the preceding line.
- The lead prepositional phrase ("After all") should be set off by a comma.

Line 11

- Parallelism is lacking in three ways: verb formation, pronoun usage, and punctuation. The four actions must be revised thoroughly, including the first two words of Line 12.

Line 12

- There is a problem of diction: "weather" should be replaced by "whether."

Line 13

- Fix the broad reference of the pronoun "this," which refers potentially to many of the ideas in the paragraph.
- Excessive subordination leads to a practically unreadable sentence. Revise to achieve more concise, clear grammar.

Line 14

- Once again, "anchormen" is an inappropriate choice of words.
- The pronoun "we" should be in its accusative-case form—"us"—because it is an object of the preposition "between." In oral discourse, this correction is counterintuitive for most people; former Prime

Minister Mulroney always used to speak about discussions "between President Reagan and I." Nevertheless, case is determined, strictly, by whether a pronoun is being used as a subject or an object.

Line 15

• Fix the sentence fragment, which lacks both a subject and a verb.

Here is how one corrected version of the quiz might look:

Anyone who watches a weather channel realizes that it provides valuable information. Regular viewers may find, however, that the anchorpersons suffer from a lack of charisma. Tuning in last Saturday evening, I was nearly bored to tears by one of them. Her rambling description of the summer hailstorm in Edmonton, Alberta, wasn't worthy of a city known for its bizarre climate. Three characteristics cause these TV anchors to be particularly tiresome: their continuous frowns, their excessive makeup, and their habit of explaining meteorological theory in monotonous voices. Of course, as television personalities, they are able to attract viewers—but this advantage should not be taken for granted. Each one of us, after all, is free to turn off the set, step into the backyard, look up at the sky, and forecast tomorrow's sun or clouds. What seems clear is the need for a higher quality of communication between weather-channel anchorpersons and us viewers. The sooner a change occurs, the better.

READINGS FOR PART III

Organization and Style

In Chapter 10, *rhetoric* is defined as "the various means at a writer's (or speaker's) disposal for influencing the views of an audience." The readings for Part III demonstrate just how important rhetorical skill can be for writers from different discourse communities.

Addressing business professionals, **Roger Martin** employs analogy to sharpen his article's focus: he aligns the "expectations market" of the corporate world with that of professional football. The result is a lively article, "The Wrong Incentive," whose *persona* is both creative and analytical. In "MSN Spoken Here," **Charles Foran** begins with a common journalistic format—presenting brief examples of his topic, addressing his readers directly, and then launching into detailed explanation of his topic. His style combines an amiable persona with persuasive reasoning.

As you might expect, articles from the academic world often follow disciplinary conventions of format and stylistic tone. **Daniel J. Mennill** and his colleagues adhere to the scientific format described in Chapter 11: "Female Eavesdropping on Male Song Contests in Songbirds" moves from introduction to methodology to results and discussion, as the writers analyze carefully the hypotheses that guide their research. Also adhering to a conventional format, which is highlighted by subtitled sections, are **Gillian Creese** and **Edith Ngene Kambere**. As part of its emphasis on systemic discrimination, "What Colour Is Your English?" cites data of personal testimony, which adds an element of pathos to an otherwise logic-centred rhetoric.

Jerome Groopman's "The Grief Industry" is an analysis of "critical-incident stress debriefing" in the wake of the September 11th attacks. Groopman, a medical doctor, directs his assessment of therapeutic procedures to an educated audience of non-specialists (readers of *The New Yorker* magazine). The attitudes and needs of that audience, whose experience predates the killing of Osama bin Laden, certainly influence the shape of his writing, which combines rhetorical elements from journalism and academia.

The Wrong Incentive*

Executives taking stock will behave like athletes placing bets

Roger Martin

Every Sunday in the season, hundreds of National Football League players put on their cleats, shoulder pads and helmets and head out on the field to compete. The teams wage an intense battle of strategy, will, experience and muscle. Offensive coordinator against defensive coordinator. Quarterback against secondary. Running back against linebackers. Wide receiver against cornerback. It is a very real game in which real touchdowns and field goals are scored. And after 60 gruelling minutes of official time there is a real winner and a real loser.

Billions of dollars are earned on television contracts and billions are spent on player salaries. But Sunday is also the culmination of an even bigger dollar game: betting on the NFL. Because much of it is done illegally, nobody really knows just how big a game betting on the NFL is, but it is probably bigger than the real game.

During the week, bettors make predictions about what will happen when the teams take the field and place their bets. Clever bookmakers continuously adjust the point spread—the number of points the bettor must give the underdog if betting on the favorite—to even the betting on each team. The magnitude of the spread is entirely based on expectations of a future event—what really will happen on Sunday. Point spreads change with the news. An injury to a key player can stretch the odds or even reverse them.

In football, there is a rigid separation of the real market—the games played on Sundays—from the expectations market, or the betting that takes place prior to the game. No participant in the real market is permitted to participate in any way in the expectations market. If they do, they risk a lifetime ban for even one infraction.

Why wouldn't you want your star quarterback to be even more motivated to win on Sunday afternoon by having placed a big bet on his team? Trying harder on Sunday is one way to score in the expectations market, but another is to manipulate expectations in order to improve betting chances. Going in the tank in Week Three could pay off in Week Four if other gamblers underestimate the team's true ability. Shaving points to score less than would otherwise be possible can lead a gambling player to throw the game and win a bet on the opposing team using the betting spread.

These second-order incentives to manipulate the expectations and real markets for personal benefit are what caused football and the other major professional sports to ban participation in the expectations market.

Vulnerable Market

There is an even bigger game in which players in the real market not only are allowed, but are strongly encouraged to play in the related expectations market—even though exactly the same incentive problems exist.

That game consists of the markets in which publicly traded corporations compete. Here, real companies spend real money to make and sell real products and earn real profits if they play with skill. This market also requires strategy, will, and experience.

Linked to this are expectations markets—the stock markets, the biggest of which is the New York Stock Exchange. Like point spreads in the NFL, prices on the NYSE aren't set by real things like sales, margins or profits, but by the collective expectations of investors concerning future sales, margins and profits. Stock prices go up only when expectations of investors rise, not necessarily when sales, margins or profits rise.

Senior executives, arguably the most critical players in the real market, are strongly encouraged and often compelled to participate in the expectations market. They are given massive stock-based compensation under the misguided theory that stock-based compensation aligns their interests with the interests of shareholders.

Stock-based compensation does nothing of the sort. Like encouraging NFL players to bet on football, it encourages executives to manipulate the expectations market and the real market to benefit themselves at the expense of outside shareholders.

There is only simplistic logic in assuming that powerful stock-based compensation incentives will cause executives to work hard in the real market to improve performance, which then will increase the stock price and make investors rich.

As in the NFL, it isn't that simple. There are much easier paths to personal riches than working hard to improve performance in the real market, then waiting and hoping that improved performance will result in higher stock prices.

Motive to Manipulate

Stock-based compensation is an incentive to increase expectations, not performance. The easiest way to do that is to hype the stock by talking up the company's prospects on TV and in newspapers and magazines. Alternatively, a hungry executive can use extremely aggressive accounting to inflate performance in the real market in an attempt to raise expectations. Or he can make a bunch of acquisitions that appear to produce profitable growth in the short run but hurt the firm in the long run. Better still: Combine all three, like Tyco International!

As NFL officials know all too well, simple exaggeration of expectations isn't the worst result. Tanking and point shaving are more nefarious and a key feature of senior executive behavior. Tanking helps reset expectations to a low level and provides a big upside potential for stock compensation that was given at the low price level. Point shaving, known in the stock market by the more popular term "earnings management," can ensure that results don't rise too high, too fast, pushing expectations to unsustainable levels.

The greatest incentive for stock-compensated managers is to create as big a gap as possible between expectations and reality—in either direction—then utilize their superior knowledge either to sell or buy stock for personal profit.

In the numerous stock-market scandals of the recent years—Enron, Worldcom, Global Crossing, Qwest, Tyco, Adelphia, etc.—observers seemed shocked that senior managers appeared so misaligned with the interests of outside shareholders, despite high levels of stock-based compensation.

There should have been no shock. Senior managers were completely misaligned with the interest of outsider shareholders because of their high levels of stock-based compensation. They had a powerful incentive to hype expectations on their stock well in excess of reality, then cash in on sales of stocks and options before outside investors understood the true picture.

Blaming the Tool

The reaction has been to blame the problem on stock options, but the real culprit is stock-based compensation of any kind. Overemphasizing any form of equity compensation provides executives with the incentive to focus on and manipulate the expectations market.

How then, should incentive compensation be structured? It should be based exclusively on features of the real market—sales, costs, investments, margins, profits. These are items over which management and employees have some control and their actions can be directly linked to such items. Compensation plans should look more like royalty streams than annual bonuses.

If there is any great utility to employee stock ownership, it is not as an incentive for enhancing performance, but rather as a vehicle for creating a feeling of warmth and togetherness in the corporation. Employees like to feel that they are all in the enterprise together and stock ownership is conducive to the warmth of feeling.

In the end, the corporate market needs to take as sophisticated an approach to the fundamentals of compensation as the NFL.

Imagine what play in the NFL would be like if Brett Favre's or Peyton Manning's compensation depended more on the number of point spreads they beat than on the number of wins they produce.

Actually, imagination isn't required. We need only look at the behavior of senior executives over the last ten years, as their compensation based on the expectations market has dwarfed compensation based on the real market.

We will see more distortion until we recognize what professional sports have long realized: You shouldn't mix the real and expectations markets.

MSN Spoken Here†

The latest street lingo springs from the computer keyboard and is changing the form of the written word

Charles Foran

Welcome, newbie. Wan2tlk, one chatfly to another? I've got NB2D ☺. What, you don't speak TxtMsg? L2K, eh. N/P. It's kewl. Promise you this: TTOYaL. :-)

If you have to ask, you're probably too old for text messaging (TxtMsg), the latest youth craze, complete with its own lexicon. All the characteristics of a hipster slang are in evidence: abbreviations and acronyms, symbols only known to the initiated, and an astonishing speed of exchange. Wan2tlk is "Want to talk?" and NB2D is "Nothing better to do." L2K is "last to know," and TTOYaL is "the time of your life. ☺" Then there are the typed characters :-), called emoticons. An emoticon works if you tilt your head to the left, the colon becoming the eyes and the bracket the grinning mouth.

Two qualities of text messaging make it unique. First, where most street argots are particular to a society, this one is fast becoming universal. Its "street," so to speak, is a vast one—the World Wide Web. Second, for all its resemblances to oral speech, text messaging isn't spoken. It is written and, even then, hardly in the traditional sense. It exists solely on the computer or cell-phone screen, and is meant to be as ephemeral as an unrecorded, real-time conversation.

The Net has a short but lively history as a generator of languages. First developed in 1969, it only reached public consciousness in the early 1980s. (The term "cyberspace" dates from William Gibson's 1984 novel *Neuromancer*.) HTML (hypertext markup language), the "lingua franca" of the Web, came together in the early 1990s. Home PCs and e-mail established themselves in the same decade. Text messaging, born in chatrooms such as MSN's and now migrating onto mobile phones, belongs to the twenty-first century. But it already has its own dictionary, *The Total TxtMsg Dictionary*, with more than 6,000 entries.

There is a distinction between text messaging and the vocabulary of "netizens," called "Net lingo," which also has its own dictionary. The latter is older and more established, and has always had a literate bent. Much Net

---

†Charles Foran. *The Walrus*, Vol. II Issue 3 (February/March 2004): 36-37. Reprinted with permission from the author.

lingo is the product of techies, paid to spend their days in front of a screen. They may be cyber-geeks, but they're also probably old-fashioned eggheads, raised on books, who enjoy showing off their wit and riffing on pop culture.

Neologisms are the specialty of Net lingo. A "drump" is a salacious middle-aged Internet surfer and a "spod" is an irritating amateur techie. "Netsploitation" involves taking advantage of the Net's freedom to push a product. "Fram" is spam from friends and "to gonk" is to embellish the truth. That term is imported from the German *gonken*, which means to pull one's leg. "You're gonking me," in cyber-speak.

Text messaging is something else. Chatrooms belong to ordinary netizens, often very young ones. Speed is imperative. Wit isn't outlawed, but it isn't especially prized. The majority of abbreviations in use are, in fact, short-forms for verbal cliches: 2T^ for "Two thumbs up" and KYSO for "Knock yourself out." Mostly, they read as what they are: simple, declarative exchanges, the way people talk on the phone.

"Speakers" of text messaging must have an almost physical relationship with the computer keyboard. Net lingo is still about inferring complex meanings through words. With text messaging, the medium—the strokes available on a keyboard, the ability to talk to someone nearby or on a different continent—is at least part of the actual message. The relationship with technology, however glib, is less mediated, and more casual, than ever before.

Then there are the emoticons, "icons" that represent emotions. Their other name, "smileys," suggests their purpose: to substitute for the "feelings" that might accompany a remark in a face-to-face exchange. At first glance, "classic" smileys, constructed from the keyboard, bring to mind primitive ideograms. Their meanings are strictly visual, and they display some of the wit absent in the messages themselves. Samples include :-0 for "wow" and X-(for "mad." There are also smileys for characters and people: +:-) for "a priest" and =|:-)= for "Abraham Lincoln."

More common, however, at least in chatrooms such as MSN's, are the smiley faces. With a click of the mouse one selects the appropriate "emotion." The smileys are intended to behave as would a wink or a shrug, more body language than verbal cue. While these symbols may not do much to make text messaging respectable, kids love them, and coat the simplest remarks with grins or contortions, as they might once have covered a letter with stickers.

For some of us beyond a certain age, though, such an argot triggers associations. The twentieth century told cautionary tales about secret dialects.

The authors of *1984* and *A Clockwork Orange* warned that language, if degraded and made cabalistic, turned sinister. Martin Amis's 2003 novel, *Yellow Dog,* has a character semi-stalking a journalist with text messages. She types sentences such as this one: "come 2 me on your return. only when u & i r 1 will i feel truly @ peace. 10derly, k8"

Amis wants the notes to be creepy, if only for their infantilism and disrespect of proper English. But he may be reading too much into the slang. His character's e-mails are overly long and burdened with an anxiety about language that doesn't exist among text messagers. She isn't using the keyboard in the proper spirit.

That spirit, the spirit of text messaging, is almost certainly closer to Marshall McLuhan than George Orwell. The communications sage foresaw the emergence of a generation rendered both physiologically "electronic" and spiritually connected by computers. Chat rooms aren't his "global village." They are, however, evolving a global dialect he would recognize: inclusive and unironic, versed in symbols as much as the alphabet. I have a Chinese friend who finds it easier to communicate in text messaging than in written English, and Mandarin chatrooms in China already employ a number of the more popular symbols.

Is text messaging in English? Clearly. But it is also being written, or spoken, online, using other sorts of linguistic signs. It communicates in a crude but ingenious manner, one that can bridge divides. The biggest barrier, curiously, may prove to be age. After a point, adults want to speak meaningfully. For that, you need words: the right ones, and more than a few.

Female Eavesdropping on Male Song Contests in Songbirds[‡]

Daniel J. Mennill, Laurene M. Ratcliffe, and Peter T. Boag

Male song reflects the quality of the singer in many animals and plays a role in female choice of social and copulation partners. Eavesdropping on male–male vocal interactions is a means by which females can compare different males' singing behavior directly and make immediate comparisons between potential partners on the basis of their relative vocal performance (*1, 2*). Using an interactive playback experiment followed by microsatellite paternity analysis, we investigated whether female black-capped chickadees *(Poecile atricapilla)* base their reproductive decisions on information gained through eavesdropping.

Black-capped chickadees are socially monogamous songbirds that follow a mixed reproductive strategy in which one-third of broods include young that are not related to their social father (*3*). From 1999 to 2001, we assessed dominance ranks in a free-living population of chickadees at Queen's University Biological Station, Canada, to predict which males were likely to be sought for extrapair copulations (high-ranking males) and which males were likely to lose paternity within their nests (low-ranking males) (*3, 4*).

At the start of the breeding season, when male-male song contests are common and females actively solicit copulations, we used interactive song playback to engage territorial male chickadees in countersinging interactions with a simulated intruder (*5*). We performed 6.0-min playback trials to dyads of neighboring high-ranking and low-ranking males from the same winter flock. In control treatments, we mimicked natural territorial encounters; we simulated an intruder that sang submissively (Fig. 1A) with the high-ranking playback subject and sang aggressively (Fig. 1B) with the low-ranking neighbor. In experimental treatments, we attempted to alter eavesdropping females' perceptions of their social mates; we simulated an intruder that sang aggressively with the high-ranking playback subject and sang submissively with the low-ranking neighbor. To test whether interactive playback altered the normal pattern of paternity in the nests of subject males, we conducted paternity analysis on blood samples collected from offspring (*6*).

[‡]Daniel J. Mennill, Laureen M. Ratcliffe, Peter T. Boag. Reprinted with permission from *Science* Vol. 296, 3 May 2002: 873. Copyright © 2002 AAAS.

High-ranking males that lost song contests with a simulated intruder lost paternity in their nests (Fig. 1C); high-ranking males that received playback simulating an aggressive intruder showed a significantly greater level of paternity loss than high-ranking males that received playback simulating a submissive intruder (control I; Fisher's exact test, $P = 0.05$) and a significantly greater level than a control group of high-ranking males that received no playback (control II; $P = 0.05$). As predicted (*3, 4*), we observed little extrapair paternity in the nests of high-ranking males that received submissive playback and high-ranking males that received no playback. Thus, females paired to high-ranking playback subjects adopted a mixed reproductive strategy after hearing brief song contests in which their mate fared poorly. This change in female reproductive decisions after short playback sessions suggests that information available through eavesdropping plays an important role in female assessment of male quality.

Playback mimicking a submissive intruder did not reduce the level of extrapair paternity in the nests of low-ranking males (Fig. 1D); paternity loss by low-ranking males that received playback simulating a submissive intruder was not significantly different than for low-ranking males that received playback simulating an aggressive intruder (control I; $P = 1.0$) or low-ranking males that received no playback (control II; $P = 1.0$). The females paired with low-ranking males that received submissive playback may have engaged in extrapair copulations before playback sessions or may have heard natural male-male song contests in which their partner revealed his low-ranking status. Whereas females paired to low-ranking males normally overhear their mate win some song contests and lose others, females paired to high-ranking males are only accustomed to hearing their mates win. As such, two short playback sessions were sufficient to alter high-ranking, but not low-ranking, females' perceptions of their partners' status.

We tested the alternative explanation that unusual patterns of extrapair paternity could have arisen from females reacting to changes in their partners' postplayback behavior, rather than from eavesdropping per se. We detected no significant changes in male behavior after playback (*5*), further suggesting that changes in female reproductive decisions arose through female eavesdropping on male song contests.

Our results support the idea that information may be transferred between individuals in a communication network rather than simply within a dyadic context (*2*) and provide a conceptual link between the attractive and repellent properties of male song where mate attraction and territory defense may be simultaneous functions of a common signal.

Finally, our results show that short playback sessions can have long-lasting and far-reaching effects on individual fitness.

References and Notes

1. K. Otter et al., Proc. R. Soc. London Ser. B Biol. Sci. **266**, 1305 (1999).
2. P. K. McGregor, T. Peake, Acta Ethol. **2**, 71 (2000).
3. K. Otter, L. Ratcliffe, D. Michaud, P. Boag, Behav. Ecol. Sociobiol. **43**, 25 (1998).
4. S. M. Smith, Behaviour **107**, 15 (1988).
5. See supplemental information available on Science Online at www.sciencemag. org/cgi/content/full/296/5569/873/DC1.
6. Paternity was analyzed by polymerase chain reaction amplification of two highly variable microsatellite loci. Offspring were considered extrapair young if they had one (n = 44) or two (n = 22) allelic mismatches with their social father. The combined exclusionary power was 0.91 given one known parent.
7. We thank R. DeBruyn, A. MacDougall, D. Aiama, A. Boone, P. Christie, L. Colgan, M. Cunningham, S. Doucet, J. Hodson, B. Meigs, S. Ramsay, N. Vreeswyck, and landowners adjacent to the study site for assistance and the Natural Sciences and Engineering Research Council of Canada, the American Ornithologists' Union, the Animal Behavior Society, the Association of Field Ornithologists, the Frank M. Chapman Memorial Fund, Queen's University, and the Society of Canadian Ornithologists for funding.

"What Colour Is Your English?"§
Gillian Creese and Edith Ngene Kambere

This paper raises questions about ways in which the "imagined community" is discursively patrolled through accents. Drawing on preliminary research with African immigrant women, we argue that "Canadian English" constitutes a border allowing only partial and provisional crossing for those with an "African English" accent. The accent border is material and figurative, affecting access to material benefits such as jobs or housing, as well as shaping perceptions of who belongs in Canada. Thus, accents form a site through which racialized power relations are negotiated and "Others" are reproduced materially and figuratively in Canada.

> When you come here, you come from a continent or a country that was originally colonized by the British. You had your education, you were taught by the British. You speak your good English, but somehow they ask you "what colour is your English"? (Focus Group, 1997)

The points system of immigrant selection rewards fluency in Canada's official languages, but perceptions of language fluency remain contested in everyday interactions. Drawing on preliminary research with African immigrant women, we highlight the need to explore the social construction of language fluency and the intersection between accents and processes of racialization.

Processes of immigration, like the projects of colonialism and nation building in which they are embedded, are simultaneously racialized, gendered, sexualized and classed (Anthias and Yuval-Davis, 1992; Bannerji, 2000; Calliste and Dei, 2000; Sharma, 2001; Stasiulis and Yuval-Davis, 1995; Strong-Boag, Grace, Eisenberg and Anderson, 1998). The "imagined community" underlying the nation-building process (Anderson, 1991) is both a literal and figurative border that immigrants of colour negotiate. As Anzaldua argues, those who inhabit the borderlands, or "the spaces in between," shift back and forth across borders, never fully belonging in either space (Anzaldua, 2000). In the Canadian context, as Ng (1990) notes,

§Gillian Creese and Edith Ngene Kambere. *The Canadian Review of Sociology and Anthropology*, 40:5, Dec 2003, pp 565-73. Reprinted with permission from CSAA.

common-sense discourses construct people of colour as immigrants and immigrants as people of colour. Immigrants of colour inhabit Anzaldua's "spaces in between," always in the process of negotiating the border crossing from "Other" to "Canadian."

This paper raises questions about one way the "imagined nation" is discursively patrolled through accents. A "foreign" accent is socially defined, such that British or Australian English accents, for example, do not seem to elicit the same treatment as described by the African immigrant women in our focus groups.[1] Accents signify more than local/"Canadian" and extra-local/"immigrant"; accents, embodied by racialized subjects, also shape perceptions of language competency. Thus, accents may provide a rationale for (dis)entitlement in employment or full participation in civil society without troubling liberal discourses of equality.

Methodology

There is little research on African immigrants in Canada and less on women who have migrated from Africa.[2] Existing research documents low socio-economic status, under-employment in the labour market, restricted access to suitable housing, and racial discrimination (Adjibolosoo and Mensah, 1998; Danso and Grant, 2000; Elabor-Idemudia, 2000; Mensah and Adjibolosoo, 1998). African immigrant women face additional demands negotiating paid work, family and child rearing in an often unfriendly environment (Elabor-Idemudia, 2000).

Our research begins to explore issues affecting African immigrant women in Vancouver. Mindful of feminist debates on research for, rather than on, women (DeVault, 1999; Razack, 2000; Smith, 1987; 1999; Wolf, 1996) we put African women's experiences at the centre of our analysis. As exploratory research, with a limited budget, focus groups allowed us to talk to a larger group of women than individual interviews, and begin the process of mapping out key issues they identified.[3] Focus groups provide spaces in which power relations are more amenable to negotiation and attenuation, creating a relatively "safe space" for the collective generation of knowledge (Barbour and Kitzinger, 1999; Pratt, 2000). One author shares the participants' "outsider-within" status (Collins, 1999) and the other author does not,[4] so we chose to construct focus groups as African-women-only spaces, thereby enhancing the possibility of candid discussions.

We did not set out to frame the focus groups around issues of language or accent. We asked eight open-ended questions that focused on experiences with employment, housing, settlement services, mothering, changing gender relations, language and policy concerns. Reading the transcripts, however, it became clear that participants identified accent as a perennial problem. The quote that begins this paper and provides its title—"What colour is your English?"—was uttered by one author to the other at our initial meeting, a multi-ethnic focus group of immigrant women conducted in 1997. It was in the process of making sense of the current research that we recovered our earlier exchange.

The following discussion draws on two focus groups that were made up of Black women who are relatively recent migrants from Africa. They were conducted in Vancouver during the summer of 2002. The 12 focus group participants migrated from 6 African countries previously colonized by Britain (Nigeria, Sierra Leone, Sudan, Swaziland, Uganda and Zambia), and one previously colonized by Belgium (Congo). The small African community is linguistically, ethnically and religiously diverse, and is characterized by a dispersed residential pattern that provides no spatial "centre" for the community.[5] At the same time, processes of settlement in Vancouver are creating a transnational "African" identity, as individual immigrants are drawn together, often in spite of significant cultural, linguistic and other differences, by similar experiences within Canada.

Almost all focus group participants defined themselves as fluent in English,[6] and in two cases also fluent in French, before arriving in Canada. Most had advanced post-secondary degrees undertaken at English-language institutions. One focus group was composed of professional women, five of whom had master's degrees that were completed in English (three of these from Canadian or American universities), and the sixth had a Canadian bachelor's degree. The second focus group was more diverse: one participant had a master's degree, two had post-secondary diplomas, and three had Grade 12 certificates. The length of residence in Canada varied from 2 to 13 years; 6 had been in Canada less than 5 years, and 5 had been here for more than 8 years. Our participants' comments about reaction to their "African English" accents are all the more noteworthy given these high levels of education in English, and the length of time they had been in Canada.

Border Crossings: Localizing Language, Bordering Accents

"Canadian English" constitutes a border allowing only partial and provisional crossing for women in our focus groups. Language is performed and interpreted within a localized context and migration from English-speaking Africa to Canada might require initial translation of colloquial phrases, pace of speech, intonation and syntax. However, the local vernacular is not only different, its difference implies [in]competence in the speaker. As the women in our focus groups made clear, perceptions that their "African English" accents imply limited English skills persist well beyond an initial period of localizing within Canada.

The most common responses to "African English" identified in our focus groups were being ignored when speaking, and being corrected rather than responding to the content of the speech. Comments by Mapendo[7] and Muhindo illustrate this point:

> It seems that somehow they put you in a spot where you become defensive. You have to defend how you talk. When they correct me, I just say well this is the way you pronounce it, but this is the way I pronounce it. You continue to pronounce it the way you do and I will continue my way I do. We are from different schools so why should I listen to what you have to tell me. It becomes ridiculous when people are correcting you and not listening to what you have to say (Mapendo).

> I feel the same way as you all do about accents. After finishing my [university degree] I feel I don't want to go and work in institutions where people will not listen to what I say, but only to correct my accent which I have no control of (Muhindo).

Both Mapendo and Muhindo adopt strategies of resistance to assert their own identities. Mapendo asserts her right to pronounce words as she sees fit, and indeed to argue for equal validation of "African" and "Canadian" styles of English. Expressing her African accent celebrates her African identity and asserts a claim for respect and dignity. Muhindo identifies another strategy of resistance: refusal to work in a context where she is not heard. The consequences of this strategy are not insignificant; so far Muhindo has not found work in her field, in spite of her post-secondary education in Canada.

At the time of the focus groups Mapendo had been in Canada for eight years, and Muhindo for ten years. Muhindo has a bachelor's degree from a Canadian university, and Mapendo has a master's degree from the United States. However, as our focus groups suggest, other people's perception of their fluency in "Canadian English" is low, in spite of their educational accomplishments and years in Canada.

The border around an "African accent" has material and figurative consequences. Materially, an "African accent" is frequently named as a rationale for not being hired in the labour market. Figuratively, daily accent policing makes it clear that African women do not really belong to the imaginary

Canadian nation. Below, comments by Caroline and Kabugho exemplify the material consequences of accents bordering employment opportunities:

> English is a major barrier because it is the major language of communication. The accent which is part of the language, my accent is very heavy… when you don't have their own accent, they don't want to accept you in areas where you have to speak like receptionist, teacher of English, customer service. It is a big barrier (Caroline).
>
> The language is a barrier to integrate in the society because if you speak English in your accent, people will know that you are from Africa… and by the accent they can not give you a job, or a house (Kabugho).

Caroline identifies particular types of occupations that are more difficult for her to enter. Since these jobs require speaking with the public, she suggests, "Canadian English" may be seen as a job requirement. If it is the case that immigrants with a "heavy accent" are typically barred from such employment, this poses problems for large numbers of workers (who can't get jobs in the service sector) and customers (who can't be served by people like themselves).

While Caroline points to specific sites on the accent border, Kabugho provides a broader picture of how accent mediates opportunities in the labour market. For Kabugho, her accent tells people who you are, "they will know you are from Africa." Kabugho's observations lead us away from the particularities of accent (is it really, as Caroline suggests, "too heavy" for most Vancouverites to understand?) and toward the processes of racialization (how can an "African accent" be separated from an African body?).

Nora provides a further example of how the embodied accent shapes her experiences in the job market:

> What I also find is I made my resume and when they read it, it was excellent and then they called me for the job interview. When I started to answer some of the questions they asked, they said, "Where are you from?" Then I said "From Africa." "When did you land as an immigrant?" Then I said "In Africa we also are trained in English." "No wonder, your accent is too heavy, we cannot understand you" (Nora).

Nora's experience of qualifications that appeared good on paper, but were discounted in person, was not uncommon. Although Nora had been in Canada for 13 years, her spoken English was so disparaged it had become an insurmountable barrier to her employment. Just as language is embodied, so are the consequences of marginalization. For Nora, the physical toll of repeated rejection for jobs for which she is qualified has contributed to a serious medical condition that now prevents her from working. As she suggests, rejection wears down the body and the spirit, and creates, at best, an ambiguous sense of place within Canada:

> For you, who is trained to be integrated, you want to be friendly, you want to be accepted. But what you get is rejection ... So I don't know. I love Canada, but I haven't gained much. I don't know if I ever will (Nora).

African women are marked as "Other" through the intonations of their voices and the colour of their skin; indeed, the former implies the latter. When women in our focus groups talked about the way their "African accent" underscored their status as immigrants, they identified a form of boundary maintenance that prevents crossing from "immigrant" to "Canadian," regardless of formal citizenship processes. Mabunda was particularly eloquent on this point:

> I think it is the fact that you remain an immigrant which is the main obstacle because you never become either citizen or Canadian. This remains a big block, because you really have to belong. It is a kind of stigma; it is how I see it. So you are not in although you are among (Mabunda).

In Mabunda's experience, an embodied "African accent" renders her an "outsider within." Whatever her legal citizenship status, she knows she will never be perceived, or perceive herself, as "Canadian."

The above examples of disparaging "African English" recounted by participants in our focus groups are not occasional random acts, they are daily encounters. While each instance might seem minor, taken together, these examples point to systemic processes of marginalizing and "Othering" African women. As Mabunda noted, an "African accent" cannot be separated from the African woman who bears it: "I am an immigrant, I am a woman and I am an African." Indeed, it may be that extra-local accents provide a rationale for discriminatory behaviour that would be considered unacceptable on the basis of skin colour. Mabunda concluded:

> I find this language as a tool that has been used against us and it is unfortunate that at this time we are still held accountable because of our accent. None of us talk English in the first place. This is another aspect of colonization. But if they could understand that,

Canadian government which accepts immigrants, this language shouldn't be a barrier for people because it is dehumanizing. It is not that we don't know English. I think I know English. It is about Canadian or English accent. If the British can not speak Nyangore as the way I speak it. I had an English lady in high school, she spoke my language fluently but when it came to accent it was different.... So I think these people who are doing this research they should highlight the language barrier as a systematic barrier that was put within the system to put us down. I went to the university, I did all the papers, and you discriminate against me (Mabunda).

Mabunda traces the systemic use of accent discrimination against African women to its roots in colonialism. Forms of English that emerged in one British colonial context are, perhaps ironically, rendered unacceptable in another former colony. As Mabunda argues: "It is not that we don't know English. I think I know English. It is about Canadian or English accent." She concludes that the accent barrier she encounters is systemic, a tool used "to put us down." It is not, after all, about communication. It is about power and exclusion, marginalization and "Othering," racism and discrimination. Mabunda came to Canada with her husband, first as graduate students and then as independent immigrants, awarded points for higher education and knowledge of English. She has been in Canada 13 years and earned a master's degree at a Canadian university. That she "knows English" is beyond dispute. That she speaks English with an "African accent," and experiences the world in an African woman's body, is also beyond dispute. The problem, she suggests, is not mastery of the English language; the problem is being an African woman in Canada.

Conclusions

We did not set out to assess the effects of "African English" accents for women who migrated from English-speaking Africa, but this turned out to be a central theme in our focus groups. Although our research is preliminary, it suggests the need for more research on how socially defined "foreign" accents shape perceptions of language fluency; how this intersects with processes of racialization, gender and class; and how it reproduces inequality in the labour market and elsewhere.

According to our focus groups, African immigrant women experience language as a problem in their daily lives not because they have difficulty with expression or comprehension but because their "African English" accents mark them as immigrant, African, Black, women perceived to have low English-language competency. As such, accents discursively patrol the borders within Canada. Although accent remains a site of community identity, resistance and empowerment as African women assert their own identities, it is also a site through which racialized power relations are negotiated, and "Others" are reproduced materially and figuratively within Canada.

Endnotes

1. We are not aware of existing research on responses to different types of extra-local accents, but this is clearly an area that merits attention.
2. For research on African immigrant women, see Agnew, 1996; Elabor-Idemudia, 2000. Other research focuses more generally on Afro-Canadian women, for example Brand, 1993; Bristow, 1994; Calliste, 2000; Daenzer, 1997; Thornhill, 1989.
3. The ability to generalize from focus groups is limited, but they may raise important questions that merit more in-depth research. These focus groups were undertaken to develop a SSHRC application for a detailed qualitative study of the settlement experiences of African immigrant women in the greater Vancouver area.
4. One of the authors is a member of, and a well-known community activist within, the African women's community in Vancouver. The other author is a White sociologist who conducts research into issues affecting immigrant and refugee families in Vancouver.
5. In the 1996 Census, only 1.2% of the population of greater Vancouver (or just over 20,000 people) were born in Africa; 0.5% claimed African ethnic origin, and 0.7% identified themselves as Black. See Hiebert, 1999; Mensah and Adjibolosoo, 1998.
6. One participant had some knowledge of English but was not fluent, and another was fluent in French but not English. Ten were fluent in English before arriving in Canada.
7. All participants are referred to by pseudonyms.

References

Adjibolosoo, S. and J. Mensah. 1998. *The Provision of Settlement Services to African Immigrants in the Lower Mainland of B.C., Part 2.* Victoria: Ministry Responsible for Multiculturalism and Immigration, Community Liaison Division.

Agnew, V. 1996. *Resisting Discrimination: Women from Asia, Africa, and the Caribbean and the Canadian Women's Movement.* Toronto: University of Toronto Press.

Anderson, B. 1991. *Imagined Communities.* London: Verso.

Anthias, F. and N. Yuval-Davis. 1992. *Racialized Boundaries: Race, Nation, Gender, Colour and Class and the Anti-Racist Struggle.* London: Routledge.

Anzaldua, G. 2000. In *Interviews/Entrevistas.* A. Keating (ed.). New York: Routledge

Bannerji, H. 2000. *The Dark Side of the Nation: Essays on Multiculturalism, Nationalism and Gender.* Toronto: Canadian Scholars' Press.

Barbour, R. and J. Kitzinger (eds.). 1999. *Developing Focus Group Research.* London: Sage.

Brand, D. 1993. "A working paper on Black women in Toronto: Gender, race and class." In *Returning the Gaze: Essays on Racism, Feminism and Politics*. H. Bannerji (ed.). Toronto: Sister Vision Press, pp. 220–42.

Bristow, P. (ed.). 1994. *"We're Rooted Here and They Can't Pull Us Up." Essays in African Canadian Women's History*. Toronto: University of Toronto Press.

Calliste, A. 2000. "Nurses and porters: Racism, sexism and resistance in segmented labour markets." In *Anti-Racist Feminism*. A. Calliste and G.S. Dei (eds.). Halifax: Fernwood Publishing, pp. 143–64.

Calliste A. and G.S. Dei (eds.). 2000. *Anti-Racist Feminism*. Halifax: Fernwood Publishing.

Collins, P.H. 1999. "Learning from the outsider within: The sociological significance of Black feminist thought." In *Feminist Approaches to Theory and Methodology*. S. Hesse-Biber, C. Gilmartin and R. Lydenberg (eds.). New York: Oxford, pp. 155–78.

Daenzer, P. 1997. "Challenging diversity: Black women and social welfare." In *Women and the Welfare State*. P. Evans and G. Wekerle (eds.). Toronto: University of Toronto Press, pp. 269–90.

Danso, R. and M. Grant. 2000. "Access to housing as an adaptive strategy for immigrant groups: Africans in Calgary." *Canadian Ethnic Studies*, Vol. 32, No. 3, pp. 19–43.

DeVault, M. 1999. *Liberating Method: Feminism and Social Research*. Philadelphia: Temple University Press.

Elabor-Idemudia, P. 2000. "Challenges confronting African immigrant women in the Canadian workforce." In *Anti-Racist Feminism*. A. Calliste and G.S. Dei (eds.). Halifax: Fernwood Publishing, pp. 91–110.

Focus Group with Immigrant Women. 1997. Community Studies Project. RIIM. August.

Hiebert, D. 1999. "Immigration and the changing social geography of Greater Vancouver." *BC Studies*, No. 121, pp. 35–82.

Mensah, J. and S. Adjibolosoo. 1998. *The Demographic Profile of African Immigrants in the Lower Mainland of B.C., Part 1*. Victoria: Ministry Responsible for Multiculturalism and Immigration, Community Liaison Division.

Ng, R. 1990. "Immigrant women: The construction of a labour market category." *Canadian Journal of Women and the Law*, Vol. 4, No. 1, pp. 96–112.

Pratt, G. 2000. "Studying immigrants in focus groups." *RIIM Working Paper Series*, No. 00-18. Vancouver: Centre of Excellence, Simon Fraser University.

Razack, S. 2000. "Your place or mine? Transnational feminist collaboration." In *Anti-Racist Feminism*. A. Calliste and G.S. Dei (eds.). Halifax: Fernwood, pp. 39–53.

Sharma, N. 2001. "On being *not* Canadian: The social organization of 'migrant workers' in Canada." *The Canadian Review of Sociology and Anthropology*, Vol. 38, No. 4, pp. 416–39.

Smith, D. 1987. *The Everyday World as Problematic*. Toronto: University of Toronto Press.

Smith, L.T. 1999. *Decolonizing Methodologies: Research and Indigenous Peoples*. London: Zed Books.

Stasiulis, D. and N. Yuval-Davis. 1995. *Unsettling Settler Societies: Articulations of Gender, Race, Ethnicity and Class*. London: Sage.

Strong-Boag, V., S. Grace, A. Eisenberg and J. Anderson (eds.). 1998. *Painting the Maple: Essays on Race, Gender and the Construction of Canada.* Vancouver: University of British Columbia Press.

Thornhill, E. 1989. "Focus on Black women." *Socialist Studies*, Vol. 5, pp. 26–36.

Wolf, D. (ed.). 1996. *Feminist Dilemmas in Fieldwork.* Boulder, Colo.: Westview Press.

The Grief Industry[1]
Jerome Groopman

Soon after the collapse of the World Trade Center, experts predicted that one out of five New Yorkers—some one and a half million people—would be traumatized by the tragedy and require psychological care. Within weeks, several thousand grief and crisis counsellors arrived in the city. Some were dispatched by charitable and religious organizations; many others worked for private companies that provide services to businesses following catastrophes.

In the United States, grief and crisis counsellors generally use a method called critical-incident stress debriefing, which was created, in 1974, by Jeffrey T. Mitchell, a Maryland paramedic who was studying for a master's degree in psychology. Mitchell had seen a gruesome accident while on the job: a young bride, still in her wedding dress, had been impaled when the car that her drunk husband was driving rear-ended a pickup truck loaded with pipes. He was unable to shake the memory. Six months later, he confided his troubles to a friend—a firefighter who had witnessed similar horrors. The friend asked him to describe exactly what he had seen. Mitchell felt greatly relieved by this conversation, and became convinced that he had stumbled across an invaluable therapeutic approach. Indeed, he came to think that if a "debriefing" conversation was held soon after an upsetting event it could help prevent the onset of post-traumatic stress disorder.

In 1983, Mitchell received a Ph.D. in human development, and he began crafting a structured seven-step debriefing regimen that could be applied to groups of paramedics, firefighters, and other professionals who regularly witnessed traumatic events. Six years later, he started a nonprofit organization, the International Critical Incident Stress Foundation, to teach debriefing and related methods. The foundation has grown steadily, and more than thirty thousand counsellors are trained by it each year.

In a typical debriefing session, crisis counsellors introduce themselves and provide basic information about common stress reactions—sleeplessness, headache, irritability—as well as more debilitating symptoms, like flashbacks and delusions. Each participant is then asked to identify himself, pinpoint where he was during the tragic event (or "critical incident"),

---

[1]Jerome Groopman. *The New Yorker*, 26 January 2004: 30-38. Copyright © 2004 by Jerome Groopman. Reprinted by permission of William Morris Agency, Inc. on behalf of the Author.

and describe what he witnessed. This is known as the "fact phase." The discussion next turns in a more emotional direction, as each participant is asked to divulge what he was thinking during the event. The purpose of sharing such memories is, in part, to draw out group members who "bottle up" their emotions. At the end of this process, the conversation enters the "feeling phase," focussing on each participant's current reaction to the catastrophe. (The counsellors ask questions like "What was the worst part of the incident for you personally?") Finally, the counsellors discuss strategies for coping with stress and suggest services that can provide additional help; by the end of the session, participants are considered ready for "reentry" into the world. The group does not meet for a follow-up session.

I recently spoke with a man who worked at a travel agency on Liberty Street, across from where the Twin Towers once stood. He had been in the subway when the towers collapsed, but after considerable difficulty he made it home safely. "I was called by the company the next day and told to report to headquarters on Thursday," he told me. His parent corporation, which was situated in midtown, and had numerous offices throughout the city, had hired an organization called National Employee Assistance Providers to give debriefing sessions. Many of its counsellors used texts created by Mitchell's foundation during their training.

Most debriefings occur between twelve and seventy-two hours after a catastrophe, according to "Blindsided: A Manager's Guide to Catastrophic Incidents in the Workplace," by Bruce T. Blythe, the C.E.O. of Crisis Management International, a company that offers psychological services. Blythe writes, "Earlier than that, people are likely too numbed to put their personal reactions into words; after seventy-two hours, people typically begin to 'seal over' emotionally." This "sealing over" is seen as dangerously "laying the ground" for P.T.S.D. In most circumstances, employees are required to attend a debriefing session. Blythe writes, "Experience has shown that if attendance is voluntary, those most in need of support will not come, out of fear or discomfort."

The travel agent sat in a conference room with co-workers from the Liberty Street branch who had witnessed the collapse of the World Trade Center and had been evacuated from the building. Also attending the session were employees from uptown offices who had not witnessed the collapse or been at risk. In all, there were between twenty and thirty participants at this debriefing session. "There were two counsellors, a man and a woman, and they encouraged us to tell our stories and vent our feelings," the travel agent told me.

When it was the agent's turn, he revealed to the group that, at the time of the attacks, he had been sitting in a subway car, just short of the Fulton Street station. The train came to an abrupt halt, the air-conditioning went off, and the conductor announced that the train's doors were stuck. Passengers managed to pry open the doors; as they stepped onto the plat-form, a tremendous blast of black smoke filled the air. It blew a woman walking in front of the agent off her feet. He ran away from the billowing smoke, and soon found himself pressed up against a turnstile exit that wouldn't budge. The crowd pushed behind him, and he began to struggle for air. ("I said to myself, 'I'm not dying here,'" he told the group.) He broke free of the mob and found a stairwell; when he arrived at street level, the air was so dark with soot that he still felt as if he were trapped under-ground. He walked north and eventually got home.

"I told what happened to me, and people started crying," he recalled. A colleague said she had made her way to the pier where she usually catches a ferry to her home in New Jersey. "She told everyone how she came across a dazed co-worker walking aimlessly in the darkness, and how they both saw people jumping into the water even though there was no boat there," he said. Another employee from the Liberty Street branch spoke vividly about watching bodies fall from the towers.

I asked the agent whether he had chosen to attend the debriefing. "Well, they felt everyone should participate," he said. When he was asked if it had been helpful, he shrugged and said that, like most of his Liberty Street colleagues, he was relatively numb during the debriefing. "Some people burst into tears," he said. "But the people who were really crying hadn't even been downtown."

At the end of the session, the two counsellors gave telephone numbers to the workers and encouraged them to call if they felt distressed. The travel agent had nightmares for weeks after the debriefing, and often felt as if he were choking. Images similar to the ones he had described during the session would flash through his mind. He didn't pursue further therapy, though. "I had to take care of my family; they rely on me," he explained. After several months, he said, the flashbacks and the sense of choking sub-sided. "You just block it out," he said. "You have to get on with life."

The director of human resources at the travel agent's company told me that she had arranged the debriefing session because "it made me feel that I was doing something for the employees." She went on, "I saw behavior that worried me, people very upset after the attacks. I didn't want the company to seem unfeeling." Another concern that leads companies to hire debriefing services is the fear of litigation. Employees who have experienced a traumatic incident on the job, and who have subsequently been sidelined by P.T.S.D., have sued their companies. The Web site for National Employee Assistance Providers claims that its debriefing program insures "that the productivity of the work unit is not impaired."

Hundreds of similar debriefing sessions took place in Manhattan in the days following the September 11th attacks. Did they help? One debriefing company told me that 99.7 per cent of the participants found the sessions beneficial. But such evaluations are subjective, and hardly scientific. In fact, only in the past few years has debriefing undergone serious scrutiny. Brett Litz, a research psychologist at Boston Veterans Affairs Medical Center who specializes in post-traumatic stress disorder, recently completed a randomized clinical trial of group debriefing of soldiers who were stationed in Kosovo. (Peacekeeping forces there were exposed to sniper fire and mine explosions, and discovered mass graves.) He summarized the academic verdict on debriefing as follows: "The techniques practiced by most American grief counsellors to prevent P.T.S.D. are inert."

Clinical trials of individual psychological debriefings versus no intervention after a major trauma, such as a fire or a motor-vehicle accident, have had discouraging results. Some researchers have claimed that debriefing can actually impede recovery. One study of burn victims, for example, found that patients who received debriefing were much more likely to report P.T.S.D. symptoms than patients in a control group. It may be that debriefing, by encouraging patients to open their wounds at a vulnerable moment, augments distress rather than lessens it.

Mitchell, the movement's founder, told me that debriefing has been "distorted and misapplied" by some private companies, and noted that some negative findings stem from studies of these unorthodox variants. His technique, he added, is meant only for "homogeneous groups who have had the same exposure to the same traumatic event," and sometimes crisis counsellors brought together people who had experienced unrelated traumas. With firefighters who had, say, all watched one of their colleagues die, Mitchell said that his method had a "proven" beneficial effect. He could cite no rigorous clinical trials, however, in support of this claim.

Scientific studies suggest that, after a catastrophic event, most people are resilient and will recover spontaneously over time. A small percentage of individuals do not rebound, however, and require extended psychological care. The single intervention of a debriefing session does nothing to alter this consistent dynamic.

Despite the influx of counsellors into Manhattan, most New Yorkers received no therapy following the attacks. Furthermore, data from surveys taken after September 11th contradicted the early predictions that there would be widespread psychological damage. A telephone survey of nine hundred and eighty-eight adults living below 110th Street, conducted in October and November of 2001, found that only 7.5 per cent had been diagnosed as having P.T.S.D. (According to the American Psychiatric Association, a patient is said to have P.T.S.D. if, for a month or more after a tragic event, he experiences several of the classic symptoms: flashbacks, intrusive thoughts, and nightmares; avoidance of activities and places that are reminiscent of the trauma; emotional numbness; chronic insomnia.) A follow-up of this survey, in March of 2002, found that only 1.7 per cent of New Yorkers suffered from prolonged P.T.S.D. This finding indicates that the debriefing industry is predicated on a false notion: that we are all at high risk for P.T.S.D. after exposure to a traumatic event.

In the wake of a catastrophe like September 11th, Litz told me, victims should not be asked to disclose their personal feelings about the event. All that is needed is "psychological first aid": victims should be taken to a safe place, given food and water, and provided with information about the status of friends and family. None of this, he added, requires the presence of a trained psychologist.

In 1917, a traumatic event on a scale similar to that of the September 11th attacks took place in Halifax, Nova Scotia. Two ships collided near the dock, one of which was carrying explosives and benzene, a flammable liquid. The crew abandoned this ship, and it drifted to the dock, where it exploded and destroyed the entire north end of the city—an area encompassing two and a half square miles. More than two thousand inhabitants were killed, and nine thousand were injured—many of them blinded and dismembered. The night after the explosion, a blizzard descended on Halifax, hindering the relief effort, and many people whose homes had been destroyed froze to death.

April Naturale is a psychiatric social worker who heads Project Liberty, a government-sponsored program that was established to coordinate the therapeutic response to September 11th. Not long ago, she went to Halifax to read archival materials on the 1917 accident. "Some of those who survived seemed psychotic, hallucinating for days," she told me. One woman continued to speak solicitously to someone named Alma—her dead child; other victims were in such a state of shock that doctors were able to perform surgery on them without using chloroform. But after a week or so these disturbing symptoms spontaneously subsided in the vast majority of cases. These accounts led Naturale to conclude that psychiatric intervention in the wake of such an event should be minimal; the mind should be given time to heal itself. In short, the "abnormal" behavior witnessed in the aftermath of the explosion was actually part of a healthy process of recovery.

Malachy Corrigan, the director of the Counseling Service Unit of the New York City Fire Department, was once a proponent of debriefing—but months before the September 11th attacks he decided that it was generally not a beneficial technique. "Sometimes when we put people in a group and debriefed them, we gave them memories that they didn't have," he told me. "We didn't push them to psychosis or anything, but, because these guys were so close and they were all at the fire, they eventually convinced themselves that they did see something or did smell something when in fact they didn't." For the workers in the pit at Ground Zero, Corrigan enlisted other firefighters to be "peer counsellors" and to provide moral support and educational information about the possible mental-health impact of sustained trauma.

"It was like one huge extended family," Corrigan recalled. "We gave them a lot of information about P.T.S.D., as well as about the burden that they would be putting on their own families. We quite boldly spoke about alcohol and drugs. And we focussed on the anger that comes with grief, because the members were more than happy to display those symptoms. You are speaking their language when you talk about alcohol and anger. The simpler you keep the mental-health concepts, the easier it is to engage them."

Naturale sees the approach that Corrigan took, with peers providing basic comforts, as the paradigm for civilians as well as for rescue workers. "Non-mental-health professionals do not pathologize," she said. "They don't know the terminology, they don't know how to diagnose. The most helpful approach is to employ a public-health model, using people in the community who aren't diagnosing you."

Scientists are now trying to determine what causes some people to fall victim to P.T.S.D. after a traumatic event like the September 11th attacks. Rachel Yehuda, a neuroscientist at the Bronx Veterans Affairs Medical Center, has studied both combat veterans and Holocaust survivors, and has found that people with P.T.S.D. have significantly lower baseline levels of cortisol, a hormone that is released in the body during moments of stress. Cortisol, Yehuda theorizes, acts as a counterbalance to adrenaline, which is thought to play a role in the "imprinting" of horrific and intrusive memories. She speculates that the lack of cortisol allows adrenaline to act unopposed, so to speak—and this contributes to the development of P.T.S.D.

Vulnerability to P.T.S.D., Yehuda added, also depends in part on the intensity and duration of the trauma. Someone who witnessed the fall of the towers from afar is not as likely to develop the disorder as someone who worked on the fiftieth floor of Tower One and only narrowly escaped. An injury can also help precipitate P.T.S.D., and the disorder is more likely to affect a civilian bystander than someone who is trained to face dangerous situations, like a police officer. A study performed thirty-four months after the Oklahoma City bombing found that the rate of P.T.S.D. was twenty-three per cent among male civilian victims and only thirteen per cent among firefighters.

Other studies have found that people who are at greatest risk for P.T.S.D. have a history of childhood abuse, family dysfunction, or a pre-existing psychological disorder. In order to properly combat P.T.S.D., Yehuda told me, we need to have a baseline mental-health profile on everyone. "Why don't we have a doctor check our stress level?" she asked. "Just like doctors check our cholesterol."

A 1996 study of American pilots who were prisoners of war in North Vietnam underscores the importance of baseline mental health. Although the pilots endured years of torture and, in many cases, solitary confinement, they showed a very low incidence of P.T.S.D.—presumably because pilots are screened for psychological health and trained for high-stress combat.

Although there are no published studies on P.T.S.D. among rescue workers at Ground Zero, Corrigan, who has assessed many of these individuals, says it is relatively low. He estimates that, of about fifteen thousand firefighters and emergency personnel, fewer than a hundred have developed full-blown P.T.S.D. "There were a lot of therapy experts here in New York who were quite happy to tell everyone that firefighters would have P.T.S.D.," he told me. "But these folks have tremendous resiliency. People say fire-fighters are crazy to put themselves at risk, but they are mentally very healthy. They can sustain enormous amounts of stress and continue to function."

Some of the most promising treatment interventions for people with P.T.S.D. have been developed by Edna Foa, a professor of psychology at the University of Pennsylvania. Twenty years ago, she began a research project involving rape victims in the Philadelphia area. "Most women recover," Foa told me. "Only about fifteen per cent will develop P.T.S.D. symptoms." For these women, Foa devised a technique to "restore resilience," based on cognitive behavioral therapy. The victim is slowly taught to restructure her reactions to her memories of the rape. First, a therapist sits with the woman and asks her to close her eyes and recount the event in detail. (Unlike group debriefing, this takes place months after the event and is performed one on one.) Then the woman is told to repeat the story. Subsequent therapy sessions span some thirty to forty-five minutes each and are taped so that the rape victim can listen to them at home. "The story changes as it is relived," Foa told me. "It becomes more organized, more flowing. A narrative emerges, with a beginning, a middle, and an end."

In contrast to classical psychotherapy, which attempts to link the patient's current feelings and behavior to previous events, Foa's treatment is focussed primarily on relieving symptoms of distress. After each session, the patient is given homework assignments that are simple and direct. She is instructed to make a list of "avoidance behaviors," such as not getting into an elevator because it reminds her of the scene of her violation, and record how anxious she feels when she listens to the tape or thinks about the rape. The therapist then instructs the woman to begin to go to places that remind her of the attack. Over time, this intentional exposure to cues and memories of the trauma shifts the so-called "locus of control" to the victim, who realizes that she can control her unpleasant and intrusive thoughts.

Foa, who is an Israeli, has taught her technique to therapists with the Israel Defense Forces. These therapists recently treated thirty soldiers who had severe P.T.S.D. Some had been in continuous psychotherapy until they received Foa's treatment, which typically requires only twenty hours of therapy. Twenty-nine of the thirty experienced a marked improvement in both their symptoms and their ability to function.

Neuroscientists and experimental psychologists are now mapping the circuits in the brain that could account for the success of Foa's treatment. For example, rats exposed to a tone and then given an electric shock learn to associate the tone with the shock, so that simply hearing the noise causes them to exhibit increased pulse, muscle contraction, and avoidance behavior—an analogue to P.T.S.D. If the tone occurs without the shock being given and is repeated on multiple occasions, the rats no longer respond with these anxiety symptoms. In a related experiment, Joseph LeDoux, a neuroscientist at New York University, made lesions in the prefrontal lobes of such fear-conditioned rats—in a part of the brain just behind the forehead. He then provided the tone without administering the shock; the animals were unable to extinguish their anxiety response, which suggests that the missing circuits play a critical role in stress management.

In recent years, Foa's technique has been used not only to treat P.T.S.D. but also to prevent it. Richard Bryant, a psychologist in Australia, has treated people who displayed sustained symptoms of acute anxiety after a motor-vehicle accident or an assault. In three randomized controlled trials, six months after the trauma, patients who had received treatment were three times less likely to develop P.T.S.D. compared with members of the control group, which received only supportive counselling.

Despite considerable evidence in the United States and abroad showing that treatments like those developed by Foa can ameliorate established P.T.S.D.—and possibly help prevent the disorder in people with acute stress reactions—her approach has not been widely adopted. Most counsellors find cognitive-behavioral techniques unappealing. Dr. Steven Hyman is a neuropsychiatrist and the provost of Harvard University; in 2001, he was the head of the National Institutes of Mental Health. "When I was N.I.M.H. director, I was upset by how few people wanted to learn cognitive-behavioral therapy," Hyman told me. "Here was a therapy proven to be effective by clinical trials. But psychologists and psychiatrists are so interested in people, and they want to cure you with their understanding and empathy and connection. The cognitive-behavioral approach is by-the-book, mechanical, pragmatic. The therapists find it boring. It's not their idea of therapy, and they don't want to do it." Debriefing holds more allure for most counsellors, for it reflects a prevailing cultural bias; namely, that a single outpouring of emotion—one good cry—can heal a scarred psyche.

Foa's method has begun to find some adherents. Malachy Corrigan, of the F.D.N.Y., now uses cognitive-behavioral techniques with several groups, including firefighters who narrowly survived the collapse of the towers. In November, 2001, Foa came to New York and trained forty therapists in her technique. Now Columbia University is offering seminars to therapists who are interested in learning Foa's approach.

At the same time, the scientific critique of debriefing has begun to have an impact. The Department of Defense, the Department of Justice, the Department of Veterans Affairs, the American Red Cross, and the Department of Health and Human Services have all abandoned it as a thera-peutic method. Bruce Blythe's company, Crisis Management International, which is based in Atlanta, recently decided to discontinue its debriefing service. This week, the American College of Neuropsychopharmacology Task Force on Terrorism will release a paper recommending that debriefing be abandoned as a mainstream prevention method. Nevertheless, many for-profit companies in the so-called "grief industry" continue to offer single counselling sessions that are fundamentally linked to Mitchell's seven-step technique. And debriefing is still widely embraced; counsellors for the N.Y.P.D. and the Los Angeles Fire Department continue to use the method.

Perhaps the solution, Hyman said, is to drop the idea that "counselling" is necessary. He told me that the way we respond to individual or mass trauma should be guided by how we behave after the loss of a loved one. "What happens when someone in your family dies?" he said. "People make sure you take care of yourself, get enough sleep, don't drink too much, have food." Hyman pointed out the different rituals that various cultures have developed—shivah among Jews, for instance, and wakes among Catholics—which successfully support people through grief. "No one should have to tell anyone anything!" he said. "Particularly not in the scripted way of a debriefing." The traumatized person should share what he wants with people he knows well: close friends, relatives, familiar clergy. "It's so commonsensical," Hyman said. "But the power of our social networks—they are what help people create a sense of meaning and safety in their lives."

Works Cited

Bednarski, Betty. "'Sameness' and 'difference' in Les Belles-soeurs: A Canadian spectator's reflections on two Polish productions of Michel Tremblay's play." *International Journal of Francophone Studies* 13.2 (2010): 515–25.

Booth, Wayne C., Gregory G. Colomb, and Joseph M. Williams. *The Craft of Research*. Chicago & London: The University of Chicago Press, 1995.

Cohen, David. "Julian Assange: The end of secrets?" *New Scientist* 16 August 2010. Available at http://www.newscientist.com/article/mg20727731.200-julian-assange-the-end-of-secrets.html?full=true.

Cole, Sally, and Elizabeth Kiss. "What can we do about student cheating?" *About Campus* (May–June 2000): 5–12.

Creese, Gillian, and Edith Ngene Kambere. "What colour is your English?" *CRSA/RCSA* 40.5 (2003): 565–73.

Curtis, Polly. "Quarter of students 'plagiarise essays.'" *The Guardian*, June 30, 2004. Available at http://www.guardian.co.uk/education/2004/jun/30/highereducation.uk1.

Eisenberg, M.B., and R.E. Berkowitz. *Information Problem-Solving: The Big Six Skills Approach to Library and Information Skills Instruction*. Norwood, NJ: Ablex Publishing, 1990.

Foran, Charles. "MSN spoken here." *The Walrus* (Feb./Mar. 2003): 36–7.

Frye, Northrop. *Divisions on a Ground: Essays on Canadian Culture*. Ed. James Polk. Toronto: House of Anansi Press, 1982.

Fulford, Robert. "My life as a high school dropout." *The National Post*, April 18, 2001.

Gibaldi, Joseph. *MLA Handbook for Writers of Research Papers*. 6th ed. New York: Modern Language Association, 2003.

Goldberg, Natalie. *Wild Minds: Living the Writer's Life*. New York: Bantam Books, 1990.

Gray, Ralph Gareth. "CEE designers and the problem, the other problem, and the other other problem." *Presentation at the CEE New Millennium Colloquium*, March 20–21, 2000, Wong Auditorium, Tang Center, MIT, Cambridge, Massachusetts.

Groopman, Jerome. "The grief industry." *The New Yorker* Jan. 26, 2004: 30–38.

Hannah-Moffat, Kelly. "Gendering risk at what cost: Negotiations of gender and risk in Canadian women's prisons." *Feminism & Psychology* 14.2 (2004): 243–49.

Hult, Christine A. *Researching and Writing Across the Curriculum*. Boston: Allyn and Bacon, 1996.

Kingwell, Mark. "The mirror stage: Infinite reflections on the public good." *Queen's Quarterly* 106/1 (Spring 1999): 51–61.

Lawrence, Steve, and C. Lee Giles. "Accessibility of information on the Web." *Nature* 400 (1999): 107–9.

Lodge, David. *The Art of Fiction*. New York: Penguin, 1992.

Loftus, Elizabeth F. "Memory in Canadian courts of law." *Canadian Psychology* 44.3 (2003): 207–12.

Lyman, Peter, and Hal R. Varian. *How Much Information?* 2003. Berkeley: University of California, School of Information Management and Systems at the University of California at Berkeley, 2003. Oct. 15, 2004. Available at http://www.sims.berkeley.edu/research/projects/

how-much-info-2003/printable_report.pdf.

Marius, Richard. *A Writer's Companion.* 4th ed. New York: McGraw-Hill College, 1999.

Martin, Roger. "The wrong incentive." *Barron's* Dec. 22, 2003.

McCall, Bruce. "The Scavenger of Highway #3." *Thin Ice: Coming of Age in Canada.* New York: Random House, 1997. 3–10.

McGroarty, Patrick. "Plagiarism row plagues German official." *The Wall Street Journal,* February 18, 2011. Available at http://online.wsj.com/article/SB10001424052748703561604576150341564716876.html.

McQuaig, Linda. "A matter of will." *Queen's Quarterly* 106/1 (Spring 1999): 9–15.

McTeer, Maureen. "Harvard mice on thin ice." *The Globe and Mail* Dec. 9, 2002.

Mennill, Daniel J., Laurene M. Ratcliffe, and Peter T. Boag. "Female eavesdropping on male song contests in songbirds." *Science* 296 (May 3, 2002): 873.

Millin, Leslie. "Idols of the tribe." *Queen's Quarterly* 110/3 (Fall 2003): 391–403.

Orwell, George. "Politics and the English language." *Shooting an Elephant and Other Essays.* London: Secker and Warburg, 1950.

Overall, Christine. "Karla Homolka has a right to study at Queen's." *The Kingston Whig-Standard* Aug. 21, 1995.

Owens, Derek. "Introduction" to *The Essay Theory and Pedagogy for an Active Form,* by Paul Heilker. Urbana, IL: NCTE, 1996. xiii.

Pashley, Robert. *Travels in Crete,* Volume 1. London: Cambridge University Press, 1837.

Paris, Erna. "What sort of people did this?" *The Globe and Mail* Sept. 13, 2001.

Posner, Michael. "Image world." *Queen's Quarterly* 110/2 (Summer 2003): 229–41.

Wynn Kirby, Peter. "Japan's long nuclear disaster film." *The New York Times* March 14, 2011. Available at http://opinionator.blogs.nytimes.com/2011/03/14/japans-long-nuclear-disaster-film/.

Index